Developing a Networked School Community

Plenty Valley Christian College

Developing a Networked School Community

A guide to realising the vision

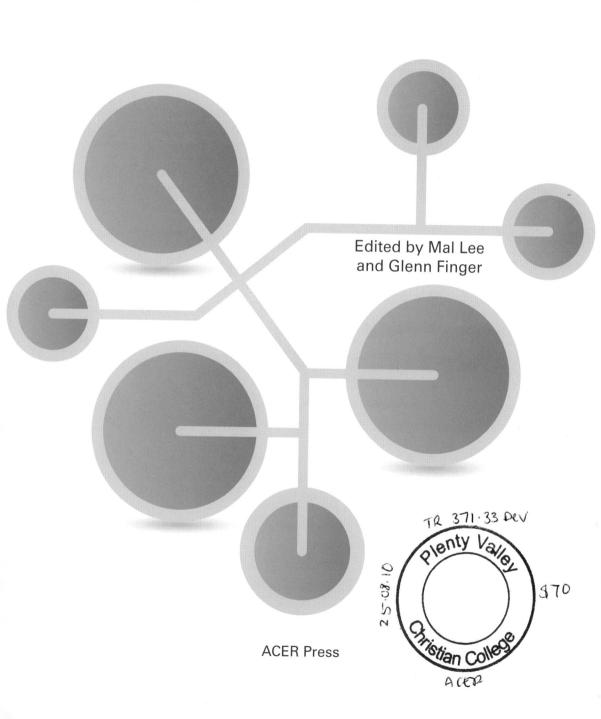

Edited by Mal Lee
and Glenn Finger

ACER Press

First published 2010
by ACER Press, an imprint of
Australian Council *for* Educational Research Ltd
19 Prospect Hill Road, Camberwell
Victoria, 3124, Australia

www.acerpress.com.au
sales@acer.edu.au

Text © Mal Lee and Glenn Finger 2010
Design and typography © ACER Press 2010

Edited by Ronél Redman
Cover design and typesetting by ACER Project Publishing
Cover images: Shutterstock

Printed in Australia by BPA Print Group

National Library of Australia Cataloguing-in-Publication entry

Title: Developing a networked school community :
                     a guide to realising the vision
                     editors, Mal Lee, Glenn Finger.

ISBN: 9780864319814 (pbk.)

Notes: Includes index.
                     Bibliography.

Subjects: Educational technology–Australia
                     Computer-assisted instruction–Australia.
                     Education–Australia–Data processing.
                     Internet in education–Australia.
                     Information technology–Study and teaching–Australia.

Other Authors/Contributors: Lee, Malcolm, 1944-
                     Finger, Glenn D.

Dewey Number: 371.3340994

Foreword

Professor Mike Gaffney, FACE, FACEL,
Chair of Educational Leadership,
Australian Catholic University

Effective schools not only are in touch with their community, especially the homes and families of their students, but also take deliberate steps to reach out beyond their local area into the world at large to provide the best possible educational opportunities for the young people in their care. A key element of the thinking of these effective schools is the concept of the 'network'—what it is, how it works and how it can be used to best advantage for students.

In this book, Mal Lee and Glenn Finger and their contributing authors have taken the concept of the network and explored how it applies to the challenge of providing teaching and learning in ways that are relevant and engaging to twenty-first century educational settings.

Growing appreciation of the value of networks is presenting some interesting challenges for school communities. While networks have always been seen as means to build and share knowledge, and as avenues for expressing one's identity and interests, for providing social support and for developing communities, accelerating developments in digital technologies are raising new questions about networks and their influence on the structure and operation of schools. Importantly, these technologies are providing greater breadth, depth and meaning to the term 'network'. In an age where communication is becoming faster and information is becoming more accessible, and where the technologies are becoming cheaper and more reliable, many of the cherished assumptions and distinctive characteristics of schooling are changing. In fact, the increasing sophistication of digital technologies is expanding the networking capabilities of schools to a point where common terms like 'school community' and familiar concerns like 'how might the school best relate to its community' are taking on new and exciting meanings and possibilities.

This book is focused on assisting educational leaders in understanding these new meanings and the possibilities they hold.

In the Industrial Age the concept of the school community was fairly straightforward. It was defined simply in terms of *local demography* (who are our students? who are their parents?) and *local geography* (where do they live? what are our school's enrolment boundaries?). Schools were basically 'stand-alone' neighbourhood or regional entities that operated between 8.30 am and 3.30 pm, five days per week for up to 44 weeks per year. They were there to provide an educational service, which relied on assumptions that young people were ready to learn and that they developed this readiness from the home, from their parents.

As we move further into the post-Industrial Age, this cosy image of 'school community' is becoming more anachronistic. Not as many young people come to school ready to learn and, increasingly, schools are doing things that used to be done by parents. At the same time, some parents—as 'purchasers of educational services' for their children—are becoming increasingly demanding. Other parents, perhaps as a consequence of their own school experience and life circumstances, are less engaged though remain hopeful that their children's interests and needs are being well catered for. And there are still others who may feel disengaged from their children's education and are quite unsupportive of the school's efforts. In other words, the relationships that a school has with parents and the home have always been and remain key element of its success. Mal, Glenn and their contributing authors provide a range of fresh insights on this theme, and argue that building and sustaining a strong connection between the home and the school is fundamental to young people's learning.

But this book goes further. It argues that the developments in digital technologies are such that the possibilities for strengthening the nexus are more urgent and more promising than ever before. The urgency comes from the need to engage young people in their learning. Continuing with the industrial models and mindsets for the development and delivery of curriculum is just not an option. In the Industrial Age, young people went to school to learn things they could not learn at home. That was the whole point: to prepare them to work and live in an industrial society. And for much of the past 150 years schools have been outstandingly successful in performing that service. But things are different now. Post-industrial society with its increasing use and reliance on digital technologies is having profound effects on the ways people—and especially young people—access knowledge and learn. The tables have turned! Through their access and use of digital technologies young people are now able 'to learn things' at home that they cannot learn (or are not allowed to learn) at school. Schools need to recognise this and use it to their advantage.

The authors make this point tellingly. They rightly argue that schools, educational leaders and bureaucrats need to overcome their fear of digital technologies and the potential pitfalls and sensationalist dangers to privacy and wellbeing, and wisely embrace the concept of digital citizenship as an outcome for all young people. Such approaches care less about fruitless banning and filtering charades, and more about informing, critiquing and building knowledge, skills, understandings and values to the point where our young people are able to confidently ask questions and find solutions that are life giving for themselves and for others. Clearly, moves by schools to embrace this challenge must involve parents and the home in new and engaging ways if a meaningful nexus is to be achieved.

Allied with these possibilities is the fact that many schools are currently developing the capacity for staff, students and parents to communicate with each other like never before. Email, websites, wikis and blogs are being increasingly used as vehicles to engage and connect local communities. But it does not stop there. The capacity of these technologies to connect with individuals, groups and organisations beyond the school, in other schools, across town, regionally, nationally and internationally is bringing new insights and meanings to the term 'school community'. Those school communities that are beginning to take advantage of digital technologies in building these connections for valued educational purposes might appropriately be labelled as 'networked school communities'. Leading these networked school communities is one of the key emerging educational challenges of our time. I am confident that this book will assist them in meeting this challenge.

Professor Mike Gaffney has wide experience as a teacher, an education system senior executive, and as a researcher, consultant and policy adviser to Australian Governments in areas of education policy, curriculum and teaching practices appropriate for twenty-first century schooling.

Contents

Figures and tables

Acknowledgements

The writing of this book ventured into largely unchartered waters in envisioning the future of schooling and providing guidance for those willing to move to networked school communities. This venture entailed significant commitment by all the authors of the chapters, extensive ongoing liaison and resilience in drafting, reworking and sharpening all of those important contributions.

We would like to thank the authors for their willingness to join this challenging journey in collectively portraying the vision of what is possible and subsequently offering guidance throughout their respective chapters for helping the reader in realising this vision.

It is important to acknowledge many who have helped bring this book from being an idea through to publication. We thank Professor Michael Gaffney (Australian Catholic University) and Allan Shaw (Chief Executive Association of Heads of Independent Schools of Australia) for their ongoing counsel in the development of the book.

We would particularly like to thank Ralph Saubern, the Managing Director of ACER Press, for supporting our vision for this book. We appreciated the ongoing advice by Maureen O'Keefe and the meticulous work undertaken by Ruth Watkins in checking various drafts of the manuscript. The collaborative liaison between Maureen, Ruth and us assisted greatly. We thank Ronél Redman for her professional editing of this book.

The valued support from Professor Claire Wyatt-Smith (Dean, Faculty of Education, Griffith University) was critical to the book's development. The research assistance provided by Dr Alison Green and Vilma Simbag (Griffith University) assisted with the development of an extensive synthesis of relevant research to inform the book.

Mal Lee and Glenn Finger

The contributors

The editors

Mal Lee

Mal Lee is an educational consultant and author specialising in the development of digital schools. He is a former director of schools, secondary college principal, technology company director and a member of the Mayer Committee that identified the Key Competencies for Australia's schools. A Fellow of the Australian Council for Educational Administration (FACEA), Mal has been closely associated with the use of digital technology in schooling, particularly by the school leadership, for the last decade. A historian by training, Mal has written extensively, particularly in the *Practising Administrator, Australian Educational Leaders* and *Access, Educational Technology Guide* on school planning for the Information Age, digital schooling and the effective use of digital technology in schooling. He has released three previous publications with ACER Press: in 2008, Mal and Professor Michael Gaffney were the editors of *Leading a digital school*; in 2009, he was co-author with Dr Arthur Winzenried of *The use of instructional technology in schools: Lessons to be learned*, and co-author with Chris Betcher of *The interactive whiteboard revolution: Teaching with IWBs*. Mal provides not only a business, research and school administrator's perspective, but also an extensive understanding of the structural, organisational, financial and technological challenges facing school and education leaders as they seek to take advantage of the immense and ever-merging educational and administrative opportunities made available by digital technology, in a networked world.

Glenn Finger

Associate Professor Glenn Finger is Deputy Dean (Learning and Teaching) in the Faculty of Education at Griffith University, Queensland, Australia. This portfolio involves responsibilities that reflect his passion—learning and teaching. Glenn has extensively researched, published and provided consultancies in creating transformational stories of the use of information and communications technologies (ICT) to enhance learning. He has contributed to the scholarship of teaching through more than 50 peer-reviewed publications (including books, chapters, articles, conference papers) and major reviews. He is the lead author of the book *Transforming learning with ICT: Making IT happen*. For his outstanding teaching related to ICT, Glenn has won various teaching awards and citations, including the prestigious 2009 Australian Learning and Teaching Council (ALTC) Award for Teaching Excellence (Social Sciences), the Australian Teacher Education Association Pearson Education Teacher Educator of the Year in 2008, an Australian Learning and Teaching Council Citation for Outstanding Contributions to Student Learning, and is a Fellow of the Australian College of Educators. Prior to his appointment at Griffith University in 1999, he had served with Education Queensland, a large education system in Australia, for more than 24 years as a physical education specialist, primary school teacher, deputy principal and acting principal in a wide variety of educational settings.

The authors

Neil Anderson

Professor Neil Anderson holds the Pearl Logan Chair in Rural Education at James Cook University, Queensland, Australia and is a senior research fellow at the Cairns Institute. His research has focused on rural education, e-learning and ICT equity themes. Current research interests include leading an Australian Research Council (ARC) funded study that involves collaborative research to examine issues associated with middle schooling and ICT. Other ARC funded studies have focused on the low rates of female participation in professional ICT occupations and education pathways. Professor Neil Anderson is the coordinator of SiMERR QLD, the state hub of the National Centre of Mathematics, Science and ICT research for regional and rural Australia, and leads the 'Wired' research community within the multi-university consortium, Eidos. He serves on the editorial board of *Australian Educational Researcher, Australian Educational Computing* and *Knowledge-based Innovation in China*. He is a member of the advisory board and conference committee for the Asia Pacific Professional Leaders in Education Conference (QSAPPLE).

Lyn Courtney

Lyn Courtney is a registered psychologist and PhD candidate at James Cook University, Queensland, Australia. She is the senior research officer assisting Neil Anderson's team working on two Australian Research Council (ARC) Linkage Grants investigating declining participation rates of girls in information and communication technology (ICT). Lyn is the Queensland ICT coordinator for the Centre of Science, ICT and Mathematics Education for Rural and Regional Australia (SiMERR), adjunct lecturer in the School of Education and associate lecturer in the School of Psychology. Lyn's PhD thesis, *Successful ageing of Australian baby boom career women: The psychosocial processes of constructing quality of life judgments*, is nearing completion.

Lyn Hay

Lyn Hay is a lecturer in the School of Information Studies at Charles Sturt University in New South Wales, Australia. Before joining the academic team at CSU, she held teaching and teacher librarian positions in New South Wales central and secondary schools. Her teaching and research areas include teacher librarianship and school libraries, effective information use, information policy issues, the use of Web 2.0 to support learning and libraries, online community building and Computer Supported Cooperative Work (CSCW), and e-learning in universities. She is the course coordinator for the Master of Applied Science (Teacher Librarianship), holds a teaching fellowship with CSU's Flexible Learning Institute (FLI), and is involved in a number of scholarships in teaching projects. She has published articles and book chapters and presented at local, national and international conferences. Lyn is a recipient of state, national and international awards for her contribution to teacher librarianship, including the Australian School Library Association's ASLA Citation (2007), ASLA (NSW) John Hirst Award (1997) and International Association of School Libraries (IASL) Commendation Award (1997).

Brenton Holmes

Brenton Holmes spent much of his professional career in education, as a teacher, media producer, lecturer, bureaucrat, ministerial officer and researcher, and has long been involved in community advocacy roles. He also spent fifteen years managing Senate committees within the Australian Federal Parliament. He now works as a freelance writer and researcher, including for the Family–School and Community Partnerships Bureau.

Romina Jamieson-Proctor

Associate Professor Romina Jamieson-Proctor is the Associate Director of Education at the University of Southern Queensland, Australia. She has had first-hand involvement with the use of computer-based technologies in classrooms since 1980. She has also been extensively involved in teacher education programs and professional development activities focusing on the use of ICT in education and demonstrating to teachers how they can effectively integrate and create ICT applications that transform curriculum, teaching and learning to meet the needs of twenty-first century learners. Romina has also had extensive experience managing national and industry-sponsored research projects investigating the impact of ICT on teaching and learning.

Kay Kimber

Dr Kay Kimber holds dual roles in a secondment partnership between Griffith University and Brisbane Girls Grammar School in Queensland, Australia. As a Research Fellow at Griffith University, she has been involved with an Australian Research Council (ARC) funded longitudinal study on secondary students' online use and creation of curricular knowledge. As an English teacher of many years' experience, she has been an advocate of new media integration into classrooms. Her research interests have included digital literacies, literacy, assessment, design of learning environments, and pre-service teacher education. The latter reflects her position as Director of the Centre for Professional Practice at Brisbane Girls Grammar School.

Colin Lankshear

Professor Colin Lankshear is Professor of Literacy and New Technologies at James Cook University, Queensland, Australia and is Adjunct Professor at McGill University and Mount Saint Vincent University in Canada. Colin is recognised internationally as a leader among scholars working at interfaces between pedagogy, learning and popular cultures of computing. His books include *New literacies* (2006), *New literacies Sampler* (2007), *Digital literacies* (2008) and a *Handbook for teacher research* (2004) jointly published with Michele Knobel. His international research collaborations include two Australian Research Council (ARC) Linkage projects and research funded by Canada's Social Sciences and Humanities Research Council.

Kevin Larkin

Kevin Larkin is Assistant Principal (Administration) at a large Australian primary school and a part-time tutor and doctoral student at Griffith University. His thesis investigates how various usage patterns of wireless-enabled Netbooks affects the classroom environment and communication patterns of four middle school classrooms. Kevin is an educator with over 27 years experience in a variety of educational and cultural contexts. He has taught in both state and Catholic primary schools in Australia and overseas, and has taught undergraduate and postgraduate university students for the past eight years. Kevin holds masters degrees in both Education and Educational Leadership and his research interests include ICT, adolescent education and Activity Theory.

Martin Levins

Martin Levins is an educator with immense national and international practical experience in the use of digital technology in all areas of education over the past 30 years. He is Director of Information Technology and Coordinator of Technological and Applied Studies at The Armidale School in regional Australia. Martin's experience goes beyond the classroom to include consultancy in office technologies, publishing, advertising and journalism. His education experience runs the full gamut from primary to tertiary, and includes significant involvement in the identification of education and training needs, and the development, promotion and delivery of education and training courses. He has built an extensive network of contacts in the education and technology fields, locally, nationally, and in New Zealand, the United States and United Kingdom, through frequent attendance and presentation at relevant conferences both domestically and overseas. An education columnist for *Australian Macworld* and regular presenter at domestic and international conferences, Martin is a team player with a wealth of experience in bringing good ideas to fruition.

Damian Maher

Dr Damian Maher is currently a lecturer in Primary Education at the University of Technology, in Sydney, Australia. Damian has worked in primary schools for over 20 years up until 2007. He started work when computers were first introduced into primary schools and has followed their evolving use with interest. His doctoral study examined the use of communication technologies in primary schools focusing on issues of access. It was during this research that the importance of a home–school link using digital technologies became clear. The focus of Damian's current research revolves around the use of computers in primary schools. He is currently conducting a research project focusing on the use of interactive whiteboards. Also of interest is how ICT can be harnessed to enhance the education of pre-service primary teachers in universities.

Judy Parr

Associate Professor Judy Parr researches and teaches in the Faculty of Education at the University of Auckland, New Zealand. An Auckland history masters graduate, she then completed a teaching diploma. Judy taught in Canberra for a number of years, later graduating with BSc (Hons) and a PhD in Psychology from the Australian National University. Literacy, with particular emphasis on writing and the interface between literacy and technology, are her main research interests within the broader field of developmental and educational psychology. Judy publishes in a wide range of international journals on literacy, technology and school change.

Bernard Ryall

Bernard Ryall is the Chief Financial Officer for the Parramatta Catholic Education Office in Sydney, Australia. He is a member of the senior leadership group with responsibility for strategy and direction in support of the mission to improve the learning outcomes for every student in all Catholic schools in western Sydney. Since his appointment in October 2006 he has developed and implemented system-wide reform to deliver value-for-money solutions, improve financial stewardship and report in an environment of greater accountability. Prior to his appointment, Bernard held senior executive positions in the financial services sector and has a record of outstanding achievements.

Pei-Chen Sun

Associate Professor Pei-Chen Sun received his PhD in Management Information Systems from National Sun Yat-Sen University, Taiwan. He has over ten years of extensive experience in e-learning practice and research. He has served as a consultant on this area to several organisations and has published over 30 refereed journal articles and 100 papers in academic conferences. His work focuses on the design and development of adaptive ICT-based education models that foster learners' effective learning at every level. Dr Sun is currently Associate Professor of the Institute for Computer and Information Education and the Computer Centre Manager at National Kaohsiung Normal University, Taiwan.

Roberta Thompson

Roberta Thompson is a sessional lecturer, tutorial leader and PhD candidate at Griffith University, Queensland, Australia. Her doctoral thesis explores the normative interaction patterns of adolescent females in digital landscapes and highlights the link between strategic vulnerabilities, relationship problems and cyber bullying. Roberta is an experienced educator who has worked in various educational contexts in Canada, Australia and New Zealand. For the last three years, she has mentored third-year teacher education students in behaviour and classroom management and has worked with local schools in dealing with safety and bullying concerns.

Ray Tolley

Ray Tolley is a highly experienced educator with years of practical experience in the use of digital technologies in all manner of schools in the United Kingdom. Ray started teaching in 1963 and has held a wide range of senior posts in schools in the UK, combining technological awareness, a keen eye for problem solving and a strong leadership in policy making and curriculum development. Following many years of innovative work in schools, he was quickly appointed as an advisory teacher for ICT as soon as the first computers became available to schools in 1981. After working for some years in this capacity he was appointed as Director of Technology, setting up the CTC in Gateshead. In 1999, he was appointed as head of ICT and project manager to assist in turning around a 'failing school' in Oxfordshire. His work is reflected in his NAACE fellowship. Since retiring from full-time teaching, he has been able to spend more time in providing online support to both teachers and technicians through his company, Maximise ICT Ltd, latterly concentrating on the development of a UK and European version of e-Folio. Recently he has produced two research papers, one on VLEs in schools, and as an outcome of that, another paper on the place of e-Portfolios—both of which are very relevant to the Home Access program.

Lorrae Ward

Dr Lorrae Ward is currently working as an independent researcher and evaluator. Her career includes secondary teaching, professional development facilitation and educational research and evaluation. She has long been interested in the potential of digital technologies to transform teaching and learning. Her PhD considered the impact of ICT on secondary teaching practice and highlighted the importance of the world-view of teachers in determining the extent to which ICT impacted on the classroom experiences of their students. Recent work has been in the area of schooling improvement and enhancing outcomes for students through increased accountability, purposive leadership and evidence-based practices.

Claire Wyatt-Smith

Professor Claire Wyatt-Smith is Dean of the Faculty of Education at Griffith University, Queensland, Australia. She has been a sole or chief investigator on a number of Australian Research Council (ARC) and government-funded projects, primarily in the fields of literacy and assessment. Central to her work is a focus on quality assessment and conceptualising multimodal assessment. With over 70 key publications in international and national journals, her research has informed both state and national curricula and assessment policies. Further, she has worked as a national adviser to government at state and federal levels for several years. Current research includes an ARC Linkage study of standards-driven assessment reform with a focus on teacher judgement and assessment to improve learning. Her most recent book is titled *Educational assessment in the 21st century: Connecting theory and practice* (Wyatt-Smith & Cumming 2009).

Jason Zagami

Dr Jason Zagami is a lecturer at the School of Education and Professional Studies (Gold Coast) in the Faculty of Education of Griffith University in Queensland, Australia where he conducts research in cognition, professional learning and expertise, and all aspects of educational technologies—with a current focus on mLearning, virtual environments and neural interfaces. Jason has 15 years experience in K–12 ICT education and has been the recipient of the Queensland Computer Educator of the Year and Outstanding National Achievement by a Teacher awards. He is also an Apple Distinguished Educator, the Australian HP Innovations in Education Mentor, president of the Queensland Society for Information Technology in Education, and a board member of the Australian Council for Computers in Education.

PART A

The digital and networked world

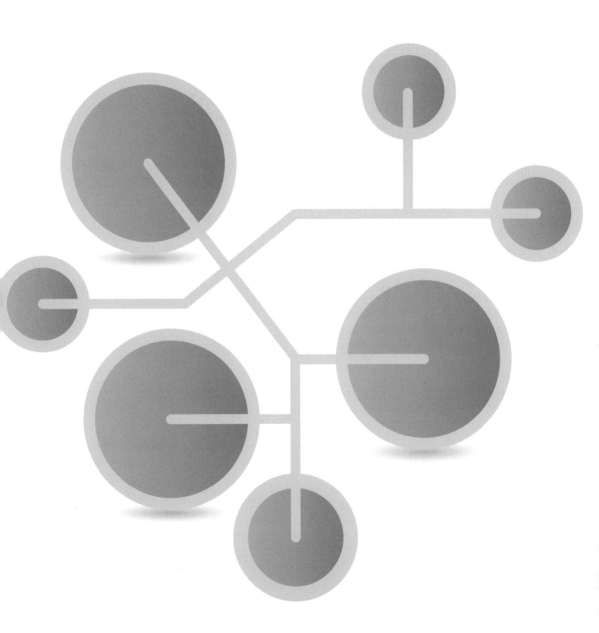

CHAPTER 1

The challenge: Developing a networked mode of schooling

MAL LEE & GLENN FINGER

Schools are being designed for a new balance that combines the best of traditional classroom learning with leading 21st-century learning methods and tools.

At the same time, federal, state and local policies must help guide the creation of learning environments that serve all students ...

Bernie Trilling (2009)

The context—the evolution of the networked mode of schooling

The move to the digital and networked world has brought with it profound and pervasive changes to most situations in our daily lives, including the global economy and changes in the nature of work. However, schooling largely remains one of the exceptions in terms of the limited impact of new technologies significantly transforming learning and teaching and the organisation of schooling. Internationally, while there are examples of pathfinding schools and education authorities that have made considerable progress in reshaping their policies, practices and organisational structures to better prepare young people for a digital future, the vast majority of the world's schools continue in their traditional form, still heavily reliant on paper-based technologies.

In 2009, the most commonly used technologies in many of the classrooms of the world—including those in the developed world—were the pen, paper and the teaching board usually located at the front of a classroom, be it black, green or white (Lee & Winzenried 2009). While the schools continue with their largely traditional ways and operate on the assumption that formal education happens within the school walls, young people of the developed and developing worlds have embraced the use of the digital, networked world and integrated it ubiquitously into their daily lives. In the process, they have begun educating themselves for digital futures. Importantly, many parents are actively supporting their children's use of those technologies in their homes and personal lives, and informally working with them to develop their digital competencies and wider life skills. Those parents are, as in previous times, playing a vital role in the education of young people.

The consequence is that we suspect that this will create an ever-widening divide between the use made of the digital technologies in the home and the school in the education of today's young people. For example, in Australia, the Programme for International Student Assessment (PISA) 2006 study reported that 96 per cent of Australian students who were part of the study had a computer for school use, and 91 per cent had access to the Internet at home (Organisation for Economic Co-operation and Development [OECD] 2009). However, only 23 per cent of students indicated that they used a computer at school 'almost every day' (OECD 2009). We suspect that many Australian students use their digital technologies at home every day and access the Internet more frequently from home than at school, and that this is a trend evident internationally.

While it is pleasing that the more prescient educational and government leaders are concerned about this development and have made early steps to address the divide, the reality is that this divide will continue to grow, and that it will be far more astute for all involved in shaping the education of young people—and in particular those in educational leadership and governance situations—to recognise the importance of shifting to a model of schooling appropriate for education in a digital, networked world.

The authors of this book appreciate the enormity of that call and the challenge of moving away from the mode of schooling most of us have only ever known—that is, the paper-based mode that operates as a discrete entity within the school's walls and timetable. The cultural impediments and resistance to change these structures of schooling are immense, and are not to be underestimated. Notwithstanding, across the developed world education authorities, schools, and indeed national governments that have moved to a quite different digital operational mode, have begun to remove the traditional school walls and disturb the traditional conception of timetabled formal lessons, and use the opportunities provided by the networked technology to move into a third distinct phase of schooling, which is strongly networked and collaborative in nature and is starting to involve the students' homes more fully in teaching and learning. (Note: the reference to 'home' throughout the book incorporates both the home-based and mobile technology.)

While these are still embryonic developments, they are sufficient to provide an important insight into the immense potential and the opportunities that exist to markedly enhance the quality, relevance and effectiveness of schools. To date, the majority of the moves are sporadic in nature and not tied to an overarching model of schooling. What the authors will suggest in the following pages is that the moves can be conceptualised as a new and emerging phase of schooling—the networked schooling mode. We argue that with foresight, strategic thinking and planning all schools can move to become what we have termed 'networked school communities' and realise the immense potential of that mode of schooling, particularly when developing a stronger home–school nexus.

Pathfinding schools across the world have moved from the traditional paper-based to the digital (Lee & Gaffney 2008). In recent years a small but significant number of the digital schools have taken another step in the evolutionary process and begun to shift to the networked mode of schooling.

What mode is your school operating within? What needs to be done to move it to a position where it is providing an education for life and work in a digital and networked world, and making astute everyday use of the appropriate technology?

The evolution and changing phases of schooling

Many have assumed, either implicitly or explicitly, that the basic form of the place we call school is well defined and has an organisational structure that would never change. Throughout the twentieth century, many innovators tried to change the structure and organisation of schooling, but, as Perelman (1992) noted, those dents were soon removed when the innovators moved on. Schools have proven to be remarkably resistant to any sustained structural change.

While there have been some exceptions, the reality is that the vast majority of schools across the developed world have a remarkably similar structure and modus operandi today to that of a century ago. Few, if any, schools in the twentieth century succeeded in getting all their teachers to use digital technologies in their everyday teaching. Significant structural changes in the mode of schooling only became apparent in the pathfinding schools in the early 2000s, and only in those schools that were making extensive use of the digital technology.

As indicated in Chapter 3, the significant change first became apparent around 2002/2003 in those schools that had succeeded in getting all their teachers to normalise the use of a suite of digital technologies in their everyday teaching. Those schools quickly moved from a few teachers using the digital technologies in their teaching to all teachers using them effectively. Lee and Winzenried (2009) described this dramatic surge as *digital take-off*.

The catalytic impact of that *digital take-off* upon those school's operations was dramatic. The schools found that virtually all of their operations, the teaching, the administration and the communications could be predominantly digitally based. Very quickly, the school's staff began to appreciate how the digital technologies enabled them to do many new things in new ways. As their expectations and excitement grew, they increasingly questioned the ways of old and discarded them in favour of more effective and efficient digitally based processes and systems. This resulted in a transition as the schools moved to a new digital operational mode, began operating within a digital paradigm and became digital schools (Lee & Gaffney 2008; Lee & Winzenried 2009). The contrast between the paper-based and digital mode is summarised in Table 1.1.

Table 1.1   Characteristics of the paper-based and digitally based paradigms of schooling

Paper-based schooling	Digitally based schooling
Industrial Age organisational structures	Information Age organisational model
Schools operating as discrete, largely stand-alone entities	Networked, incorporating the total school community and its homes
A segmented organisational structure, with a widespread division of labour	Integrated synergistic operations
Discrete and constant instructional technologies in paper, the pen and the teaching board	Suite of changing, increasingly sophisticated, converging and networked digital instructional technologies
Individual lesson preparation	Increasing collaborative lesson development
Reliance on mass media	Interactive multimedia
Staffing hierarchical, with fixed roles	Changing flexible team-oriented staff roles
Well-defined and long-lasting jobs	Uncertainty, untapped potential, rising expectations and frequent job changes
Slow segmented paper-based internal communication and information management	Instant communication and management of digital information across the organisation
Long-established operational parameters	Few established operational parameters

(Source: Lee & Gaffney 2008)

Fundamental aspects of the traditional school's operations had not only changed, but had changed forever. Where schooling previously had been characterised by its constancy and stability, once the schools became digital, and in a sense on an innovation phase, they found it important to continually review and improve their operations, seeking to make informed, strategic decisions about the use of the digital technologies available and emerging, and adopt new ways of providing the best possible schooling.

It is that quest that has prompted schools operating in the digital mode to appreciate that the networked technology provides opportunities to discard the physical constraints of the school walls and traditional timetabled lessons, and to opt for an even richer, broader mode and conceptualisation of how, when, where and why schooling can take place—that is, one that is networked and envisions a collaborative, interdependent relationship between educators, school, home and the wider community.

Significantly, this development is happening in a small sample of pathfinder school contexts at the same time as the aforementioned divide between what is happening with digital use in the home and the school is growing. What the authors are suggesting is that this is an opportune time to unite these two developments and consciously embark on the quest to develop a mode of schooling that better integrates the very significant digital capacity of students' homes with that of the school's digital capacity. This can achieve a shared vision of creating a home–school nexus through networked school communities.

That shared vision can capitalise on the digital capacity of the home with the already extensive, important, informal teaching that parents provide every day to their children, and more consciously enhance the vital informal education that young people acquire beyond the school gate. For example, through focusing on *quality teachers*, rather than the shared and more sophisticated concept of *quality teaching* where teaching is seen as a shared responsibility, most developed societies have lost sight of the fundamental importance of the informal education occurring outside the schoolroom. The consequence has been that blame and responsibility has shifted to individual schools and teachers, and this excludes the potential for the contributions of learning in the home, which remains a vast, largely untapped and unacknowledged national resource in terms of human resources and access to digital technologies. The belief is that by combining the learning that young people are undertaking in their everyday use of the digital with a more pronounced parent and home involvement in learning, nations should be able to significantly enhance the educational outcomes of their young people.

Central to this ongoing evolution of schooling has been school leadership. That will remain so, even as schools make further use of the networked mode, and involve the school's wider community and in particular its parents and students in the collective education of young people. While some education authorities and national governments have provided invaluable support to the quest to harness the technology and provide a mode of schooling appropriate to the twenty-first century, ultimately the successful development of any school has to come from the individual school itself and its leadership. The focus of this book will be very much on the development of the individual school and the adoption of an organisational mode appropriate to its particular context.

It will become ever-more apparent that while it will be important that schools are provided the appropriate support and direction and are obliged to play their role in the development of the specified national educational outcomes, how each school fulfils their commitment will be best decided by the individual school community.

The way ahead

What we suggest throughout this book is that you are encouraged to step back from the day-to-day approach and take a more global view of your school and beyond your school. After identifying and examining the key variables at play, major trends, opportunities to capitalise upon the digital and networked technology and to build upon the educative power of the home, the book aims to assist you to chart a way forward for the development of a distinctly networked mode of schooling that utilises available opportunities to better prepare young people for their digital futures.

We are sure that this will lead to a greater appreciation of the dramatic technological developments occurring, particularly within the homes and with the new and emerging mobile technologies, a much stronger recognition of the part the parents and the students themselves should play in the education of society's young people, and that schools can no longer be 'stand-alone' entities but need to now be part of the networked world. We are not suggesting that schools can or should make dramatic changes overnight, but that they simply move from their current starting points, develop a clearer appreciation of the kind of teaching and learning environment they want to provide, understand the opportunities available, and commence charting the changes they want. Having done that homework, most will appreciate that they can embark on that quest immediately.

In advocating the adoption of a networked mode, the authors have in mind developing a model where the school dismantles the present school walls, takes advantage of the digital and networked technologies to allow the parents/caregivers, the students and any other people or organisations to work with the teachers in educating the students for a digital future. A think tank organised by the Illinois Institute of Design, which involved thinkers like Charles Handy and Gary Hamel, in exploring the nature of future digital schools, observed:

> Schools need to become network institutions, establishing themselves as the centre of diverse, overlapping networks of learning, which reach out to the fullest possible range of institutions, sources of information, social groups and physical facilities. To solve this problem schools need to become nodes on a network instead of isolated factories.

> Illinois Institute of Design (2007, p. 25)

At the moment, most schools and education authorities are unsuccessfully trying to replicate in the classroom the level of digital technology in the home. While it is important that all teachers have in their classrooms the appropriate digital technologies to provide the requisite teaching and learning (Lee & Winzenried 2009), not all that technology has to be acquired by the school to be used in the school for only a limited number of days a year, and number of hours each day. In a networked school community, where there is a successful nexus between the school and the home, a significant proportion of the digital technology could be that owned and maintained by the home.

A home–school nexus

The authors' consistent call throughout this work is to focus on the positives and the potential, and avoid the reactionary and resistive—to take advantage of the myriad of opportunities being opened almost daily by the digital technologies to enhance the quality, relevance and appropriateness of schooling. The preoccupation in the literature and educational policy making thus far has tended to focus heavily on the perceived negative aspects and dangers of young people working in the networked world.

Our approach involves a search for the pathfinders—the schools and education authorities—who have taken the alternative approach to bridge the digital difference between the home and the school. We are positioning the discourse around 'difference' rather than 'divide', though we recognise that a divide exists in a number of areas. Our rationale is to capitalise upon the difference rather than accentuate the wedge politics by focusing on the language of divide. For example, many governments and education authorities have perceived the use of the Internet by students in their personal lives as a threat from which they must be protected. As a consequence, one sees across the world's schools student access being increasingly curtailed, except in the more proactive, visionary settings.

While we appreciate there are some legitimate concerns that do need to be addressed in the school's use of the digital and online, what we are currently experiencing in the majority of school situations is the now historic negative reaction that has accompanied the introduction of all new major technologies. Learning and teaching in the twenty-first century requires a fresh look at the possibilities in a globalised knowledge economy where the digital technologies are the lubricants of that globalisation and increasingly networked world.

While other sectors such as business and industry have moved in this way, education, apart from the pathfinders, is rapidly becoming seen as irrelevant by young people through its antiquated division between the home and school learning environments. To illustrate, it is taken for granted that we can undertake financial transactions anywhere in the world, in face-to-face or online environments at a time and place of our own choosing. While online fraud, privacy and security are issues to be addressed, these have not prevented a transformation of the way we do our personal financial business which is now more effective and efficient than the more restricted practices in the past. This transformation is certainly not reflected in widespread educational changes. It is with this in mind that the authors argue for the adoption by all associated with school development of a positive approach that recognises the current reality, the major trends and shifts, and seeks to take advantage of the plethora of opportunities available.

In this changing, uncertain world, it is important that school communities take control and shape the school they want, and not be reactive, in order to shape their desired future.

Developing networked school communities—organisation of the book

The potential advantages of developing a networked school community are immense, but in light of the natural propensity to view an entity like schooling through what we have known, most will not be immediately obvious, even to those working in schools. The aim of this book is to flesh out those many advantages, and then in turn to indicate what school communities can do, starting today, to markedly enhance the attractiveness, quality, relevance, appropriateness and effectiveness of the education provided to students in schools.

While the traditional school has served society well for many years, most would recognise that, despite the efforts of many dedicated staff, it has significant and sometimes disturbing shortcomings. In addition to the contrasts between the digital developments in the home and the school, there are shortcomings that are far greater in terms of the declining relevance of the education provided. The traditional school has difficulties in adequately catering for the full range of students, with many today still being alienated and marginalised, with student suspensions, exclusions, drop outs and 'turn off' rate remaining far too high. In most developed nations, the Year 12 retention rates have remained well below the desired 100 per cent vision.

The technology has provided society the chance to build on the good aspects of the traditional school and create new, more effective, improved schooling variants. It would be an important missed opportunity for schools to not capitalise upon this.

In examining a possible networked mode that will entail a close and collaborative working relationship between the school and the students' homes, the authors are conscious of the importance of drawing the parents (and in particular parents in school governance positions), parents' political representatives, and school and education authority leaders into the discourse. We have thus consciously pitched this publication at the general reader, seeking to provide a work that all associated with the development of the school community can use to shape the desired future. Importantly, there is a need to balance the readability of such a book with supporting scholarly references to evidence-based research. Therefore, this book serves both the general reader and those looking for further research and to pursue scholarly inquiry.

This book is organised in four sections. Part A introduces the reader to the call to develop a networked mode of schooling that bridges the school–home difference, the form it can take and the state of play today. Part B examines the home and school scene today, particularly as it relates to the use of digital technology, Part C moves our thinking to the opportunities associated with developing networked school communities, and Part D addresses the practicalities of implementing a networked mode of schooling.

The home–school scene today

A continuing theme throughout this book is the emphasis on the opportunities for 'school designers' to build on the ever-expanding, ever-evolving richness of the human and technological resources available within the home and create a home–school nexus, rather than seeing the difference as a divide and therefore as being problematic.

However, before one can build on the resources, a situational analysis is needed to understand and recognise the present situation, the resources available and the use being made of them, and the issues to be addressed in seeking to develop a networked school community. The key is to be positive, optimistic and hopeful, and to focus on creating an effective, collaborative nexus between the home and the school through developing a mode of networked schooling appropriate to the times and the context.

The networked school community: The opportunities

Your school has far more to gain over the long term by forming a working nexus with homes and moving the school to the networked mode, than seeking to redress the current home–school divide. In developing solutions, the approach for schools should not be to try and replicate the level of home digital technologies in the school, but to understand ways in which schools can take advantage of the differences that exist. It is vital for schools to recognise that the level of digital technology in the average home already markedly exceeds that in the average classroom. Furthermore, since the early 1990s, the differences have continued to grow (Lee & Winzenried 2009), and the conditions in favour of the average home are such that the authors believe the differences will continue to grow.

You will soon come to appreciate the many opportunities that exist in every facet of school and education authority operations to create a meaningful nexus between the home and the school that will help enhance the quality, appropriateness, effectiveness and indeed the efficiency of the schooling—whether it be in the school's understanding of students' needs, the teaching and learning, the school development or governance, planning, evaluation, access to and management of the instructional technology, student assessment and reporting, student health and welfare, administration, communications, accounts, finance or the facility to work with industry. The intention is to provoke your thinking about the possibilities, to examine the work of the pathfinders, to engage with relevant research, and to identify the issues that you will need to address if you are seeking to create and develop a home–school nexus.

It is becoming increasingly evident that not only does the average home have appreciably greater digital technology than the average classroom, but that the nature and level of learning emanating from young people's everyday use of that technology are markedly enhancing their digital competencies, to the extent that already nations like the UK are appreciating that home Internet access for young people needs to be universal and harnessed if a country is to use education to enhance national productivity.

One of the greatest stumbling blocks to schools harnessing digital technology is the limited recurrent funding they receive from what is in essence a model designed to resource the traditional paper-based school. In addition to that shortcoming is the fact that schooling is one of the last major endeavours not to restructure its workforce. In contrast to other industries that have reduced their workforce and made greater use of technology over the past 50 years, schooling has steadily increased its workforce based on teacher-to-student class ratios and, as a consequence, increased the percentage of the recurrent budget spent on staff salaries. That development has markedly limited the school's ability to fund the ever-growing technological needs. That shortfall has usually been addressed by a series of ad hoc, Band-Aid solutions that draw on the parents or on short-term government funding. Networked school communities need a regular and known body of funds they can rely on in their planning.

A key understanding often overlooked by governments and schools is that families globally have made, and continue to make, a vast investment in digital technologies, most of which will be used extensively by young people in their play and entertainment as well as their formal schooling. In making that investment, particularly on personal computers, Internet access and mobile phone technologies, the majority of parents believe the outlay will enhance the education, future job prospects and life chances of their children. The authors will contend that it is time for schools and governments to recognise the national importance of that investment and explore the adoption of recurrent funding models for networked school communities that factor in that ongoing investment by parents. It is appreciated that this represents a fundamental change in the assumptions of the past 150 years that the state should fund schooling. But today we live in a very different, technological, globalised world from that when the original education policies were formed. Today, across the developed world, students' homes have, and will continue to have, far greater and more powerful digital instructional technology than the average school.

Despite these developments the response by the vast majority of schools, education authorities and often governments has been to either ban or restrict the use of that technology in the school, and to impose numerous impediments to accessing the Internet and mobile technologies, all of which simply serves to aid young people's largely unfettered use of that technology outside the classroom, with none of the school support and guidance so important to their appropriate education. There appears to be the simplistic assumption that if the technology is excluded from the classroom and the school, all will be fine.

While the call to recognise the learning of the home has been there for decades, and while some significant moves have been made in some schools and education authorities generally, there is a reluctance to recognise learning that occurs outside the timetabled, physical classroom learning. That needs to change. Brenton Holmes sheds some light on this in Chapter 11, by exploring the home perspective and the opportunities opened by parents working collaboratively with the school to educate young people for a digital, networked future. In shaping new thinking, careful thought needs not only to be given to how best to capitalise upon the learning occurring in the home, and the role the home can play in a more networked mode of learning, but also how to attune the present, sometimes very traditional school curriculum to better develop the key attributes of the twenty-first century. Transformation of the curriculum, pedagogy and assessment will be needed. Brenton, who has had extensive experience at the national level in Australia in fostering the involvement of parents in schooling, examines the perspectives of both the parents and the students that ought to be borne in mind when forging the desired collaborative nexus. It is very easy for even the most sympathetic of school leaders to forget the different perspective they bring to any school–home relationship, and the importance of factoring in the desires and wants of both the parents and the students in any initiative.

However, one needs to look far beyond the current pathfinding efforts to use the home learning to bolster the traditional approaches to curriculum, pedagogy and assessment and design new conceptualisations of schooling. The curriculum should not only formally recognise the key academic achievements possible through learning outside of the formal school day, but also factor those attainments into the overall 'school' teaching and learning program. In addition, there are opportunities for the home–school collaboration to relatively quickly enhance both individually and collectively schools', systems' and a nation's performance on the student learning performance tables and rankings.

Implementation

There is little to be gained from reading and thinking without converting ideas into action— to make things happen in positive ways for schools, teachers, students, their parents and communities. In looking to work collaboratively with the home there is much to be said for starting small, to move in only a couple of areas initially and to learn from your experiences and those of other pathfinders as you gradually extend the links across all of the school's operations. Our belief is that you will soon come to appreciate the general issues to be borne in mind in operating within and developing a networked school community.

If you are contemplating a significant move into this area it is strongly suggested you also have a close read of *Leading a digital school* (Lee & Gaffney 2008) as many of the issues addressed in it complement the guidance here for implementing a successful home–school nexus. It is appreciated that in many instances you will be moving into uncharted waters. Our hope is that the opportunities flagged, experiences documented and the issues identified will assist your journey.

The authors contend that if nations want to provide the best possible education for all its young, the home needs to be involved in a significant, collaborative form that:

- takes advantage of the opportunities of the digital, networked technologies;
- recognises the busy lives of the parents; and
- obligates the professionals to develop appropriate modes of teaching, learning and collaboration.

The facilities of the digital, networked world have the capacity to fundamentally transform the traditional involvement of both parents and students, to reassert their partnership and responsibilities for learning outcomes appropriate for life and work in the digital world. The approaches taken are perhaps remarkably similar to the Internet-based grass roots strategy used so successfully by President Obama and the Democratic Party to extend and enable the engagement of people in the 2009 US election. It is a model that can readily be used by every school community and education authorities and, as is being seen in the US today, as part of a national change strategy in relation to policy and practice. Inevitably, the developments will challenge the bureaucracy's close control of the information flow and the decision making will be questioned and its appropriateness queried by the authorities. However, the reality is that it merely reflects the way decision making and communication occur in a networked world.

What we are witnessing in the shift to the networked mode in both the home and the pathfinding schools is a pronounced move away from mass, to a far more individualised mode of schooling. The potential implications of adopting such an approach are profound and immense, not only for the educational bureaucrats and governments, but also for the opportunities they provide every school community—small and large, poor and rich— to develop a model of schooling far more appropriate to the networked world than the traditional 'stand-alone' school. Thinking and action are needed.

Implementing a home–school nexus is long overdue and needs to be enacted now to provide the platform for dealing with the imminent, dynamic, rapid technological changes and affordances in the next ten to 20 years. Twelve key principles are identified in that chapter for particular attention.

The final and concluding chapter draws all the major elements together and succinctly lays out the challenge and opportunities ahead.

Conclusion

In compiling this book on the next phase of schooling, the editors and authors could readily have addressed every variable associated with the operation of a school. That is not the purpose of the book. Space does not allow us to identify and explore in depth all the issues that will require attention; nor is it possible at this embryonic stage of the evolution of the networked mode.

The desire is simply to open the reader's mind to what is possible, to explore what is happening now, to identify the kind of organisation that will best allow your school community to provide the desired education, to appreciate the kind of relationships and learning culture you will want to create, and to show how you might go about the quest of developing the desired networked school community. Essentially, this book enables you to position your thinking to consider: what is the next phase? It makes a significant contribution by suggesting that the next phase, now evident already in pathfinders, is the networked school community developed through creating a home–school nexus.

Schools are complex human organisations. A move to a networked mode that aims to harness ever-more sophisticated technologies will increase that complexity. It is why at the outset we encourage a macro perspective that will make it that much easier for you to appreciate the many interlocking variables you will need to address in order to develop the desired networked school community. What you will soon appreciate is that within a networked world we should be looking for solutions appropriate for a networked paradigm, not those of an Industrial Age.

Postscript: Throughout this book, the authors have chosen to use the term 'digital technologies' consistently to refer to the ever-evolving suite of digital software, hardware and architecture used in learning and teaching in the school, the home and beyond both home and school environments. The literature is replete with various terms, such as 'educational technology', 'computer-based technologies', 'learning technology' and the more frequently used 'ICT'. The authors suggest all have shortcomings and, most importantly, do not adequately communicate the full implications of being digital, with its facility for increasing convergence and integration, and its impact upon traditionally discrete operations.

By referring to digital technologies, one accommodates the evolution of a suite of integrated digital technologies that can be accessed virtually anywhere, any time. They are far more than just a few discrete technologies. Rather, it is about the use and impact of an ever-evolving suite of increasingly integrated digital technologies conceptualised as part of a digital ecosystem that can be adapted, based on needs and context. To illustrate: the Smart phone, viewed as a digital technology rather than a discrete technology, can be used as a phone, a camera, an MP3 player, or computer, or any blended combination of those functionalities, and in seamless conjunction with other digital technologies. In this way, digital technologies become defined in terms of the user's need and context, shaping the ways in which the digital applications are used in multiple ways and with multiple digital applications.

Guiding questions

After reading this chapter, consider your context and propose your ideas in relation to the following questions.

1   Are there differences between young people's personal and home access to and use of digital technologies, and their use of digital technologies in the school? What are the differences? What paradigm is the school mostly operating in—paper-based or digital?

2   Can you identify examples of ways in which the school:
   • acknowledges young people's understanding and use of digital technologies?
   • builds on and enhances the informal 'teaching' and learning in the home?
   • builds relationships with homes and families?

Key messages

• We are seeing schooling in pathfinding situations across the developed world evolve from the traditional paper-based mode to becoming digital, and now moving to become networked school communities for learning and teaching.

• The potential advantages of developing a networked school community are immense, and are associated with the emergence of a distinct form of schooling and an organisational mode appropriate for the digital, networked world in which we live.

• Developing networked school communities seeks to markedly enhance the attractiveness, quality, relevance, appropriateness and effectiveness of the education provided to students in schools.

The networked school communities today

MAL LEE

The Age of Networked Intelligence is an age of promise. It is not simply about the networking of technology, but about the networking of humans through technology. It is not an age of smart machines, but of humans who through networks can combine their intelligence, knowledge and creativity for breakthroughs in the creation of wealth and social development. It is not just an age of linking computers, but of Internetworking human ingenuity. It is an age of vast new promise and unimaginable opportunity.

Don Tapscott (1996, p. xiv)

The move to networked school communities

With the provision of network access to all classrooms in the school and across education authorities, the way is opened for formal schooling to build upon the work of the traditional school and its more recent digital form and develop a networked mode of schooling that has the capacity to take the quality of schooling to previously unimagined levels.

Boundaries are conceptual not physical in virtual workplaces and need to be completely reconceived so that 'physical site' thinking is no longer a limitation (Lipnack & Stamps 1994, p. 15). Most classrooms in the developed world will soon find themselves in this position, with this opportunity. The challenge for educators and societies is to ensure that their schools realise the many and diverse opportunities and benefits made available by that networking. The challenge is human, not technological.

The task is to conceive a model of schooling that will enable the many educational, social, economic, organisational and political benefits discussed in the following chapters to be realised and for schools to move to a position where they can readily accommodate ongoing change and continue to provide an education that prepares all young people for a digital future. The author's belief is that the answer lies in the development of networked school communities, the creation of a far greater nexus between the home and the school, and a shift to a more collaborative and socially networked form of teaching and learning.

The answer also lies in articulating the desired education, in identifying the kind of organisation that will best facilitate the realisation of that vision, in appreciating the increase in marked shortcomings of the present organisational model, and how best to take advantage of the digital and networked technology available to help redress those shortcomings while at the same time enriching the schooling. Also significant is understanding the organisational principles inherent in developing a networked school community, those facets of the traditional school you wish to retain in the new organisation and the elements of the digital school mode to be incorporated, appreciating the kind of relationship you want to establish with your homes, and identifying the path forward for your particular situation.

The evolution of school networks

The networking of school communities, where the networks are harnessed to enhance the quality and appropriateness of the formal schooling, is a relatively recent and still evolving development. While schools have for centuries had their distinct and important social networks, the concept of schools reaching out beyond their physical boundaries and developing a more networked mode of schooling gained real traction only since the advent of the Web in the mid 1990s and the ready facility for all members of that community, wherever they are in the networked world, to communicate and share ideas.

Until the 1990s those involved with the school had to, in the main, physically attend events at the school, although there were always those few who communicated by paper. Anyone who has participated in or lived within an independent school community, and has attended the ritual sporting events, religious ceremonies and school-based activities at the school, would appreciate how important the actual school facilities were in fostering the school community's social network and its culture. All those activities served to reinforce the discrete, stand-alone nature of the school and to largely exclude those parents who did not have the time to physically attend school events. Schools operated largely as discrete entities, with limited links with its own parent community, let alone the wider educational community.

With the advent of personal computers, and in particular the World Wide Web, the importance of the physical location began to wane, and by the start of the twenty-first century it was apparent that one could have vibrant and powerful social and work-related networks based, if so desired, solely on the use of the online world. When that development was coupled with the other advances in the use of digital technology and changes within society, the more prescient education observers, school and education authority leaders and politicians realised that not only did the new digital and networking technology offer immense opportunities to enhance the quality and appropriateness of schooling, schooling also needed to change and move away from its stand-alone mode if it was to prepare young people for a digital future where networking was a norm of life and work.

Those same leaders also appreciated that the traditional, paper-based mode of teaching and learning had long since maximised its potential and that if schools and nations were to significantly improve learning, educate young people for a digital world and assist and enhance national productivity it had to harness the ever-evolving digital technology. What they were slower to appreciate was that the traditional hierarchical organisational mode and the bureaucracies that controlled schools and the educational process would be major impediments to the desired change, and ultimately schools and education authorities would need to adopt an organisational form appropriate to a digital, networked and rapidly changing, uncertain world that would assist and not impede the quest to provide the desired education. Lewis Perelman, in his usual forceful language observed in 1992 that 'education in its less than two-century old modern form is an institution of bureaucracy, by bureaucracy, for bureaucracy' (p. 119).

The reality is that since the early 1990s, while the ease of accessing and using the networked world has improved dramatically and while the more proactive schools, education authorities and nations have gone a long way to providing the network infrastructure to enable schools to make extensive use of the online world, the influence and control exercised by the educational bureaucrats in many situations have grown. In probably most developed countries the national and regional bureaucracies and the network managers have assumed considerable control over the school's networks and have used that control to strengthen the bureaucracy's—and in turn the government's—micro-management of state or public schools. It is a significant trend apparent in virtually all developed nations, but it is a phenomenon seemingly being questioned by few commentators.

Ironically, what we are seeing is the strengthening of an organisational model that is ill equipped to accommodate rapid and uncertain societal and technological change and is daily making schooling more irrelevant. The increase in the centre's control of schooling, and the diminution of the independence of the individual school, is in fact the antithesis of the model adopted by business, where one has seen since the 1980s both in practice and in the literature a strong advocacy for a shift to networked organisations that have the inherent flexibility to accommodate rapid, uncertain, ongoing change.

Interestingly, it is nearly impossible in the educational administration literature to find any support for the use of a strongly bureaucratic mode, but on the ground that mode continues to strengthen. It is surely time for parents, students, concerned educators and the elected political officials to seriously question the wisdom of that development, and to begin adopting a school organisational structure that will provide an education appropriate for an ever-changing world where the parents' and students' needs are paramount.

There will always be a place for some degree of hierarchical bureaucracy, but it ought to be limited and designed primarily to support an organisational mode appropriate for the times.

As indicated later, governments should rightly expect schools to report on key performance indicators but that does not require the type or extent of bureaucratic control currently being used.

Interestingly, not only is it time for schools to adopt a far more networked mode of organisation, it is also time for the bureaucracies to do so. Whether they can is a moot point, but at a time when school operations are becoming increasingly integrated, interconnected and networked, most bureaucracies remain highly segmented and hierarchical and find it very difficult to operate as interconnected support organisations.

In 1995, Louis Gerstner, the then Chairman and CEO of IBM, suggested the reason why there was so little use made of technology in schools, in contrast to industry and the home:

> ... is that because schools are regulated bureaucracies, they are not organized in ways that lead them into the introduction of technologies. They are like eighteenth-century farms, not even ready to dream about the agricultural revolution that would sweep the world into the nineteenth and twentieth centuries.

Gerstner et al. (1995, p. 35)

A networked school community—the concept

Very little has as yet been written about the concept or practice of networked school communities. A Google search will bring up few entries on any kind of networked school organisation. While many educators have over the last decade, in particular, talked about the educational and administrative opportunities made possible by the online world, in 2009 few of those ideas had been fleshed out on paper.

This publication is one of the first comprehensive studies of the development and the current situation. In advocating that schooling more consciously move from its traditional paper-based and hierarchical mode, and even its more recent digital phase, we found it interesting to note the dearth and spotted nature of the studies undertaken in this area, the absence of any macro perspective and indeed the absence of any agreed terminology.

We have opted to use the term 'networked school communities'. In so doing we wanted a simple term that embodied the essence of what was both happening and desired. While there are terms in use like 'collaborative networked learning' or CNL (*Wikipedia* 2009a), 'networked learning community' and 'networked organisations', none of these adequately describes the concept we have in mind.

When we talk of networked school communities we have in mind a mode of schooling that is evolving and will continue to grow and take on its own distinct form, as did the paper-based and more recent digital mode of schooling, and which in the years ahead is likely to morph into another, as yet unidentified mode. After years of constancy, schooling is on the move. 'Networks are an organic form of organisation, which means you need to understand them as a process as well as a structure.' (Lipnack & Stamps 1994, p. 19)

The term covers all facets of the school operations, not just the teaching and learning. In days of old, the term 'the hidden curriculum' was used to cover those aspects of school life, the socialisation of the students, the ability to relate to and network with others, the education acquired on the playing fields and in the cafeteria, and those many aspects of a school education not specifically addressed in the formal teaching program. 'Networked school communities' also encompasses the administration and communication of the school and the facility for the wider school community to contribute to its ongoing development. It includes all those activities, plus the myriad of others that now impact on the education of young people by virtue of the networked technology's removal of the physical limitations of the 'stand-alone' school and the many opportunities possible in a networked society.

It also relates to the identification by Lee and Gaffney (2008) of what they call 'digital schools'—schools that make extensive use of digital technologies in everyday teaching and in the school's learning, administration and communication systems. While one might assume digital schools would make extensive use of their networks and the Internet, the reality is that at this stage many digital schools have not sought to take advantage of the networking facilities to involve their wider community—and the parents and students in particular—in the school's operations, but rather are still at a phase where the professional educators are using the technology, largely unilaterally, to control the educative process, and the schooling takes place within the existing walls.

The contention is that both students and parents have a vast amount to contribute to the appropriate education of young people, that the quality and effectiveness of the education provided can be markedly enhanced and the students' scores on the vital international comparisons improved (Chapter 5) by schools taking fuller advantage of the networking technology and working collaboratively with the parents and students. The desire is to shift to a model of schooling that is in keeping with the ways of the contemporary world, is inclusive, and makes much greater use of social networking and teamwork and appreciably less use of the 'we know all' approach that has come to be associated with hierarchical and bureaucratic organisations.

> Networks are making the world evolve faster, and cities, communities, and schools in the 21st century will thrive because of their connectedness, where ideas, capital, and talent can play together and recombine. Digital technology can enable talent to play and work together through its ability to support different learning styles. Having the ability to network with others, share original thoughts and creations, and work together will only become more important in the future, as will tools to leverage the power of community members, students, and others to contribute within schools.
>
> Illinois Institute of Design (2007, pp. 24–25)

Over a decade ago, Tapscott observed in *Growing up digital* (1998) that developed societies had for the first time a generation of young people who knew more about a technology than their teachers. While one might query the finer semantics of that claim, few today would dispute that young people from kindergarten onwards have an awareness of and an interest in digital technology and a set of digital skills that should be harnessed by educators. As yet that has barely happened.

What we are advocating is the adoption of a mode of schooling where that can happen, and where the parents are able to use the technology to return to playing a significant role in the formal educative process. A networked school community is thus a legally recognised school that takes advantage of the digital and networked technology, and of a more collaborative, networked and inclusive operational mode to involve its wider community in the provision of a quality education appropriate for the digital future. It can be envisaged as follows.

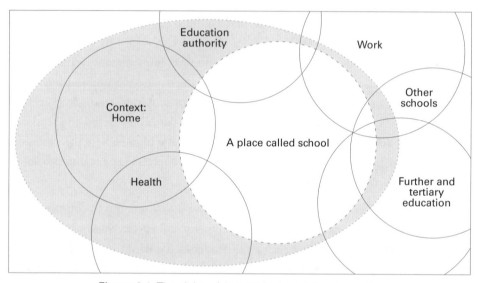

Figure 2.1 The vision: A networked school community

The networked organisation

The concept of the networked organisation and its use within business has been with us for decades. Any scan of the business management literature or descriptions of the organisational models used by business since the mid 1980s will reveal the extensive use of the network-centric approach, and a strong advocacy of the model's facility to accommodate and indeed thrive on rapid and uncertain change. Tom Peters wrote his famous work, *Thriving on chaos*, as far back as 1987.

The studies by Lipnack and Stamps in the 1980s and 1990s (Lipnack & Stamps 1982; 1988; 1994) are particularly pertinent. Their 1994 publication, *The age of the network*, warrants close scrutiny by anyone contemplating a networked school community. The work provides an excellent overview of the evolution of organisations and their form and an insightful examination of the shortcomings of the bureaucratic mode and advantages of the networked.

> The network is emerging as the signature form of organisation in the Information Age, just as bureaucracy stamped the Industrial Age, hierarchy controlled the Agricultural Era, and the small group roamed in the Nomadic Era.
>
> Lipnack & Stamps (1994, p. 3)

In a subsection aptly titled 'Fasten Your Seat Belt for Take Off', Lipnack and Stamps make the point that networked organisations need to be smarter than their predecessors,

> because the ride into the 21st century is going to be very fast indeed. Bureaucracy creates cadres of specialists who know only their particular little bailiwicks. Hierarchy limits access to information with its one-way, top down stream of command and control. Networks increase communication, multiply information, and bring people into the loop. (p. 4)

Undoubtedly one of the greatest shortcomings of modern schools is the inability of their bureaucratic and hierarchical organisation to cope with the pace of the change. According to Lipnack and Stamps, 'Today's complexity outruns bureaucracy's ability to organise it' (p. 40)—they urge that, 'If you want a more flexible organisation, be prepared not only to tolerate but to vigorously support risk taking' (p. 91).

> In the Age of the Network, social capital is continuously being formed and degraded. It increases and decreases through dynamics fed by history, circumstances, crises and creativity. (p. 197)

They make two telling observations to bear in mind in your planning:

- Any new organisation will, and should, draw upon the strengths of the earlier organisational mode.
- The networked organisation will make use of a mix of earlier organisational modes.

> To develop healthy, flexible, intelligent organisations for the 21st century, we need to harvest the best from the past and combine it with what is really new. Surely some learning from thousands of years of organisational life must be worth keeping. There must be continuity as well as change. (p. 4)

It is thus important in your planning that you seek to marry the best of the traditional school and that of the digital mode into the networked. You will continue, for example, to use much of the current instructional program, the quality teaching and the teachers' bond with the students within the new organisation. You will also use the staff's normalised use of the digital. Indeed, as will become increasingly obvious, you will be unable to move into the networked mode until you have moved into the digital mode. The new school will have to use some form of hierarchical structure with clear positions of responsibility and most assuredly a school principal.

A facet of Lipnack and Stamps' 1994 research that warrants particular attention are their five organisational principles for twenty-first century organisations:

1 **Unifying purpose:** *Purpose is the glue and the driver. Common views, values and goals hold a network together. A shared focus on desired results keeps a network in synch and on track.*

2 **Independent members:** *Independence is a prerequisite for interdependence. Each member of a network—whether a person, a company or a country—can stand on its own while benefiting from being part of a whole.*

3 **Voluntary links:** *Just add links. The distinguishing feature of networks is their links, far more profuse and omni-directional than in other types of organisation. As communications pathways increase, people and groups interact more often. As more relationships develop, trust strengthens, which reduces the cost of doing business and generates greater opportunities.*

4 **Multiple leaders:** *Fewer bosses, more leaders—networks are leaderful, not leaderless. Each person or a group in a network has something unique to contribute at some point in the process. With more than one leader, the network as a whole has great resilience.*

5 **Integrated levels:** *Networks are multilevel, not flat. Lumpy with small groups and clustered with coalitions, networks involve both hierarchy and the 'lower-archy', which leads them to action rather than simply making recommendations to others.*

Lipnack & Stamps (1994, p. 18)

Few are likely to question the fundamental importance of the unifying purpose, the voluntary links, the integrated levels and even the idea of the networked school community having multiple leaders. There will however be many—particularly within the bureaucracy and even government at this point in time—who will question the idea that schools need to have a high level of independence to respond rapidly to the continually changing circumstances of their situation or that staff within the school should have a similar kind of independence.

Networks fail at one extreme when their participants—whether organisations or individuals—cannot behave independently, the source of many network failures in large bureaucratic cultures ... If you want a more flexible organisation, be prepared not only to tolerate but to vigorously support risk taking.

Lipnack & Stamps (1994, p. 91)

The more you come to explore the possibilities opened by opting to operate as a networked school community, and appreciate the benefits that are possible, the more you will come to appreciate how important it is for the key independent units—the school, the principal, the teacher and the student—to have the desired independence. Related to the facility to respond readily to ongoing change is the importance of recognising that when schools move to a digital mode, they will move from a mode of schooling characterised by constancy—and some might say inertia—to a situation where handled astutely they can and should continually be changing and evolving. Lawler and Worley (2009), in their writings on organisational structures, argue the only way to overcome the propensity for organisations to default to stability and inertia is to consciously build them to change.

When the school moves to the networked mode it will continue its inclination to ongoing evolution and change. As the school's networks change, as new technologies open new possibilities and, most importantly, as the expectations of the members of the school community grow, so will the school be open to change in order to better meet its clients' needs, provided it has an organisational structure and leadership that foster that change. As indicated in the opening quote to this chapter, Don Tapscott in his 1996 work, *The digital economy* (interestingly subtitled 'Promise and peril in the age of networked intelligence'), reinforces the observations of Lipnack and Stamps (1994) and Lawler and Worley (2009).

While the business literature provides an important insight into the possible form and nature of the networked school community, ultimately you are going to need to develop a model appropriate for schools and most importantly for your situation. There is nonetheless much to be gained by scanning the more recent writings and, increasingly, interviews like that with Eric Schmidt, the CEO of Google, and Google's networked organisation and culture (*Washington Post* 2009).

State of play

As we approach the start of a new decade, globally we are still at a very early phase in the development of networked school communities. At this stage there are across the world significant pathfinding developments at the school, education authority and national levels seeking to take advantage of the digital and networked technology to more fully involve the parents and students in the school's work, but as yet there have been few efforts to articulate, let alone consciously pursue, the concept of a networked mode of schooling.

Indeed, as yet there is still little written on the concept of the digital school, a precursor to the development of networked school communities. The current interaction between most schools and their homes is summed up in Figure 2.2.

Throughout the early twenty-first century there are schools, education authorities and nations seeking to enrich the schooling and its efficiency through the new school networks. The initiatives range from the minute, started and run by a lone teacher, through to extensive, highly ambitious national programs. You will readily find examples of the new networks being used to:

- provide home access to the school's library holdings
- provide online tutoring of gifted and talented students
- handle the booking of parent–teacher interviews

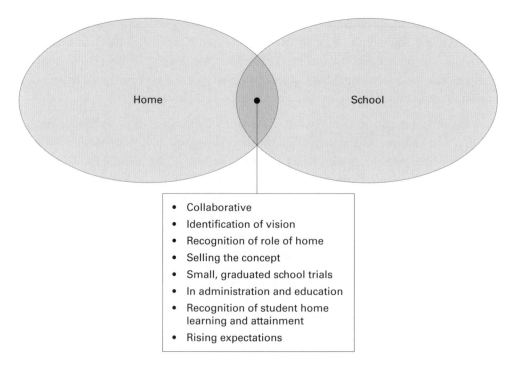

Figure 2.2 The networked school community—pre-structural change

- reach into the parents' homes and endeavour to enhance performance in key school subjects
- provide multifaceted online learning platforms
- involve the parents at home through the use of wikis
- conduct virtual schools—usually a step on from the old correspondence schools
- provide the disadvantaged across the nation with home Internet access
- conduct a plethora of what might appear to many small, unrelated student classroom links with the students' homes.

(Source: Johnson et al. 2009)

These programs have invariably been initiated and controlled by the educational professional in the school or the central office. Few are mounted at the behest of the students or the parents. Virtually everyone uses the technology to try and improve the ways of old. They aim to improve the students' attainments in the existing curriculum or the efficiency of the school's current operations. As yet there have been few moves that question the relevance of the current curriculum to harness student learning within the home, particularly that which is acquired in using the various digital technologies, or to use a more networked or collaborative method of teaching.

Significantly, there is little evidence at this stage of the students—Prensky's (2006) 'digital natives'—having any great voice in the development of the networked school communities. While there is recent research (Project Tomorrow 2008) eliciting the students' views, and while the author has recently had the pleasure of working with the students of a secondary school in visioning the future of their school and had reinforced his beliefs on the level of student digital use and understanding, few schools as yet appear to be building upon this very considerable resource. Rather, one continues to see the 'digital immigrants' deciding what is appropriate for the 'digital natives'.

There are, however, several developments that fall outside the aforementioned pattern. One is the growth of digital teaching hubs, where classroom teachers are using the interactive whiteboard as a hub to bring together a suite of digital technologies to enable the class to network and interact with folk outside the school. There are examples of peer tutoring with other schools that makes particular use of the video in Skype. Skype links with students in other nations and the use of wikis with the parents' homes (Betcher & Lee 2009).

Another is the emergence, particularly in the US, of parents using the Web 2.0 forums to critique the work and in particular the instructional program of their local school. A potentially significant development is that elaborated upon in Chapter 17, which sees several of the world's major technology corporations working with a group of nations to develop a model of student assessment that will assess a suite of twenty-first century competencies using the tools of the networked world.

While there are some signs of change, there have been as yet few moves to position these initiatives, even those by the national authorities within the wider macro context, and relate them to an overall model of future schooling. Lee and Gaffney in *Leading a digital school* (2008) set out to position the very significant developments in the school-wide uptake of digital technologies in its wider educational context. What they found was a pronounced shift in the nature of schooling provided by those schools that had achieved digital take-off. Often unwittingly those schools were operating in what Lee and Gaffney described as the digital operational paradigm. They summarised the characteristics of the shift in Table 1.1 (page 6).

Of note is that the compilation of the comparison in Table 1.1 was undertaken in early 2007, based extensively on the 2003–2006 period. While the table makes reference to the use of networks, teams and collaboration, what has become increasingly evident in the past three years is that schools can operate within the digital mode, where the use of the digital is normalised in the school's everyday teaching and administration while at the same time operating within the existing school walls, retaining the traditional hierarchical organisation and ensuring that the educational professionals continue to control the curriculum and what is taught.

However, once those schools that have normalised the use of the digital begin to lower or remove the school walls, reach out and take advantage of the teaching and learning possibilities outside those walls, they move into a very different world and begin to appreciate the kind of changes needed to realise all the opportunities available. The desire is to place these early networking developments in their wider educational context, to suggest the organisational form the pathfinders are seemingly unwittingly entering, to alert them to the possibilities, to explore in the following chapters the many potential benefits of schools developing as networked school communities, and to explain how they can move their school into that mode.

Before embarking on that task, however, it is vital to appreciate how important human relationships and the development of an appropriate teaching and learning culture will be in the creation of successful networked school communities.

Relationships and culture

For any networked school community to succeed there has to be a close bond between the school and its teachers and the home and the evolution of a supportive learning culture that is sustained over time. This relationship and the desired culture will not simply happen. They will have to be consciously worked upon and factored into any developmental program.

If yours is a school—like many urban schools—that has extensive and often foreboding fences that separate the school from its community, the challenge of reaching out and forming a bond with even a proportion of the homes will be immense. If, however, your school already collaborates extensively with the parents and has in place a strong bond between the parents, students and teachers, the way forward will be that much easier and faster.

It is therefore essential in contemplating the developmental path for your school to ascertain the current relationships, and in particular the parent and student perspectives, and to factor the situation into your planning. Sadly, in some situations the current relationship could markedly impact on what can be done, and when. The unique nature of each school's relationship with its homes makes it ever-more essential that each school has the organisational independence needed to devise a development strategy appropriate for its context.

Conclusion

If yours is a school that has begun or soon wants to create a home–school nexus, and in time wants to reap the many dividends of operating as a networked school community, it is important that you locate your school on the school evolution continuum, ascertain the relationship between the home and the school and then identify the steps you need to take.

Is your school still operating within a hierarchical mode where the teaching is still predominantly paper based? Have you achieved digital take-off and normalised the everyday use of the digital in all school operations, and in particular the everyday teaching?

Your answers will determine your next steps. As you work your way through this book it will become increasingly apparent that before a school can contemplate moving to the networked mode it has in general terms to become a digital school, ready to move to the next phase. It is only when you have a critical mass of staff able and willing to use the digital and networked technology, the requisite digital technology in place in every classroom and at least a cadre of teachers and homes willing to collaborate, that you can begin the quest to develop a networked school community.

Guiding questions

After reading this chapter, consider your context and propose your ideas in relation to the following guiding questions.

1   In your community, what do you believe are its main social networks? Which of those networks have grown, and which have waned in the last few years? Can you describe examples of networking beyond the classroom and school walls?

2   To what extent:
   - do students believe that learning occurs mainly in classrooms and at the school?
   - do teachers believe that learning occurs mainly in classrooms and at the school?
   - can change be initiated by the school, the principal and individual teachers?
   - do students, the parents and the community participate in decision making about the development of the school? Is there real collaboration?

Key messages

- To date (in 2009), there is still little written on the concept of the digital school, which is developmentally a precursor to networked school communities.
- We are still at a very early phase in the development of networked school communities.

PART B

The home–school scene today

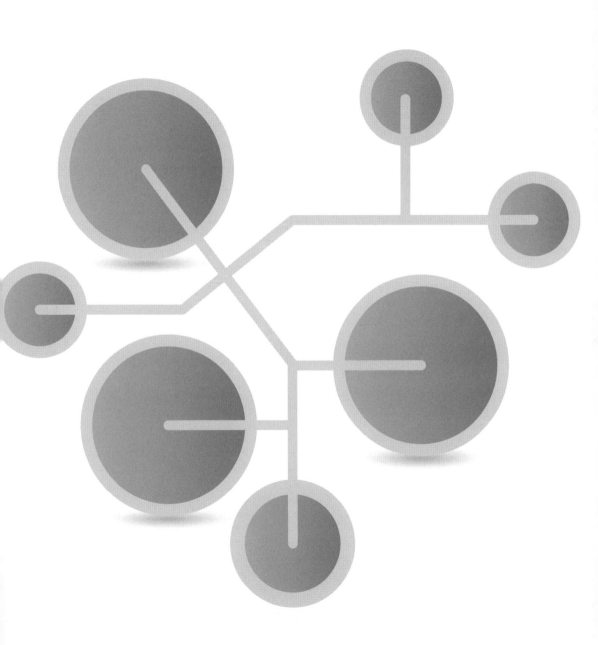

Schools and the digital technology: An overview

MAL LEE

It is disturbing ... that in 2008 the combination of astute leadership and appropriate technology was limited to a relatively small proportion of situations. The most commonly used instructional technologies ... throughout the developed world were still the pen, paper and teaching board ... That said ... in different parts of the world there were schools and education authorities finally using digital instructional technologies in everyday teaching to enhance student learning ...

Mal Lee & Arthur Winzenried (2009, p. 1)

Mapping the technological developments in schools

In seeking to develop a networked school community and build upon the opportunities provided by the digital and networked technology it is important to appreciate the current situation in your school and that with which you have to work. In a networked world it is also important to understand the wider context, to appreciate the recency of the developments, the often significant difference between the rhetoric and the on-ground reality and extent to which teachers and students in particular are actually using the technology in the everyday teaching and learning.

This chapter provides an essential overview of the global scene. If you would like to secure a fuller appreciation of the developments, it is suggested you consult Lee and Winzenried's *The use of instructional technology in schools* (2009) and Friedman's *The world is flat* (2006).

1995–2010

All of you can well remember the major happenings we are about to comment on, and indeed may find it a surprise how quickly those events have become history. The history of the use of digital and networked technology in schools from the mid 1990s falls into two general periods.

'Ramp up': 1995–2002

The first phase from 1995 to around 2002 can be termed the 'ramp up' period. It was in those years that the more proactive schools and education authorities recognised that if they were to prepare their students for a digital future they needed to prepare the groundwork required for the mounting of a comprehensive, long-term strategy that would facilitate the teachers' and students' shift to the everyday use of the digital in teaching and learning.

Remember the mid 1990s were the years of the 'information super highway', of the recognition of the educational potential of broadband to enhance national productivity and the impact globally of the Clinton–Gore administration's decision to network all US classrooms by 2002. However, it was also a time when governments and school leaders recognised the aptness of Al Gore's famous observation that schools were telecommunication deserts, with scarcely a classroom in 1995 having even a phone connection, ill-equipped to take advantage of the Internet.

The proactive schools and governments soon appreciated that the first priority was to markedly enhance the networking of schools and provide the desired high-speed access to the Internet. One thus saw throughout the developed world in the latter 1990s concerted efforts at the school and education authority level to enhance telecommunications by upgrading the networks within the schools and network access to the school. The US, for example, building on the Clinton–Gore initiative, set in motion the National Infrastructure Initiative (NII) and introduced its E-Rate scheme, Canada embarked on its Canadian School-Net program, Korea and Denmark set about on national broadband connectivity, while the UK began assembling its national grid for learning (NGfL) that would in time provide all UK government and Catholic classrooms with broadband access (Meredyth et al. 1999). On reflection, many schools and education authorities moved from virtually nothing to having broadband connectivity to all teaching rooms in six to seven years.

The other reality of this period, particularly for schools, was that there remained a sizeable gap between the promise of what was possible with the Internet and the technology that was available at a price schools could afford to make the best classroom use of the Internet. Although work was underway on a suite of digital technology that teachers could use, such as data projectors, interactive whiteboards, digital cameras, cell phones, scanners and interactive multimedia software, most of that technology remained immature and well out of schools' price range in the 1990s.

While homes could readily use the Internet and email with a single PC and a 56K modem, that kind of setup in a school—although played up in the media and the education public relations units—was of limited use. Schools would have to wait a few years before they would have ready access to the desired technology.

It is important to appreciate the kind of homework done by your school during these years and understand how well or otherwise it succeeded in preparing the groundwork and developing a culture within the school where significant priority was attached to harnessing the undoubted educational potential of the technology. You will appreciate the importance when you look at Table 3.1 (pp. 38–39).

Digital take-off: 2003–2010

The second stage, the digital take-off period, emerged in late 2002 and early 2003 and continues on an upward path today. It built on the groundwork done in the latter 1990s and was markedly stimulated by the confluence worldwide of a suite of technological developments, all of which served to add another level of sophistication and functionality to what could be done at work, in the home and in the school.

Friedman, in *The world is flat* (2006), speaks of the 'triple convergence' and its profound impact in flattening the world. While Friedman's focus is industry, the same confluence of technological developments opened the way for the astute schools and education authorities—and in particular those who had already done their homework—to harness all manner of digital technology across K–12. During 2002/2003, we saw the 'emergence' of two technologies that finally provided teachers with a digital tool that could generate a digital image for whole-class viewing and teaching. Until interactive whiteboards (IWBs) and data projectors reached a level of maturity and a price point where they could be used in every teaching room, teachers had to rely on personal computers with their small screens.

Personal computers, as the name aptly communicates, are designed for personal use and not whole-class teaching. As Larry Cuban's 2001 work rightly indicates, personal computers were *Oversold and underused*. The research (Cuban 2001; Lee & Winzenried 2009) reveals that the vast majority of teachers did not use that technology, which they regarded as inappropriate for their everyday teaching of class groups. At the same time as the IWBs and the data projectors reached the desired maturity and price point, so too did digital still cameras, video movie cameras, surround systems, MP3 players, scanners and a burgeoning suite of interactive multimedia applications software. Google had revolutionised the search engines, Skype was unveiled and the first of the Web 2.0 and social networking applications appeared.

These developments finally meant all teachers K–12 could have in the classroom a suite of digital technologies they could use for whole-class teaching. It is worth noting that it was not until around 2003, after nearly a century of notable failures, that we saw schools where all the teachers and the students were using electronic instructional technologies in the everyday teaching and learning. The use of the instructional technology in those schools had become normalised.

It is important to appreciate the recency of this development. As you will be aware, since 2003 the range and sophistication of the digital technologies—hardware and software—have evolved and continues to evolve at pace. Today, primary schools, and to a lesser extent secondary schools, have access to all the requisite technology—that is, if they have the funds and the commitment from the leadership. It is no longer the technology constraining its everyday use, but rather the capacity of the educational leaders to get all teachers and students using that technology as a normal part of everyday teaching and learning.

Disappointingly, by 2009, only a minority of the world's schools had normalised the use of the digital and networking technology in their everyday teaching. While we now understand the suite of human and technological variables needing to be simultaneously addressed to achieve that normalisation (Lee & Winzenried 2009), and while the number of schools in the different parts of the world that are achieving digital take-off and operating as digital schools is increasing rapidly, the vast majority are still not. As indicated earlier, until your school has at least a critical mass—and preferably all the teachers using the digital technologies normally within the everyday teaching, and as such displaying their willingness to use that technology—the school will be unable to move successfully to the networked mode. The key variable is the willingness to use the technology.

What is important to appreciate—as Naisbitt identified in his work on *Megatrends* in 1984, and reinforced by others since—is that all new technology will be used initially to try to better perform the ways of old and it will only be in time, as the users become more competent and confident in its use, that they will use it in new ways. Most teachers, not surprisingly given the recency of the key technological developments, are still using the technology to better perform their traditional teaching.

While many long-term users of computers are critical of this use of technology, the reality is that it is a natural phase virtually every teacher will move through, particularly if they have not been provided with the requisite development in their teacher training. The research reveals that once the teachers have accepted the value of using the technology, they will then be open—when given the requisite support and training—to use it differently. Where your school sits in the total teacher and student use of the digital is worth checking because it will shape the nature of your development strategy.

The proactive–reactive digital divide

In commenting on the developments since the mid 1990s, regular mention has been made of the proactive schools, education authorities and nations. What Lee and Winzenried (2009) have noted in their analysis of the period is that the successful uptake and normalisation of the use of the digital and networking technology have been restricted to but a subset of all schools, education authorities and nations—the proactive. They were those that have been implementing a concerted whole-school development strategy to prepare young people for a digital future, usually since the 1990s; hence the importance of appreciating the homework undertaken by your school.

The majority of schools, education authorities and nations continue to be reactive, to tinker with the technology, to make fine-sounding political statements, but in reality to be generally negative about embracing the online world; and as a group they have not adopted substantive, well-reasoned, appropriately resourced, holistic development strategies that will facilitate the desired normalised use of the technology by the teachers and students. Lee and Winzenried (2009) suggest that the divide between the proactive and reactive is steadily growing, with the proactive now well positioned as a result of their groundwork to make ever-greater use of the digital and network technologies in order to provide their students with a marked educational advantage over those students in the reactive schools.

Indeed, the homework done and the understanding acquired by the proactive are such that it is going to be extremely difficult for the reactive to remove the growing divide. The major attributes of the reactive and proactive situations are compared in Table 3.1. While the model provides contrasting attributes, the reality is that schools, education authorities and nations will be at different points along a continuum, and along different points on the continuum with each of the attributes.

The other point to bear in mind is that while schools within proactive education authorities and nations have had appreciably greater support than those in reactive ones, there are a significant number of proactive schools in all situations that have normalised the everyday use of the digital with all teachers and students, almost despite their governing authority. Think about where your school and education authority sit on this table and once again note the attributes the school will need to address if it is to achieve the desired development. The understanding of where you sit will be important when you consider the school's student Internet access situation in Chapter 16.

Schools and digital technology today

While you need to be mindful of where your school's efforts, and indeed those of the government, sit on the proactive–reactive continuum, it is also important in your planning to understand the current and planned use of digital technologies in your total school community, in the home, on the move and within the school. The home and digital technologies, such as mobile technologies, are addressed in the next chapter.

Despite the assumption that everyone understands the situation with the use of digital technology in schools, the reality is that remarkably little research has been undertaken or written on the actual use being made of the various digital technologies in schools and the factors impacting on that use. Below are a few general points. They are written particularly for parents in school governance situations but should be of value to all in school leadership situations. It is appreciated that some of the observations might seem blunt and not accord

Table 3.1 Attributes of proactive and reactive schools, education authorities and governments

Proactive	Reactive
Educational vision for networked world/digital future	Belief in traditional schooling—with the technology existing to enhance it
Nexus between education for digital future, national productivity and funding	Disjointed, reactive responses to key technological developments
Positive outlook to using the emerging digital technology wisely to enhance schooling	Negative attitude to the emerging digital technology, and preference for traditional ways
Holistic developmental strategy for implementing desired vision that addresses human and technological variables over time	Policy seemingly developed 'on the run', reacting to media pressure Use of discrete ICT plans
Development strategy given priority funding	Regular complaints re the lack of adequate funding. Blame always accorded others
Concern to provide appropriate network infrastructure, bandwidth and network support	Inadequate infrastructure and support, with major shortcomings Low speed and low-level teaching room connectivity to the Web
Use of market position to choose or to have developed digital technologies and solutions that facilitate the attainment of the desired educational requirements	Use of a series of short-term, high-profile initiatives that focus on the 'in' technology— with little attention accorded infrastructure and human change Marked propensity to go with the market in the choice of instructional technology
Recognition of the lead role to be played by the school principals and education authorities	Minimal development provided to existing or potential leaders to lead digital schools
Focus on enhancing teaching and learning	Focus on the technology, with a continued reliance on the use of personal computers
Teacher acceptance and involvement central to the wise use of digital instructional technology	Teachers disenfranchised
Appropriate digital technology placed or scheduled for placement in each teaching room	Digital technology concentrated in specialist rooms—with controlled access
Significant support provided to assist in the development and teacher acquisition of interactive multimedia teaching materials	ICT perceived by most staff as the prime responsibility of the ICT teachers Interested teachers obliged to acquire their own digital teaching materials, as cheaply as possible
High-level, if not total, teacher and student use of a suite of digital instructional technologies in everyday teaching	Low-level teacher and student use of digital technology in everyday teaching Teaching boards, pens and paper remain the most commonly available technology in most teaching rooms

Proactive	Reactive
Importance attached to, and funding provided for, ongoing teacher and leadership development	Little or no school-based funding for the development of teachers' digital competencies
Digital technologies being increasingly used and integrated in all school operations	Limited digital integration Extensive use made of dated technology
Prime role of network and digital support staff is to assist the prime purpose of education—the provision of desired education	Network managers have major responsibility for network use by students, teachers and school leaders Inadequate ICT support, usually provided by the teachers
Increased wider educational use of the Web, and in particular the Web 2.0 facilities encouraged, with minimal access constraints	High-profile publicity of and warnings on the negative features of the Internet Significant constraints imposed by authorities and network managers on student access to and use of Web 2.0 facilities
Digital take-off, shift to digital operational paradigm and development of digital schools Ever-rising teacher, student and parent expectations of the digital technologies Responsiveness to rapid change	Inflexibility and difficulty of the schools and bureaucracy accommodating rapid change Schools continue to operate within traditional paper-based mode
Recognition accorded the educational importance of the digital technology in the home and the potentially disadvantaged students	Schools continue to operate as largely stand-alone entities with little recognition of the use and educational impact of digital technologies in the home on young people
High expectations placed on whole school and staff, supplemented with regular monitoring of performance	Minimal or unrealistic expectations placed on the school's or teachers' use of digital instructional technologies
Increasing dependence on quality information services and information management	Low status or abolition of teacher librarians Inadequate or ineffectual information management systems
Strong total school community acceptance of the use of digital and networked technologies	Growing frustration and alienation among students and teachers wanting to take advantage of emerging technologies
Extensive research undertaken and published on the use and impact of the digital technology Development builds ongoing research, evaluation and professionalism of the educators	Little, if any, research undertaken and published on the impact of digital instructional technology Reliance on PR spin to secure political advantage

(Source: Lee & Winzenried 2009, pp. 217–19)

with the line projected by many of the public relations cells, or even your school, but if you are to succeed with your planning you need to understand from where you are actually starting.

Both government and technology corporations have been very good for many years in creating the illusion that school children are using the latest technology every day. As indicated earlier, that is not necessarily true. A viewing of *Mr. Winkle Awakes* on YouTube (http://www.youtube.com/watch?v=lm1sCsl2MQY) succinctly sums up the situation in many schools.

The staff's tools

It might appear incredibly basic, but for a school to operate in the digital and most assuredly in the networked mode the staff need to have the core digital tools. They will need to have:

- an appropriate desktop, laptop or Netbook computer with the requisite software and wireless facility
- a work email address
- an appropriate work-related Internet usage service or allocation.

Some might argue that rather than a laptop they ought to have a Smart phone. The bottom line is that employers need to provide their staff, directly or indirectly, with the core tools needed to work within a digital and networked world. The history of schooling over the last 15 years reveals that many education employers have been slow to provide the teaching staff with their digital toolkit. In 2009, at the time of writing, there are still many schools across the developed world where that is not so, and teachers are obliged to share a desktop computer and/or provide their own.

Interestingly, while none of the employers would expect the staff in the front office of the school—and most assuredly in the central office—to work without their computer, it is somehow alright for teachers to do without or to make do with aged and ineffectual technologies.

The suspicion gained by observing the comments made on global mailing lists is that, in 2009, the majority of teachers in the developed world have use of 'their own' desktop or laptop computer, and many have a work-related email address. However, it appears unusual in 2009 for employers to provide for or to recompense the education professionals for their work-related ISP and Internet communications costs. In some nations those costs can be claimed as a tax deduction, but the feedback from several international teacher mailing lists suggests there appears to be scant effort being made or even contemplated by employers to meet this significant cost. Interestingly, at the same time, those employers pay some of their staff members' work-related phone bills, even when the charge covers web-enabled Smart phones!

In a networked school community, particularly as one dismantles the traditional walls and makes greater use of the new work environment, it is important that careful thought is given to meeting the costs of both the teachers' toolkit and the Internet communications. This is a small outlay for potentially huge returns. It would be as well to check the current thinking and situation in your school.

Availability of digital technology in the school

It is suggested that another of the early tasks is to ascertain the situation with the digital technology in the school and the school's plans for future acquisition. A rapid and very telling audit of the current situation can be done by seeking out from the school executive the information on the following key performance indicators (KPIs).

- What percentage of the school's teachers has normalised the use of digital technology into their everyday teaching?
- What percentage of the school's teaching rooms and staff offices has high-speed broadband access to the Internet?
- What percentage of classrooms has a suite of whole-class digital technologies that allows the teacher to use them when desired?
- For what percentage of time is the school's network up and available for use during the teaching hours in the year?

The desired answer for each question would be 100 per cent. If it is, you are very well positioned and can proceed at pace with your planning. If not, you have some significant work to undertake.

You might note that no mention is made of the school's current and planned computer-to-student ratio. As you will come to appreciate, it is a largely meaningless indicator as far as the school's operations go. It might make great media copy for governments and computer companies, but there is scant correlation between it and the actual use of the appropriate technology in the school or within a networked school community.

Deployment of the technology

The ideal at this stage in the development of technology is to have in every classroom a suite of digital instructional technologies, with broadband Internet access, that can be used to teach the whole class. You then need a suite of digital technologies the students can use to create their work.

On top of that you might want a couple of specialist computer labs, such as for media studies, art, etc., and probably another suite of digital technologies in the library or learning centre(s). To provide an image that the whole class can see and discuss, one will basically want a data projector, or an interactive whiteboard (IWB) which in most situations will use a data projector.

Where the students work within the one teaching area, such as a primary or middle school, one can readily complement the whole-class technology with pods of desktops, scanners, digital cameras, digital microscopes, surround-sound systems, pay TV feed and the like. Where the students move between places, they will want a highly portable wireless handheld computer. You could either opt for a Smart phone—of the iPhone/Android ilk—or a Netbook type of unit, preferably owned by the students.

The key is that every teacher and student has to have the appropriate technology (Lee & Winzenried 2009) if they are to use it anywhere near as ubiquitously as it is used in the home.

Teacher and student use of the technology

Closely allied to the deployment of the technology is the extent of teacher and student use of the digital technologies, particularly in the classroom. A very basic point you need to remember is that if the teachers don't use the digital technology in the class, neither will their students. Schools appear to be of the mind that students are not to be trusted using the school's technology, even if they may know far more about it than the teacher, and that a teacher has to facilitate or oversee its use.

In the pathfinding schools where there is appropriate digital technology and Internet access in every room, and the school has succeeded in getting all the teachers to use that technology as a natural part of everyday teaching, so too will the student use be normalised.

If, as is the situation in many schools today (Lee & Winzenried 2009), only a minority of teachers—say, 35 to 40 per cent—use the technology, the students will miss out. If yours is a school that has built its digital strategy around computer labs, the students will probably be restricted to using the technology for two to three hours a week, often appreciably less.

In addition to the deployment and availability of the technology, there is also a range of other factors that will impact on the teacher and student use of digital technologies in the school, and why—on reflection—the school use of the technology will only ever constitute a small, almost minuscule, part of its overall use by students. Schools operate for only six hours a day, five days a week, for around 200 days each year. Within that limited time there is only a portion when the technology can and ought to be used. The contrast with the time and opportunity young people have to use it outside the classroom is dramatic, as will be discussed in the next chapter.

Approximately half or maybe two-thirds of the digital technologies used every day outside the classroom by young people are currently banned from use by most schools or education authorities. The majority of schools block the use of computer games, MP3 players, iPods, cell and Smart phones, the social network facilities, Skype, Instant Messenger, many of the commonly used Web 2.0 facilities like YouTube, and most websites to varying degrees. Ascertain the current situation in your school. The level of constraint on student access to the Internet and in particular the Web will in many schools be extensive (something amplified upon in Chapter 17). While the constraints will be significantly less in the more proactive schools, they will nonetheless be there.

In brief, in many current school settings, there are constraints on the use of the digital and networked technology. Some will always exist, but many should be removed if the school is to better harness the digital technology. The key is to ensure that the use of the digital is normalised in every classroom.

Online learning platforms

A significant development that has considerable potential and bears close scrutiny, particularly for use within a networked school community, is what Becta has called 'learning platforms' (Becta 2009a). They are also called VLEs (virtual learning environments), MLEs (managed learning environments) and CMS (content management systems). In brief, they are comprehensive and increasingly more sophisticated web-based teaching and learning systems that can be tailored for use by each student in the school (*Wikipedia* 2009b).

The hype surrounding their potential has been considerable, but despite more than a decade of development and promotion the level of student and teacher use remains relatively small, even in nations like the UK where the national government mandates their use by each school (Becta 2008a). The theory suggests learning platforms should be an ideal teaching and learning facility, but not only have most been used in only a limited way, the current technology largely restricts their educational capability. Few, if any, have the wherewithal to foster the development of higher-order thinking skills and creativity (Lee & Gaffney 2008).

Most of the commercial offerings are expensive and thus it is easy for schools to waste considerable monies—as many have already done. There are open-source offerings such as Moodle (2009) that appear to offer a less expensive entrée, but once one costs the time the staff need to invest in shaping and maintaining the system they too are expensive, particularly if the development is undertaken by just the one school. There are significant educational and economic advantages in groups of schools using the one system. Indeed if yours is a school within an education authority it is most likely that the authority will decide on the system you will have—regardless of whether you use it or not. Most assuredly have a look at this development and what is happening in your school and, if relevant, the education authority.

However, we suggest that you move cautiously, explore all the possibilities and consider how such a system would be used within your ideal networked school community before making a decision. The issue is complex and does require some within the leadership team to acquire an in-depth understanding and to appreciate the short- and long-term implications of the decision, as it is usually not easy or quick to transfer data from one system to another.

Note it is very easy to adopt a technical solution that will actually work against the desired educational outcomes.

We strongly recommend reading Chapter 13 of Lee and Gaffney's *Leading a digital school* (2008) to further that appreciation. Ironically, today a combination of the Web 2.0 tools that are available free of cost, when used astutely, could well achieve better educational outcomes than many of the expensive and now dated solutions. In considering your options, bear in mind the problem might have more to do with low teacher use of the digital technology (addressed below) than the actual learning platform.

Normalised teacher and student usage

There are nine main variables entailed in achieving normalised usage. Each is elaborated on by Lee and Winzenried (2009, p. 225). In brief, they are:

1   Teacher acceptance
2   Working with the givens
3   Teacher training and teacher developmental support
4   Nature and availability of the technology
5   Appropriate content/software
6   Infrastructure
7   Finance
8   School and education authority leadership
9   Implementation.

You can use the list as a guide in ascertaining the situation at your school.

Teacher acceptance

If the teachers, who are the gatekeepers to what happens in their classroom, do not perceive the educational benefit of the technology and are not comfortable using it in their teaching room, they will not use it—despite what the leadership or government says. At the very least you will want a critical mass of your teachers (60–70%) having normalised the use of the digital in their teaching before you can contemplate developing a networked school community.

Working with the givens

There are many, largely unwritten givens all teachers have to work within, not least of which is that teachers teach classes and have to manage those classes within a room with size limitations and complete an invariably crowded curriculum in a specified time. They are thus reluctant to waste valuable teaching time moving their students out of their normal teaching room. Too often these basics are forgotten in the strategic planning.

Teacher training and teacher developmental support

In an ever-evolving digital world it is imperative that all the teachers, and indeed other school staff, are provided with appropriate ongoing training and developmental support. Again, it is basic but too often neglected. While there are now some excellent initiatives in pathfinding schools that employ a battery of arrangements within the school's everyday operations and are well resourced, that is not the norm. Unless (as is discussed in Chapter 14) the teachers have the requisite capabilities and working conditions, there is only so much that is possible.

Nature and availability of the technology

Interestingly, history reveals that scant attention has been given to the appropriateness of the particular technology for use in the classroom. All too often the major technology companies 'convinced' the decision makers of the wisdom of acquiring their technology, even when it did not assist the teachers with the teaching of their classes in their teaching room. It is one of the very real problems with personal computers. It helps to explain why the interactive whiteboard is revolutionising the teachers' acceptance and everyday class use of digital technology. No other electronic teaching tool has had such widespread and rapid teacher and student uptake as the IWB (Lee & Winzenried 2009; Betcher & Lee 2009). In the UK alone the percentage of teachers using IWBs rose from 5 per cent in 2002 to 74 per cent in 2008 (Becta 2008a). While in 2002 just over 70 000 IWBs were sold globally, that figure had risen to over 650 000 in 2008. By 2012, the figure is predicted to at least double (Futuresource Consulting 2009).

Becta, the government agency charged with overseeing the harnessing of technology in the UK's schools, observed in its 2007 annual review:

> This sharp rise in the use of ICT resources in the curriculum has been driven to a large extent by the adoption of interactive whiteboards (IWBs) and related technologies. Interactive whiteboards are a popular technology, in heavy demand by schools and practitioners. They offer transparent benefits to learning and teaching. That is, it is easy for institutions and teachers to recognise how IWBs enrich and enhance learning and teaching—something which may not always be so immediately transparent to practitioners in the case of other technologies.
>
> Becta (2007a, p. 66)

Infrastructure

Schools have to have the requisite network infrastructure and support if they are to operate successfully within the networked world. Without it you can forget all your ambitions. Mention was made earlier of the connectivity to each room and the network operating 100 per cent of teaching time. The vast majority of schools are well networked these days, with most having all classes with network connectivity. How well they are placed to handle the heavy multimedia traffic they are likely to experience in a networked school community or, more particularly, have the appropriate network support required to achieve the 100 per cent up-time, is a more moot point. Check it out.

In a networked school community seeking to take advantage of the new and expanded playing field, the demands are likely to be ever-greater and the time the network needs to be up appreciably longer. Consequently the level of support and capability of the network could require attention. However, increasingly the research is revealing (not at all surprisingly) that if use of the network—and in particular access to the Internet—is too tightly controlled, the students will (as per Gilmore's Law mentioned in Chapter 16) opt not to use the school network but rather will use their own technology to circumvent those controls.

A colleague tells the revealing story of a recent visit to a Japanese secondary school where much to his surprise he found the school's very expensive, extensive and tightly controlled network only being available for school administration. The comment was made that the students preferred to use the technology they had in their pockets for unfettered Internet access! A careful balancing act is thus required.

Finance

Suffice to say, the vast majority of the schools in the developed world are struggling to fund the desired digital and network developments and the requisite human support and development from their recurrent funding. Today's schools (as is discussed in Chapter 7) are still basically funded using a formula developed for paper-based schools, with only a few per cent of the annual allocation available to spend on the burgeoning technological needs. While the pathfinding schools have achieved much with limited funds, invariably other school operations have been curtailed or stopped.

Leadership

It is almost impossible to over-emphasise the importance of the role of the school leadership and in particular the school principal in the astute acquisition, deployment and use of the appropriate technology in the school. The principal will have a profound impact whatever she or he does. Whether proactive, apathetic or vehemently opposed to change, the principal will, knowingly or unwittingly, influence all that the school does.

While this impact is analysed in depth in *Leading a digital school* (Lee & Gaffney 2008), you will find throughout this book an ongoing highlighting of the importance of the leadership position in shaping the desired networked school community. Research reveals that many existing and prospective school principals lack the expertise expected of the principal educational architect of a digital school or in particular a networked school community (Moyle 2006; Lee & Gaffney 2008), and still tend to rely on their middle-level 'ICT experts'. Globally, there has been and still is today a pronounced lack of opportunities for school and education authority leaders to acquire, either at the postgraduate level or within the education authority, the up-to-date macro understanding of the digital technology required to lead a digital or networked school.

It is appreciated that there is a very real challenge to secure and maintain that understanding with a rapidly evolving technology, but as the technology becomes more sophisticated and integrated, so too must the leader's understanding of how best to use that technology, and so must the school principal take ultimate responsibility for the acquisition and deployment of the technology throughout the school and the provision of the requisite support. As indicated in Lee and Gaffney (2008), while principals don't need to be digital experts, they ought to have a macro appreciation of how to get the most from that technology. You will need to ascertain how well your school is placed.

Implementation

History and the research reveal—perhaps not surprisingly in light of the comments made about the digital understanding of many school principals—that most schools' and education authorities' implementation of new technology have been handled poorly. Almost universally the preoccupation has been with the actual technology, with only incidental attention given to the human dimensions for effectively implementing change. The classic example has been the school ICT plan. Invariably developed by a committee of school 'experts', the plan usually focused on the actual technology and was developed in isolation from the school's main development plan. In most instances, the plan became another 'bolt on' venture that had the same limitations in terms of impact as many occupational health and safety, gender equity, inclusiveness and indigenous education committee plans that were not enacted.

What will become increasingly apparent as we explore the development of networked school communities and seek to create the home–school nexus, is that the main challenges will be human. Indeed by moving as most schools will from a digital mode, the vast majority of the technological facets of the new model will already be in place. The real challenge will be to develop an astute human and organisational change strategy that incorporates the wise use of the technology, which in turn is able to accommodate an ever-changing world. The school most assuredly does not need a discrete 'ICT plan', even though the local bureaucrats may well demand one.

Bureaucratic and hierarchical control

Ironically, while many school and education authority leaders might lack the high-level understanding of the digital world, you will find in most instances that they will still very much wish to maintain their control of the acquisition, deployment and use of that technology. Indeed, don't be surprised if many challenge your right to question their understanding and expertise.

What appears to be happening across much of the developed world is a growth in the power and control exercised by the bureaucrats over the technology acquired and used by schools. It does not appear to matter that this is antithetical to the development of a networked organisation able to respond rapidly to change, and indeed the conduct of schools in a democracy. It is now common for the central bureaucracy to use the networked technology to exert greater control over the schools' operations, all in the name of efficiency. It is a variable you will need to address, probably politically.

A telling 2008 US national study of school principals and highly ICT-competent students (Project Tomorrow 2008) revealed that while all the principals surveyed believed they had an excellent appreciation of the education required for a digital future, the students seriously questioned that assumption and believed only 30 per cent of their principals understood what was required. That pattern is likely to be replicated globally; but, regardless, those atop the hierarchy in both the schools and bureaucracies will invariably insist they know what is best and are likely to want to maintain their control.

Administration and communication

While most schools in the developed world now use digital administration and communication systems, a sizeable proportion of them are dated, limited in their capability, expensive and not particularly user-friendly, and often add to the workload rather than providing the promised efficiency. Most are configured to cater for and serve to reinforce the status quo and to maintain the control of the particular educational bureaucracy.

You may well find in your school that the educational and school administration and communication systems are still physically separated, with little interoperability. Virtually all of the school management systems strongly reflect the local educational bureaucracy's current agenda. Very few of the systems currently open their arms to a fuller home–school collaboration. That said, if your school is fortunate enough to be proactive, there should be the opportunity to use the systems to better work with the homes.

As indicated, the major stumbling block to using these systems to forge a closer home–school nexus is human and not technological; it is that desire by the bureaucracy to retain control. Most web-enabled systems can readily be attuned to cater for all manner of user if the system administrator so allows. Look at your local situation. We suspect there will be the ready facility for your school, if it so desires (and the bureaucratic controls can be overcome), to make extensive use of the ever-evolving suite of Web 2.0 and social networking facilities, particularly in enhancing the participation of both the parents and students in the school's development and its communications.

Interestingly, at this stage even the more proactive schools and education authorities have been very slow to use those collaborative and what some describe as disruptive technologies—that is, those technologies whose functionality challenges the old ways.

Impact of the technology corporations

In examining the current situation in your school it would be as well to appreciate that the major multinational technology corporations have had and will continue to have a profound impact on the choice of technology used in schools, some good but much historically to the detriment of teaching. The prime purpose of all those companies is rightly to sell product and make a profit regardless, ultimately, of schools' and teachers' needs (Lee & Winzenried 2009). While at first glance this comment might appear harsh, it is a reality that is often forgotten.

The power of the marketing arms of companies like Microsoft, Dell and Apple is immense and will usually sway the less astute. Provided one deals with the technology companies and their marketing and salespeople with this in mind, one can achieve win–win outcomes. But, sadly, the school industry has a very poor track record with those win–win scenarios, more often than not acquiring technology that does not enhance the teaching or the efficiency of the school's operations. It is important to go into any negotiations well informed and take a measured approach.

Conclusion

As you will appreciate, it is difficult to generalise on the use of digital technology in the schools of the developed world, but hopefully you are now aware of the significant variables to bear in mind in seeking to move onto the networked stage. It is our intention for you to also appreciate where your situation sits on the proactive–reactive continuum. That appreciation can help you quickly identify what is the rhetoric and what is the reality.

As schooling moves deeper into the changing and uncertain digital and networked worlds, no one—least of all the educational bureaucrat—has charts to guide the way. As Lee and Gaffney (2008) indicate, while the trend lines offer some guidance, the reality is, as Steve Jobs famously noted, that even visionaries like him have little chance of foretelling the technology that will be available to schools and homes in five to ten years time.

What we do know is that there will be dramatic change, the technology will become more sophisticated and smarter, some of the technological developments will succeed and others will fail, but overall a host of new opportunities will emerge for astute educators. Approach its use positively and with an open and flexible mind and you are likely to succeed, albeit with an occasional glitch.

Guiding questions

After reading this chapter, consider your context and propose your ideas in relation to the following guiding questions.

1 Where would you position the school on the proactive–reactive continuum in Table 3.1?

2 Has the school become a digital school and achieved digital take-off?

3 What digital technologies are the staff provided with?

4 Do all classrooms have a suite of whole-class digital technologies that allows the teacher to use them when desired?

5 What percentage of the school's teachers has normalised the use of digital technology into their everyday teaching?

6 What percentage of the school's teaching rooms and staff offices has high-speed broadband access to the Internet?

7 For what percentage of time is the school's network up and available for use during the teaching hours in the year?

8 Do all teachers and students use the school's online teaching facilities?

9 How ready is the school to move into the networked mode?

Key messages

- There will be dramatic change, the technology will become ever-more sophisticated and smarter, some of the technological developments will succeed and others will fail, but overall a host of new opportunities will emerge for astute educators.
- The real challenge will be to develop an astute human and organisational change strategy that incorporates the wise use of the technology that, in turn, is able to accommodate an ever-changing world.

CHAPTER 4

Homes and the digital technology: A home–school difference or digital divide?

MAL LEE & MARTIN LEVINS

Kids lead high-tech lives outside school and decidedly low-tech lives inside school. This new 'digital divide' is making the activities inside school appear to have less real-world relevance to kids. A blend of intellectual discipline with real-world context can make learning more relevant, and online technology can bridge the gap between the two.

Illinois Institute of Design (2007, p. 24)

Digital technologies in the home

The level of digital technology in the average home has always exceeded that in the average classroom, but since the mid 1990s the difference between the digital holdings of the home and those in the average classroom and the use made by young people of that technology in both situations have diverged rapidly. So great is the difference today that prescient leaders and writers across the developed world (Fairlie 2005; Buckingham 2007) speak of an alarming digital divide between the school and home and the need for societies to urgently redress the situation. The e-Learning Foundation, the organisation charged with implementing the UK's Home Access Project, commented in 2009 on the project's desire to 'help close the digital divide' (Hawkins 2009).

The authors view the development not as a matter of concern but rather as an opportunity to help develop a mode of schooling appropriate to a digital and networked world. What many see as a divide we see as but a difference and the evolution of a suite of resources and learning opportunities that, employed wisely, can significantly enhance the quality and the appropriateness of schooling. As discussed below, the authors appreciate there are situations where there is still a digital divide and where students are likely to be disadvantaged educationally.

Challenges in seeking to harness the opportunities opened by the digital resources in the home are to:

- secure an in-depth appreciation of the current and evolving situation across the developed world;
- identify the differences between the home and school situations;
- appreciate that most homes have normalised the use of digital technology by young people and that it is the schools that lag behind;
- understand that there are a number of growing digital divides that ought to be of concern.

In examining the nature of the difference between the technology in the home and the school it will soon become apparent that one is not looking at a black-and-white situation but rather a complex scenario that needs to be approached cautiously and without making false assumptions about the situation with all young people in schools.

What will remain obvious is that the level and use made of the digital technology by young people in their homes are on average appreciably greater than in the average classroom, with the difference growing rapidly. In 2009, one is not talking two or three times greater but rather (as explained in Chapter 7) conservatively in the region of approximately 14 to 15 times greater. It is by any measure a vast and growing difference. While the actual figures are likely to vary between developed nations, the reality is that in all—whether Australia, Spain, Taiwan or Finland—the difference will be great, and in situations like Spain and Taiwan probably even greater than the figures mentioned. (It is worth noting that when the authors speak of the 'home' they are in fact commenting on all the digital technology owned and used by all within the home, including the rapidly escalating suite of mobile and wireless technologies.)

In seeking to better understand the difference between the home and the school, look in particular at the trends and not so much the current state of play. It is a mistake that many of the early and even more recent analysts of the 'digital divide' have made. The rate of technological development is so rapid that within 12 to 18 months your situation can have changed significantly. Plan for the evolving scene and not around the snapshot-in-time that you have taken. Similarly, position the developments in your situation within the wider macro and global context. In reviewing the literature this is a mistake that some have made in extrapolating from their country and assuming that it will be so globally. It is apparent that that will not always be so but, that said, you are likely to find remarkably similar differences between the homes and schools across the developed world.

In your planning for all the students in the school, appreciate there is likely to be significant variation in student access to technology in the home. Don't work simply on the average picture, as the education of every one of your students is important. There will be students who do not have Internet access at home, sometimes because of economics, sometimes because of family beliefs, and sometimes because the family has no interest in the online world. It is therefore important to analyse the situation in your school community, the trends, the opportunities available and the areas needing particular attention.

In seeking to get a fuller understanding of the technology and the use young people make of it in the home, note:

- the use made of the various technologies, being sure to look at both the hardware and software;
- those used by special interest groups, such as the complex game players;
- the differences between the various age cohorts and genders;
- the time available to use the technology, and the degree of control exercised by the home over the use of the particular technology;
- the impact of changing fashions;
- the extent to which the technology constitutes part of the developmental process of young people in contemporary society;
- the impact of increasing digital convergence and the challenge of categorising multifaceted technologies like 'the phone';
- the uptake of mobile and, in particular, wireless technologies; and
- the contrast between the home and the school.

Don't make the mistake many researchers and policy developers have made of assuming that students in homes without Internet access are automatically disadvantaged. Granted those students might not currently have conventional computer access to the Web, but many may well have a suite of digital technologies, such as digital TVs, DVD players, MP3 players, games consoles and cell phones on which they are developing many of their digital competencies. Some of that group may well have regular web access through friends and relatives. Don't forget also the grandparents who care for many young people after school and their Internet access.

The home–school difference

The origins

The origins of the current significant difference between the home and the classroom are to be found in the emergence of the first of the digital technologies, the personal computers in the late 1970s and 1980s, the global expansion of the consumer electronics industry and development of the networked world (Lee & Winzenried 2009). Throughout the 1980s and then particularly in the 1990s, every day young people in their homes across the developed world were using the instructional technologies that had at some stage been projected to revolutionise teaching. By the latter 1980s the vast majority of homes were using colour TVs, video recorders, video cameras, 35-mm cameras, hi-fi systems, radios, audiocassette players, telephones and—increasingly—personal computers every day, while most classrooms struggled to acquire, let alone actually use, those technologies (Cuban 1986; Saettler 1990; Lee & Winzenried 2009). The beginnings of today's 'divide' between the home and school use of technology were clearly evident.

The reality is that historically, as attested by Cuban in his *Teachers and machines* (1986) and Lee and Winzenried in *The use of instructional technology in schools* (2009), the availability and use of 'instructional technology' in the average home have always exceeded that in the average classroom. That 'divide' was accentuated in the late 1980s and early 1990s by the emergence of GUI software for personal computers, the ubiquitous use by both Apple and Windows users of Microsoft Office, the surge in the availability of quality computer games, the advent of CD-ROMs and the emergence of a suite of software applications that made it easy for all—both the young and the old—to create quality digital multimedia materials in their homes.

In Australia in 1995, 57 per cent of households with school children had a personal computer (Australian Communications and Media Authority [ACMA] 2007). The figure was comparable in the other developed nations. In brief, one in two children had ready home use of a PC. In contrast, most schools across the developed world were fortunate to have two PCs with a class of 30 students, or a student-to-computer ratio of 1:15 (Tabs 2003; Meredyth et al. 1999). The computer-to-student ratio in the US in 1998 had, in no small part due to the efforts of the Clinton–Gore administration, reached 12.1:1 (Tabs 2003). While the media lauded the introduction of computers into the schools (and published many photos of the new computer labs), the reality is that the lab often contained all the school's computers and afforded students less than an hour's computer use per week. The contrast with the home was pronounced.

It was, however, the introduction of the World Wide Web's web browser, initially in the form of Mosaic and then Netscape in the mid 1990s, that markedly amplified the differences between students' use of technology in the home and the classroom. While in the mid 1990s virtually every home had a telephone that could be immediately linked via a modem to the Internet, most classrooms—as Al Gore (1994) aptly noted—were telecommunication deserts. Few teaching rooms anywhere in the developed world had a telephone or indeed were linked via a network to the Internet. Moreover, few schools had the high-speed connectivity or school-wide network needed to connect classrooms to the Internet. The US, while well to the fore internationally in 1995, had only 8.1 per cent of its classrooms linked to the Internet (Tabs 2003). It would take the more proactive schools and education authorities most of the latter half of the 1990s to install the requisite network infrastructure.

In the same period, home access to the Internet, either by modem or broadband, grew rapidly as did the uptake of personal computers, the associated computer peripherals and most importantly email. What this meant was that young people in their homes had everyday use of emails several years ahead of when they were provided by the school. It is little surprise that they were unimpressed by those schools and education authorities that made great noises about providing some students with email accounts four to five years after the homes started using emails.

The uptake of the Internet was particularly strong in homes with school-age children, with the parents from the mid 1990s believing that access to the Internet would enhance their children's education and life chances. Thus, from the mid 1990s on, across the developed and developing world Internet access in homes with children was always greater than those without. What is important to note, particularly in light of the earlier comment re the professional educators' desire to retain unilateral control of the education for a digital future, is that while parents instantly identified the educational potential of PCs and the Internet, the schools showed little if any leadership in the area. The uptake in the home was spontaneous and prompted in no significant way by the school leadership.

As indicated in Lee and Winzenried (2009), Mal Lee can well remember sighting confidential market research from the International Data Corporation (IDC) in 1995, which revealed that well over 90 per cent of parents believed the purchase of a PC and the acquiring of Internet access would benefit their children's education. In 1996, Lee wrote of the folly of schools seeking to replicate the technology of the home, and yet today there is still scant evidence of schools responding to the needs of a networked world (Lee 1996a). The comprehensive study of digital technology in Australia's family homes undertaken by ACMA in 2007 identified the same belief with regards to both computer and Internet use (ACMA 2007, p. 10).

While the availability of computers and Internet access provides a quick and important indicator of the differing situations in the home and the school, and is the one most cited in the literature, the authors contend that in terms of educational development it is more important to examine the suite of digital technologies available to young people in the home and school, in that it is the holistic use of those technologies that is the key.

As you will appreciate, what we have seen in the past ten to 15 years is an expansion of the variety of technologies available in the home, a growth in their sophistication, a reduction in its size, increased portability, a relative drop in price, a move from analogue to digital technologies, and with that shift ever-greater digital convergence and the emergence of integrated technologies. Allied to those developments has been the growth, particularly in young people, of a set of generic digital competencies and a confidence that allows the users to quickly learn how to use a new digital technology, whether it is a computer, games console, digital camera or iPod. The nature of that confidence and those competencies are important considerations.

It is our belief that it is young people's use of the suite of technologies that is the key variable and not simply the use of a part, important though it is. Educationally it is therefore vital to note the total suite of technologies used by young people, and to identify the use made and impact of those digital technologies not generally used within classrooms. The research is suggesting the contribution made by the likes of the complex computer games, iPods and MP3 players, Smart phones, and even digital television, all of which are rarely used in the classroom, is significant (Prensky 2006; Gee 2007). Think about your own home and the kind of use made of the suite of technologies you had in the 1990s, in the early 2000s and today, and the use your children made of that suite of technology.

2002–2003

Take your memory to the early 2000s and think about the suite of technologies you had in the home, the changes that had occurred in only five or six years and the use made of that technology by young people. The impetus that impacted on schools around 2002–2003 had a similar if not greater effect on the average family home. With the money and freedom to spend those monies when they wished, on what they wished, the home was able to secure the latest technology when it appeared. Without the structural and legislative constraints of the school, one saw family homes and young people therein both acquiring and making ever-greater use of the converging technologies.

The analogue technology was being phased out and gradually replaced by the digital. DVD recorder sales passed those for VCRs in 2003 (*Wikipedia* 2009c). The audiocassette joined the record player in gathering dust, to be replaced first by the CD and then the MP3 player, and most notably in 2001 by Apple's iPod. By the early 2000s, the iPod and Apple's iTunes store, which opened in 2003 (*Wikipedia* 2009d), dramatically changed the domestic audio scene. The distinctive white iPod earphones soon became common with young people around the world.

The movement towards digital convergence and the creation and use of multimedia applications were stimulated by the release in 2001 of Microsoft's XP software and Apple's OS 10.1—its UNIX-based operating system. The analogue cell phone had been replaced by increasingly more sophisticated and more multifunctional digital phones. By 2003, the vast majority of teenagers had their own cell phone. The external modem of the 1990s, which connected to a basic phone line, has been superseded by broadband technologies that use the same wires in an intelligent way, or via mobile phone radios. Combined with the growing number of computers in the home, and as users realised the benefits of 'always on' access, the home needed more sophisticated routers than many small businesses.

The early 2000s saw the release of a suite of online facilities that we have come to know as Web 2.0, offering opportunity for all Internet users to publish to or communicate via the Web. In addition to the blogs and general wikis, *Wikipedia*, the free encyclopedia, emerged in 2001, while Skype was released in 2003. Between 2002 and 2004 three significant social networking facilities appeared, namely Friendster, Bebo and the most successful of all three, MySpace (*Wikipedia* 2009k).

What was clearly apparent by 2002–2003 was that young people had taken into their lives a set of sophisticated digital technologies, all of which were excluded globally in the classroom, namely Smart phones, computer games and consoles, MP3/MP4 players and social networking facilities. Indeed, Cassell and Cramer (2008) argue that the use of those 'non-school' technologies had become very important to the social development of young people in developed societies. There is little doubt that their use and impact on the lives of young people, even by 2003, were immense.

The cell phone, in particular, had become an integral part of the teenager's social existence by 2003, as had SMS texting and instant messaging. Not only was the growth in the uptake of this technology profound, but so too was the shift from using the new technology to replicate the old ways to adopting a completely new way of using the technology—the use of SMS texting. A similar kind of development occurred in the use of computer games (or what some term 'video games'), although with the games the embracement was skewed to the males and hence the number who embraced this technology was less than the mobile phone. The early 2000s saw the release of the first games on mobile phones and the emergence of what is termed the sixth generation games, those associated with Sony's PlayStation and Microsoft's Xbox (*Wikipedia* 2009e).

The schools in 2002–2003

By the early 2000s, proactive schools around the world were networked, with high-speed Internet access and with extensive collections of personal computers, but they were few in number. While the proactive nations had, as mentioned, developed the network infrastructure, even they had made little progress in providing the teaching rooms with the digital tools. In the US by 2002, even after the efforts of the Clinton–Gore administration, 92 per cent of the nation's teaching rooms were networked, but the computer-to-student ratio was still only around one computer for every five students (Tabs 2003).

In the UK, the figure for 2003 in secondary schools was much the same, with the primary figure being only one computer to 7.9 students (Becta 2007a, p. 7). The actual time spent using the technology in the classroom remained small, usually only an hour or two a week, in marked contrast to young people's everyday use of the suite of digital technologies in their homes.

2003–2010

When you consider and examine the technology in your home today, you will appreciate the considerable advancements made since the early 2000s. There has been a marked increase in sophistication of the technology, the shift to virtually all digital technologies, rapid and ongoing digital convergence and miniaturisation of the technologies, an explosion in the use of mobile and wireless networked technology and a burgeoning in the 'smarts' in the manner of software. You will also appreciate the sophistication and the learning opportunities afforded young people by the aforementioned 'non-school' technologies. The multifaceted cell phone of the early 2000s had morphed, with the likes of the iPhone, into a 'Smart phone' or what was in essence a wireless handheld computer. The iPod, with sales of over 150 million units (*Wikipedia* 2009d), has become a portable multimedia entertainment unit and digital storage facility, while the computer games consoles have become networked multimedia entertainment and communications technologies. The same kind of sophistication and digital convergence is now to be found in the plethora of social networking and Web 2.0 facilities available, with most linking to complementary online services.

When used in conjunction with the other technologies in the home, of the kind mentioned below, you will appreciate why the home has and will continue to play a vital role in developing the digital confidence and competence of young people, and in fostering the development of the kind of skills set and competencies discussed in the next chapter. What many educators and policy makers forget is that young people born after 1985 in developed economies have grown up in homes where the digital and networked are a normal, everyday part of life, and have been educated in schools where for the most part that technology is a limited add-on. In its 2007 study of the homes of Australia's young people, ACMA found that of the homes surveyed the following average emerged: three mobile phones, three televisions, two computers, two DVD players, two portable MP3/MP4 players, one VCR, two games consoles (ACMA 2007, p. 49).

The ACMA study succinctly captures the changes we have been examining when it observed that 'communications and media technology available to Australian families has changed significantly since 1995. Then, less than 10 per cent of families had access to the Internet. Now, less than 10 per cent of homes are without it' (ACMA 2007, p. 5). It noted the following trends:

- In 1995, more than 90 per cent of homes had a video player or recorder, while in 2007, DVD players are in almost every home.
- Children and families have greater access to gaming devices than in 1995, with games consoles now in three-quarters of homes.
- Families have also embraced portable digital music players, with about three-quarters of households having a device such as an iPod or MP3 player.
- Other technologies now found in Australian homes include portable DVD players, DVD recorders and hard-drive recorders, though these are present in less than one-third of households.
- Home Internet access seems to be partly a function of means; 94 per cent of households with incomes of more than $35 000 are online, compared with 75 per cent of those on less than $35 000.

- The type of Internet connection is even more closely correlated with income; broadband Internet is present in 91 per cent of households with incomes of more than $100 000, down to 50 per cent of those on less than $35 000.

- In 1995, less than 10 per cent of families had access to the Internet. Now, less than 10 per cent of homes are without it.

- Televisions were ubiquitous in 1995, and remain so in 2007. In 1995, three-quarters of families had two or more televisions. In 2007, 90 per cent of families have two or more televisions and one-quarter of homes has four or more. One-third of families (32%) has access to digital free-to-air television.

- An analysis of household income suggests that electronic media and communications devices are important to all families, even where their income is low. Of households with an income of less than $35 000, three-quarters have Internet access and greater proportions have at least one DVD player, game console and mobile phone. However, household income does have a considerable impact on the likelihood of having subscription television, digital free-to-air television and devices such as DVD recorders, hard-drive recorders or portable DVD players.

(Source: ACMA 2007, pp. 5–6)

In relation to young people, the survey also found that nine out of ten teenagers had their own phone (ACMA 2007, p. 7). The Pew study of US homes, undertaken by MacGill in 2007 similarly found:

> The role of digital technology in families continues to grow. Many of the results in the most recent survey are compared to another survey conducted by the Project in October 2004. More parents and teens are online. Some 93% of youth are online and 94% of their parents are online. Overall, 87% of parents who have a child aged 12–17 use the Internet, up from 80% in the 2004 survey. (p. 2)

What the studies do not reveal is that the same homes were also likely to have numerous radios (although fewer battery-driven ones), at least one sound system, which in view of the DVD players was likely to be a home theatre surround-sound system, several boom boxes, and a fixed line telephone system using multiple handsets that was integrated with the home's use of broadband. At least one of the TV sets was likely to be a flat-screen digital unit, integrated with the surround system and the games console. The older cathode-ray TVs were likely being phased out and moved down the pecking order into the spare and kids' rooms.

It was highly likely that a sizeable proportion of the mobile phones mentioned was multifunction Smart phones, web-enabled and with digital camera and MP3/MP4 capability. In 2006, New Zealand, in keeping with the other developed economies, had over 90 per cent of its teens with their own mobile (Statistics New Zealand 2007). If the survey was taken in

2009, those mobiles were likely to be wireless handheld computers, such as the iPhone or Android-powered phones. It is also likely, as was identified in the 2008 UK study by Hart, Bober and Pine, that the students at home had access to the Internet not only via computers, but also by way of the mobile phones and the games consoles.

> *Most children (91%) used a computer or lap-top to access the Internet at home ... 20% of children used their mobile phones to get online, 17% used their games console and 15% used a handheld gaming device.*
>
> Hart, Bober & Pine (2008, p. 5)

The playing of video games by young people in 2009 across the developed world was near universal. The following Pew survey results on the use of the games in 2008, while drawn from US data, are common in all developed economies:

- Video gaming is pervasive in the lives of American teens—young teens and older teens, girls and boys, and teens from across the socioeconomic spectrum. Opportunities for gaming are everywhere, and teens are playing video games frequently. When asked, half of all teens reported playing a video game 'yesterday'. Those who play daily typically play for an hour or more;

- 97% of teens aged 12–17 play computer, web, portable or console games;

- 50% of teens played games 'yesterday';

- 86% of teens play on a console like the Xbox, PlayStation or Wii;

- 73% play games on a desktop or a laptop computer;

- 60% use a portable gaming device like a Sony PlayStation Portable, a Nintendo DS, or a Game Boy;

- 48% use a cell phone or handheld organiser to play games;

- 99% of boys and 94% of girls play video games. Younger teen boys are the most likely to play games, followed by younger girls and older boys. Older girls are the least 'enthusiastic' players of video games, though more than half of them play. Some 65% of daily gamers are male; 35% are female.

(Source: Lenhart et al. 2008)

The survey does not reveal the profound explosion that has taken place in the use and sophistication of the social networking facilities in the last five years and young people's embracement of these facilities. As any parent will know, the likes of MySpace and Facebook, with links to other online facilities like YouTube, Ning, Twitter and Digg now constitute an important part of the lives of most young people. The 2007 Pew Internet research noted over 55 per cent of 12–17 year-olds in the US were involved in a social network, with the older girls being the biggest users (Lenhart & Madden 2007, p. 1). MySpace, the breakthrough social networking facility, had 230 000 members joining each day in 2006. Facebook, which began operations in 2005, was by 2009 the most popular of the social networks, surpassing MySpace and Twitter (*Wikipedia* 2009f).

Dretzin and Maggio's excellent 2008 PBS documentary *Growing up online* provides a revealing and stimulating examination of the impact of the social networks on young people and their parents. The social significance of these facilities can be appreciated by going to barackobama.com (Obama 2009), and noting under 'Obama Everywhere' on the homepage the US President's use of the various network communities. Despite the importance of the social networks in the lives of young people, and the outlook they engender, most in 2009 were still banned in the vast majority of schools in the developed world. Ironically, while President Obama is one of the most high-profile users of the networks, existing US legislation (cited by Cassell & Cramer 2008) makes it very difficult for schools to use them.

The 2007 ACMA study makes the telling observation that 'From age 14 onwards, 70 per cent or more of teenagers are engaged in some form of web authorship' (ACMA 2007, p. 8). The implications of those figures—given they were assembled in mid 2007 and were steadily trending upwards—are profound, particularly when compared with the scene in the schools. Once again the use of a powerful educational facility is largely restricted to outside the classroom.

Home Internet access

What you will find when you examine the level of Internet access in those homes with young people in 2009 is that the aforementioned figure of 91 per cent for Australia's homes is at the high end internationally. When you look at the findings of the World Internet Project (WIP), the Pew Internet studies and the latest OECD figures you will note countries like the US, Canada, the UK, Denmark, Finland, Norway, Sweden, New Zealand, South Korea, Hong Kong and Japan are all akin to Australia with the vast majority of the family homes having Internet access (USC Annenberg School for Communications 2008; Bell et al. 2007; Ewing, Thomas & Schiessl 2008; Findhal 2008; OECD 2009). However, you will also note, particularly if you examine the OECD figures, that many developed nations are appreciably lower, with the likes of France and Spain falling well below the abovementioned.

In looking at the latest home Internet connectivity figures, one will often find it hard to explain some of the variability in some of the national figures. While those associated with WIP appear reliable, some of the other sources are more dubious. For example, a study by a group called FreshMinds (2007) that was used in shaping the UK's Home Technology Access initiative, not only suggested that only 65 per cent of the UK's family homes had Internet access, but that market conditions were such that the UK could not expect any marked increase. When one contrasts the observation with the following comments by Hart, Bober and Pine (2008) one begins to wonder.

Almost all children had access to a computer and the Internet at home.

92% of children said they used a computer or laptop at home.

This corresponds to the findings of Becta's Harnessing Technology Review 2008, where 92% of parents of school-aged children said they had Internet access at home.

The majority had access to handheld devices, games consoles and mobile phones. (p. 5)

An often hidden element in many of the home Internet access figures is the breakdown in plain old telephone (POT) and broadband access. The important development to note, particularly as it relates to the home–school nexus and the development of networked school communities, is the trend towards increasingly higher broadband and the openings that bandwidth provides for ever-more sophisticated interaction between the home, the school and other educational offerings. The 2008 USC Annenberg School for Communication's Digital Future study of the US found:

The number of hours online per week continues to increase—rising to an average of 15.3 hours per week, up by more than one hour per week from 2006, and the highest level in the Digital Future studies. (p. 4)

The universal picture would appear to be that the time spent on the Internet in the home is now on par with that spent watching TV. While some (particularly those with a vested interest in free-to-air television) will dispute that claim, the following research finding, while relating to UK homes in 2008, is now typical of homes in the developed world.

How the Internet fits into family life

On a typical school day, these children spend twice as much time on their computers as they do watching television.

On aggregate children spent 79 minutes on the Internet and 48 minutes on computer games—a total of 127 minutes on their computers, compared with only 68 minutes watching television.

Hart, Boder & Pine (2008, p. 5)

The widespread acceptance of the Internet by young people in the home today can probably best be encapsulated in the following observation by Findahl (2008) on the Swedish situation with those not yet at school:

The time we spend on the Internet has tripled in the last seven years, while the Internet has spread to younger users, down to pre-school age. Internet use for children under the age of 7 has doubled during the last few years. Nowadays, one of three pre-schoolers uses the Internet. For school children, from grade one and on, the Internet is already well established. Virtually everyone is an Internet user. School children have become the group, out of all the age groups in the study, with the largest percent of Internet users. (p. 6)

Points of clarification

Time availability and usage

It is very easy to overlook the amount of time young people have'at home'to use the various digital technologies, particularly when one factors in the increasing use being made of mobile technologies, and the limited time available in the school week and indeed the school year. The combination of home-based and mobile technology allows young people to use it 24 hours a day, 365 days a year. In reality they don't use all that time but, interestingly, a 2007 AAPT study found that 80 per cent of the 16–34 age group left their mobile or cell phones on 24 hours a day (AAPT 2007). In contrast, young people can only use that in the school a limited number of days each year, for around six hours a day. Globally the use of the digital and networked technologies is growing rapidly. In Canada it is noted that 'overall, time spent online using mobile and wireless technology has increased, from 1.6 hours per week in 2004 to 2.6 hours per week in 2007' (Zamaria & Fletcher 2008, p. 23).

Commenting on the 2008 US scene, the *Digital futures* study reported:

> *The number of hours online per week continues to increase—rising to an average of 15.3 hours per week, up by more than one hour per week from 2006, and the highest level in the Digital Future studies.*
>
> USC Annenberg School for Communications (2008, p. 4)

It would appear from an analysis of a series of recent surveys in the main developed nations that young people use the information and communications technologies around two to three hours a day, most days of the year. The actual hours used in the 'home' is being complicated by the marked propensity of young people to multi-task and to use a range of technologies at the one time. The ACMA study revealed, as you will already be aware, young people's seeming ease in almost simultaneously using the likes of a computer, listening to an iPod, instant messaging and the TV. Similarly, a 2007 Canadian study found that:

> *The media use behavior of Canadians is evolving towards increased concurrent activities and multi-tasking across several platforms and media; it is therefore becoming more difficult to isolate and measure specific media use as Canadians, more and more, attend to many media simultaneously.*
>
> Zamaria & Fletcher (2007, p. 26)

Before rushing to quick conclusions, think about how much you multi-task, both at work and at home, readily moving from one activity to another, in an often seemingly chaotic manner. The contrast with the desired carefully controlled learning in many classrooms is pronounced. The research indicates that young people prefer to use the technology, and in particular to use the computer and access the Web in the afternoon after school and early evening. The ACMA research pointed to a preference to use the two to three hours before the evening meal and then for several hours after the meal, with 'the most popular time for children and young people to watch television … [being] between 6.00 and 9.00 pm, followed by 3.00–6.00 pm, whether during the week or on weekends' (ACMA 2007, p. 4). A similar pattern of use was found in a 2008 UK study.

> Going online has become part of children's regular evening routines. The fact that many children use the Internet as soon as they get home from school shows how important this technology has become in their daily lives. On a typical school day, nearly six in ten children say they go online as soon as they come home from school (58%). Slightly fewer children use the Internet after their evening meal (56%). One in four goes online just before they go to bed (24%), and almost two in ten before school (18%). Older children are more likely to access the Internet before bedtime but less likely to access before they go to school.

> Hart, Boder & Pine (2008, p. 20)

These findings match research that Mal Lee undertook in 2003 (Lee & Boyle 2003) with one of the early schools to use interactive whiteboards throughout. Although located in a low socio-economic community, the focus group discussions with both the students and the parents revealed the students' preference to use the time at school for collaborative and social interaction and at home for individual work. As many primary age children get home mid afternoon, they often have several hours before their parents come home from work. While one can debate the actual hours of use of the various technologies by young people at home, the bottom line is that they have had all their life, and will continue to have throughout their schooling, appreciably more time and opportunity to use the various digital technologies at home than in the classroom.

Probably the most important message to come out of the 2007 ACMA analysis of the use of technology in the home by young people is that the vast majority are very astute in retaining an appropriate balance in their lives, particularly as it relates to their play, participation in sport and recreational activities and use of technology.

> Parental mediation is a balancing act, and seven out of 10 parents say they are happy for their child to maintain his or her current balance between electronic media and communication activities and other activities. This proportion is down a little from 1995. This figure reflects the broader picture provided by the community research, that while parents have some concerns, overall they appear reasonably comfortable with their children's engagement with electronic media and communication activities.

> ACMA (2007, p. 14)

Control of use

In general terms, it would appear from experience and the research that young people are far freer, far more trusted at home to use the various technologies than at school. While a significant number of parents have misgivings about aspects of the Internet, and in particular the social networking, they don't appear to place too many actual controls. These misgivings appear particularly strong in the US, with both the Pew (MacGill 2007) and Annenberg surveys (USC Annenberg School for Communications 2008) noting the concern. Young people are generally free—albeit within some general family operational parameters and guidance—to use the full suite of digital technologies whenever they wish, with few controls being imposed. That holds from the very young pre-schoolers upwards.

The degree of parental control exercised over the content and nature of use made of the mobile technologies would appear to be minimal, with use basically unfettered. While most families, directly or indirectly, control usage costs there are few such constraints on the nature of the communiqués. A recently reported small survey of student mobile use in classrooms revealed what most of us would suspect— the students use the phone's web and communication capabilities quietly and subtly in class, even when banned (Brown 2009). Some of us who are old enough can well remember transistor radios in the same situation.

It is appreciated that the level of control will vary from family to family, within social groupings and between nations, but when one compares the controls exercised in the home with those in the classroom the difference is pronounced, further elevating the degree of usage in the home relative to the classroom. What is clear is the high level of parent support for young people's use of the various technologies and their belief in the educational benefits young people can derive from the wise use of the Internet and computers. That support is evidenced pointedly in the parents' willingness to spend on the technology and in numerous surveys of the type mentioned earlier (ACMA 2007).

Most parents are today aware of the downside of the Internet, express that appreciation in surveys and keep a watching brief on their children, but one suspects they also place considerable trust in their children's ability to operate within a digital world and to do the right thing. It is appreciated that the degree of control is likely to vary between nations and social groups therein. In contrast to schools where there are Internet filters even in the most liberal of settings, the vast majority of homes do not use them on either their home computers or mobiles. The Howard Liberal government in Australia, for example, mounted a national Net Alert program highlighting the dangers of the Web and set aside funding for every family to download a home filter free of charge. Only a fraction of Australia's homes took up the offer and this initiative proved to be largely ineffective.

What one has to be wary of is the line projected from the many companies promoting home Internet filtering and protection services, whose prime concern is the making of profits. What also needs to be appreciated is that when filters are used in the home, young people— sometimes with a little help from their friends and the search engines—are very adept in using proxy servers to bypass the blockages, often unbeknown to their parents. It is now apparent from the research that parents, not surprisingly, place constraints on the newer technologies and ease these constraints as the technology becomes normalised. This trend is well documented in ACMA's 2007 study, revealing how the earlier concerns about television use have long since disappeared with most families (ACMA 2007, pp. 10–11).

One might surmise that as the parents come to know the new technology they relax their vigil and leave it to the young people to act responsibly. The concept of digital citizenship is discussed later in Chapter 18. In general terms, particularly when one compares the controls exercised in the home with those in the schools, young people today have immense freedom at home and with their mobile technology. It would appear that after nearly 15 years association with the online world, and a growing parental appreciation of its importance in everyone's lives, both the parents and the young people have in most homes adopted a well-balanced view on the use of the various digital technologies. The use of the technology has been normalised into contemporary home life.

Granted there will always be those who become addicted to certain technologies and will need greater direction than others, but it appears most homes have learned to accommodate the burgeoning digital technology, to accord it an appropriate place and to have young people use it wisely. The challenge is to assist the schools to normalise their use of the digital technology and to strike an appropriate balance commensurate with what is happening in the home. A key point—and anomaly—to grasp is that the students are operationally responsible for the use and care of their digital technology everywhere except in the school.

Use by gender

The last five years have seen a reduction of the earlier concerns about gender differences in use of the digital technology, particularly by the girls, and a growing recognition that males and females have different interests and as such will make greater or lesser use of the various digital technologies. Early in the use of the various digital technologies, and in particular the Internet, some commentators were expressing major concerns, based on the snapshots at the time, about girls' use of the digital technology, expressing the belief that there was a major digital divide between boys and girls. While implications from a research study are discussed later in Chapter 15, the following observation on the Canadian scene by Looker and Thiessen in 2003 (in an article that is unfortunately no longer available online) was not uncommon; that is, that 'male youths also tend to use computers and ICT with greater frequency and for a more diverse set of tasks than do their female counterparts' (Looker & Thiessen 2003, p. 3). There was also the inclination, forewarned against earlier, to extrapolate upon a snapshot in time and not view the trend lines.

All parents today will appreciate that both the boys and the girls make extensive albeit slightly different use of the various technologies, and in so doing undoubtedly develop slightly different skills sets. The ACMA study and Pew studies note that girls, for example, are more likely to make greater use of the SMS and IM facility of cell phones than boys. A similar gender difference is to be found in girls' greater usage of the iPod technology and the desire to use it when exercising. Conversely boys, for example, have been found to show a greater interest in the playing of complex computer games, although interestingly the difference with girls is not now as envisaged in the 1980s.

Cassell and Cramer (2008) outlined the importance of the digital and networked technologies in the social and sexual development of today's young women. It not only places the use of the technology by the girls in its historic context, but also provides an invaluable insight into why girls in developed societies place so much importance on having and being able to use an appropriate suite of digital technologies.

> It is clear that online participation is a key way of engaging in developmentally important activities for all young people, in the relative safety of the Internet, where Web profiles can be erased and replaced with new and different representations of the self.
>
> Teens' use of instant messaging, e-mailing, game playing, and Web site creation are key ways by which they grow into adults who manage, produce, and consume technology intelligently on an everyday basis. In particular, for young women, the Internet appears to be a way to explore aspects of identity that may not be welcome in the real world, to project more forceful agentive personalities than they feel at liberty to do in the physical world, and to explore their technological prowess.
>
> With luck, there will be a single difference between the moral panic surrounding the telegraph and the telephone, and that surrounding the Internet: that we will come to recognize young women as more likely to be empowered by technology than damaged by it.
>
> The Internet allows for a tremendous potential of creative expression that has not necessarily first been vetted by adults. Ultimately, it is when young women construct sexualized images of themselves, or contact strangers, that communication technologies are felt to become dangerous.

Cassell & Cramer (2008, p. 68)

Moreover, this provides an excellent explanation for the folly of the mother in *Growing up online* forcing the daughter to close down her MySpace account (Dretzin & Maggio 2008). If there are young women in your school community, Cassell and Cramer (2008) is not only a must read, but an excellent discussion starter for the key stakeholders. This appreciation of the different ways girls and boys use the technology within the homes has undoubtedly been helped by the ever-widening range of digital technologies, and the development of market-driven applications specifically tailored for market niches. As Cassell and Cramer note: 'The Internet, on the other hand, has hardly suffered from a gender divide, and Web 2.0, where media creation trumps media consumption, seems to have brought the participation of women and girls to the fore.' (2008, p. 69)

Market forces

The authors' analysis of the now extensive body of educational research on the use of digital technologies points in a number of situations to a failure to factor in or to accurately address the impact of market forces on the uptake and use of the various technologies. At times, though, the research agenda appears to be naïve. There has been, and there still is, a propensity to argue for public policy changes based on snapshots and not to let the market forces address in time the perceived shortcomings. This has been most apparent in the public uptake of the Web, and the contention in the late 1990s and early 2000s that it was necessary for government to intervene, leaving little time for the natural market forces to redress the situation.

Of note is the contention by the research group FreshMinds (2007) that no more than 65 per cent of UK homes with school-age children would have Internet access, despite the fact that there were already comparable economies with well over 90 per cent uptake. Lee and Winzenried (2009) have documented the fact that all instructional technologies move through a common, finite life cycle, features of which are an ongoing enhancement in the technology and a reduction in the price of the product or service. That is what we are seeing with the Web, with the users being able to secure appreciably greater bandwidth at lower costs. That trend will continue, as will the user update and most importantly, as indicated, the technologies used to access the Internet.

Anyone who has noted the rapid developments with digital technology and the pace and uncertainty of change would be reluctant to proclaim what the market situation will be ten years hence and suggest public policy plans based on those assertions are moving into territory where even the likes of Steve Jobs will not move. Note the trends, but also be flexible in your planning and implementation. Already education has had the experience of validly implementing the best technical solution for the time, only to find it archaic within five years.

Averages and actual use

When contemplating a home–school nexus it is important to identify the actual level and nature of Internet access across your community. While the national averages provide a very good general insight, even in the most advanced of nations, there can be significant regional variations on both the up- and downside. Mostly it is on the downside, usually in the regional areas and the bush, but while in general terms the urban areas are being provided with higher speed broadband one can still encounter significant pockets therein where the Internet connectivity is poor.

In large nations like Canada, the US, India, Russia, South Africa and even the likes of France and Spain there will be regional pockets that for geographic and/or socio-economic factors do not have broadband available, or have it available at a price most homes can afford. Get to know your context well, and its ISP provisions.

Socio-economic status and digital technologies

While socio-economic standing has been and will continue to be a factor in the availability and use of digital technologies in homes in developed nations, it is an ever-changing situation and the current trend, in keeping with the earlier comment re the life cycle of technology, is for the cost of products and services to fall, for fewer and fewer young people to be unable to secure them and as a consequence to be able to access the digital technology. Zamaria and Fletcher (2007), commenting on the Canadian scene, make a similar observation to that made earlier about Australian Internet use among the lower income bracket:

> Within Canada, gaps in Internet use across income levels have diminished greatly; lower income households have shown the largest increase in home Internet use compared to all other income categories (59% of individuals with household incomes less than $40k use the Internet). (p. 22)

It is important when considering the availability of the technology in your school community to also consider the importance that the poorer attach to the desirability of having the technology, the technologies they have, the facility to acquire all the emerging technologies in their basic form at a continually reduced price, the fact that many of the disadvantaged have ready access to the Internet via friends and relatives, and the increasing options available to access the Internet.

What we have seen over the last five years, as the cost of the various digital technologies has dropped and the perceived importance of young people having the key technology has risen, is that the proportion of young people without the key technology and in particular Internet access in their homes is declining. It would appear that it is less a case of not having the technology, but rather of the more affluent having the more expensive versions of the technology. Some schools have opted to look after these families by providing them with the equipment, while the likes of the UK and Singapore governments have opted to address the issue nationally.

One of the first home–school nexus initiatives you might want to consider is identifying the families in your school community in need of Internet access, how long they will need the support, the kind of monies required and how those resources will be found. It could be a vital educational initiative for your school and students.

The non- or low users

What you may well find is that it is not only those without the funds that are being disadvantaged, but rather there are families, social and religious groups within your school community who see little value in their children using the technology. That challenge could in many ways be harder to overcome. For example, the early research in countries like New Zealand and Canada—nations that at first glance would appear affluent—suggested there could well be indigenous groups within developed societies that set little store by the acquisition and use of the digital technologies. Williamson (2006) has, for example, noted in New Zealand that the Internet use among the Polynesians is both appreciably lower than the general population and not rising anywhere near the same rate. Looker and Thiessen (2003) expressed the same kind of concern with the Canadian indigenous population.

However, later studies in those two countries question those assertions. Bell et al. (2007), in commenting on the New Zealand scene in 2007, note the complexity of variables at play in the indigenous community's use of the technology. You could well have students in this category who will need support but who could well be disinclined to take it.

Differences or divides?

The concept of the digital divide emerged in the literature and indeed in government reports from the mid 1990s and has continued to play a significant role in the study of Internet use, particularly in education since. In reality, the focus of the divide was on Internet access and far less on the use of the other digital technologies. In retrospect, the early researchers did have to contend with unknown, global phenomena of new technologies and the uncertainty of the impact of market forces, and in retrospect made some poor reads.

DiMaggio and Hargiatti in their 2001 seminal paper on the Digital Divide succinctly identified the finer nuances of the divide and most importantly underscored the likelihood that the market would remove much of the divide. Notwithstanding, throughout the 2000s one saw increasing reference to the digital divide between what was happening with the technology in the classroom and the home. Now that we all have a better appreciation of the impact of the Internet, and indeed all the other digital technologies, can see both their strengths and shortcomings and are conscious of how they can be used to enhance the quality and appropriateness of the schooling, we are able to view the technology far more positively.

As soon as one takes the positive outlook and recognises that in the home there is the immense resource base that astute educators can build upon, one begins to appreciate the possibilities. What is now apparent is that there is a digital divide between nations, with the citizens in many—both developed and developing countries—being disadvantaged. There is also a digital divide between homes, with there being young people in all developed nations whose lack of the basic digital technologies or Internet access at home disadvantages them educationally. There is moreover a significant divide between the proactive and reactive schools, education authorities and nations, with young people in the reactive situations being disadvantaged. However, the difference that we have been examining between the situation in the average home and classroom is simply that: a difference in circumstances.

Conclusion

While it is essential in a digital and networked world that all teachers and students have ready use of the appropriate digital instructional technology in each classroom, it is also vital that the education providers, and indeed the politicians overseeing the operations of the education providers, recognise that schools need to work with the current reality while at the same time shaping the desired future. The situation with the average home is working well. They have normalised the use of the digital into the lives of their young people and are making a significant contribution to their education and in turn to enhancing national productivity. As Clay Shirky has so perceptively noted:

> It's when a technology becomes normal, then ubiquitous, and finally so pervasive as to be invisible, that the really profound changes happen, and for young people today, our new social tools have passed normal and are heading to ubiquitous, and invisible is coming.
>
> Shirky (2008, p. 105)

The challenge is for schools to overcome the mindset where they are struggling with the resourcing and educational models of another era. The time has clearly come for politicians, concerned parents and the educational providers to recognise the educational capability in the nation's homes and build upon it befitting the digital era to create a home–school nexus.

That need becomes even more apparent when we provide compelling evidence in the following chapter of the importance of the kind of learning already taking place in the home.

Guiding questions

After reading this chapter, consider your context and propose your ideas in relation to the following guiding questions.

1   How do the digital technologies young people have in the home compare with the digital technologies in the school?

2   When do young people use the home digital technologies the most?

3   Are there home and personal digital technologies that are not used or permitted in the classroom?

4   What differences have you noted in the use of the home digital technologies by young people and older children, and by girls and boys?

5   Where do young people mainly turn for help in using the home digital technologies?

6   What level of trust do you give your own children in using the technology wisely, including the Internet?

Key messages

- Since the mid 1990s, the difference between the digital holdings of the home and those in the average classroom, and the use made by young people of that technology in both situations have diverged at pace.

- In your planning for all the students in your school, appreciate that there are likely to be significant variations in student access to technology in the home. Don't work simply on the average picture, as the education of every one of your students is important.

- The time has clearly come for politicians, concerned parents and the educational providers to recognise the educational capability in the nation's homes and build upon it befitting the digital era to create a home–school nexus.

CHAPTER 5

The learning in the home: Importance and implications

GLENN FINGER & PEI-CHEN SUN

The bedroom of the average connected young person today is a much more powerful learning environment than most classrooms in most schools. Think about it.

In the comfort of their bedrooms, connected learners can access all the information they wish, freed, mostly, from the petty and pointless restrictions that are being placed in their way by most classroom connections. They can communicate and collaborate freely with their friends, near and far, when they choose, in the way they choose, using the tools and applications they are most comfortable with. They can choose to work in peace, in quiet isolation, or they can work in distributed groups using collaborative tools of many kinds. And, most powerfully of all, they can learn what they want to learn and at the pace that suits them.

Even when they are working on tasks set by their teachers, they are still able to work and learn within an environment that is considerably more appropriate in so many ways to effective learning than their classroom at school.

John Connell (13 October 2007)

The significance of learning in the home

This chapter acknowledges the informal and formal learning that takes place beyond the timetabled formal school learning. It highlights the importance of learning that takes place by young people in their homes and personal lives as they go about life in an increasingly networked world. It examines the learning in the home within a context of its wider potential for contributing to learning, by conceptualising its role in creating the home–school nexus to shape new modes of schooling that factor in young people's everyday ubiquitous use of digital technologies. As Pushor (2007) indicates:

a broad school community, parents, community members, and educators work to create a shared vision which represents both parent and teacher knowledge, which articulates the hopes and dreams that together they hold for their children, and which establishes schooling as a collaborative endeavour (p. 7).

While few would argue otherwise, how well is this realised in terms of digital technology use at home and at school? How well is the home connected to creating a networked school community? The answers are largely determined in how well schooling systems, politicians, teachers, parents and students better understand and recognise the vital importance of the education occurring in the home. The central question then becomes: Are the technologies that students use at home well understood by schools?

For example, in the new networked learning environment we can consider young people to be able to use technologies to access information and communicate for all of the 365 days of the year, for 24 hours of every one of those days, which equates to approximately 8760 hours. This compares with a more restricted, pre-digital age structure of formal learning taking place for approximately 200 days and about five contact hours with teachers for those days, which equates to approximately 1000 hours. While we obviously do not advocate for students not to have a study–life balance with appropriate time for leisure, recreation and sleep, even a conservative recognition of enabling home and personal use of technologies could suggest at least a doubling of the time—an additional 1000 hours of home and personal use of technologies—for greater study and learning. This was highlighted more than a decade ago by Mal Lee in his writings 'Harnessing the power of the home' (1995), and 'The educated home' (1996). This chapter builds upon and complements the previous chapters in this section to establish the importance of learning in the home.

In reviewing the literature related to learning in the home, much of the twentieth-century literature focused on equality of opportunity to access schooling and the socio-economic factors of the home that related positively and negatively as predictors of success in schooling. For example, throughout the twentieth century access to schooling became progressively more widely available, and it wasn't until the late 1960s that access to secondary schooling was not reliant on an externally administered entrance examination or requirements of some kind. Many readers might be able to identify with this as their parents and grandparents might not have undertaken secondary schooling. Even now, we are seeing on many campuses in Australian universities more than half of first year university students being the first in their family to undertake university studies.

Until the late 1970s, sociological and psychological studies focused on attempting to identify factors that could explain achievement. To illustrate, Woolfolk (2001) provides a synthesis of well-documented relationships between low socio-economic status students and achievement, and identifies a range of variables that impact, including poor health care, low expectations, low self-esteem, learned helplessness, peer influences and resistance cultures, and tracking (which refers to students placed throughout schooling in 'low ability' classes). Importantly, many of those factors relate to home contexts. Furthermore, Woolfolk discusses at length the importance of child-rearing styles and the home environment and resources.

In relation to child-rearing styles, it has been well established that children from homes that have values similar to those of the school perform more successfully in schools. Woolfolk (2001) appropriately refers to research that has shown that parents can assist children in ways that reflect Vygotsky's suggestions for providing intellectual support through scaffolding in the children's zone of proximal development. We have known for some time that the congruence between home values and those of the school and the parents' interactions with their children are influential in student learning achievements.

Similarly, Woolfolk (2001) notes that recent research has shown that home and neighbourhood resources explain the greatest impact on young people's achievement when not in school:

> When parents of any SES level support and encourage their children—by reading to them, providing books and educational toys, taking the children to the library, making time and space for learning—the children tend to become better, more enthusiastic readers … White (1982) found that **the actual behaviors of the parents were more predictive of their children's school achievements than income level or parents' occupation**. [emphasis added by the authors] (p. 165)

The technologies in the twentieth-century homes that were highly influential for learning in the home were print materials such as books and magazines, to some extent educational toys, and pen/pencil and paper. The typical scenario for students undertaking an assignment was for them to be given the task at school, with most of the research gleaned from a prescribed textbook, with some recommended visitation to a library to attempt to locate a book on the topic. A feature of this schooling as it interfaced with the home was homework, and this model has been enduring. Homework designed in this way is now problematic and in a digital, networked world needs redefining.

In stark contrast, in examining the more recent research of the importance of learning in the home, the key characteristic evident has been a transformational access by young people and their parents to digital technologies in the home. As explained comprehensively throughout the previous chapter, in many instances there is now a home–school difference, with young people having greater access to information and communication through digital technologies available in the home than at school. This has been transformational in terms of access to information and communication through the Internet, particularly from home and independent of permission from schools, teachers and librarians characterised in previous generations.

Psychological, educational and practical justifications for using computers as tools for thinking, with an emphasis on learning *with* computers, have been made by researchers such as Jonassen (2000). He proposes that digital technologies can be used by students as both productivity tools and as Mindtools or intellectual partners—which the authors argue are more powerful than the previous learning technologies of pen and paper. To illustrate, Jonassen refers to Mindtools as computer-based applications that require students to think in meaningful ways in order to use the application to represent what they know, and 'when learners enter into an intellectual partnership with the computer' (Jonassen 2000, p. 4). This approach contrasts with Jonassen's reference to the use of digital technologies used by students to complete tasks in productive ways, such as word processing their assignments and using software applications to publish their work in acceptable forms for assessment.

The key difference between earlier learning in the home and learning in the home in the twenty-first century is that there is now a pervasive access to and use by students of digital technologies in the home. This is reflected in the emergence of e-learning (defined as 'electronic learning'), and m-learning (defined as 'mobile learning'), in which central to learning is the human dimension of learning that is now able to take place anywhere and at a time and place of the learner's own choosing—including in the home. Nalder (2009) goes further in his work *The dawn of ulearning: Near-future directions for 21st century educators* by suggesting that this pervasiveness of digital technologies through the learner being mobile with m-learning, and being able to undertake e-learning remotely from traditional schools seen as physical places, has given rise to the equation e-learning + m-learning = u-learning, where u-learning is defined as 'ubiquitous learning'. Nalder argues that:

> the 21st century is different to the 20th, in part because of the effects of the Digital Revolution and subsequent developments in mobile, wireless and networked technologies ... Education, which normally would be expected to be preparing students to thrive in this period, has been slow to adapt to these changes. When integrated into learning however, the opportunities which connected, always-on technologies present for facilitating rich learning experiences can be described as providing a uLearning, or ubiquitous learning, environment ... Educators can become designers of learning, and allow students to become active, collaborative participants in knowledge making. Administrators can implement mobile, wireless and Cloud Computing-based options to potentially replace today's classrooms. (p. 1)

As discussed earlier, prior to the emergence of digital technologies, studies in educational research have established the significant role home and family background play in young people's education. When this is coupled with studies that demonstrate the integral role digital technologies can play in the lives of our young people, referred to as the 'digital natives' (Prensky 2001) and outlined in Chapters 3 and 4 of this book, we have a potentially powerful learning environment (referred to by Kimber and Wyatt-Smith in Chapter 17 as 'new networked learning spaces'), enabling the development of networked school communities.

As outlined comprehensively in the preceding chapter, this requires an improved understanding of the different technologies being accessed by young people at home, the meanings and values they attach to the technologies, how these home technologies are shaping them and influencing their learning, and identifying and dealing with the risks of home digital technologies. The following discussion outlines further the benefits of digital technologies for learning in the home.

Learning in the home and digital technologies — the research

Studies confirm the educational and other benefits of young people's access to digital technologies at home. In the UK, Becta (2008a) has argued that the educational outcomes alone justify the significant investment that is being required to give more access to home computers and the Internet. (The UK Home Access program is presented as an interesting case study by Ray Tolley later in Chapter 12.) Despite some anecdotal and empirical evidence on the negative impact of digital technologies, such as decline in social involvement (Kraut et al. 1996), 'wasting' time (Becker 2000a) or getting exposed to damaging information, parents are generally convinced that having these technologies available to their children is beneficial. In reality, this is almost a commonsense observation as most secondary school students are unable to complete many of their assessment tasks without home access to a computer, the Internet and a printer. Handwritten assignments are generally not accepted and insufficient time is provided during the school timetabled day for assessment tasks to be completed.

Beyond the commonsense observations there is substantial evidence that young people who regularly use computers and the Internet are more engaged and empowered learners (Becta 2008a), with improved attainment or higher grades (Subrahmanyam et al. 2001). This could be due to more developed cognitive skills and visual intelligence (Subrahmanyam et al. 2001), high confidence, self-esteem, competence and understanding (Becta 2008a; Owen & Moyle 2008; Marsh 2004), and better communication and social skills (Subrahmanyam et al. 2001), developed through activities such as regular and constant communication with teachers and peers using mostly their personal and home digital technologies.

There is growing research evidence that digital technologies are recognised as a rich resource in twenty-first century learning (Chien et al. 2009; Stephen et al. 2008; Zevenbergen & Logan 2008; Prensky 2001; Subrahmanyam et al. 2001), with the homes being the space that provide young people with more access to these digital technologies (Becta 2008b; Wellington, 2001). The use of digital technologies through increasing interest and usage (Silverstone & Hirsch 2004) has led to some concerns about the risks these technologies have on young people (Becta 2008a; Marsh 2004). The response by some authors is that the way young people use digital technologies is influenced by household norms (Roberts, Foehr & Rideout 2005). Subsequently, the implication is that household members, particularly parents, working with schools can minimise the risks associated with young people's often liberal usage of these technologies at home.

Home as an authentic environment for digital learning

The influence of home and family on a child's learning, and how that learning is expressed, is well established in educational research (Wellington 2001). The household, being a social, cultural and economic unit engaged in the consumption of objects, symbols and meanings (Silverstone & Hirsch 2004), provides a significant influence on how young people attach meanings to digital technologies. A trend occurring in universities noted by Lomas and Oblinger (2006) is that the development of contemporary technologies and learning theories have occurred, so too have financial constraints impacting upon the time a teacher actually spends on face-to-face teaching with students. Referring to universities in Sweden, but evident elsewhere, for students this means that they to a larger extent than before have to act—and learn—in environments outside the formal classroom (see p. 2 at http://www.ou.nl/Docs/Campagnes/ICDE2009/Papers/Final_paper_090hedestig.pdf).

For students, the Internet is part of their everyday functioning outside of schooling and it allows them to discover, uncover, create, synthesise and integrate knowledge that is instantaneously available to them through fast connections at home. This is in contrast with the slow-paced connection and accessibility available in many schools (Becta 2008c; Siemens 2008) resulting in a wide disparity between what students use at home and at school. By moving to a home–school nexus, this becomes seen as a difference rather than as a divide, and the connection between students and the home as both social and spatial contexts (Ramaley & Zia 2005) can be established.

The ability to learn is directly influenced by the learning environment (Siemens 2008). Thus, home as a space for digital learning needs to provide the required functionality, a 'sense of place' and comfort (Horan 2001) to young people. It must promote 'productivity, creativity, and engagement' and offer 'cognitive effectiveness, social support, emotional functioning, and physical function' (Gee 2006, pp. 10–12). In contrast to learning that occurs in classrooms, which is generally controlled, structured and managed (Siemens 2008), digital learning at home offers more freedom and flexibility thus giving rise to self-regulated learners who believe that learning:

- is a social process (e.g. knowledge of classmates, appreciation of class diversity, collaboration, development of friendships);
- is exploratory (i.e. involving thoughtful processes);
- is a complex activity that involves taking account of multiple viewpoints;
- should be concerned with real-life and lifelong issues (i.e. it is authentic, personal, interesting, and develops knowledge of new tools);
- uses information resources;
- requires the organisation of information; and
- is satisfying, enjoyable and rewarding.

(Source: Levin & Wadmany 2006)

At home, as Marsh (2004) indicates, young people can be scaffolded by parents and siblings to provide support for the rising pressures as they explore what the Web, the new software and the other technologies can offer (Siemens, 2008). Ironically, the greatest barrier to the recognition of that learning can be the education institutions themselves, their educational bureaucrats and credentialling authorities with their resistance to acknowledging new ways of learning. While it is quite common to see family members appreciate, and often rely on, the digital capabilities of their young people, similarly school leaders and teachers globally should not feel challenged by the use of digital technologies by students. Schools are no longer necessarily the place where knowledge creation commences and is controlled. For example, research such as that by Meredyth et al. (1999) in Australia has revealed that students are far more likely to acquire their digital competencies at home than in the classroom. On eight of the 13 advanced information technology skills in Meredyth's study, students were found to be more likely than teachers able to create music or sound, draw using the mouse, play computer games, create a website or home page, copy games, create multimedia, create a program, and undertake creative writing. (Meredyth et al. 1999, p. 92)

Importantly, and relevant to this book, students were also found to be more likely to have acquired those skills at home, with the exception of programming abilities. Meredyth et al. (1999) reported that slightly more of the students indicated that they acquired this at school. Since that time, there has been the emergence of Web 2.0 social networking technologies used by students in their personal lives, arguably to a greater extent than the software applications examined by Meredyth et al. in their study more than a decade ago. It is time for schools, school systems and governments to recognise the considerable learning that is occurring with young people's everyday use of the digital technologies.

Student use of digital technologies at home

Mal Lee and Martin Levins very effectively established that homes are now what might be considered to be havens of digital technologies. In the discussion here we also reinforce that digital technologies are becoming part of so many households and are vital in the formation of the home's identity and security (Silverstone & Hirsch 2004). More and more homes, especially those in the forefront of technological revolution, are being referred to as digitised, wired and networked 'digital spaces' (Siemens 2008; Zevenbergen & Logan 2008; Horan 2001; Becker 2000b). Digital technologies are found in the majority of homes. Factors such as downward trend in costs, better features, (Norris 2001) and other external pressures (Wellington 2001) could have influenced this increasing home computer use, Internet access and other digital technology consumption. This provides us with the important understanding that it is no longer appropriate to talk about homes and digital technologies as being separate, discrete objects of study. Rather, homes and digital technologies have become new networked spaces.

Surveys showed that parents acquire home computers and subscribe to the Internet to offer educational opportunities for their children and to prepare them for the 'information-age' (Subrahmanyam et al. 2001) despite the relatively longer time spent on other 'non-educational' activities such as games and Internet browsing (Becker 2000b; Kraut et al. 1996). Home computers with Internet support are useful tools in sourcing information and developing presentable school projects, reports and homework, even after school hours, within the confines of the home (Chien et al. 2009; Ramaley & Zia 2005; Levin & Arafeh 2002; Becker 2000a, 2000b). They are also used by students to communicate with their peers and teachers about school-related issues and activities through discussion boards and electronic mails (Becta 2008b; Becta 2008c; Levin & Arafeh 2002; Subrahmanyam et al. 2001). Home computer and related technologies have become tools for students to cope with 'the distributed nature of knowledge and the growing complexification of all aspects of society' (Siemens 2008, p. 12).

What is able to be differentiated is that home computers, the Internet and other digital technologies are not used solely for educational purposes determined by the school. Studies have documented how students use digital technologies for entertainment and social activities, as well as for educational purposes (Blanchard, Burns & Metcalf 2007; Lomas & Oblinger 2006; Subrahmanyam et al. 2001). Playing games, watching videos, listening to music, surfing the Internet for information on anything that interests them and connecting with their 'cyber mates' through emails and chat rooms (Chien et al. 2009; Roberts et al. 2005; Becker 2000b) are among the popular 'pastimes' of young people at home. Kvavik (2005), in contrast, found that students use computers more for educational purposes than for other activities.

Studies have shown that students' home computing and use of other digital technologies have been influenced by a number of factors such as age, gender, socio-economic status, household experience and background, computer features and peer pressure (Steinkuehler & King 2009; Chien et al. 2009; Becta 2008b; Blanchard, Burns & Metcalf 2007; Kvavik 2005; Haddon 2004; Hayward et al. 2003; Subrahmanyam et al. 2001; Becker 2000b). In general, older boys from high-income families with professional parents use home computers and other digital technologies more than their counterparts. Tertiary students use digital technologies more for their studies and other educational activities compared with primary or secondary students who use technologies more for entertainment (Kvavik 2005). DiMaggio and Hargiatti (2001) also noted the digital inequality among those who have access to technology and attributed this to factors such as differences in equipment, autonomy of use, skill, social support and purpose.

In an enlightening study, *Students' voices: Learning with technologies*, Owen and Moyle (2008) observed that while students are at the centre of the work of education and training institutions, there has been little research listening to the student voice in relation to learning with technologies. They argue that:

Listening to the student voice though is important because they are the main stakeholders in education or training ... Overall, this generation of students is well versed in how to use technologies; various technologies are a normal part of their lives. It is time to bring together their understandings of technologies with the wisdom of educators to jointly construct learning futures and synthesise the best of both sets of experiences. (p. 3)

Their 'student voice research' provides a synthesis of literature about access and use, learning environment and digital skills proficiency, cognition and student learning, motivation and engagement, and communication. This report is recommended reading to gain insights through evidence-based research. For example, Owen and Moyle refer to the study of Dutch students (Wijngaards, Fransen & Swager 2006) that involved more than 400 students aged between 13 and 15. The study confirmed the students use networking sites to communicate with each other and a major topic of communication is their school work. They identified that students use networking technologies to help them do their homework, to help them with their studies and in finding information, and to learn from the opinions and ideas of others. They reported that more girls than boys used networking applications, and also found that in general girls networked with more people than did boys, and that boys had more classmates in their network than the girls.

Those are fascinating findings, which are examples of findings elsewhere in the literature that demonstrate the increasing use of digital technologies by young people to undertake tasks that can assist learning. The question for you to consider is: Where is the locus of power and control for this learning in the home? That is, has this use been funded and required by schools and teachers?

In a study that the authors undertook of students in Taiwanese senior high, junior high and elementary schools, the aim was to understand student use of digital technologies. Specifically, students were provided with a range of specially designed scenarios to respond to. For example, one scenario asked students: 'If your parents asked you for the password of your blog or website to enter it, what would you do?' The findings indicated that generally students at all levels felt that their communications were private and when parents asked, only elementary school subjects would obey the parents' request. Almost 80 per cent of junior high and senior high students indicated that they would refuse to provide passwords of blogs and any privacy information about their online activities to their parents.

In relation to gender differences, males were found to be more likely than females to be less concerned about privacy in their Internet use. In terms of being part of social networking sites, female senior high school students were the highest users and, interestingly, they also emphasised their right to privacy more than any other group. They were also less likely than any other groups to accept consequences from their parents, with most indicating that they would strongly defend their rights to personal privacy from their parents.

Importantly, based on the overall data analysed, the authors found that the students were increasingly being immersed in online environments from elementary school level. While we tended to find differences between groups in terms of use of various applications, and the relationship between students of various year levels and their parents, there was compelling evidence that the students of all school levels could instantly adopt the latest technologies; though they were somewhat measured in their approach to acquire the latest technologies. For example, in response to the question 'How important is it that you own the newest "gadgets"?', the data suggest that this doesn't significantly change over time, as it is slightly more important to elementary school students (53% males, 47% females), and generally as both males and females grow older this is comparatively slightly more important to males than to females (junior high: 46% males, 30% females; senior high: 48% males, 34% females).

Students were generally confident in using the Internet for searching for information they needed and frequently engaged online with friends, and for some time junior high students have been transforming their friendships from previously face-to-face to online social networking interactions with friends. While female senior high students (82%) and female junior high students (86%) were the highest groups to have published on the Internet, more than half of the elementary students (59% males, 65% females) indicated that they had published on the Internet.

An interesting scenario involved the students being asked that if they had created a digital movie and uploaded this to YouTube, who would they share this with first? Both male and female elementary students' first choice was either their family members or friends, and they tended not to wish to share it with their teachers. Furthermore, when asked what they would do if they didn't know how to create a video, only fewer than one in three students (31% of males, 34% of females) indicated that they would ask a teacher. Generally, both female and male students conveyed that when they post any video on the Internet they feel that it is fresh and interesting. Putting the finished products online gives them a sense of accomplishment and they felt that it is okay if their teachers know what they have done, but that their teachers are not necessarily their intended audience or motivation. Also, most of them hoped that their skill of editing videos can be improved by reading relevant books, practising more, or asking teachers and their classmates.

The implications from this research are:

- Students of all levels of schooling are increasingly acquiring and using digital technologies in their homes, with immersion in using digital technologies happening at a younger age.

- While they are generally interested in sharing with teachers what they publish online, and/or asking teachers for help, students tend to share and ask for help more with families and friends than with their teachers.

- Considerable digital technology use occurs in the home by students in elementary, junior high and senior school, irrespective of access at school.

A new model—creating the home–school nexus

From the preceding discussion and analysis, the importance of learning in the home and the ways in which the digital technologies now available are being used by young people provide an essential context for developing networked school communities through creating a home–school nexus. As we have suggested elsewhere, it is important to undertake a situational analysis of your current school context, and we add here that it is important to make integral to that analysis the affordances available for learning in the home. As you move towards this new model, we have also deliberately referred to this as a home–school nexus rather than a school–home nexus.

The positioning of the home is important in focusing attention on the largely untapped potential of the home for delivering improved student learning and for adding substantially to the resource base of your learning organisation. We refer you to Figure 2.2 (p. 26), which provides a conceptualisation of the networked school community—prestructural change; many of the current relationships between school and home are captured in that figure. As you move to develop and realise the vision of the networked school community portrayed in Figure 2.1 (p. 22), we suggest that you consider the characteristics of the paper-based and digitally based paradigms of schooling listed in Table 1.1 (p. 6) and strategies to position the home in helping to realise the networked school community vision. This will need considerations to reflect the following key features, which relate specifically to learning in the home:

- Adopt an Information Age organisational model to guide links between home and school, and to understand the scale of student access to information in the home.

- Become networked, incorporating the total school community and its homes.

- Recognise and encourage a suite of changing, increasingly sophisticated, converging and networked digital instructional technologies that connect home and school.

- Design the technological architecture and infrastructure to enable a seamless, ubiquitous communication and management of digital information across and beyond the organisation.

Conclusion

This chapter concludes Part B: The home–school scene today. It built upon and complemented the preceding two chapters that examined schools and the digital technology and homes and the digital technology. Collectively the three chapters have provided the context for developing a networked school community through creating a home–school nexus. The following chapters provide further insights into your journey towards understanding the opportunities of the networked school community.

Guiding questions

After reading this chapter, consider your context and propose your ideas in relation to the following guiding questions.

1 In relation to young people's use of digital technologies at home, has the use of digital technologies become pervasive?

2 What knowledge, skills and values do you believe home use of the digital technologies has fostered? How were these learned? Were they learned differently from learning that takes place at school?

3 Do some members of the family use some of the digital technologies better and/ or more often than others?

4 Do you think that the school is aware of the knowledge, skills and values being acquired in the home? Does it recognise them, build upon them and take advantage of the style of learning young people use with the digital technologies?

Key messages

• This chapter acknowledges the informal and formal learning that takes place beyond the timetabled formal school learning, and highlights the importance of learning that takes place by young people in their homes and personal lives as they go about life in an increasingly networked world.

• The central question is: Are the technologies that young people use at home well understood by schools?

• The key difference between earlier learning in the home and learning in the home in the twenty-first century is that there is now a pervasive access to and use by young people of digital technologies in the home.

PART C

The networked school community:
The opportunities

CHAPTER 6

The rationale

MAL LEE

Modes of learning have changed dramatically over the past two decades—our sources of information, the ways we exchange and interact with information, how information informs and shapes us. But our schools—how we teach, where we teach, who we teach, who teaches, who administers, and who services—have changed mostly around the edges...

... Implicit in a sincere plea for transformation is an awareness that a current situation needs improvement.

Cathy Davidson & David Goldberg (2009, p. 8)

Developing the rationale for networked school communities

The reasons for developing a networked school community and seeking to create a home–school nexus lie in the eternal quest to enhance the quality, appropriateness and effectiveness of the education of young people, coupled with the desire to ensure that schooling is relevant and attractive to all and does prepare young people for life and work in the years ahead.

Other reasons include the importance of education enhancing the national productivity of the nation, accommodating the societal and technological megatrends impacting on the education of young people, and appreciating the profound impact digital and networked technology has had and will continue to have on life and work in the contemporary world. Furthermore, it is important to recognise the immense opportunities that the digital and networked technology provides education and the potential for significant short- and long-term educational, social, economic, organisational and political benefits, and to understand that the digital capability of young people's homes will continue to grow at pace while that of the classroom will always be limited, and that therefore it is in society's interest to better utilise the considerable digital capability in the home.

The potential of the traditional paper-based school has long since been maximised. Moreover, the capacity of the traditional form of schooling to provide an appropriate education for 100 per cent of school-age students is constantly declining as most schooling becomes less relevant. Digital and networked schooling has tapped but a minuscule percentage of its undoubted and as yet unidentified potential. One has only to look back a decade and note how dramatically the digital technology has changed work and life, and then to project ahead five years and try to envision the kind of 'smarts' that will be available for use in a networked school community to appreciate the immense opportunities those technologies afford astute school communities, both today and into the future.

However, in addition to all these many benefits is the everyday reality we have mentioned before, that while the digital technology in the homes of young people will continue to grow, the technology in the classroom will always be limited and its use constrained. The astute development of a new mode of schooling, a networked form, can not only help maximise the use made of the capability of the classroom and the home but more importantly can also provide a new dynamic type of formal schooling that can assist in overcoming many of the current shortcomings and better prepare young people for a digital and networked future. It is thus imperative that schools, education authorities and nations attune their schooling to the times and adopt an approach that takes advantage of the opportunities presented to overcome the considerable limitations of the formal classroom.

Accommodating the megatrends

Today we are all aware of the profound changes science and technology has made and will continue to make to our world. We are also now highly conscious of the importance of identifying and accommodating the megatrends in work and life. Since the release of John Naisbitt's seminal work in 1984 on *Megatrends* we have consistently been informed by all parts of the media of the major trends, their likely impact and the importance of leaders factoring those developments into their planning, in what we all know will be a constantly changing, ever-more uncertain future.

As Thomas Friedman indicates in *The world is flat* (2006), most of those trends relate to the macro developments in technology and the impact they are having, and will continue to have, on life and work. As we have indicated, their impact on the education of young people is already profound. In seeking to provide the desired education, schools can opt to disregard those developments and continue as they always have, or choose to identify the desirable megatrends, to build upon their momentum and to astutely accommodate them into the desired form of schooling.

What should now be apparent is that schooling has in many quarters been slow to accommodate the megatrends and been obliged to constantly and ineffectually react to the major forces, slowly but surely reducing the effectiveness of the education provided to young people. The concept of the networked school community, with its close ties with the students' homes and their very considerable digital capability, is strongly premised on the desire to harness the desirable developments and to take advantage of the opportunities they provide to better educate young people.

It is appreciated that there will always be risks in seeking to accommodate the unknown, but if approached wisely and addressed in graduated steps those risks are appreciably less than allowing schools to become archaic in an information economy.

Benefits

In shifting to a networked mode of schooling, schools and nations will be able to derive the benefits not only in the areas mentioned above, but in fields where the highly desirable rhetoric has rarely been matched in reality.

Democratisation of schooling

In the early 1900s, John Dewey rightly advocated the democratisation of schooling (Dewey 1916). Since then many schools have endeavoured to realise those ideals, but one would have to concede that today those succeeding are few in number. Most school operations are decided upon by the school and education authority executive—an oligarchy—with little input from most staff, the students, the parents or the interested community. One of the impediments, aside from the desire to control, has been the logistical wherewithal to swiftly and accurately ascertain the ideas of those outside the school or authority executive. As Jason Zagami and Glenn Finger discuss in Chapter 13, there are now teaching and learning opportunities made available through the tools, smart software and techniques that allow every school to more significantly democratise the schooling. Dewey's observation in 1916 is still highly apposite:

> A democracy is more than a form of government; it is primarily a mode of associated living, of conjoint communicated experience. The extension in space of the number of individuals who participate in an interest so that each has to refer his own action to that of the others, and to consider the action of the others to give point and direction to his own, is equivalent to the breaking down those barriers of class, race and national territory which kept men from perceiving the full import of their activity. These more numerous and more varied points of contact denote a greater diversity of stimuli to which an individual has to respond; they consequently put a premium on variation in his action. They secure a liberation of powers which remain suppressed as long as the inclinations to action are partial, as they must be in a group which in its exclusiveness shuts out many interests. (p. 101)

Over the last couple of decades the home has largely been excluded from the decision making in formal schooling. The digital technology provides the opportunity for the home to once again be involved, in a manner befitting a democracy and at a level busy families can easily accommodate.

National productivity

Another area where schooling lags well behind the rhetoric is in its contribution to the enhancement of national productivity and the part it ought to be playing in educating young people for a knowledge-based economy. Today there should be little question that schools ought to be preparing the nation's young people for a digital future, doing their utmost to ensure all complete Year 12 and contribute to the quest to have 40 per cent plus of the nation secure a tertiary degree. Those outcomes should be paramount in the school's planning and everyday operations.

Across the developed and developing world national leaders regularly speak of the part to be played by the schools in preparing young people for a digital future, but ironically at this stage that role is being performed primarily by the home and not the classroom. When one considers the still small use made of the digital in most classrooms it is little surprise that the think tank on digital schooling conducted by the Illinois Institute of Design (ID) (2007) observed:

> Schools aren't preparing kids for the world of work in the 21st century.
>
> As much as we know and repeat that one cannot teach all the skills necessary for life after school in K-12 public education, we still teach as if it were so. Schools are still organized to teach children to work in the Henry Ford world, with set job descriptions, lifetime employment, and low career mobility ...
>
> ... As competition becomes global, kids need to be educated to work in an environment that embraces change and works across cultures and countries. When kids are excited and engaged by a new subject, they should be allowed to explore that subject in more detail. Schools need to discover ways to bring real-world relevance into the classroom to engage children at higher levels. (p. 26)

The UK Government in its Home Access initiative has recognised the economic imperative of a nation, ensuring all its young people have in their homes the digital technology to advance their education.

> The evidence base underpinning the home access initiative is largely centred around the educational benefits that could be accrued from it. However, it was also understood that the initiative might also contribute to a number of other policy agendas, including personalising learning, narrowing the attainment gap, raising standards to increase the competitiveness of 'UK plc', and assisting the transition to a knowledge-based economy, as outlined in the Lisbon Strategy [http://europa.eu/scadplus/glossary/lisbon_strategy_en.htm].
>
> Although the primary beneficiaries of the initiative would be learners aged 5 to 19, it was understood from very early in the scoping stages that the initiative could have important spin-off benefits for parents, teachers and the wider community.

Becta (2008a, p. 11)

The UK policy makers, while appreciating that British schools have moved further in the school harnessing of technology, also appreciate the fundamental contribution the home has played and should play in a knowledge-based economy, and that it is essential that all young people are able to contribute to the national development.

Educational

The potential educational benefits, even with today's technology, are immense and almost boundless. What those benefits might be in ten or 30 years' time we can only guess. The key (as Glenn Finger and Pei-Chen Sun identified in Chapter 5) is to immediately begin to position the school to take advantage of those benefits, appreciating they will be ramped up over time.

Using the new technology to enhance the old

The natural inclination is to begin by using the new technology to better perform the ways we have always known (Naisbitt 1984). This is what we are seeing as the norm globally at this point in time. This characterises the initial moves by both schools and government, and indeed the research thus far in this area. It is a case of how well the home technology enhances the student's performance in the traditional curriculum and its impact on the likes of grade point averages (GPA), A-levels and national benchmarks.

What we are seeing at the moment at the school and authority level are efforts by the professional educators to enhance performance in the traditional instructional programs, within the existing curriculum, without questioning the appropriateness of that curriculum for a networked world. While these moves are to be applauded, they are nonetheless limited and ought to at best be considered as a transition to a more holistic, networked and appropriate education.

Opportunity to revisit the underlying philosophy of formal schooling

One of the unintended benefits of the shift to a digital and in turn networked mode of schooling, fundamentally different in many respects to the traditional schooling, is the chance to revisit the underlying philosophy of schooling and check its relevance today.

One of the core decisions the original curriculum developers had to make was to decide which aspects of the life experience should be incorporated in formal schooling and which should be left as informal educational experiences. Nearly a century ago in that context, John Dewey (1916) made the telling observation that:

> ... there is the standing danger that the material of formal instruction will be merely the subject matter of schools, isolated from the subject matter of life experience.

> Dewey (1916, p. 10)

Dewey concluded his analysis of the desired balance between the formal and informal education by making the telling observation:

> *This danger is never greater than at the present time, on account of the rapid growth in the last few centuries of knowledge and the technical mode of skills. (p. 11)*

Dewey's warning is as relevant today as a century ago. It is thus vital when seeking to make best use of the networked school community that you not only question using the new technology to merely better perform the ways of old, but also ask whether the present formal school curriculum has the right kind of balance for a networked school community. The striking of the right balance is critical to its success.

As you read through the chapters, you will gain a fuller appreciation of the elements that ought to be considered for inclusion in the revised curriculum, but it should already be apparent that there are competencies fundamental to a digital future not addressed or given priority in the current curriculum. In the same way that schooling has been increasingly controlled by the educational professionals over the past three decades, so too has been the curriculum development and the decisions made regarding what is addressed in formal schooling. Ask to see the curriculum of your school. Don't merely take the word of the vested interests in control of the curriculum that all is right. Check its appropriateness.

Educational impact of the home

The area that we know has had a profound impact on student educational attainment is the family learning culture (Reynolds 2006). This impact always has and always will be immense, on the up- or downside. In the past a key indicator was the availability of books within the home. Today it is increasingly the extent and nature of the digital and networked technology (Meredyth et al. 1999). While it took some time for schools to recognise the vital importance of books in the home in the education of young people, one might have hoped schools would have been quicker in recognising the comparable impact of the digital resources. Sadly, as we have seen, that was not to be with most schools and education authorities.

Interestingly, some preliminary efforts have been made—particularly in the UK—to build on the home digital culture, but all the efforts have sought to use the home resources to supplement the traditional teaching program and have achieved little success. One senses the benefits that will flow from taking account of the nature of learning favoured by young people, and developing collaborative programs in keeping with that learning.

Home learning and attainment

One of the greatest educational benefits lies in recognising the nature of learning used by young people, appreciating the competencies and attributes they are developing, creating a formal curriculum for the networked school community that incorporates the development of the desired competencies, developing an instructional program that astutely takes advantage of both the classroom and home learning environments and appreciating the continued importance of the informal learning. And, most importantly, for teachers to adopt an instructional approach consonant with the nature of learning favoured by young people.

It is appreciated that this scenario cannot be created overnight. Nonetheless it is imperative if schooling is to be relevant to this and future generations that it urgently begins making the move.

> *To serve the future, schools need to learn how to teach, use and assess each child's need to excel not just on the linear path laid down in state guidelines, but also through the now impossibly large body of knowledge in which each child can find for him or herself the joys of chopper repair, calligraphy, or string theory. For learning to be relevant to the future, it must be personalized, and only digital media provide the means to bring personalization to the classroom.*

Illinois Institute of Design (2007, p. 26)

How that might be achieved and indeed phased in is discussed more fully in the later chapters. The point nonetheless remains that the informal learning young people are acquiring in their homes and with their mobile technology is at a stage of development where parts of it can be factored beneficially into the formal curriculum, and other aspects can be enhanced by the parents' and students' metacognition and reflective learning capability being more consciously improved.

As you will have appreciated from earlier observations, one is talking about according greater attention to the development of key process skills and their infusion throughout the curriculum rather than the addition of any new areas of learning. The idea is to ensure that the likes of writing for specific audiences and medium, of using multimedia communication, developing generic digital competencies, problem solving, collaborating, understanding and refining one's networking capacity and information literacy, and managing and securing one's digital holdings are integrated and addressed in various parts of the formal curriculum.

There is another facet of learning in the home that is worth noting, and that is the impact that the use of the home digital technology has upon the wider family—the parents, the grandparents and often other relatives. The existence of that technology, as recent UK research attests, can markedly enhance the productivity of the parents as wage earners and the grandparents as carers and mentors. The British research notes the particularly important role it is playing in the informal education of the older new arrivals and those who arrive in the UK with little English, often aided by the children. The educative power of the technology thus impacts upon the whole family.

An attractive and relevant schooling for all

The other great benefit can be the provision of a mode of schooling that is attractive and relevant to potentially all young people. While young people have long since embraced the digital into their lives, most are expected to endure a mode of schooling that not only makes limited use of 'their technology', but is in many respects antithetical to their preferred mode of learning.

It is interesting to watch on the various education mailing lists the number of teachers still scornful of young people's use of the various digital technologies, dismissing its use as mere play. Little is the wonder that so many students—both capable and struggling—find schooling irrelevant and unattractive.

The only real difference today is that probably more of the capable students are alienated by the irrelevancy of much of their schooling. When one notes, as mentioned, that 70 per cent of the capable students surveyed by Project Tomorrow (2008) found that only 30 per cent of the small number of visionary principals understood the needs of a digital world, this ought to come as no surprise.

Mal Lee had the rare opportunity in the 1970s to work in a new education authority with a blank slate in developing a model of upper secondary education that sought to cater for 100 per cent of students. While considerable progress was made and the Year 12 retention rates moved well into the 90 per cent range, there is little doubt that a significant proportion of the less academically inclined—the 'burnouts'—found schooling irrelevant. What is important to note is that in most developed nations the Year 12 student retention rates have largely reached a plateau over the last couple of decades, suggesting the time has well come for schools and nations to explore the use of different modes of teaching and learning, particularly in the upper secondary years. Mere compulsion and the upping of the school leaving age are not going to redress student alienation and disenchantment. As we all know, students soon learn the art of attending but then switch off.

While no one model of schooling is likely to suit all students, a networked school community with all its inherent flexibility should be able to go closer than most of the existing arrangements.

> If the school experience is unconnected to the world outside the classroom, it will fail to engage a substantial percentage of capable learners. It is predictable that students who are motivated in unit-based instruction sometimes lose interest when methods shift to the study of isolated, specialized intellectual disciplines in middle school or earlier.
>
> For the 20% of the population with the valued linguistic/mathematical learning style, success continues, but among the remainder, work in formerly attractive subjects becomes drudgery. The problem is that the connection to the real world has been severed, a connection that doesn't return in some fields until graduate school, which is a place beyond the reach of those who most need to see the practicality of what they learn. To keep students connected to education, education has to remain connected to reality.
>
> Illinois Institute of Design (2007, p. 26)

A new, rich and expanded playing field

A networked school community that integrates the resources of the home and the classroom has at its disposal a new, vast and rich playing field upon which to operate. Where schools operate largely within the walls of a building, work with only its limited resources and operate for only six or seven hours a day for around 200 days a year, a networked school community is able to remove the traditional walls, and to factor into its instructional program the digital resources of its homes, the classrooms and if it desires many parts of its networked community. It can, if it wishes, extend the instructional period each day, for more days a year, and if it is astute build upon young people's informal use of the digital most of the time they are awake.

Approached wisely, the networked school community can also take advantage of the various settings within which young people can learn. Such schools are not restricted to the formal class time but could, if they wish, use much of scheduled class time for social interaction, and the often extensive home or student travel time for personal study.

Similarly, the new schools should consider when some or all students might physically have to come to the place called school. This is particularly pertinent for post-compulsory students, but it also could apply to students involved in work placements, indigenous settings, students assisting on the land or those in remote locations. Bear in mind also the developments taking place with virtual schooling and home schooling, both of which could be incorporated into the immensely flexible networked school community concept. The potential benefits of the new scenario are immense. All that is required is some wise leadership within the new, networked school community to decide how best to use the new playing field.

Appreciating the role of the informal

A similar kind of leadership could also assist the parents, the students and the teachers to appreciate the important role that the informal plays in the education of young people, and why in a rapidly changing society it is so important that the students, teachers and parents have that understanding, are able to reflect upon and analyse the skills and competencies being acquired and, when appropriate, to shift aspects of that learning into the formal curriculum.

While it is appreciated that the metacognition and reflective facilities will develop as the students age, nonetheless they are vital learning facilities schooling could do more to foster. The application of those facilities and desirability of consistently monitoring the ever-changing informal educative process hold equally with the educational leaders. In *Educating the reflective practitioner*, Schön (1987) identified the vital part reflection should play in all endeavour, but in particular in the development of professionals.

The immense pace of change, particularly that associated with the emerging technology, makes it near impossible for school communities to use many of the conventional evaluation measures. With a little preparation the students, the parents and the educators can be taught how to pause, reflect and, if necessary, enhance the effectiveness of the informal educational process.

Formal recognition for home learning

Logistically it would be easy for the networked school community to assess and formally recognise the attainments acquired by young people outside the classroom, be it in the workplace or the home. The recognition of those achievements would not only be a great fillip for the students concerned but would save the government and the school valuable staffing resources. While it is appreciated that the teachers' unions and the gatekeepers within the credentialling authorities will invariably resist these moves, the time has surely come to use the scarce resources to best educational advantage.

The concept of recognition of prior learning (RPL) has been with us for decades but today is only grudgingly being recognised formally, and even then usually for attainments in the workplace. The increased scope of a networked school community should, when coupled to some astute politics, help overcome the present impediments and provide the desired benefits.

Enhancing the effectiveness of the online learning platforms

A greater nexus between the home and the school could enhance the schools' and national efforts to use online learning platforms, of the type analysed by Ray Tolley in Chapter 12. They could, if designed wisely, become a fundamental facet of teaching and learning within the networked school community and be an ongoing expression of the formal curriculum of that community.

Most of the existing learning platforms would, however, need to shift from their highly traditional, control-over form and adopt a far more collaborative, constructivist approach where there is a clear consonance between the desired learning outcomes and the teaching mode employed, before they are likely to be used extensively.

Summary of educational benefits

In brief, the educational benefits are to be found in:
- Using the new technology to enhance the old
- Revisiting the underlying philosophy of formal schooling
- Recognising the learning culture of the home

- Enhancing the home learning and attainment
- Seeking an attractive and relevant schooling for all
- Taking advantage of a new rich and expanded playing field
- Appreciating the role of the informal
- Formal recognition for home learning.

Social

The importance young people today attach to the possession and use of their various digital technologies will be apparent to you. You will have seen it with your own children, you will have noted its impact on their learning at home, and you will have appreciated the revelations of the likes of Cassell and Cramer (2008) and Ito et al. (2008) on the importance young people attach to the technology in their daily lives and social development. You will also appreciate that it has been so for all the generations of young people born in the developed world since around 1985.

And yet, all these years later, we continue to see the schools—society's educator—having little appreciation of the social importance of that technology, let alone assisting young people in using it wisely. The development of a networked school community not only offers teachers the chance to better understand the part the suite of digital technologies plays in the educational and social development of their students, but also the opportunity to appropriately shape that development.

Where in the past many schools prided themselves on the part they played in the social and values education of young people, virtually all have thus far put their heads in the sand when it comes to providing direction and support in the use of the various technologies and opted to leave that facet of the lives of young people to the home. Interestingly this has been equally so of both government and religion-based schools. The vast majority (as will be apparent in Chapter 19) have opted to ban or markedly restrict the use of the technology in the classroom. A home–school nexus provides the opportunity for educators to once again play an astute and sensitive role in a vital area of values education.

Economic

The considerable economic benefits have already been mentioned. There is, however, an important observation that should be added. The shift to a networked mode of schooling will not place an additional financial burden on the nation but has the potential to actually save it money, while at the same time enhancing the national productivity (see Chapter 7). While some government funds will need to be spent to support the minority of homes unable to afford Internet connectivity, the savings will come by recognising and building upon the very considerable investment the nation's families are already investing in their digital capacity.

At the macro level there is a very real chance to actually use education to enhance the national productivity, and to build on the contribution already being made by the home. While the government rhetoric is normally directed at schools performing this role, it should be clear from the earlier observations about the use of digital technology in teaching that most nations have some time to wait before classroom teaching will make a significant contribution.

As we have seen, the home is already making that contribution, a fact noted in the UK in the *Harnessing technology* initiative (Becta 2008d). It is imperative that all politicians not only appreciate the contribution being made by the home but consciously assist in the development of national and regional public policy that builds on that base. As indicated earlier (and considered in greater depth in Chapter 7), it is also time for the politicians, the public policy developers and those in school governance to fundamentally rethink much of the funding of schools and to factor in the considerable and growing resources of the home, and derive those benefits.

As the team at NFER noted in 2005 (Atkinson et al. 2005), it is time for governments to fundamentally rethink the recurrent funding of schools in the digital era, but as yet little has been done. Basically, today's schools are funded on a paper-based model that emerged at the inception of public schooling in the Industrial Age (Lee & Winzenried 2009). At that point in time few homes, except those of the upper class, had the requisite educational resources or know-how, and thus the government needed to provide.

Today, across the developed world the opposite seems to apply, where the vast majority of homes have appreciably greater digital instructional technologies than in the past. While all developed societies do have family homes lacking in that technology and will require some support, as indicated they constitute an increasingly smaller proportion of the population. Both the homes and the government stand to benefit by opting for a new resourcing model that recognises the contribution the home can play. As we indicate in Chapter 7, that contribution can begin immediately.

While it is appreciated that the national, or even the provincial, adoption of a fundamentally new school recurrent policy could take years to sell and implement, there is the facility at both the school and government levels to phase in—and in a sense 'road test'—the desired changes, starting now. Pathfinding schools are already beginning to use some of the students' digital technology in the classroom. That can soon be ramped up.

Similarly, pathfinding governments have also introduced subtle changes that reward parents' acquisition of 'educational' digital technology for their children. For example, the Rudd Labor Government in Australia provides tax breaks for parents acquiring computer technology and Internet access for their children. While it is important to go after the desired big change there is much to be said, both politically and logistically, for introducing the changes incrementally, while always having the vision in mind. The ultimate financial benefits for digital societies can be immense.

Organisational

The network technologies also provide schools with the opportunity to markedly enhance their organisational effectiveness and efficiency. While the focus of the use of the emerging technologies is rightly on improving the quality of teaching and learning, there is ample scope to use the increasingly smarter online technology to greatly improve organisational capability of the school and its operations.

Interestingly, the 2008 Becta review of the UK Government's efforts to better harness the digital and networked technology noted the significant enhancement in efficiency that had been achieved and the part the technology had played in reducing teacher lesson preparation time.

> *The strongest general impact of technology across education relates to improvements in efficiency, notably the impact on the use of teachers' and practitioners' time. Studies have demonstrated that practitioners generally re-invest time they save into core tasks (PwC, 2004), thus giving rise to benefits in quality. Technology has delivered significant benefits to teachers in the use of their time. For example, overall around half of teachers who use technology for lesson planning report gains in time from this use, with just one in ten reporting losing time. Over 60 per cent of teachers report saving time reporting on pupil progress, with 8 per cent reporting losing time. A considerable proportion of those who say they save time report on average saving more than two hours per week (Smith et al. 2008).*

Becta (2008d, p. 11)

In a world where the load on teachers and school administrators has seemingly grown every year and when time is so vital in achieving the desired improvements, this is a very significant finding. Put bluntly, the technology should have been enhancing the effectiveness and efficiency of the organisation some time ago. That has not been realised as much as it should have and needs to be addressed.

The school administration and communication should, for example, mirror that available to the average home, and be consistent with that employed by any astute medium-sized business. Importantly, all the members of the school community, and not just a select subset, should have instant access to their information and to general workings of the school. In brief, schools should be providing what we as everyday consumers and users of the online and networked world regard as the norm.

Pause for a second and reflect on the kind of services provided by your Internet service provider (ISP). You can instantly check your account details from anywhere in the world, when you want, and make any adjustments or payments to your account without calling on the ISP staff. Can you do that with your school? If not, why not? The inexpensive technology exists to provide that service. Is it the lack of know-how or is it more the traditional mindset of the bureaucrat who decrees that only a few should control the information flow?

One of the many potential benefits, and indeed vital needs, of a networked school community is the opening of the information flow, of creating networked communities, of promoting collaboration and providing the ready facility for all the members to contribute to the ongoing development of the school community.

Political

It will now be apparent how many political benefits can be derived from creating a home–school nexus and, in time, networked school communities. It is an exciting vision that is likely to appeal to all parents, to the ever-expanding Net Generation, the many older generations that are now embracing the online world and in turn to most politicians and governments.

When one combines the many educational and economic benefits with an appreciation of the current home and school scenarios, the selling of the concept ought to be easy. That said, in looking to create a home–school nexus, be conscious of selling the concept and in the implementation to pay due attention to your small 'p' politicking, and probably also your large 'P' politicking as well, with the key political representatives. See if you can win the key politicians over to your move(s) and have them extol the benefits.

While the point will be elaborated on in Part D we cannot stress enough the difficulty of getting adults to perceive a mode of schooling different to what they have only ever known. You will need to factor in a concerted 'big sell' of your planned initiatives. Having the requisite political support and getting the politicians to own and promote the concept will not hurt your efforts.

The current reality

A key facet of winning that political support is to convince the politicians, their education authority bureaucrats and those in school governance of the current and future reality with the home and the school. While the digital richness of most homes seems blindingly obvious to most people, and indeed most educators and politicians, the same people have yet to appreciate its educational potential and undertake the kind of analysis we have done above. Nor, most importantly, will they have considered the very considerable constraints that will always hold back formal schooling. Most at this stage, like the UK Government, believe it will be best to simply redress the home–school digital divide.

Factors favouring the home

The following is but a sample of the factors that are working in favour of the vast majority of the nation's family homes continuing to enrich their acquisition and use of an ever-emerging suite of digital technologies.

Home priority

As mentioned, both the parents and young people place considerable store by and priority to having a significant suite of the current digital technologies in the home. Not only do the parents want those technologies themselves but they have long since believed—rightly— that computers and Internet access will improve the life chances and education of their children, while mobile phones are perceived to be an important part in the organisation of family life and the security of the children.

There will be very few young people who don't aspire to having the 'in' digital technologies, be it a games console, a Smart phone, an iPod or wireless broadband access. Both the parents and the children place a high priority on having the key technology.

Unfettered decision making

The home is free to acquire whatever type of digital technology it desires, whenever it wants, at whatever price it wants and to replace it when it so chooses. The home is not bound by any purchasing or replacement program. Moreover, it is only accountable to itself for its acquisitions and not subject to anyone else for the use of that technology provided it operates within the law.

User embracement

Parents and in particular young people invariably make extensive and immediate use of the newly acquired 'core' technologies. Technologies like digital TVs, DVD players, Smart phones, iPods, instant messenger (IM) and the various social networking facilities are embraced immediately, often months or years before they become available in the formal classroom. As indicated earlier, the use of a significant proportion of the school's digital technology by the students is limited and highly controlled.

Unlimited and largely free usage

It is easy to forget how much time young people have available to use the various technologies in the home and on the move, particularly when we compare the situation in the school. Most teenagers' Smart phones are left on for 24 hours a day. Not only do they have the time but they also have very few constraints on their use of the technology, particularly compared with the school setting where the use of all technologies will be controlled or monitored by a teacher.

Responsibility for a known few

In contrast to the school situation, the parents or the carers have only to 'supervise' the use of the technology by a few young people they know well. It is very much a dispersed set of responsibilities to folk who can soon ascertain how much trust they can apportion to their wards. Our experience suggests that the greatest challenge with young people is to keep the sound levels reasonable!

Ever-increasing resources with no controls

The vast, increasing majority of homes with children have the money to spend on buying the desired current technology. While socio-economic standing will impact on the choice of the brand and sophistication of the digital technologies, even lower-income families can and will acquire the cheaper makes of virtually all the technologies. Significantly homes do not have to go through complex and restricted purchasing processes. They can acquire the current technology as soon as they wish.

Responsiveness to change/flexibility

Consequently, the home can respond rapidly to the constant changes in the technology, try the new offerings, immediately use the latest software upgrades and, very importantly, use the technology as they wish. There are scant impediments to having the current technology.

Devolved infrastructure

In a networked school community, the actual network infrastructure in each home—its acquisition, setup, maintenance, support and upgrade—is devolved across the parent community. The homes are free to decide on the type of network they use and the costs they wish to incur. Not only does the government not have to meet any of those costs, it most assuredly does not need to handle any of the implementation logistics.

The school constraints

As you think about each of the following you will soon appreciate why the homes will continue to enrich their digital resources and their use at pace, while the schools will fall ever further behind. These many deep-seated constraints make it near impossible to overcome any digital divide, even if that was desirable.

Bureaucratic/hierarchical controls

In 1995, in *Reinventing education*, the then CEO of IBM Lewis Gerstner and his team questioned the ability of educational bureaucrats to successfully administer ongoing technological change in schools. He observed that:

> ... because schools are regulated bureaucracies, they are not organized in ways that lead them into the introduction of technologies. They are like eighteenth-century farms, not even ready to dream about the agricultural revolution that would sweep the world into the nineteenth and twentieth centuries.

Gerstner et al. (1995, p. 35)

As a former educational bureaucrat who had watched many Australian bureaucracies struggle to remain abreast of the digital and successfully implement whole-authority instructional technology initiatives, the author has to admit there is much in Gerstner's observation. The challenge for bureaucrats today is many times greater and appreciably more complex than in 1995. There is the old joke that a camel is a horse designed by a committee. One found far too many committees that had provided schools with 'camels'—as Winzenried and Lee (2009) did in researching the implementation of instructional technology programs over the last century. Only recently we noted a tender for interactive whiteboards where the bureaucracy concerned opted to use four companies to provide different facets of what was an as yet untried solution. Not surprisingly that rollout struggled, as has the teachers' use of the provided solution. Sadly, that has happened across the world and continues to happen.

The problem is amplified when internal bureaucratic politics intervene and when the elected officials attempt to micro-manage the implementation process to achieve the best political, and not educational, outcome. Allied to the bureaucratic procedures are the hierarchical approvals, with few if any teachers free to acquire the desired technology without the signature of those in charge.

Slowness and inflexibility

Related is the time required to get the new technology into schools and the processes that must be followed. With even the most efficient and effective of bureaucracies, the time taken between the formation of a major policy initiative, its approval, budget approval, choice of solution and school implementation can be two, more likely three, years. The contrast with the home is pronounced.

Structural/legislative impediments

The number of structural impediments, years of legislation and public policy that practice has invariably imposed can lengthen the time taken. The vast majority of central offices are reluctant to devolve all the financial responsibility to the schools. Full school-based financial management is found in only a minority of the world's public schools. While independent schools that have full control over the use of their monies are normally far less constrained than the government schools, most still have their own committees, buying procedures and approval processes with which to contend.

Public accountability

All schools—government and independent—have ultimately to account publicly for all their technology acquisitions, either to their councils or their central office and/or government. They are increasingly obliged to show how the acquisition contributed to the specified outcomes.

Politics/media pressure

Education authorities, government and even independent schools are constrained in what they can do by politics and likely media pressure. Those constraints will always be there when the technology is new and largely unknown by the general public. Once its use is normalised the pressure is invariably markedly reduced. While today there is likely to be little comment (even by the most rabid of tabloids) on the use of biros in schools, some of us are old enough to remember the outcry surrounding their introduction and the demise of 'quality handwriting'.

As discussed in Chapter 18, the current political and media pressure on most schools, and in particular government schools, about the dangers of young people's use of the Internet in schools has in some situations almost reached a point of paranoia evidenced through Internet filtering and censorship controls. Ironically, scant mention is made of the fact that students with web-enabled handheld computers are able to surf the Internet at leisure up to the classroom door. History reveals that this has always been the way with schools and all new technology, and it is likely to be an issue unless handled very astutely in developing networked school communities.

Antipathy?

Mention was made earlier of the technology antipathy that appears to be strong with some senior educational administrators. Whether it is antipathy, disinterest or lack of understanding by many of the school and education authority, it does not matter greatly. What matters is that a significant number of senior people do not have the same kind of commitment to the preparation of young people for a digital future as do most in the home. It is appreciated that many senior bureaucrats and politicians still strongly favour a traditional education. In the former Bush administration in the US and the former Howard administration in Australia there was little priority accorded to educating young people for a digital future. In any bureaucracy, if a policy is not given priority by the government of the day and, in turn, the executive, it is not likely to succeed.

Limited and controlled funding

Where most homes in the developed world have the finances that allow them to go out tomorrow and buy whatever digital technology they want, schools have no such capacity. As indicated in Chapter 7, most schools in the developed world have only around 2.7–3 per cent of their annual recurrent budget to spend on information and communication technology. Most homes spend around 8.5–9 per cent of their annual income on the various forms of communication and digital technology. Moreover, a sizeable proportion of homes are prepared to acquire the desired technology and communications on credit. Not only are the school funds limited but their spending is invariably tightly controlled and able to be spent on specific items, often within the parameters set on high.

Centralised infrastructure

Schools and education authorities have long since moved away from the time when each little cost centre could acquire its own networked technology. Rather the trend is towards ever-greater centralised decision making about the nature and use of the network infrastructure, with the control seemingly inexorably being vested in larger, centralised and remote authorities.

Limited and controlled usage

Mention has been made on a number of occasions of the limited time schools have in the day and week to use the digital technologies, even when it is normalised into everyday teaching. After one takes out time for assemblies, roll call, pastoral groups, recess, lunch, class movement and the occasional sporting or musical event, the time left is small—there is only so much that can be done. The hours available to use the technology in the school and to acquire the requisite prowess will always fall a long, long way behind that available in the home and on the move. Allied is the fact that virtually all use of the technology in the school is monitored or indeed controlled by the teachers, even in the senior school years.

Responsibility for multiple students

Lastly, but by no means least, schools have statutory responsibilities for the care of often hundreds of students. It is a very different situation for teachers managing a significant number of students in a class than a parent or carer monitoring the activities of a few young people they know well. As you can plainly see, the odds are heavily in favour of the home continuing to enhance its acquisition and use of the current digital technologies at pace and for classrooms to fall further behind.

Table 6.1 The home–school contrast

Home	School
Unfettered decision making	Hierarchical/bureaucratic control
User embracement	Limited acceptance
Ever-increasing resources, with no controls	Limited and controlled funding
Responsiveness to change/flexibility	Slowness/inflexibility
Family accountability	Public accountability
Home priority	Antipathy?
Control and agency	Structural/legislative impediments
Unlimited and largely free usage	Limited and controlled usage
Responsibility for a known few	Responsibility for multiple, relatively unknown students
Personal privacy	Political/media scrutiny
Devolved network infrastructure	Centralised network infrastructure

Pitfalls

The shift to a more networked mode of schooling, like any major human organisational change, will have its many potential pitfalls. The earlier analogy to e-commerce is apt. There will be ongoing challenges that astute leaders and politicians will need to address. Most will be human, linked to the retention of the known and existing power bases, but as with the e-commerce the way forward can be readily managed provided it is approached wisely and positively.

Conclusion

In *The world is flat* (2006), Thomas Friedman made the telling point that the confluence of technological and political developments that occurred around 2002/2003 fundamentally changed life and work across the globe. In education, as mentioned, it had a similar impact on the proactive schools and education authorities. Since then, those schools and authorities have been exploring the ever-opening possibilities of the digital and networked world, and have set themselves the task of educating young people for a digital future.

What they have yet to do is articulate their vision for the model of schooling that will best enable them to provide that education. The concept of the networked school community that we described earlier is an attempt to articulate that vision. In opting for that model we sought to use a form that would let educators continue their quest to provide the best possible education for all, while at the same time building on the now clearly discernible major trends in school and technological development and the burgeoning digitally related resources of the home.

As you will now appreciate, the potential benefits of such a model are considerable and diverse. However, taking the pragmatic perspective, it is appreciated that there is much to be done, much to be learned, major hurdles to be overcome and inevitable mistakes to be made before that vision can be fully realised. Notwithstanding, the rationale for the vision does provide direction as you begin to take the steps towards creating the desired home–school nexus and networked school communities. One of the yet unstated benefits of the suggested model of schooling is that it is a natural extension of the shift in the mode of schooling already underway, and does allow schools, education authorities and governments to move forward in graduated, readily achievable steps.

Guiding questions

After reading this chapter, consider your context and propose your ideas in relation to the following guiding questions.

1   Would you say your school is best described as a democratic, collaborative organisation or a hierarchical organisation?

2   Does it understand the kind of digital technologies in all its homes? If you believe that it does, does it build upon those technologies in its teaching?

3   Does it recognise or foster the learning culture of its homes?

4   What kind of incremental moves do you think that the school could make to take advantage of the home's technology and its learning culture?

5   Are there significant barriers to the school beginning to dismantle its walls and shift to the networked mode? If so, what are they?

Key messages

- There is a compelling rationale for developing a networked school community, including recognition of the immense opportunities that the digital and networked technology provides education and the potential for significant short- and long-term educational, social, economic, organisational and political benefits.

- The astute development of a new mode of schooling, a networked form, can help maximise the use made of the capability of the classroom and the home and, more importantly, provide a new dynamic type of formal schooling that can assist in overcoming many of the current shortcomings and better prepare young people for a digital and networked future.

CHAPTER 7

Financing the networked school community: Building upon the home investment

MAL LEE & BERNARD RYALL

I feel additional concern about attempts to supply every student with continuous access to high-performance computing and communications because of the likely cost of this massive investment. Depending on the assumptions made about the technological capabilities involved, estimates of the financial resources needed for such an information infrastructure vary (Coley, Cradler, & Engel 1997). Extrapolating the most detailed cost model (McKinsey & Company 1995) to one multimedia-capable, Internet-connected computer for every two to three students yields a price tag of about ninety-four billion dollars of initial investment and twenty-eight billion dollars per year in ongoing costs, a financial commitment that would drain schools of all discretionary funding for at least a decade. For several reasons, this is an impractical approach for improving education.

Chris Dede, Professor of Educational Technology, Harvard (1998, p. 2)

Investment challenges

Over the last decade there have been numerous government initiated and funded programs across the developed world based on the idea of school-wide student use of computer laptops, 1:1 or 'ubiquitous' computing and, more recently, Netbooks. Ten years later than Dede's statement (quoted above), the education authorities in Okanagan School District in Canada made the 'startling' observation that not only could the district not afford the 1:1 laptop program, but the students already had the technology in their homes (*Vancouver Sun* 2008). And all this was before the 2008–2009 global financial crisis and the substantial debt accrued by most developed nations. While at the time of writing the authors were unable to identify how many other Okanagan examples had transpired, it is likely that many other school districts across North America and the rest of the world now realise that they cannot afford to maintain laptop or 'ubiquitous' computing programs and, also, that most of their students already have better technology in the home.

It should now be clear that the parents of school-age children are making a vast investment in digital technology for both their own use and that of their children. Moreover, it should be apparent that investment will continue to grow while that available to the schools will always be limited and its use constrained. The authors' contention is that the time has arrived when public policy makers and school decision makers need to recognise the very considerable and growing investment the nation's families are making in digital technologies, actively encourage and support that investment and begin to develop a model of financing where at least part of the operations of a networked school community are financed by the home investment.

Related is the reality that no developed nation can afford to fund from the public purse the level of digital technology needed by schools in a digital and networked world over a sustained period, and that within a networked and collaborative world where the digital and educational capacity of the students' homes is largely untapped it is inappropriate to do so.

School funding

Today's schools are still funded in general terms using a model created for traditional paper-based schooling. Not surprisingly all but the richest schools struggle to finance and support the best use of the desired digital technologies. The vast majority of the school's annual recurrent funding is spent on its staff, both the salaries and the on-costs. While that proportion varies across education authorities and indeed between independent schools in general terms, around 85–90 per cent of the annual funding is spent on staff, with the remainder having to meet all the school's operating costs, such as its textbooks, library stock, insurance, maintenance, debt repayment, administration and increasingly its information and communication technology (Lee & Winzenried 2009).

As you will soon appreciate, the amount available in the remaining '10–15 per cent' to acquire and support the burgeoning digital technology is minuscule. A US national study by Anderson and Becker (1999) revealed that only 2.7 per cent of the 1998 US education budget was spent on ICT. The indication is that the UK, which has for the past 15 years led the way internationally in resourcing and seeking to harness the use of digital technology in its schools, still only allocates approximately 6 per cent of its national education budget on ICT. Figures prepared by the authors that relate to the figures in Table 7.1 (pp. 118–19) suggest that in the Australian context the average family outlays around 8.5–9 per cent of its annual budget on digital technologies and communications. As George Megalogenis, writing in *The Australian* in September 2009, observed, the mobile phone alone was consuming a greater proportion of the average family budget than petrol.

> A study by The Australian *using unpublished official data shows spending on motoring fuel was at historic lows of just 2.4% of household expenditure in the June quarter national accounts, while the share that went to telecommunications was 0.1 points higher at 2.5%. (p. 1)*

Try if you can to ascertain the proportion allocated by your school, and if you succeed don't be surprised how small it is—well below the kind of proportion available in virtually all other knowledge-based industries. Think about how much you spend on digital and communication technology in your home.

Schooling globally is not going to succeed in getting a significantly greater proportion of the national budget. With an ageing population it will do well to retain its present share. It has basically to work with its existing government allocation. One of the main reasons for the present shortcoming is that schooling is one of the 'last of the dinosaurs'—those industries that have not as yet restructured, reduced their dependence on labour and made greater use of the technology. Indeed, if over the past 50 years, with the near universal political push to reduce school class sizes and in turn employ more teachers, the proportion of the education budget spent on staff has steadily increased, further reducing the money for other operations. The likelihood of any significant industry restructuring in the near future is remote, but as you will note in Chapter 8 it is suggested that some initial moves should be made.

Thus far, schools, education authorities and nations have opted to redress the shortfall by turning to the parents to fund the technology or to use highly political, short-term, often one-off supplementary payments. Both approaches are Band-Aid solutions that will not provide the requisite level of financing for all the nation's schools over a sustained period, nor provide the school leadership with the financial surety needed for wise long-term planning.

As societies continue to become more digital and networked and the technology more sophisticated, schools are going to want and will be expected to make ever-greater use of the appropriate technologies. They will need the requisite funding. Moreover, they will want a far more secure source of funding, sheltered if possible from the whims of the short-term political life cycle. Ironically, all of this is happening at a time when the digital resources and indeed digital capability of the average student's home is outstripping that of the average classroom.

It is time for society to pause, to reflect upon what is happening, to ask some hard questions, to realise that the assumptions that underpinned the current mode of recurrent school resourcing have fundamentally changed and that it is time to rethink the funding of at least part of the digital technology in a networked school community. The present model of school funding emerged in the Industrial Revolution, along with the free and compulsory schooling movement of the 1870s, at a time when few homes had the resources to school their children. The only way was for the state—with 'state' here meaning the body politic—to provide that funding in a place called school.

As indicated, that situation has over the last 20-plus years in particular changed dramatically and all the signs are that the riches of the home will continue to grow steadily while those of the classrooms will continue to struggle, unless something very different, more sustainable and appropriate is done.

What we are suggesting in this chapter is a possible solution. Schools and governments need to begin exploring using a public–private funding model that recognises and harnesses families' considerable investment in digital technology and allows the networked school community to use the total basket of resources available. The UK has shown how the public–private model can be applied successfully to the development of schools. All we are suggesting is for the concept to be taken a step further. While any major structural change will ultimately need to be made by government, self-managed and independent schools can, as we indicate below, begin making significant moves and trialling various options immediately.

Traditional funding allocation

School funding remains largely secret in most education authorities. While virtually all independent schools and education authorities in the developed world publish their annual financial reports, the reporting modes employed make it difficult to accurately determine the actual break-ups and compare the situation in different education authorities and nations.

That said, there are facets of the funding that are common globally and that bear remembering when seeking to adopt a model appropriate for schools operating within the networked mode. The vast majority of the funds spent on schools in developed nations are provided by the state, even in many of the supposed independent schools, and the majority of that money is spent on staff, with only a limited proportion available for all the school's other acquisitions.

Most of the digital technology acquired by schools is only available for use (as indicated in Chapter 4) for a limited proportion of the calendar year. As indicated, virtually all in-school use of the technology is teacher controlled and available for student use at most for six hours a day, five days a week, for around 200 days a year. Aside from the mobile technology that some schools allow the students to take home, the technology remains largely unused, rapidly depreciating in value most of the day. That ought to be a concern when the average life of computers is only around three to four years.

In the more bureaucratically controlled education authorities, the educational effectiveness of even the limited proportion of the overall funding is further minimised by the central office's determination of how the money will be spent, and often how it will be spent on technology chosen by the bureaucrats and not the school. History consistently shows the bureaucrats are more driven by securing what they perceive to be the best deal, rather than whether it meets the teachers' and learners' educational requirements. Many of those 'great deals' paid little regard to the total cost of ownership of the technology, had scant if any impact on improving the teaching and student learning, and in the end often obliged the interested schools to fund the shortfall and clean-up of the mistakes made (Lee & Winzenried 2009).

History (Lee & Winzenried 2009) also reveals the marked propensity for the central bureaucracies to spend most of the limited monies primarily on the technology and to allocate little or nothing for the vital human element so essential for the effective use of the technology. While some of the proactive education authorities have made considerable progress in this area, today there are still many schools and education authorities continuing to make this mistake. Often it is the desire to acquire technology that will make the elected representative look good, but sometimes it is the segmented nature of the central bureaucracy that brings that about. Check on the situation in your school. Whether it is intentional or simply the by-product of the bureaucratic mindset, there is in many education authorities a marked inclination to assume increasingly greater control of the limited public monies available, to take advantage of the increased broadband to centralise the technology's operations, and to largely leave the individual schools as 'dumb terminals' in the quest to bring about what the bureaucracy decides is the 'desired' school change.

The likelihood of significantly changing the current break-up of the monies in the foreseeable future is remote. The power of the teachers' unions and education lobbyists, and indeed the current parent perceptions, are such that politically all but the smallest of shifts will be near impossible across the developed world. While the seminal McKinsey research by Barber and Mourshed (2007) makes it clear that class size has little impact on student learning except in the early childhood years, and while the technology as mentioned allows schools to take advantage of a new and expanded educational playing field, the chances of shifting monies away from staffing are small. What is worth noting is that if schools, particularly the larger schools, could work with several fewer staff the considerable money saved would make a significant difference to the school's technology acquisitions.

Globally, all but the wealthiest of schools in 2010 are struggling to resource the acquisition of the desired digital technology and the support required to obtain the best educational and organisational use of that technology. While the pathfinding schools have made significant advances, they have invariably had to do without in other operations to fund the desired technology.

The changing balance

The shift of the educational capacity from the public authority and the school to the students' homes is a historical development that few have commented upon let alone analysed for its public policy implications. It is a fundamental societal megatrend with considerable ramifications. As indicated in Chapter 4, it is not (as many would contend) a home–school digital divide that can and should be quickly rectified, but rather two different situations with very different capacity to deal with rapid and ongoing change. When one understands that difference, one can also begin to appreciate the positives and the opportunities on offer, provided schooling is seen as something far more than an education behind classroom doors.

One of the major opportunities that the changing balance provides existing schools and governments is the facility for the home's digital capacity to be factored into the overall ongoing resourcing of the networked school community, and for the home's financial contribution to the education of the nation's young people to be formally recognised. How that might be done is considered below. In commenting on the shift the authors are fully aware that this shift has not yet occurred in all family homes and that the group as mentioned needs to be recognised and, if required, resourced.

Band-Aid solutions

What we have today with the recurrent resourcing of the digital technology in schools is a classic example of a model that was designed for another era being taken well past its use-by date and a number of ineffectual Band-Aids being applied, rather than the key decision makers appreciating that a fundamentally new model appropriate to the times is required. The authors would be among the first to acknowledge that that is a very considerable task, particularly within an unstructured industry, but eventually a new model will have to be adopted.

The current approach does not provide the kind of resources required, nor is it sustainable over a period when the digital requirements will escalate. If governments want education to contribute to the national productivity in an ongoing manner they will need to move to a sustainable model that will produce.

With the advantage of hindsight one can see schools and governments struggling with the adequate provision of digital technologies and the associated support for the past 25-plus years—really since the advent of the PC clones and the first of the school computer networks in the mid 1980s. As the technology developed and society's expectations grew, so schools and governments looked for ready sources of finance.

They found those monies initially with the parents. The early requests were initially small and manageable, but as soon as the desire to increase the number of machines and the reach and sophistication of the school network grew, and the parents were asked to fund the replacement of rapidly dating personal computers, so too did the demands quickly grow. Today not only are few school parent communities able to find the very considerable monies required by the school, but rightly a growing number are beginning to question the logic of their funding, directly from their own purse or via fundraising digital technologies they already own. This is particularly so with the 1:1 computing thrust advocated so strongly by the major computing companies. The strain becomes that much greater when a school mandates that all families have to buy a brand 'X' unit for their son or daughter, in addition to the unit already acquired because it makes it more manageable for the teachers.

With the vast majority of family homes already spending around 9 per cent of the family budget on digital technologies—appreciably more than the school—and on technology that is generally more capable than that of the school, the capacity for the schools, and indirectly government, to ask the parents to fund the school's technology will increasingly diminish.

Reflect for a moment on the situation at your school, and ask how the pressure on the parents to cover the shortfall in technology funding has grown. Do you have concerns about the seeming desire to duplicate technology already owned by the parents, and indeed to ask the parents to fund that duplication? Are there not more rationale and economic ways of meeting the need?

The second source of funding was the infusion of supplementary government monies. This has been happening for decades with national and regional governments, and continues today. Designed in part to address a significant shortfall in the government's resourcing and to generate political capital, this infusion of money or actual technology has in most instances done little to enhance the quality of teaching and learning, particularly over a sustained period.

In researching *The use of instructional technology in schools*, Lee and Winzenried (2009) explored the use of supplementary government funding of technology for schools over the past 50 years across the developed world. In general terms, while there has been some significant achievements by the more proactive, visionary governments particularly since the mid 1990s, overall one would have to rate the performance of governments and the allied education bureaucracies on the poor side. The mistakes made 30–40 years ago are still being made today in many situations, and as a consequence it is difficult to discern any significant impact of these investments on the efficiency or effectiveness of the schools, or on enhanced student attainment.

Let us be quite clear before fleshing out some of the shortcomings: there are many excellent initiatives by governments that rightly deserve praise, but overall they are the exception. Again think of your own situation and the impact of the supplementary funding provided over the years. Has it worked?

The one area where governments have been particularly successful is in the provision of the network infrastructure both up to and in schools, and negotiating with the telecommunication carriers on an appropriate Internet traffic pricing structure. The proactive schools, education authorities and nations as mentioned earlier moved swiftly in the second half of the 1990s and early 2000s to move schools from a position where they were telecommunication deserts to having broadband connectivity to all teaching rooms (Lee & Winzenried 2009).

In general terms, the supplementary funding model has been characterised by the following:

- its strongly political nature, both in the technology selected and the decision where to spend the monies;
- the short-term nature of the funding, which often coincided with the short political life cycle;
- its preoccupation with the technology, and invariably a particular piece of technology; think back over the years to educational television, video, computer-aided instruction, interactive multimedia CD-ROMs, laptop programs and more recently Netbooks;

- the failure to learn from history and invest in open and objective research;

- the focus on large-ticket items with media appeal, and propensity to exclude vital supplementary funding for the likes of Internet traffic, teaching applications software, teacher release, program evaluation, network backup and infrastructure support;

- the reluctance to provide appropriate ongoing support for the human parts of any strategy;

- the propensity to exaggerate what will be achieved, leaving a significant gap between the rhetoric and the reality;

- its association with a major multinational technology company or two, as if this adds to the credibility of the spending;

- the continuing disenfranchisement of the teachers and their growing scepticism with all 'on high' funding;

- its imposition on schools and school communities, and in turn lack of school and teacher acceptance of the initiative;

- the lack of flexibility allowed individual schools to attune the funding to their particular situation;

- the failure to evaluate the effectiveness of the government's implementation strategies, and to publish those findings. It is invariably the schools' work that is evaluated even though it had little control on what was imposed.

(Source: Lee & Winzenried 2009)

Invariably, the supplementary funding programs stopped or were markedly curtailed upon a change of government, and in particular the coming to power of a conservative government.

Reflect on your situation. Are you one of the few fortunate ones where the government supplementation has been deployed astutely or is your experience akin to the scenario described above? The sudden dose of economic reality through the global financial crisis might be beneficial if only because it obliges school and education authorities to review their use of scarce public resources. It is appreciably cheaper and smarter for young people to transfer data between the home or school or a USB drive or the SD card in their Smart phone than the government spending considerable resources duplicating expensive technology.

That said, there are nonetheless education authorities worldwide still persisting with the much-wounded supplementary, state-funded model. The Australian Labor Government, for example, embarked on a national 'digital education revolution' (Australian Government 2009a) in 2008 that aimed to provide all Year 9–12 students with a computer. Why Years 9 to 12, and why just computers? We'll let the Australian Government explain. The telling point is that the government set aside $2500 for each student to cover the cost of the acquisition of the computer, its software and its support, for the period 2009–2013. In 2009 alone, it will need to allocate $2500 for 970 000 students. Each year thereafter up to and including 2013 it will need to set aside $2500 for an additional 270 000 Year 9 students. Overall, that will cost the Australian taxpayer in the region of $2.425 billion for the first year and $675 million for each of the next four years—an overall cost of around $5.125 billion.

It is important to remember with the Australian program that by the end of 2012, 50 per cent of computers are at least four years old and obsolete; 12.5 per cent are at least three years old and obsolete; 12.5 per cent are at least two years old and nearly obsolete; 12.5 per cent are approximately one year old, and 12.5 per cent are near new.

In the program documentation there is no funding mentioned for:

- external research
- program evaluation
- the teacher's acquisition of interactive multimedia teaching software
- school-based teacher development, teacher time release or mentoring programs
- the acquisition of school or student information systems, or any type of learning platform.

Most importantly, there appears to be no specific funding provided for the school network upgrades that will inevitably come with the upsurge in use associated with the networking of the Year 9–12 PCs. This is a lesson learned by the UK in the mid 2000s, and well documented in the Becta annual technology reports (Becta 2006, 2007a, 2008d).

In addition to this money, there will be the as yet unannounced proportion of the 45 billion national broadband network dollars set aside to provide broadband connection to every Australian teaching room. One can rightly argue that the broadband connection of the classrooms in any education authority is a valid long-term infrastructure outlay of the state, and as such should not be included in this short-term, supplementary state funding category. It is nonetheless an extra cost that has to be borne by the taxpayer.

When one considers what the Australian family is already spending on all manner of digital technology annually and that the home has what it usually perceives to be better technology than the school, one suspects the Australian Government is going to find it hard to justify in 2013 making another massive outlay of around five to six billion dollars for the 2014–2018 period. And that assumes that the current investment in the Year 9–12 computers enhances teaching and learning in the school! On current indications the likelihood of that success is already remote. Interestingly, at the time of writing in latter 2009, Australian education authorities were informed that the Australian Government's contribution was to be regarded as a one-off payment.

The great problem with the Band-Aid solutions is that individual school communities have little financial surety on which to plan. When the source of a significant and ever-growing proportion of the school's budget is uncertain it is only natural for principals and indeed the school governance to be cautious. The development of networked school communities is strongly dependent on the availability of adequate monies over a sustained period, and the school's extensive control over the best use of those monies.

The educational resources of the home

As indicated, the vast majority of young people's homes in the developed world—be they in Australia, Spain, Taiwan or Finland—have extensive and ever-growing digital resources and an immense and as yet largely untapped digital educational capacity. The suggestion is that developed societies should be tapping that capacity, and more consciously recognising the contribution those homes are making and can make to the education of young people and the enhancement of national productivity.

It is appreciated that within all developed societies there will be a proportion of the student population that lack the money to acquire the requisite digital resources in the home. Our contention is that the group needs to be supported, either in the way the UK has opted to do or by the school community itself. It is also recognised that there will be families that have the monies but for some reason have chosen not to provide their children access to the digital technology or the networked world. That is their choice.

A gauge of the digital capacity of most homes can be gained by identifying the expenditure in the home on digital technology (detailed for Year 6 students in Table 7.1). While the costs are based on the Australian scene in 2009, the picture that emerges might be generally representative of all the leading developed nations. Table 7.1 offers a comparison of the monies spent on digital technologies in the homes of 30 Year 6 students and that spent in their classroom.

Table 7.1 Average home–classroom digital technology difference (approx.), based on 30 Year 6 students in Australia, 2009

Home			
Items	Cost	Qty	Total cost
TV HD digital LCD 32"	$1 200	45.0	$54 000
HDD recorder	$500	30.0	$15 000
DVD player	$120	30.0	$3 600
VCR	$120	30.0	$3 600
PC Lenovo	$1 270	25.0	$31 750
PC Mac	$1 400	20.0	$28 000
Printer/Scanner/Copier MFDs	$500	30.0	$15 000
Net connection (PA)	$1 000	28.0	$28 000
Surround-sound home theatre	$8 000	25.0	$200 000
Digital camera	$250	30.0	$7 500
Digital video camera	$600	15.0	$9 000
Data projector	$1 750	4.0	$7 000
Interactive whiteboard 78"	$2 850		$0

Home			
Items	Cost	Qty	Total cost
Games consoles Wii/PS3/Xbox	$350	25.0	$8 750
iPods	$200	30.0	$6 000
Mobile Smart phones	$900	15.0	$13 500
Fixed phones	$300	25.0	$7 500
Instant Messenger/Skype		30.0	$0
		Total	$438 200

Classroom			
Items	Cost	Qty	Total cost
TV HD digital LCD 32"	$1 200	1.0	$1 200
HDD recorder	$500	1.0	$500
DVD player	$120	1.0	$120
VCR	$120	1.0	$120
PC Lenovo	$1 270	6.0	$7 620
PC Mac	$1 400	6.0	$8 400
Printer/Scanner/Copier MFDs	$2 000	1.5	$3 000
Net connections	$1 000	0.8	$800
Surround-sound home theatre	$8 000	0.1	$800
Digital camera	$250	1.0	$250
Digital video camera	$600	1.0	$600
Data projector	$1 750	0.4	$700
Interactive whiteboard 78"	$2 850	0.2	$570
Games consoles Wii/PS3/Xbox	$350		$0
iPods	$200		$0
Mobile Smart phones	$900		$0
Fixed phones	$300		$0
Instant Messenger/Skype			$0
		Total	$24 680

The figures are based on the average situation in Australia. While one might challenge the veracity of every figure, what is revealed is that the resources in the home are not two or three times greater than the classroom but, conservatively, in the region of 14 to 15 times greater. The difference is immense. The suspicion is that in many other developed nations such as Spain, Taiwan, Hong Kong and France the factor in favour of the home could be well above the factor of 15 mentioned for Australia.

A public–private solution

Developed nations should consider shifting away from the traditional 'fully' state or public funded model of schooling to a new public–private recurrent funding model for networked school communities that makes astute use of the considerable digital resources of the home, and in turn recognises and actively encourages families to maintain their investment in and use of those technologies.

As indicated earlier, most developed nations have in fact moved into that de facto situation by virtue of the usually unwritten reliance on parent funding. The suggestion is that the shift is formally recognised and an appreciably clearer and more sophisticated model openly adopted. We are not advocating any particular approach, simply the concept.

We recommend shifting incrementally in that time will be needed to model the various possibilities, to trial and evaluate the options and to prepare schools and their communities and the education authorities for the change. The move can and should be graduated. It will be important to identify appropriate quantifiable key performance indicators that provide all within the school community and government with a ready indication of the effectiveness of the investment. If it can be done in areas like health, it can be done in schooling.

The ramifications of this kind of shift are considerable, and thus time should be allowed for all the elements to be analysed, policy to be formulated and budgeted, implementation strategies shaped and the concept sold to the general community. There will be many within the education industry unable to countenance anything other than a state-funded model. Lewis Perelman, while renowned for his somewhat right-wing views, did note in *School's out* in 1992 that:

> *Education is our most labor intensive industry; at 93% of output (or total costs), education's labour costs are nearly double those of the average US business and more than twice those of such high-tech information industries as telecommunications. In 1956, education's labour costs were 85% of total costs ... (p. 99)*

> *Academia would now be the largest, and probably the last socialist economy on earth. By the way the 'socialist' label applies quite literally; American academia is 90% owned, operated and/or financed by government and most of the remainder is government regulated. (p. 107)*

As mentioned earlier, with the seemingly shrinking class sizes, education's labour costs are likely to have grown since Perelman's 1992 analysis. The reality is that the world has moved a long way since these observations were made 18 years ago, and yet both comments still remain pertinent for most schools and the funding of the digital technology therein. In seeking to recognise and support the families' use of digital technologies it will be important for government to factor in the benefits associated with the education of not only young people but also, as the UK has identified (as discussed in Chapter 12), the lifelong learning of all the family members, and the impact that the enhanced digital competence of the older members of the family will have upon the improved work prospects and the overall learning culture of the home.

In brief, the digital resources of the family home serve not only to enhance the education of the school students, but also their parents, grandparents and relatives. The UK work in this area—most notably that of Schmitt and Wadsworth (2004)—bears noting. Conscious of the increasingly evident shortcomings of the present model of recurrent school funding and the lag time involved in developing and implementing a new one, it is suggested homework begin now. An early part of that homework would be to identify the moves already being made by various governments. In Australia, for example, the Rudd Labor Government recognised in part the contribution digital technology in the family home makes to the education of young people by providing them with taxation relief up to the value of $A750.00 (Australian Government 2009b). Undoubtedly there are comparable moves being made elsewhere.

The possibilities

The more independent schools could begin building upon the home's investment in digital and networking technologies immediately, and in the process provide public policy officials and politicians with valuable information on the way forward in developing a public–private mode of funding. While ultimately government will have to address and oversee the implementation of a new funding model, there are many aspects of the concept that could be applied and tested now as part of the overall development of a networked school community.

A simple move would be to promote with the parents any government support or tax relief relating to the purchase of any digital and networked technology. A more significant development would be to begin trialling the use of the students' digital technology in the classroom. The possibilities are extensive, but in a larger school several of the student technologies could be trialled simultaneously. The school could, for example, trial the use of students' individual:

- laptops, initially with a limited and in time wider group of students, addressing specifically the everyday management of that technology;
- iPods/MP3 players/Smart phones for use in music or the learning of foreign languages;
- wireless technology with the school providing the Wi-Fi outlets;
- Smart phones to handle all the students' diary entries, replacing the traditional paper school diary;
- Smart phone cameras/editing applications in the creation and presentation of a photo journalism exercise;
- Smart phones/SDs or USBs as portable hard drives;
- Smart phone interfaces with interactive whiteboards and data projectors.

It is appreciated that work is already underway on some of the above, but interestingly most of the trials entail the school buying and owning the technology. Significantly within the business world, there is already a trend for employers to use their technology in the workplace and for the network managers to accommodate that use. *The Australian* newspaper's IT section reports the shift as 'BYO laptop trend extends office' and observes:

> *BYO, or bring your own, machines give employees the freedom to use their own computers at work. Portable personal devices can deliver massive savings to a company, which can pick any hardware supplier to use, as budget airline Jetstar has done. Gartner says the benefits of a BYO plan include greater worker satisfaction, increased productivity, and a reduced burden on the IT department.*
>
> *It also makes the employer more attractive for job applicants, especially generation Y.*
>
> *Gartner research director Robin Simpson said the main drivers of the BYO and portable personalities approach were cost and flexibility.*
>
> Foo (*The Australian*, 22 September 2009)

The authors suggest the BYO model has much going for it within a networked school community. Interestingly the US research by Project Tomorrow in late 2009 noted:

> *When asked how their schools would make it easier for them to work electronically the students' number one response was '... let me use my own devices and tools in the school day.' Students are becoming free agent learners, seeking control of their own education.*
>
> Project Tomorrow (2009a, p.8)

Table 7.2 offers a possible public–private scenario you might like to use as a discussion starter. Of note is that the model:

- sees the students/home as responsible for the care and maintenance of its digital technologies;
- can be phased in over time, allowing for trialling of the concept and the run out of leases/commitments;
- provides significant wins for all associated—the students, parents, community, politicians, and professional educators;
- would need to be accompanied by a phased preparation of students, parents, the community, politicians, as well as the professional educators.

Table 7.2 Possible public–private school technology funding model

Private	Public	Employer
• Home/mobile Internet access • Home/mobile suite of digital technologies • Personal telecommunications • Personal applications software • Personal digital storage • Personal mobile multimedia hardware and software—apps, cameras, audio recording, etc.	• Cater for disadvantaged • Tax/government technology incentives for families with school children • Public policy promotion/sell • Network infrastructure • Free school network Wi-Fi access for students • Provision of digital systems—administration/ communications/learning • Whole-class instructional technology • Instructional software/ applications • Specialist instructional technologies • Staff development • iCentre (Chapter 9) • Archival digital storage and management	• Provision/subsidised use of mobile computing facility of choice • Assisted telecommunications • Relevant applications software • Access to school(s) network(s)

Conclusion

The logic of the student's home contributing the use of its burgeoning digital technology to the education of young people in a networked school community, and gaining societal recognition for that contribution, appears so powerful that it is hard to believe the proposition would be rejected. However, the authors appreciate how immersed schooling is in the ways of the past and that it appears, particularly with funding, to be unable to contemplate any variation on what it has always known.

The ground-breaking work of public–private partnerships in the UK has shown what is possible. We are suggesting that similar thinking might be applied to the funding of some of the technology used within a networked school community.

Guiding questions

After reading this chapter, consider your context and propose your ideas in relation to the following guiding questions.

1   In relation to your school, what proportion of the total school budget—not the actual monies—do you estimate is spent on the use of digital technologies? If possible, seek to verify your estimate.

2   How great is the parent contribution to the ongoing acquisition of the school's digital technology?

3   Are students able to use their mobile technologies in the home, on the move and in the classroom?

4   How does the situation described in Table 7.1 mesh with your situation?

5   Is the investment in the home digital technologies being taken into account by the school?

6   What is your vision for schools taking advantage of the substantial investment in digital technologies in the home?

Key messages

- The time has arrived when public policy makers and school decision makers need to recognise the very considerable and growing investment the nation's families are making in digital technologies, actively encourage and support that investment and begin to develop a model of financing where at least part of the operations of a networked school community is financed by the home investment.

- The UK has shown how the public–private model can be applied successfully to the development of schools.

Networked school communities: Possible nature, organisation and leadership

MAL LEE

Networks allow you to build on what you have ...

... The Age of the Network includes all that has gone before, reshapes it, and brings a new spirit and set of capabilities to organizations of every kind and size.

Jessica Lipnack & Jeremy Stamps (1994, p. 28)

Formulating the networked school communities options

As Lipnack and Stamps (1994) suggest, the possible form of the networked school community is almost boundless. In contrast to the traditional school and its years of constancy and fixed walls, the networked school, devoid of those limitations, will always be varying its form as its networks change and as the opportunities to enhance the quality and appropriateness of the offerings emerge and are pursued. This will be so whether one is looking at a two-teacher school catering for a widely dispersed rural community, an inner-city multi-campus school seeking closer links with its diverse community, or an international school operating campuses in different parts of the world.

In the foreseeable future virtually all networked school communities will evolve out of an existing school, will build on the many excellent things that that school is doing, will incorporate the best of the old in the new and will gradually take on an increasingly networked mode. It is likely, in creating the home–school nexus and developing networked school communities, that one is simply attuning the existing mode of schooling to better meet the needs of the times. There is nothing to say that networked school communities couldn't be started anew from the ground up, but that is likely to be some time off, and with all the prerequisite conditions even then with only a few situations.

In beginning the quest to identify the desired form of the networked school community, remember there is no one optimal organisational model that will assist you in realising your desired educational outcomes, but simply some forms that will make the task easier than others. The adoption of the new form ought to be graduated and balanced. You can, if you wish, begin creating the desired home–school nexus and networked school community tomorrow. There are many areas where some schools fall well behind society's and astute educational leaders' expectations of schooling and where, with some astute 'selling', one could soon convince the stakeholders to introduce changes.

It would probably be wise to start small, to ensure you have the support of the key parties and the opportunity to learn from and build upon your experience. All going well you can then ramp up the rate and magnitude of the enhancement. The key, as indicated previously, is to ensure all the changes are designed to contribute in time to the realisation of the desired big picture—the vision you have for your networked school community. We suspect that you will be able to, and indeed will be encouraged to, ramp up your development as the students, teachers and parents begin to realise the many benefits. This has been abundantly evident in those schools that have achieved digital take-off and moved to a digital operating mode (Lee & Gaffney 2008). Structural change might find legislative limitations, be restricted by industrial agreements, be embedded in the dictates of education authorities or simply ingrained in the local culture.

Ultimately, you might need to vary some of those 'structures' to realise your vision, but there is much you can do within the existing parameters. Start by working within them, and then in time when you win the vital political support, seek to overcome the structural impediments. In the same way, you should look to a graduated approach to structural change. You would do well to adopt a similar path in expanding the level of networked collaboration between the professional educators and the parents and students. Many educators, teachers and school and education authority leaders will be wary of expanding the current, even limited collaboration and adopting a more networked mode of operation. They could well find collaboration with the parents and the students and the art of digital networking alien and threatening. They will need to be convinced of the value of both, and the ability to engage in them in a way and at a speed that will add to the educational and/or administrative performance of the school.

Networked organisations bring with them quite different staffing and organisational models. Schools, like industry in the 1990s, will need time to adjust before they can thrive with the new ways. Related is the need to decide the extent to which the school should draw upon the resources of the home, which resources and when. It will be a balance that will be affected by your context and the nature of your homes. That balance will be strongly influenced by the current relationships between the school and the students' homes and the work needing to be done to get the relationship to a point where at least some of the homes and the school can work collaboratively.

Linked is how you want to address the balance between the formal and informal education, those aspects of the informal that ought to be incorporated into the instructional program of the networked school, and the efforts the school should make to highlight the educational importance of the students' informal education. As indicated earlier, the out-of-school student education receives little or no recognition and thus it is an area schools can move into in a graduated form easily and quickly, and which can soon reap significant dividends.

Appreciate that once one removes the traditional school walls and adopts a more networked form, the opportunity to keep the organisation fluid and ever-evolving is considerable. It is a significant variable you need to bear in mind when determining the nature of the networked school community you create and the type of organisation you opt for. You need to also consider the school's facility to capitalise on the major societal and technological trends and indeed shifts within schooling. As discussed earlier, schooling and society are undergoing significant and rapid change, prompted in large by the increasingly sophisticated technology. The art will be to identify the megatrends, to factor them into the school's development and to capitalise on the momentum already underway. Related is the need to balance the achievable with the vision. By removing the school walls, the possibilities are virtually boundless. There is the very real chance that governments and education authorities, probably more so than schools, will overreach in their quest to sell an attractive future. An important potential counter to that overreach, in addition to astute school leaders, is the use that can now be made of high profile Web 2.0 facilities and the media.

Another important safeguard is to involve the politicians in the creation of your desired networked community and thus position yourself against potentially unpopular and ill-conceived propositions from the bureaucrats. For example, if a small rural community moves with political support to realise its desired vision before the bureaucrats conceive their grand plan, it becomes more likely to win the desired high-level support. In considering the desired form of your networked school community and the various options described below, bear in mind the following matrix (Figure 8.1), which has on the one axis the extent of the home–school nexus and on the other the extent of structural change required. For modelling purposes the pre-structural–structural change point is set midway. As you will see from the possible options outlined below, there is actually much that can be done within the existing structures.

Possible options

In suggesting the following options the desire is to simply open your minds to where you might move. You could run with several of the options at the one time, or indeed variations of the ones suggested. Designed astutely, one could integrate several of the options in the one project. The options move from the simple to the increasingly complex, from those in Quadrant 1 through to those in Quadrant 4 where there is a high level of home–school collaboration and significant structural change. These are options that can be taken up by schools anywhere, rural or urban, rich and poor, small and large.

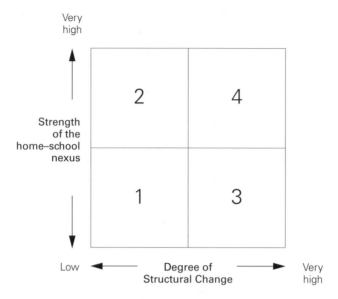

Figure 8.1 A networked schools options matrix

All of the options involve the school leadership and the education authority leadership playing significant roles, and all necessitate the appropriate politicking. In addition, they will need to be addressed by schools conducting full programs already. You are thus going to have to be astute and weave the initiative into the existing operations.

Toes in the water (Quadrant 1)

You can if you want begin to dabble in a host of areas. You could, for example, take advantage of the school's library system, some of the Web 2.0 tools, handle the booking of school functions or parent–teacher interviews online, or simply encourage the teachers to set projects that oblige the students to use the digital resources in their home. Be sure to position each of the developments into a wider vision for the school.

Using the new to improve the old (Quadrant 1)

As mentioned previously, at this point in time virtually all the home–school initiatives are using the new technology basically to improve the ways of old. They have generally been initiated by the professional educators and administrators and are designed to enhance student attainment in the traditional curriculum or to enhance the efficiency of the existing administration. Indeed, most of the learning platforms are characterised by the traditional highly linear, tightly structured instructional programs. Content is 'all important'. Let us be clear that there is nothing wrong in using technology to try and enhance the old ways—for a short period of time. As Naisbitt indicated in *Megatrends* in 1986, this is a normal part of the evolutionary process and is often essential in helping to get all to use the new technology. By all means look to take advantage of the facility, but consciously aim to use it as an introductory phase in the overall development program.

The online learning platforms, as many will be aware, do provide an excellent opportunity to form a greater nexus between the home and school and will in some form be increasingly central in a networked school community, but their focus is going to need to change dramatically if they are to be used successfully in a networked and collaborative teaching and learning community. There has to be genuine collaboration if they are to play the desired role. Many of the current unilateral operations are struggling to gain user acceptance. Of note is that the teacher and student use of the learning platforms is still very low, even in the UK. It is a concern noted by Becta in its 2008 review (Becta 2008a).

This is an excellent potential home–school initiative for both the parents and students to consider, but it is vital to get a birds'-eye view of the current offerings and then decide on the changes to be made if they are to contribute to the desired vision for your networked school. Already it is apparent that online learning offerings can be expensive white elephants. Chapter 13 in *Leading a digital school* (Lee & Gaffney 2008) provides an excellent up-to-date overview of what can be a challenging topic.

Updating the administration and communication (Quadrant 1)

One area where you can make significant improvements in the home–school relationship is within those facets of the school administration and communication that involves the home, both the parents and the students. Parents and students are entitled to expect that schools, like any medium-sized business, should provide the same kind of online services of comparable businesses. It is not unreasonable for families to expect of their school that:

- accounts could be paid online
- permission forms are provided online
- student assessment and report information is available online
- parent–teacher interviews can be booked online
- parents can readily access and edit their account and contact details
- parents can readily identify online the current situation with the processing of any form they submit
- school communiqués are sent electronically, personalised and tailored (e.g. ask if the school newsletter is sent electronically and if not, why?)

- all electronic communiqués invite the parents and students to interact and provide comment online if desired
- they can communicate by email with the teachers.

You can undoubtedly think of other areas where there could and should be far more efficient, effective and inexpensive electronic communication between the home and the school.

Digital teaching hubs (Quadrant 1)

Interestingly, one is seeing across the developed world the rapid evolution of what Mal Lee (2004) has called 'digital teaching hubs', and teachers using the hubs to take teaching into the networked world. This is a rare case of a new technology being used early in its life cycle (Lee & Winzenried 2009) in a significantly different manner to the ways of the past.

The hubs have evolved from the introduction of interactive whiteboards (IWBs), their facility to act as a digital integrator, and astute teachers' realisation that by using the IWBs as a digital hub they are able in their classroom to draw upon an ever-expanding digital toolkit and the networked world to enrich the teaching and learning. Overnight every classroom can become a state-of-the-art library, a largely independent teaching and learning centre and a vehicle for the students to use the networks to enrich their learning. However, each digital teaching hub could markedly enhance its educational capability by networking with like digital teaching hubs elsewhere in the school, the region or, if it wishes, elsewhere in the world. All the technology is in place, and to make it happen requires vision and support. If your school already has IWBs and digital hubs it would be very easy in a pilot, and then in the longer term, to have the digital hubs play a key role in creating and sustaining the desired home–school nexus.

Collaborative vision setting (Quadrants 1–2)

Early, even while discussing the aforementioned type of entry-level initiatives, it is important that the school community begins to discuss the desired big picture, such that all the initiatives contribute in time to its realisation and desired student outcomes. Be collaborative, and be seen to be collaborative. It is likely to be a vital first step on a much longer journey and if handled poorly could be damaging. Open the way for all the stakeholders to be involved and actively promote that opportunity. Appreciate that after years of exclusion many parents and students will take some convincing to contribute, and that it will take some collective acumen to involve those alienated, scared and diffident or disenchanted with schooling. Ensure that extensive use is to be made of the online networking facilities. A tool like Ning (http://www.ning.com), particularly when coupled to the other networking facilities like Twitter, will cost the school community nothing, is quick to configure and can help to engage the wider school community remarkably quickly.

In undertaking this exercise the goal should be to develop a general vision, being conscious that that vision will change as expectations grow and the emerging technology opens new and as yet unimagined opportunities. A simple shift from a 1-mg link to a 100-mg network link, for example, changes the equation dramatically. Handled wisely, you can integrate this initiative with the next.

Networked and collaborative development (Quadrants 1–2)

Many educators and parents have not really participated in online social networking, have not used the facilities in a collaborative exercise and as such don't fully appreciate what one is talking about when one uses the term 'social networking'. They rely on their own traditional frame of reference. It is thus important to acquaint them with those facilities in a meaningful development project, thus fulfilling a series of objectives simultaneously. While it is difficult to explain a facility like automated tags, one can soon see its impact on a social network. Similarly, many have difficulty in appreciating that seemingly impersonal technology can markedly enhance collaboration, particularly among busy people.

Another project you could well consider is one that involves all parts of the school community, the students, the parents and the teachers, and that is how the school and the homes can collaborate in an ongoing manner to both enhance the students' digital citizenship and open discussions on the values of the allied to using the digital technology. This could well be conducted in a primary or secondary school. Such a project could be:

- woven into most social science and communications programs, used as a major integrated project or even incorporated in a religious studies course;
- used to develop the students' research skills, networking, information literacy and interactive multimedia communication and presentation skills;
- employed as an opening to also discuss the role of the home in learning and values formation, the importance of informal learning and the importance of identifying megatrends and their impact.

Recognising student home learning (Quadrants 1–2)

One of the more significant steps you can take is to secure a school community-wide understanding and recognition of the importance of the student learning in the home and to build upon its nature and output. It is very important that all your teachers, parents, students and your politicians appreciate this development. The suspicion is that the majority of teachers, school and education authority leaders largely dismiss the learning taking place in the home as mere play and as such are reluctant to even begin to seriously analyse the learning in the home. The more astute teachers and school leaders are only slowly coming to appreciate the kind of findings found in Chapter 5.

That recognition can be graduated and much can be done at the school level within the existing structures. In many instances the pressure to do so may need to come from the parents and students, but recent experience in running seminars for the leaders of digital schools would suggest that many of the younger principals are conscious of that need. You can start small, even with a particular student cohort. Identify an area or two you want to examine. It might be the use made of peer support, the nature of the social networking employed, multi-tasking or the seemingly chaotic nature of their learning style. Once again contemplate using the online facilities or indeed the various brainstorming programs now available. The initial moves might be for the school's curriculum designers to factor the understanding into the school's instructional program.

Further along the way there could be some recognition of specific attainment, its inclusion in the school's reports, full recognition of prior learning (RPL) and the giving of credit for learning attained or, as mentioned, the school placing priority on educating its students and parents on the importance of informal learning and applying reflection to better understand the place of that learning. Integral to all this work is gaining a fuller appreciation of both the strengths and shortcomings in the home education, and an awareness of those of your families needing learning support. If government does not look after the home technology of the disadvantaged, the wider networked school community could well do so.

Harnessing the home technology (Quadrant 2)

The harnessing can take many forms as there are pathfinding initiatives underway with virtually all of the digital technologies at the moment. Think about where you would like to begin. Take on board suggestions made in this book about the management of that technology. Similarly, ensure the disadvantaged are looked after. Once again start small, and ensure that the students, the parents and the teachers are involved in shaping the initiative and collectively identifying how the chosen technology might enhance the desired learning or administration.

Bear in mind in all you do that the desire will always be to normalise the students' and teachers' use of that technology. Sadly there are too many failures by well-meaning schools obliging parents to spend sizeable money on technology that already exists in the home and is used infrequently in the classroom. In a secondary school, the logical area to start is with the students' Smart phones. A very small development might have to do with the students accessing their own electronic organisers rather than being obliged to have a paper school diary they will never utilise.

Two significant obstacles that will need to be addressed and overcome are the perceptions by teachers and educational administrators that in teaching:

1   all students have to have the same kind of digital technology; and

2   the school has to look after the problems with the students' technology, be it the failure to charge the batteries or to rectify any technical problems.

No business, university or public sector organisation obliges everyone to have the same Smart phone. Outside the classroom, young people successfully take responsibility for their own technology. If they cannot get it working, lose it or fail to charge it they deal with the matter, usually very successfully. One of the challenges you might well take on board is to allow the students to assume that responsibility when they use their technology in the school, and to stop teachers mollycoddling the students. It would save the school significant support monies. Schools might consider providing Wi-Fi download facilities in areas of the school and so allow the students to bypass expensive telecommunication charges.

Most Smart phones not only have organiser or synchronising capacity with the students' desktop, but also have digital cameras, MP3 capability and data storage. Why try and replicate those facilities? What we are suggesting is a significant mindset change on the part of the school, a building upon what is now normal practice in the real world, and the adoption of a set of operational parameters in the classroom in keeping with the real world.

Capitalising on the student expertise (Quadrant 2)

A natural offshoot is to develop the students' appreciation of their digital competencies as well as their communication, personal relations and community service skills by including in the curriculum a program where the older students go into the homes to assist in developing the digital competencies of those in need of assistance. Such an initiative could be woven into existing programs, be used to develop a plethora of key skills, competencies and values, and be a win to the students and the wider networked school community.

Online community forum (Quadrant 2)

The tools of the online world provide a great opportunity for networked school communities to adopt a more democratic type of operation than is currently experienced in most of the schools. Thus far, all the suggested options call for action by the professional educators. A school's parent and/or student community could if it so desired create very quickly and at no cost an online forum that allows all members of the school community to collaborate in the development of the desired network mode. Ideally such a forum ought to be open to all the members of the school community, but if for example the staff did not for some reason participate, there is nothing in a democracy preventing the parents and the students from commenting on the school's operations and, if desired, bringing in the media to place considerable pressure on the school.

This is what has begun to happen in the US. As Brenton Holmes indicates in Chapter 11, there are parent communities that have taken the lead and are exercising their democratic rights by using the tools of the online forum to pressure the school to improve its performance. This potentially powerful facility is one no school administrator can afford to dismiss. It has the capacity—as evidenced in Clay Shirky's management work *Here comes everybody* (Shirky 2008)—to bring about the dismissal of school principals and members of local education authorities. Indeed, in many respects, this facility has far more capacity to shape a school than any league table.

The strong suggestion is that your school community considers very early on taking the lead and creating and actively supporting an online forum, which can take an ongoing, central role in the development of the desired school. Be proactive and avoid placing yourself in the position where you have to react. Take advantage of the many social networking tools available. Encourage the parent and student communities to take the lead. Bearing in mind the kind of bureaucratic controls described earlier and the constraints on web use imposed on many schools, it could be advisable to have the school's parent community take responsibility for the creation and operation of the facility. There is much to be gained by school communities embarking on a quest to harness this facility and its capacity to effectively and efficiently contribute to the ongoing development strategy of your school.

Catering for all (Quadrants 2–3)

Reference was made earlier to the sizeable proportion of school students disenchanted with what schools are offering today, and the inability of schools over the last couple of decades to significantly improve the Year 12 student retention rate. The signs are that this long-term disenchantment is being fuelled by the growing difference between the use of technology in the home and that in the classroom, even among the highly capable students.

If you have not yet viewed on YouTube *A vision for students today* (Wesch 2007), do so and you will appreciate why so many capable young people are finding the current mode of schooling lacking relevance. It is a very powerful video to use as a discussion starter, and indeed 'rationale' for the development of a mode of schooling that is more relevant to today's young people. Give thought to possible home–school and also home–school–work initiatives that take advantage of the networked technology that might make the schooling more relevant, accommodating and attractive.

Look in particular at what can be done with indigenous students and those from social and ethnic groups whose embracement of school has been limited. The digital and networked technologies offer the opportunity for young people, hopefully 100 per cent of young people, to participate in a new kind of 'school game'. Your challenge is to identify how that might be done.

Post-compulsory networked teaching and learning (Quadrant 2)

The post-compulsory school zone is one area that you might examine. This is traditionally where some students drop out, cease applying themselves, and/or don't complete their schooling with the desired credentials and competencies. While it is appreciated that this drop-out is invariably the product of years of disenchantment, hopefully by taking advantage of aspects of the digital, networked technologies more students would be engaged and succeed in an environment they enjoy and respond to, and where there is appropriate support for them. It has not been an easy task in traditional schooling. Many dedicated teachers have tried numerous strategies to lift the success of this group.

The digital, networked technologies and networked school communities offer students, their parents and teachers a new and exciting playing field. The post-compulsory years provide the chance to try new ways of teaching and learning. Not only are the students not compelled by law to attend a physical entity called a school, but also the students are mature enough to take greater responsibility for their actions. In all your thinking with the post-compulsory group, bear in mind their age, their taking on ever-greater responsibility and the desired educational outcomes. Give thought to the following:

- Allow the students to attend only a reduced number of traditional classes blended with online provision. Start with a few select courses. The class time can then be largely given over to discussion and student presentations.

- Use online technologies, such as Skype's video conferencing facility, to conduct tutorials, particularly where families are in geographically challenging locations.

- Draw upon the now extensive experience in online education in the tertiary area to design more collaborative teaching and learning approaches.

- Use the networks to merge the teaching of the senior school with other areas of learning— be it the workplace, community projects, vocational training or tertiary education.

Collaborative teaching and learning (Quadrant 2)

The option that offers very considerable potential to markedly improve the attractiveness of schooling and student achievement is collaborative teaching and learning. What we are suggesting as an option is a marked extension of the current classroom collaboration where the professional educator determines what is appropriate, such as advocated in the writing of Apple and Beane (1999). This involves a genuine collaboration between the home and school, which:

- involves the professional educator collaborating with the parents and the students;

- allows the students of all ages to have their say; and

- provides the opportunity for busy parents, possibly grandparents and/or carers to support the students' learning that takes advantage of the distinctive nature of learning in the home.

Ultimately, the professional educator will be responsible for deciding on the desired teaching, but there is much that the students and the parents can contribute if given the opportunity. We are suggesting that the teachers adopt a far more collaborative, networked mode, rather than one restricted to within the classroom. There are any variations that could be used that take advantage of the digital resources of both the home and the school, at all levels of learning and within all parts of the curriculum. The advice again is to move incrementally and as one learns to ramp up the use.

No mention has been made thus far of the most traditional home–school connection—homework. This is a very dated concept and very much in keeping with the Industrial Age school where the professional educator unilaterally decided on what was appropriate. We suggest that you continue to consider the contemporary education scene from a bird's-eye view to shape your thinking by constantly referencing your desired vision for your networked school community. For example:

- How does the existing homework of your school fit within that vision?
- How might the student endeavour in the home be made more profitable?

Reshaping the playing field (Quadrant 2–3)

Mention was made earlier of the fundamentally different, larger, richer and more flexible playing field one has within the networked school mode on which to play the game called school. Give thought to how your school can best take advantage of the new situation. You should appreciate that there is much you can do within the current structures, but that ultimately some existing structural and legislative impediments will need to be removed before the full field can be used. In the first instance give thought to the following:

- Organise the teaching and the instructional program such that the students and teachers can take best advantage of the group social interaction in the scheduled class time and undertake much of the personal research, with the desired peer support, in the students' very considerable out-of-school time.
- Take advantage of the sizeable proportion of the calendar year when young people are not physically attending school. Young people are involved in a host of informal learning situations—be they travel, musical, dramatic, work related or outdoor education programs outside the normal school times—that could with wise use of the technology and assessment be recognised as part of the networked school curriculum. Similarly, why prevent students undertaking further individualised or indeed peer group study out of the standard 200 school days?

- Provide parents, students and the wider community with a fuller appreciation of the national and personal importance of that learning and give young people and their parents the tools to help enhance that learning. If young people are developing much of their capacity to thrive in a digital world at home, it would be wise to build upon that skill base.

You can use a graduated implementation strategy, carefully experimenting with incremental options rather than being swamped in a vast unknown situation. Take a balanced approach through identifying the options collaboratively with the students and the parents, clearly spelling out the new operating parameters within the school community, and integrate this initiative with others.

Enhancing the role of informal education (Quadrants 2–3)

An option that could have a swift and dramatic impact on student achievement is to mount a concerted school community-wide program to enhance the informal education of your students. In earlier times, great value was placed on the informal education of young people. One of the unintended by-products of developed societies formalising the education of all young people has been to focus virtually all attention on the formal curriculum and markedly diminish the attention and support given to the informal education of young people.

As John Dewey in 1916 presciently flagged the importance in these rapidly changing times of carefully watching the balance between the informal and formal in designing the formal school curriculum, today informal education receives inadequate attention in any debate on the national curriculum. Ironically, this has happened at a time when the educative capacity of the home, accompanied by the immense, growing digital capability discussed earlier, has grown steadily and has assisted developing in several generations of young people a set of competencies and values that have been little impacted by formal schooling. Young people, aside from the occasional support of their parents and their peers, have learned—rightly or wrongly—to educate themselves for their digital world.

The suggestion is that networked school communities could provide educational programs that could quickly and markedly enhance the informal learning of young people, refining competencies and values that could in turn eventually improve overall the nation's performance on the international comparative tables. If educators worked with the parents and the students in highlighting the educational importance of the informal learning, and engendering an understanding and application of the metacognitive and the everyday use of personal reflection, significant educational improvement could be made. Any such program should naturally involve all the members of the school community and in particular the students, the parents, the students' carers and the teachers, be highly collaborative and use the facilities of the home, the classroom and the online world.

Structural change

The following options, as you will soon appreciate, are well along the continuum and would entail the making of structural changes to realise the networked school community's vision conceptualised in Figure 2.1 (p. 22).

A networked school curriculum (Quadrant 4)

Ultimately, networked school communities require a curriculum that accommodates the total 'structured' teaching and learning within the school. By structured we have in mind an instructional program that consciously seeks to develop the formal and informal learning within the chosen playing field. It thus embraces (as shown in Figure 2.2, p. 26) the learning both inside and outside the traditional school walls. The concept might be provocative, particularly to the more reactive and traditional education authorities. It would represent a fundamental mind shift for many educators, bureaucrats, parents and politicians.

Handled in a graduated and balanced manner, this is a logical extension of the earlier thinking and moving beyond the digital school. Many of you will be in schools that largely determine their own curriculum, albeit within the general parameters laid down by the government. Consider your school and ascertain how much freedom it has to vary its instructional program. We would be surprised if it did not offer the school and the leadership the freedom to 'move' at least part of its teaching outside the school walls, to work far more collaboratively with the homes, and to begin the quest of developing a curriculum for a networked school.

Networked towns (Quadrant 4)

A far more ambitious option would be to create a networked school community that networked all the schools of a regional town or city, entailing a mix of early childhood, primary, middle and secondary schools. A strategy would be to launch the initiative in a town with a similar interest—for example, a university town, a major regional hub, a port, a tourist community—to develop a knowledge precinct. With that common interest it is likely the town leaders, the local businesses and the local administration would support such an integrated venture. The potential educational, social, political and economic benefits could be immense.

In a networked world, distance is no longer a significant obstacle, but commonality of interest becomes helpful in a unifying purpose. That common interest would allow the networked school community to make significant efficiencies in the administration of the school, while the independence of the units—the campuses that go to make up the new school—would allow each to readily and flexibly cater for the needs of its particular group of students. The common interest, and the school's overarching unifying purpose, should in turn serve to hold the new, networked school together.

There are likely to be few structural impediments, other than the formal legal standing of the existing schools to bringing the town's schools together. The far bigger issue will be in deciding how many schools to bring together before one loses the community of interest and unified purpose. Theoretically, it is possible to include every school in a province in the one networked school community. In contemplating bringing existing school units together, one does need to strike a balance with how many to include. Where the balance sits is best determined by your community.

Like school communities (Quadrant 4)

A similar kind of networked school community could be developed among a group of like schools situated almost anywhere in the networked world. They could be international schools, possibly belonging to a particular religious order or based on a particular educational philosophy. Again, the community of interest and reciprocal respect are vital. For this option, bear in mind you can always aim for a graduated uptake and decide from that experience the desired configuration.

The nature of the leadership

The role of the leadership in networked school communities will be vital. The challenges facing the school leadership will be considerable. Initially, this will require courage, having to contend with the known, the many opportunities and the pitfalls that will come their way as the school moves into uncharted waters, dealing with constant change, new and emerging digital technologies and an increasingly interconnected digital ecosystem.

In all your thinking and planning for the networked school community do not underestimate the importance and the challenge facing the leadership and the necessity to factor in and resource the leadership's ongoing development. In *Leading a digital school* (Lee & Gaffney 2008), the many interconnected human and technological variables which digital schools had to contend with were identified. The development of networked school communities shifts schooling further along the evolutionary route. In so doing, this presents the leaders with another set of challenges, not least of which will be reconciling elements of both hierarchical and networked organisations.

The organisation of networked school communities provides a paradox in that, while there will be a growing need for leaders to be able to work the networked world, it is essential that schools have and continue to develop leaders who are able to provide leadership in hierarchical positions of responsibility as well as promote less hierarchical forms of organisation. In all networked school communities—as with any other networked organisation—there has to be a person in charge, and people in charge of key operational areas.

The aim (as discussed in Chapter 2) is to create multiple leaders throughout the organisation, leaders who can lead networked project teams, leaders who can show the way in the use of digital teaching hubs, student leaders who can help to ensure that the education provided is both appropriate and effective, and parent leaders able to ensure that the new instructional program maintains the desired formal and informal instructional elements. All need to be able to lead in a collaborative, networked manner.

The reality is that virtually all networked school communities will evolve from an existing school out of its existing leadership team. The principal's challenge, working in collaboration with the community, will be to develop an organisational structure appropriate to the new circumstances. This will take time, and he or she will be obliged to astutely balance the hierarchical, including the bureaucratic elements of the organisation, and the networked.

Your task in identifying the desired vision for your networked school community will be to adopt an organisational model that will support your vision, will facilitate networking and collaboration, will develop, support and sustain multiple formal and informal leaders and will be flexible enough to change as the need arises. Be cautious in understanding that if the school is to develop as a networked school community, it cannot do so using a strongly organisational mode where those in authority decide what is done. Retain that mode and the school can forget any significant shift in its operations. Changing the existing organisational mode can be a major challenge, particularly in some highly bureaucratic educational authorities, but with the astute assistance of potentially immensely powerful 'Internet Age' parents, that challenge is not insurmountable.

All organisational change will entail some kind of small 'p' politicking. In some situations some large 'P' politics may need to be invoked to bring about the desired change. The reality is that all school leaders need to apply the art of politicking change. While education authority employers may be unable to be involved in large 'P' politics, there is nothing—as Shirky (2008) aptly indicates—stopping the school's home community using the tools and power of the online world to help the leadership bring about change.

Conclusion

The potential of the shift to a networked schooling mode is immense. You can combine all the best of the traditional school while at the same time move to a digital school and subsequently become a networked school community. Most importantly, you can undertake that quest in graduated steps, planning, implementing, reviewing and making improvements as you move forward.

Appreciate that schools internationally will also be making these same kinds of steps and that the social networks allow you to learn not only from your own experiences but also from those pathfinder schools and education authorities. With the networks, removal of the old school walls and the associated limitations provides you with the potential and possibilities for adopting a far superior form of organisation made possible by digital technologies than what you have at the moment.

Guiding questions

After reading this chapter, consider your context and propose your ideas in relation to the following guiding questions.

1   What is your vision for your school as a networked school community in the next three to five years?

2   In what areas could your school make its initial moves to become a networked school community?

3   What are some of the more substantial developments you would like your school to make?

4   What are the major changes that will be needed in the organisational structure to facilitate the desired changes?

5   What leadership will be needed to realise the desired changes?

6   What are your thoughts about the ways in which government could provide support and encouragement? For example, consider tax incentives for families and addressing the needs of disadvantaged families.

Key messages

- In the foreseeable future virtually all networked school communities will evolve out of an existing school, will build on the many excellent things that that school is doing, will incorporate the best of the old in the new and will gradually take on an increasingly networked mode.

- In considering the desired form of your networked school community and the various options described in the chapter, bear in mind the extent of the home–school nexus, and the extent of structural change required.

CHAPTER 9

Developing an information paradigm approach to build and support the home–school nexus

LYN HAY

Collaborative, networked learning alters also how we think about learning institutions, and network culture about how to conceive of institutions more generally. Traditionally, institutions have been thought about in terms of rules, regulations, norms governing interactivity, production, and distribution within the institutional structure. Network culture and associated learning practices and arrangements suggest that we think of institutions, especially those promoting learning, as mobilizing networks. The networks enable a mobilizing that stresses flexibility, interactivity, and outcome. And the mobilizing in turn encourages and enables networking interactivity that lasts as long as it is productive, opening up or giving way to new interacting networks as older ones ossify or newly emergent ones signal new possibilities. Institutional culture thus shifts from the weighty to the light, from the assertive to the enabling.

Cathy Davidson & David Goldberg (2009, pp. 33–34)

A paradigm shift

Only now are we experiencing the potentials and challenges of networked school communities. In Chapter 2, Mal Lee argues that the challenges schools now face are not technological, but human. While this chapter supports this view, it also presents another important element in effectively forging and shaping the home–school nexus. This element is the development of an information paradigm approach to integrating information, technology and learning within a networked school community. An information paradigm approach views the world through a lens of *information*, where schools develop an information vision encompassing information as philosophy, skills, product, process and policy (Hay 2001; 2004), and where the technical and administrative aspects of technology management are secondary to the learning agenda within the school. In this digitally driven age, we are constantly confronted with new technological possibilities and the digital skills and understandings that students are required to develop are being translated, expanded and transformed into an ever-increasingly complex set of functionalities and capabilities. The development and continual reinforcement of this complex set of functionalities and capabilities are at the heart of an information paradigm approach.

This concept of an information paradigm as central to a networked school's world view facilitates the breaking down of silo-based mentalities where information, technology and learning are compartmentalised and disjointed, rather than integrated as one movement that underpins the daily work and learning practices within a school. In this chapter we explore the changing nature of school-age learners as the 'connected generation' and their information behaviour and needs as digital citizens; and we examine the traditional provision of information and technology services in schools and propose the concept of an iCentre as a vehicle for achieving greater integration of information, technology and learning efforts, both in the school and home, to support the development of young people as digital citizens. The chapter concludes with some ideas about how a networked school community can implement an information paradigm approach as a solution to building and supporting the home–school nexus.

The 'connected generation'

School-age children born in the 1990s have grown up surrounded by a world of high technological sophistication. The world of digital citizenship is the only world they have known. A recent UK report for the Committee of Inquiry into the Changing Learner Experience (2009) describes this generation as having 'a strong sense of a community linked in its own virtual spaces of blogs and social networking and gaming sites; a similarly strong sense of group identity; and a disposition to share and to participate', who are also impatient learners who have 'a preference for instant answers; a downgrading of text in favour of image; and a casual approach to evaluating information and attributing it, and also to copyright and legal constraints' (Committee of Inquiry into the Changing Learner Experience 2009, p. 39).

The digitally driven, socially networked world is both the reality and future of young people as the 'connected generation', and it is not going to go away. Our young people know no other life than the techno-filled one in which they have grown up. They are gamers, they are 'iPod-ders', they are far more connected with their friends (via social networks) beyond school hours than their teachers will ever experience. Their PCs and mobile phones are their lifeline. These give them the privacy to network with their friends. With one or more digital devices as their daily personal toolkit, they need to be connected to some level or levels of activity, usually while doing more than one thing at a time. They are multi-taskers, they lead very busy, digital info-entertainment lives, and they seem to cope with this much better than their Baby Boomer or Gen X parents ever will (Hay 2008).

The tension and challenge for education systems worldwide is to embrace the shift digital technologies can afford schools and learning as we know it. A recent *New York Times* interview with an Orange Country School District superintendent (as a result of the Californian governor's announcement to replace high school science and math texts with free, open-source digital versions) called for schooling to finally get out of that 'brick-and-mortar, 30-students-to-1-teacher paradigm' and start 'having 200 or 300 kids taking courses online, at night, 24/7, whenever they want' (Lewin 2009, p. A1). Solomon and Schrum (2007) argue that Web 2.0 is an opportunity for schools to adopt a 'new way [of learning which] is collaborative, with information shared, discussed, refined with others, and understood deeply' (p. 21). They argue if schools are to prepare students to become part of a 'nimble workforce that makes decisions and keeps learning as the workplace changes', students need to be taught twenty-first century learning and life skills 'using a flexible approach rather than teaching just what will be tested' (p. 21). This paradigm shift extends to the way schools support the information and technology needs of students.

Today's students are the 'one click' generation, they want immediate access to information with minimal fuss and, for many, home has become where the majority of their online learning takes place. Reporting on the Student Learning through Australian School Libraries project in a 2006 conference paper, 'Are Internet–savvy kids@home the new information poor?', the author concluded:

> *With the increasing number of students in Australia with Internet access at home, 24/7 access to a range of quality online resources and services through the school library is essential if school libraries are to remain central to students' informational and technological worlds.*

> Hay (2006c, p.10)

This message resonates in much of the writing of US-based media specialists such as Valenza (2005/2006), Church (2005), Harris (2006) and Hauser (2007), who strongly campaign for teachers and information specialists to find new ways of connecting with their students online and at the point of need.

As we move towards the next decade, are we there yet? How successful have schools been in 'connecting' with students at home, and why this urgency to do so?

Digital information behaviour of young people

The new and emerging field of research examining the digital information behaviour of young people, commonly referred to as 'the Google generation', is central to the business of school libraries and education in general. Students prefer to use search engines to find information, with the Internet being their first 'port of call' (Conole et al. 2006).

The research report, *Information behaviour of the researcher of the future* (Rowlands & Nicholas 2008) presents what we currently know about young people's information behaviour.

The authors conclude that there are a number of problems or weaknesses in students as information users:

- The information literacy of young people has not improved with the widening access to technology.

- Young people have unsophisticated mental maps of what the Internet is, often failing to appreciate that it is a collection of networked resources from different providers.

- Many young people do not find library-sponsored resources intuitive and therefore prefer to use Google or Yahoo instead.

- As a result, a search engine, be it Yahoo or Google, becomes the primary 'brand' that they associate with the Internet—this also relates to 'brands' of Web 2.0 tools—with a tendency to adopt the tools their friends use.

- The speed of young people's web searching means that little time is spent in evaluating information, either for relevance, accuracy or authority.

- They tend to move rapidly from page to page, spending little time reading or digesting information and have difficulty making relevance judgements about the pages they retrieve.

- Observational studies have shown that young people scan online pages very rapidly (boys especially) and click extensively on hyperlinks, rather than reading sequentially.

- Young people have a poor understanding of their information needs, thus find it difficult to develop effective search strategies.

- They make very little use of advanced search facilities, assuming that search engines 'understand' their queries.

- Faced with a long list of search hits, young people find it difficult to assess the relevance of the materials presented and often print off pages with no more than a glance at the value of the information, or copy and paste into a Word document.

(Source: Rowlands & Nicholas 2008, p. 12)

These findings are also supported by the research of others with regard to young people's lack of sophisticated information-based competencies and understandings (Hay in press; Gross & Latham 2007; Large 2006; Heinström 2006; Heinström & Todd 2006; OCLC 2005; Broch 2000; Ebersole 1999). A major concern for educators is that young people are increasingly gaining greater access to information and technology at home compared with that afforded at school. This minimises opportunities for instructional intervention at the point of need, which is critical given the growing body of research evidence showing that young people need to develop greater understanding of information ethics in terms of their own privacy and online safety, as well as respecting the privacy and online safety of others. Acquisti and Gross (2006) found that young people are very willing to reveal personal information to strangers as well as friends on sites like MySpace, Friendster and Facebook, with changing cultural trends, familiarity and confidence in technology use, and lack of exposure or memory of the misuses of personal data by others all playing a role in such information revelation.

Young people desire privacy from their parents and teachers. The phrase 'Get out of my space' aptly captures this desire for privacy, and digital technology supports them in achieving this. Research about young people's social use of the online world has found it not uncommon for young people to live 'undercover lives' using fake profiles within their friend networks while maintaining the G-rated profiles that their parents monitor (boyd 2007), and students frequently use instant and/or text messaging to keep their conversations private from parents and teachers (Livingstone 2007). The following quote by danah boyd (2007) illustrates the tenuous relationship between parents and their children with regard to online safety:

> Teens often fabricate key identifying information like name, age, and location to protect themselves. While parents groups often encourage this deception to protect teens from strangers, many teens actually engage in this practice to protect themselves from the watchful eye of parents. (p.15)

In addition, the increasing number of cyber-bullying cases in schools has become a national problem for many countries including the US (Brydolf 2007; Szoka & Thierer 2009; Wang, Iannotti & Nansel 2009), UK (Carter 2009; Lipsett 2009; *The Guardian* 2009) and Australia (Abrahams & Dunn 2009; Bazley 2009; Dikeos 2009; Internet Industry Association 2009). The fact that education systems are only now grappling with the impact of digital technologies on student behaviour, and with few parents having the knowledge and skills to engender ethical information and technology use, we are seeing a widening educational, psychological and sociological gap between the face-to-face and online worlds of adults and young people. Without informed and cleverly targeted instructional interventions in schools, what young people learn about living in an online world they will continue to learn from their social networks.

So what can we do to educate young people in terms of values, morals, ethics, civic rights and responsibilities, if students are not provided with access to Web 2.0 tools and experiences as part of their school education?

A school community needs to develop a much stronger and explicit information ethics curriculum that becomes integrated across subjects—this cannot just be taught in computing classes! While some would argue the Human Society and Environment and Health and Professional Development curricula lend themselves to the teaching of information ethics, wherever Internet and Web 2.0 tools are used to support the learning activities (no matter what subject or grade level), teachers and information specialists need to ensure that measures are in place to teach students at the point of need about an aspect of information ethics when issues, problems or opportunities arise (Hay 2008). Every teacher in our schools must become information ethics aware. So too, must parents of school-age children. Ethical information behaviour is not just a school-based phenomenon, it is central to students' information- and technology-based 'worlds' within the home environment. Schools need to recognise the fundamental importance of informal education, and seek new ways to support parents in developing more independence in terms of learning assistance within the home environment to support what students 'do' or experience at school. This has been identified as a key goal for UK schools in *Harnessing technology for next generation learning: Children, schools and families implementation plan 2009–2012* (Becta 2009a), and is attainable for schools that have developed an information paradigm that acknowledges and supports the home–school nexus. In the latter part of this chapter we will explore ways of achieving this goal.

Information technology access versus developing digital citizens

A recent Australian study in students' use of Web 2.0 technologies to support inquiry learning identified the different ways access can be an inhibitor or enabler to the effective use of technologies to support student learning (Hay in press). The study concluded that accessibility is a critical determinant of technology adoption and use, with students highlighting a range of home-related and school network issues that impact on their access to technology tools, programs and services, and potential information sources. Technology access issues affecting student learning when doing schoolwork from home included personal computer (PC) ownership, PC quality in terms of age and speed, and type of Internet access at home (in terms of speed and availability).

Students interviewed as part of this study also identified a range of school network issues that affected their access to and use of technology (Hay in press). Levels of 'up-to-dateness' of computer technologies throughout the school were identified as problematic for some, especially those living in boarding house facilities on the school premises, where students' PCs were considered 'old' and 'too slow' to complete tasks in a timely manner. The different levels of Internet access across the school precinct (e.g. in class, school library, boarding house and remote access) in terms of the time one has to access the Internet before, during and after school, was identified as an issue, as were filtering issues such as blocked web resources and web tools and students needing to use web proxies to by-pass the school's firewall. As one student explained:

> ... another thing that really set me back was the school filter thing. Because whenever I was trying to search for information, the school said, this has been blocked for ... I don't know whatever reason ... So, basically 80 per cent of the work was done at home.
>
> (Hay in press)

The study found that inconsistency of access between school and home can determine whether a student will use or not use a particular technology. Limited Internet access at school due to network filters can either restrict student access to potentially valuable educational resources or encourage students to employ unethical technology behaviours to gain 'better' access to the Internet; for example, students' use of web proxies to access those websites blocked by the school filtering system, such as the following:

http://peachsurf.info/

http://www.gtnetwork.net/

http://www.ibebo.info/

http://www.webproxyonline.info/.

(See http://forums.digitalpoint.com/showthread.php?t=301819 and http://www.gotgames.com.au/forums/general-discussion-165/proxy-sites-32276/ for examples of thousands of potential proxy addresses that students could register for themselves or use if registered by others.)

The above examples reinforce the need elaborated upon in Chapter 16 for schools to rethink their approach to information and technology access.

Devaney (2008) argues that 'public education is social networking' (p. 3), so why not help students learn how to properly socially network within the digital world? In a recent Consortium for School Networking (CoSN) webcast, Devaney explored how schools can use Web 2.0 tools to foster collaboration and innovation in classrooms, and the message of 'think before you ban' was presented. In other words, before school systems and school administrators prohibit teachers and students from accessing certain websites and resources, they need to explore the positive impact those sites might have on education. How many teachers work in, or have worked in, a school or education system where this 'thinking before banning' approach is the norm? My guess is very few! Restricted network access and Internet filtering is a worldwide problem in compulsory education, an agenda which is fuelled by regulatory and technical controls instead of being based on a foundation of informed technology use, effective learning design and sound pedagogy. Devaney (2008) advises when it comes to Web 2.0 technologies:

- Find those technologies that 'lend themselves very well to teaching 21st-century learning skills ... to prepare kids for the workforce they'll be facing when they leave school'. (p. 1)

- Focus on the use of tools that support *learning*, helping students understand the processes and potential application of particular tools, and help them develop the skills in 'knowing how to adapt' tools that can be translated to use personally and in life beyond school. (p. 2)

- Educators need to find a balance that allows for creativity, collaboration *and* safety as digital technologies rapidly evolve.

This is strongly supported by Internet safety and child protection organisations such as UK-based Childnet International, whose report on young people's use of social networking sites (SNSs) argues the importance of students being able to access SNSs at school to help students develop sophisticated technology, literacy and communication skills, and to help them become informed, digital citizens:

> *E-safety covers a range of online issues but ties in firmly to the real world: staying safe, keeping personal information safe, protecting yourself and your belongings. Making sure that we don't participate in bullying or other anti-social behaviour, and helping out other people who might be affected by these issues, is a key part of digital citizenship.*

Childnet International (2008, p. 15)

In terms of information infrastructure, Hay and Foley (2009) recently identified additional challenges for schools in terms of resourcing the curriculum and supporting twenty-first century learning. Those not previously mentioned include:

- an information landscape containing a growing e-book industry, publishing-on-demand and other electronic publishing initiatives that use mobile and Web 2.0 tools;

- the development of library systems that are more user friendly, integrated and seamless in their delivery as information and resource portals (blended digital collections, federated searching);

- the effect of the diversification of access platforms on remote and digital information service provision;

- the increasing popularity of data mash-ups, transforming the way information is represented, making it harder to determine the authority and authenticity of information.

(Source: Hay & Foley 2009, p. 20)

The impact(s) of these will be explored later in this chapter. Based on what we now know, how can schools develop an information paradigm to effectively build and support the home–school nexus? The author proposes that the answer lies in firstly addressing the existing divide between the library/information and technology units within schools, out of which emerges a new information-based, technology-enriched learning centre.

Introducing the concept of an iCentre in schools

It is essential that library/information service and technology departments be re-engineered to achieve synergy and functionality that transcend the traditional paradigms of twentieth-century schools. In the mid-1990s, Australian educators and school administrators were challenged with the idea of transforming the traditional school library into an information services unit with a Chief Information Officer at the helm (Lee 1996b, 2004; Hay & Kallenberger 1996; Hay 2001, 2004). While few schools have embraced this challenge, in the past decade a number of universities and colleges have been exploring new ways of providing integrated information technology learning spaces that also draw upon a sense of community and meeting the social needs of students (Cook 1995; Oden et al. 2001). This has led to the design of 'information commons' or 'knowledge commons' (Lippincott 2006).

Oblinger's (2006) work on learning spaces (see http://www.educause.edu/LearningSpaces) features many ways of thinking differently about 'learning spaces' in educational institutions. One major advantage of this 'commons' approach is marrying (and in many cases, reconciling!) existing library/information and technology departments (including people, resources and services) within an educational institution to better reflect this convergence of information and technology within a digital society. The Australian National University's (ANU) Division of Information is an example of this 'marriage', with combined information and IT help desks on the ground floor of each of its refurbished library ('commons') buildings. Stanton (2003) states the main purpose of this convergence was 'to balance resource allocation and priority setting', thus re-engineering the universities' information infrastructure. Of particular note is the emphasis on 'i' and not 'IT' infrastructure!

It is time that twenty-first century schools consider this convergence of facilities, technologies, people and resources. Hence this proposal to introduce the concept of an 'iCentre' for schools. What is an iCentre? It is the central facility within the school where information, technology, learning and teaching needs are supported by qualified information and learning technology specialists. It is a centre that provides students and teachers with a one-stop shop for all resourcing, technology and learning needs on a daily basis. Flexible access to computers, printers, Internet and other digital resources, including teaching expertise, before school and at non-class times, is valued highly by students, and they link their academic success to such support (Hay 2005; 2006b).

Findings from the Student Learning through Australian School Libraries research project demonstrated that students have an increasing dependence on and demand for a school library facility that provides them with access to state-of-the-art technologies, resources, services and teaching to support their learning. Students in this study identified their school library as a dynamic and unique place within the school precinct, compared with classrooms, computer labs and other specialist rooms, because of the availability and flexibility of the resources and services of the school library as a facility and the individualised and customised attention the information specialist and library staff could provide them at the point-of-need (Hay 2006a). The vision these students had of their school library is significantly similar to the concept of an 'iCentre', especially in smaller primary schools where the information specialist has also held the position of learning technologies coordinator.

While the iCentre is a high-end multimedia production facility, it is also a flexible learning space or 'place for collaboration, performance, creativity, interactivity and exploration, both online and offline' (Schibsted 2005). The philosophy underpinning the iCentre is similar to that employed by information schools (known as iSchools) in universities around the world— that of bringing information, technology and people together to support the machinations of the knowledge society. The concept of 'i' also builds on the successes of Apple Corporation's i-generation of digital technologies which are iconic of twenty-first century life. Ken Maher, Sydney-based architect and Professor of Architecture at the University of New South Wales, was recently asked what he thought was the most innovative product design. His answer?

The continuing editions of Apple computers, including iPod and iPhone—a communications and education revolution of outstanding design, lineage and adaptive reinvention.

Q Magazine (July 2009, p. 80)

Schools need to consider how this proposed iCentre concept can contribute to the 'education revolution' required for schools to re-invent themselves as twenty-first century learning organisations. It is time! A school's iCentre should reflect what Solomon and Schrum (2007) call 'those features of the global economy that represent the changing nature of the 21st century workplace (interconnectedness, immediacy, interactivity, communications and community)' (p. 24). Add to that the nature of inquiry learning, information fluency, learning innovation, explicit instruction and the development of students as independent, informed digital citizens, and we have just described the core business of an iCentre.

Schools can re-shape their existing information and technology infrastructures to 'build' an iCentre. For many schools, the school library facility could be the place to begin because an iCentre builds on and expands the portfolio of school libraries as we have traditionally known them. School architects and change agents for education Prakash Nair and Annalise Gehling (2007) support this view, stating that while libraries continue to evolve 'the purpose and experience of libraries will change, and change again, in their physical and virtual iterations' (p. 6). Research shows that a school library program contributes to building student confidence, independence and sense of responsibility for learning (Kuhlthau 2004; Lonsdale 2003; Dyer 2001; Murray 1999).

With the merging of information and technology resources, services and instruction, an iCentre will be better equipped to support learners in the twenty-first century with relevant, flexible, 24/7, customised information, technology and learning services, and provide customised 'i' support for teachers, school administrators and parents. At the heart of an iCentre is a qualified team of information, technology and learning experts whose knowledge, skills and motivations reflect the Chinese philosophy of 'yin-yang', the 'process of harmonisation ensuring a constant, dynamic balance of all things' (Wang 2006).

Jorge Madrid (founder of edutechnia.org) in his presentation 'Why technology is failing in public schools' argues 'For technology to be effective, truly cohesive teams is a must'. He provides five critical ingredients to achieving such cohesiveness:

1   Trust one another.

2   Engage in unfiltered conflict around ideas.

3   Commit to decisions and plans of actions.

4   Hold one another accountable for delivering against those plans.

5   Focus on the achievement of collective results.

Madrid (n.d. Slide 36)

This advice is fundamental to the success of an iCentre with a shared vision and synergistic partnerships between team members resulting in collaborative and concrete actions.

Pedagogical fusion—strengthening the home–school nexus

Pedagogical fusion is the ultimate goal of an iCentre—bringing information, technology, people and pedagogy together to support student learning, both in school and at home. Pines (2007) argues that classroom instruction is supplemented by personal tutoring, 'either at their kitchen table, in the library, in a retail centre, on the Web, or at school' (p. vii). The philosophy underpinning pedagogical fusion in terms of instructional support and intervention is that people value opportunities for 'teachable moments' with regard to technology use, information ethics, higher-order thinking skills and knowledge construction—*any time, any place, anywhere, anyhow.* The power of pedagogical fusion stems from the fact that students, teachers, iCentre staff, parents and the broader school community are all working together to achieve informed technology use and effective learning through information, through innovative and authentic learning experiences at school and in the home, thus transforming and consolidating the home–school nexus.

Anderson (2006) argues that in a Web 2.0 world, the 'come to us' model of library service is over. We need to:

> ... *find new ways to bring our services to patrons rather than insisting that they come to us—whether physically or virtually. At a minimum, this means placing library services and content in the user's preferred environment (i.e. the Web); even better, it means integrating our services into their daily patterns of work, study and play.*

The concept of the iCentre embraces this philosophical shift in service provision to be relevant to learners in the twenty-first century, where quality customer service and satisfaction underpin the 'service ethic'. The work of Bishop (2006) and his team in a rural school district in the United States captures this 'ethic' when he states, 'Our goal is to make the total customer experience satisfying, pleasurable and resulting in an end-product that meets or exceeds their expectations. Students should always feel welcome.' Some examples of online information services and 'learning through information' scaffolds that an iCentre could provide to support the home–school nexus include access to the following:

- An integrated Web 2.0-enhanced library catalogue (Google-ised) and learning management system (LMS) (such as Drupal or Moodle), which allows seamless access to resources and learning materials, collaborative learning spaces, and teacher and student personal folders both at school and from home (Note: http://fish4info.org/ is an excellent example of a next-generation school library catalogue);

- An extensive collection of free and subscription-based quality e-texts, e-books, e-journals and online reference services, with functionality to add user-generated entries for rating and recommending these resources (think Amazon.com);

- Custom-designed assignment-, subject- and class-based portals within the LMS that provide direct access to purposefully selected digital resources (the aim being to provide ready access to information with 'one click' or minimal 'clicks'), integrated with learning support documents such as at assignment tasks and criteria, checklists and rubrics;

- Online templates and scaffolds to support the research process, which reinforces the language and strategies of the information process model adopted by the school community;

- Online pathfinders and topic-based resource guides that include recommended search terms for relevant databases, subject directories and search engines, and online tutorials and downloadable handouts on selecting appropriate search engines (including Google), evaluating web resources and how to correctly cite and reference sources;

- Online guides providing advice on unpacking assignment questions, developing topic outlines using concept mapping software, note taking and essay construction;

- A rich collection of audio books and downloadable podcasts, with MP3 players available for loan, as well as a selection of wireless laptop computers, Netbooks and digital cameras for loan for both in-school and at-home use;

- Assistance for teachers to use the LMS to provide a range of learning experiences using Web 2.0 tools to support knowledge construction and collaborative learning activities for students from home (particularly for those students absent from school due to illness);

- Encouragement for students and teachers to trial the use of online tools that allows them to have any time, anywhere access to projects, assignments and 'learning or construction spaces', e.g. Google Apps for Education and VoiceThread;

- Encouragement for teachers to use sites like SchoolTube, which support collaboration and teach responsible use of sharing video;

- Information sessions and training workshops for school administrators, teachers and parents about information policy issues that impact on the daily life of teachers and students, such as students' online safety, cyber-bullying, privacy, intellectual property rights and copyright, plagiarism;

- An innovation 'space' within the iCentre where students, teachers, information and technology specialists have access to 'explore, test, play and invent' with new and emerging technologies without the constraints of network and filtering restrictions.

(Drawn upon and adapted from Hay 2006b, 2008; Bishop 2006; Usher 2009)

Each of the above contributes to the iCentre's goal of achieving pedagogical fusion and building and supporting the home–school nexus.

Shifting towards an information paradigm: Where to begin?

A networked school community can gradually shift its philosophy and infrastructure towards an information-based world view by drawing upon some of the implementation variables referred to in Chapter 19 of this book. For example, **identify and pursue the unifying vision** of an iCentre for your school. What information, technology and learning infrastructures already exist in your school, and how can these be transformed to achieve a more holistic approach to building and supporting the home–school nexus? How can the people, resources, facilities and budgets of your existing school library and technology departments be re-engineered to create an iCentre?

As an administrator, school board member, classroom teacher, information specialist or parent, think of ways you can **sell the concept** to others by employing a WIIFM ('what's in it for me') approach to stakeholders: How can an iCentre better meet different stakeholders' goals and needs? How can an iCentre improve the quality of learning and teaching in the school? How can an iCentre approach allow the school to achieve greater returns on its investment in terms of resources, technologies, people, pedagogy, access and time?

Plan and implement holistically in terms of digital citizenship across the curriculum. Grappling's Technology and Learning Spectrum (Porter 2002) provides an instructional framework for assessing and organising three broad categories of technology uses with students, with a focus on sustaining and improving student achievement, and ultimately an iCentre team will assist teachers in developing skills and practices in moving beyond the teaching of 'technology literacies' to transforming uses of digital technologies (i.e. **openly use the new to improve the old**). Churches' (2009) digital taxonomy of Bloom's Revised Taxonomy provides teachers with guidelines on how to build a student-centred, constructivist pedagogy through the integration of technologies to facilitate complex learning and higher-order thinking skills. This taxonomy is designed 'to account for the new behaviours, actions and learning opportunities emerging as technology advances and becomes more ubiquitous' (Churches 2009, p. 3).

In addition, extend the capacity for mentoring beyond iCentre staff to **develop greater independence** in networked school community members. For example, how can an iCentre program **contribute to greater staff readiness** in terms of achieving pedagogical fusion? Consider tapping into the skills of students, with an iCentre-led e-tutoring program where students in, say, Year 6 support students in Year 3 with technology support via email or instant messaging out of school hours, or a school might collaborate with a local college or university with a teacher education program where trainee teachers are partnered with students in Year 8 to collaborate on e-learning projects or homework help (Johnson & Bratt 2009).

Valenza (2003) argues that with the Internet now affording 'students a great deal of independence, often removing adult consultation from the research process', and with many students working independently at home on information-based tasks and research projects, parents need to consider the ways they can help students 'create quality research products and encourage them to reflect on their work' (p. 30). So don't forget to **strengthen the parent-home connection** within your networked school community. Valenza (2003) suggests seven ways parents can become more involved in their children's learning at home:

1   Ask your child if he or she has used subscription databases to support their research and gain access to quality online references, e-books and journals through your local school, public or state library.

2   Ask to help as your child brainstorms potential research questions and thesis statements.

3   'Good researchers search for credibility, authority, accuracy, and relevance', so ask your child to show you the list of different resources they have used to support their research, and talk about the quality of the information they have found.

4   'Look for research holes' Has your child used the best words to search for the most relevant information they need for their project? Help them develop a list of search words to 'fill the gaps' in their project.

5   'Is your child in a search engine rut?' Not all search engines have the same function, focus or resource pool they draw upon. Refer to a recommended list of search engines from your school, public or state library website to help your child develop a 'suite' of possible search engines to use for future school work.

6   Offer to proofread your child's work to see if they have been able to present their ideas in their own words and support their own argument, thesis or debate with evidence from their references.

7   If the Internet is not supporting your child with all of the information they need to inform a project, think about searching for books and other print or digital materials. In Valenza's words, 'does your child need to put the laptop down and get a lift to a library?'

(Source: Valenza 2003, p. 31)

School administrators and leading staff and parents who are keen to realise the iCentre vision will need to **opt for graduated and balanced change** within their networked community. Such change requires a carefully, well-crafted program of consultation, collaboration and policy development that involve all levels of administration, teachers, specialist staff, parents, students and the community. Finally, remember to **measure your attainments** throughout the process—collect and analyse data, seek and document evidence, share your experiences and results, and celebrate your achievements (Todd 2007; Loertscher & Todd 2003).

Conclusion

In this digitally driven age we are constantly confronted with new technological possibilities, and it is through these digital technologies that young people are challenged to become 'social participants and active citizens', 'content creators, managers and distributors', 'explorers and learners' and 'collaborators and team players' who need to develop a voice and build trust, develop independence and build resilience, and develop critical and real-world skills (Childnet International 2008, p. 14).

This chapter has argued that an information paradigm approach can assist schools in developing an information vision encompassing information as philosophy, skills, product, process and policy, where the technical and administrative aspects of technology management are secondary to the learning agenda within the school. This vision can be realised through the creation of an iCentre, transforming the resources, technologies, people and expertise of library/information services and technology departments into a high-end multimedia production facility and flexible learning space, which provides teachers, information and learning technology specialists, students and parents opportunities to collaborate, create, interact, explore and learn—both online and offline—at school and in the home.

Networked school communities need to achieve greater integration of information, technology and learning efforts, both in the school and home to support the development of young people as digital citizens as we move towards 2020. An information paradigm approach is one solution to building and supporting the home–school nexus. Is your school community ready for this challenge?

Guiding questions

After reading this chapter, consider your context and propose your ideas in relation to the following guiding questions.

1   In relation to your school's information paradigm, where do young people go initially when searching for information? The school? The home?

2   How well does your current school library/information services unit feature in that search for information?

3   What do you think could be done by the school to develop young people's use of digital technologies for accessing, selecting, managing and analysing information?

4   Do you think that there is collaboration between the school's digital technologies infrastructure staff and the school's library/information services staff?

5   What changes would have to be made to create the kind of iCentre suggested in this chapter? What could be the first moves?

6   To what extent should the home and the students be responsible for the storage and management of their own digital resources? What should be the role of the school, and the role of the education system, and government in storing information?

Key messages

- An important element in effectively forging and shaping the home–school nexus is the development of an information paradigm approach to integrating information, technology and learning within a networked school community.

- An information paradigm approach can assist schools in developing an information vision encompassing information as philosophy, skills, product, process and policy where the technical and administrative aspects of technology management are secondary to the learning agenda within the school.

CHAPTER 10

Collaboration in the development of twenty-first century learning: Reality or dream?

LORRAE WARD & JUDY PARR

The way we think about learning environments is changing. Because technology is so pervasive in our lives, the learning environment is no longer limited to a physical space. Today, the notion of a 'classroom' includes experiences, experts, collaborators, peers, and resources located all over the globe and available twenty-four hours a day. To take advantage of this trend, institutions must reflect and support the transformation of the learning environment that make it possible ... that facilitate collaboration, communication, and learning.

Johnson et al. (2009, p. 4)

Connecting and collaborating — the stories of three schools

This chapter articulates the potential relationship between two powerful notions relating to education for the twenty-first century. The first of these is the idea that to strengthen learning there should be a stronger and more seamless connection between the home and school, and that this should be focused on student learning. There is strong evidence to suggest that when families, schools and communities work together, higher student achievement, improved student behaviour and more positive school climates are found (Henderson & Mapp 2002). The second is that schools should become digital in the same way that the world around them has. This latter notion is driven, at least partially, by a desire to promote twenty-first century learning ideals in terms of the knowledge, skills and dispositions needed to have agency as a citizen in the twenty-first century (Scrimshaw 2004), although there are other economic and social rationales (Parr & Ward 2004).

Both these notions have resonance theoretically in that both are aimed at enhancing learning. There is, however, a disconnect between the ideals they express and the realities of implementation. Examples of the successful integration of digital technologies into classrooms in ways that enrich and extend the learning experiences of students, while increasing, remain limited (Cox et al. 2003a, 2003b; Hayes 2007). Further, the clear delineation between school and home still exists both physically and in terms of roles and responsibilities (Epstein & Sanders 2006; Timperley & Robinson 2002). This is particularly true in low socio-economic communities, with engagement more likely to occur with families from more educated and economically stable backgrounds (Sheldon 2003).

We make the argument that the successful digitalisation of schools should make home–school connection and collaboration in the form of a learning partnership easier to achieve. Timperley and Robinson (2002) argue that partnerships are about relationships and that they must be focused on a task. In this instance, the task is to improve student achievement and to enrich their learning experiences through a home–school connection. Digital technologies have the potential to break down many of the existing barriers of time and space that limit the extent to which homes are able to be involved in student learning. However, issues of equity are also raised in terms of the readiness and capacity of the home to engage digitally.

In this chapter, we highlight the stories of three very different schools, the ways they are currently using technology and their readiness to expand that use in order to promote connection and collaboration between home and school. Both the potential benefits and the inherent difficulties are explored.

We first provide a brief description of the three schools. These schools were participants in a larger, longitudinal study of the use of teacher laptops in primary schools in New Zealand. Fictitious names have been given to all three schools. The data gathered provided information related to the positioning of the laptops in a wider classroom context. The data was not gathered with the intention of considering home–school partnerships.

We then describe actual digital technology usage across these schools within three themes: enriching teaching and learning in the classroom, extending/dismantling the classroom walls, and bridging the gap between home and school. Finally, potential scenarios depicting the extension of this use to allow for connection and collaboration between home and school are outlined, along with a consideration of what is required for such to work.

Introducing the three schools

Each of the schools is purposively using digital technologies in a manner that specifically meets the learning needs of their students. A logical next step for these schools would be to allow for greater connection and collaboration with their home communities. The extent to which they, and these communities, are open to this next step cannot be ascertained from the current study. However, greater home engagement and greater accountability to the home is a cornerstone of the New Zealand education system (New Zealand Ministry of Education 2005), as it is in many others.

Wedgewood School

This is an urban school in a low socio-economic community, catering for Kindergarten to Year 8 students. The school roll is approximately 500. The students are predominantly from Pacific nations (57%) and Maori (39%) cultural backgrounds. Many of the students at this school—and others like it—enter school already disadvantaged in terms of literacy skills in English and, not unrelated, in numeracy. In some instances they remain below national norms throughout their schooling. A core concern at the Wedgewood School is the poor oral English language skills of the students, and technology is purposefully used as part of the solution to this problem.

School leaders described how the school had initially been 'technology driven' (technology for technology's sake) but that technology was now seen as a 'tool for making teaching more powerful'. The underlying philosophy was that teaching is empowered through the learner being more engaged and more independent. Technology also allowed for more purposeful interaction with others, including between students.

The school is well resourced in terms of digital technologies and has made a concerted effort to find the necessary funding (canvassing sources like charitable trusts) to ensure this level of resourcing. The school's extensive media centre was provided through external funding and sponsorship and is available to the wider community. The school has also been part of a government-funded professional development project aimed at increasing teacher skill in the use of digital technologies.

Its digital technology infrastructure includes the following:

- a school server
- all classrooms are networked
- a computer suite with 20 desktops and a data projector
- a data projector and sound system in the theatre
- a media room with five desktops
- plasma screen in the atrium
- all classrooms have a data projector, computer, sound system, teacher microphone and pass-around microphone, tape recorder or CD player and digital camera
- all teachers have their own laptops
- an interactive whiteboard in one classroom
- eight wireless headphones for two junior classes
- a Polycom, movie camera, DVD player and multimedia unit for teacher use
- sets of digital cameras.

Bryant School

Bryant is also a Kindergarten to Year 8 school; however, it is from a high socio-economic, semi-rural area. The families it draws from include farmers, those employed in local businesses and those who commute to the nearby city for employment. The school has a roll of approximately 330 students who are predominantly New Zealand European (85%). The school has retained a distinctly rural character despite its close proximity to both a provincial town and major urban centre.

The school provides students with a wide range of cultural and sporting activities as well as having a strong academic focus. Technology is purposively used to enrich and extend the learning experiences of students. This is achieved through the use of different media and the addition of new dimensions to the learning experience. There was clear evidence at this school of a push-pull effect, with the teachers having to work hard to 'keep up' with what the students knew or wanted to do.

The digital technology infrastructure includes:
- a school server
- two computers-on-wheels (COWs) sets (16 laptops each) with a network connection
- a media room—12 desktops and a data projector linked to a networked teacher computer
- a pod of desktops in the library computer suite
- a data projector in the school hall
- all classrooms have a digital camera, a desktop computer and a data projector
- all teachers have laptops.

Mason School

Unlike the other two schools this is a Year 7–8 school only. It serves a high socio-economic community in a major urban area. The majority of its students are New Zealand European (54%) with a large immigrant community including Koreans (10%), Chinese (9%), British and Irish (8%) and other Europeans (6%). Other nationalities, including South African, comprise 11 per cent of the school roll which is approximately 840.

The culture of this school is founded on a philosophy of invitational learning. This is learning that is personalised and individualised. The underpinning belief is that students will 'run to school excited about their learning'. The school is innovative in its approaches and teachers are encouraged to take risks and try new things. Digital technologies are critical to this philosophy and are widely used throughout the school. Indeed, there is a complex synergy between the schoolwide view of learning and technology.

The digital technology infrastructure includes:
- at least 12 thin client desktops in every classroom
- full client access for all teachers in their classrooms through their laptops

- Internet access in all classrooms
- still and video digital cameras
- a design studio with ten Macintosh G5 computers
- a television studio
- an interactive whiteboard in every classroom
- an ICT suite
- a set of iPod touches
- all teachers have laptops
- a school learning management system that enables students to create their own online web content for documents.

Using technology in twenty-first century classrooms

In this section, we highlight the ways in which the digital technologies listed above are currently being used across the three schools. These uses are grouped into three thematic areas: teaching and learning in the classroom, extending the classroom walls, and bridging the gap between home and school. Of particular relevance to this chapter are uses that could be readily adapted to allow for increased connection and collaboration with the home; these are briefly discussed within each theme.

Teaching and learning in the classroom

Across the three schools the key use of digital technologies was to enhance and/or extend the teaching and learning that was occurring within the classroom. This occurred in different ways, dependent on the educational philosophies and intentions of teachers in individual schools. However, in all three there was a clear focus on the use of technology in the professional work of teachers, whether for planning, preparation or presentation. There was also a clear focus on purposive classroom use related to the learning needs of the students.

In both Bryant and Wedgewood schools we saw examples of teachers recording formative assessments of students in real time. This could be as simple as electronically recording an observation about an individual student or students' progress or needs (e.g. not understanding forward number sequence) to inform the next day's planning. Or, as we saw at Wedgewood, it could involve actual recording of activities such as students speaking into the teacher's laptop as they practised positional language.

In all three schools digital technologies were also used in a range of ways to enrich and extend learning experiences. These uses were across the curriculum and included the use of digital cameras to explain positional language, professionally publishing student work, and students modelling and sharing their learning with the class using a range of media. In all three schools there were multiple examples of students presenting their work to each other, whether through animation, PowerPoint, booklets or posters.

At Mason School, this idea of sharing and modelling was extended to include the use of blogs. Students were able to read and comment on each other's writing via their individual blogs, promoting the exchange of ideas among the students. The teacher was able to review all posting and, in this way, could assess each student's ongoing progress. The blogs also served a broader function of coordinating learning through the posting of tasks and resource material.

The use of the digital cameras to record learning experiences was a common means of promoting learning. At both Bryant and Wedgewood visual records of events or experiences were used to enable students to be more descriptive and authentic in their writing and in its publication. At Wedgewood this was taken even further with new-entrant students using different props to recreate a story. They took pictures of each stage of the story, which were then turned into a movie using Photo Story and which they narrated.

iPod touches were used at Mason School as a means of providing students with detailed instructions on how to complete a project. Teachers recorded the instructions and provided exemplars of what was required. Students could refer to these at any stage during a lesson, removing the need to ask the teacher constantly. This enabled the teacher to work with groups of students who had specific needs rather than focusing on the whole class.

Extending the classroom walls

Digital technologies such as the Internet and iPods provide ready access to the broader world from within the classroom and, as such, are able to break down barriers such as time and space and to extend the classroom walls. They also remove dependence on the teacher as the source of all information and allow for more flexibility and diversity both in and beyond the classroom. In all three schools the Internet was used regularly to access resources, for research and for learning activities.

At Wedgewood School, a television news website was used each morning to engage the students with what was happening in the wider world. A particular, relevant news item would form the basis of a class discussion, a vocabulary lesson and a brief writing session. Technology was used to experience the world through the use of email at Bryant School where students communicated with a biologist in the Antarctic while they were working on a research unit about the continent. They told her what they were learning and she commented and added to their knowledge.

At Bryant School, the authors observed a Year 3 numeracy lesson where students were working on different online activities, depending on their capability. These activities were graded and students moved through them at the appropriate pace. At the same school, a teacher explained that accessing material on the Internet provided valuable opportunities for reading mileage and for differentiated activities.

At Mason School the teachers used iPods to download podcasts of speeches by famous people. The students used these when they were working on their own speeches as examples to emulate. In this way the teacher was no longer the only resource available and students were able to work at their own pace and away from the classroom. At the same school, students log onto an Australian-based mathematics system where they can study online at their own level. At the end of the course they can join a live competition with students from around the world.

Bridging the gap between home and school

There were examples across the schools of the use of technology to provide a greater connection between the home and the school. All three schools have websites with varying amounts of information available. Principals at each of the schools are contactable by email, although direct teacher access appears limited. There were also instances where connections had been made between classroom learning and the home. At Bryant School, students had taken turns to take a soft toy home and photograph its experiences at their house with a school-provided digital camera. These experiences had then been collated and written about for a school in Sydney, Australia, who had done the same thing with a soft toy crocodile. The two sets of stories and the soft toys were then exchanged.

Some of the students at Bryant School were also provided with CDs of photos taken during activities such as camps that they could take home. In a reverse process, one parent had provided the school with a CD of photos he had taken at a sporting event, an exchange also bridging the gap between home and school. Students at Bryant School who had conversed electronically with the scientist from Antarctica took copies of her emails home with them and discussed these with their parents. The emails provided a focal point, which enabled students to talk to the adults about what they had learned.

Teachers at both Bryant and Mason spoke of students who brought a rich skill set to school, enriching not only their learning experiences but also those of others. Such students pushed the boundaries of teacher knowledge and provided an impetus for teachers to extend their own learning. Interestingly, they also spoke of how what students learned at school better enabled them to utilise the technology available to them at home.

Teachers spoke of the importance of their laptops, the value of their portability and the greater flexibility and access provided to them as a result. For the teachers, technology had meant their homes could readily be an extension of their workspace. Some also appeared aware of the potential for the classroom to be similarly extended for students. At Mason School there was an understanding that the blogs could be readily extended to the home and, indeed, to others in the community. Wedgewood School expressed a plan to podcast students' videos through the school website so that they could be viewed at home.

A networked, collaborative learning community

The authors argue that the culture and infrastructure that exist in these schools already and the current use of technology could be readily utilised in a more inclusive manner to broaden the immediate school community. They also argue that in-school use such as that described above is a critical first step in a journey towards a broader, networked learning community. The second step is to include the home more directly, in the school and the learning that occurs, through the use of digital technologies. Finally, a learning culture within each context, home and school that is connected and shares a common vision can be developed. In this way resources at home and school can be used to augment one another and to enrich and extend the learning experiences of students.

Networked home–school communities

In a networked home–school community greater access to the teaching and learning context of the school can be provided to the home, along with more timely and detailed information. Doing so would enable the home to engage more readily with their children and the school about their learning. The easiest way to achieve this is to extend what is currently available on the school website.

All three schools are already creating published work using a range of applications. Student work is also often electronically archived at all the schools. In addition, there are examples of the use of digital cameras to record learning experiences. Technically it would be a simple step to provide access to such materials on the school website. Parents could log into a password-protected site, select their child's portfolio and browse through the work. Technologies such as Dropbox (http://www.getdropbox.com) and shared folders would readily facilitate this sharing. Such a portfolio could include podcasts of speeches or other performances. The students could manage the portfolio, providing them with greater ownership of their work and further developing their skills. Already in one of the classrooms at Wedgewood students are able to manage their work within class portfolios. To allow for space it would be possible to copy the portfolio onto a CD or other external drive once a term or when certain units of work are completed. Students could make decisions about which pieces of their work to retain in the main portfolio for the end of year; they could develop criteria for these decisions, helping them to develop evaluative skills.

Electronic formative and summative assessment records could also be made available to parents through the school website. As teachers record assessments, they could be automatically published onto an individual student's record, which stayed in their portfolio (or students could simply keep their own record up to date). Parents could then track their child's progress, preferably against class, school and national norms and expectations (information which could be available on the school website). Such ready access means that parents would not need to wait for parent–teacher nights or for reports to determine how their child is progressing and achieving. This means that potentially the home can be a partner to any necessary intervention at an earlier stage. These results could be linked to an electronic calendar for each class, which lets parents know when particular tests will be occurring and to check for new results.

Many of the key events in these schools are already recorded using video and/or still photography. Students also frequently publish work related to such events. Again, it is a relatively simple step to make such material readily available to parents who may not have the time or capacity to attend in person. In this way, they can be part of what is occurring, at least in a virtual sense.

Networked, collaborative learning communities across home and school

In this section we look at how the idea of greater connection through an electronic network, as described above, can be extended to include the home as part of a networked, collaborative learning community focused on enriching student learning. Such a learning community would involve a partnership between the home and the school that is both electronically facilitated and also utilises technology available within each context in an independent but mutually supportive manner. It would include the uses of the website described in the previous section, but allow for greater interactivity and communication.

The first steps towards this notion of partnership between home and school were readily apparent at the two high socio-economic schools. Students were already utilising home technologies and the skills they had learned there to augment resources available at school. However, this was occurring in a serendipitous rather than a planned manner. There was no apparent focus on utilising what was at home when teachers planned in-school activities or on letting parents know, in an ongoing way, what was happening so they could better support the school.

Information on the projects students are undertaking, on the websites being used across the curriculum and on the types of software the students are using may allow parents to provide complementary resources at home. There is a ready acknowledgement that students who have access to books at home are more likely to be strong readers. The same could apply to a range of technologies. Critical to this is understanding by parents that technology use is not an extra-curricular activity but central to curriculum learning.

Greater interaction could also be achieved through allowing parental access to interactive portfolios using tools such as blogs and wiki spaces. Parents could readily participate in the development of work beyond that which is done for homework. They could clearly see what the designated tasks were and how their child was progressing through a project. More importantly, they could make comments directly and be part of the learning process, providing feedback to the child and the teacher. A simple alert could let the teacher and child know that a new comment had been added. Similarly, some kind of email alert could let parents know when something had been added to the portfolio.

Achieving a networked, collaborative learning community

Electronically, the scenarios depicted above are relatively simple to achieve. However, there are infrastructural and human capacity issues to consider both at home and at school. There are also questions of equity and how to provide access to all students and their families, particularly in low socio-economic areas. Our work in these three schools highlighted a number of factors, or building blocks, that were common across all three and appeared to be prerequisites for the successful integration of digital technologies into schools. These were:

- The natural and unforced use of technology, appropriate to a school-wide clearly articulated and shared vision for learning;
- A strong professional learning culture across the school where teachers engage in learning conversations and where peer modelling and coaching are common;
- Supportive formal leadership working towards facilitating the implementation of an agreed vision;
- Collegial support and pressure from teacher champions who are highly skilled and innovative practitioners willing and able to model best and next practice to their colleagues; and
- Sufficient infrastructure, the nature and extent of which is determined by the school culture and climate and the needs of the students. Ease of access to hardware and the Internet is critical.

The presence of these factors in each school had enabled them to be successful in integrating digital technologies into the classroom and the teachers' professional lives. Achieving the next two steps—a networked community and a collaborative learning community—requires an extension of these factors within schools and the acquisition of similar building blocks in the home.

A networked learning community requires the home to be able to readily access the school network and for those at home to understand and value the role of contributing directly to the learning of their children at school. It also requires the school to commit to an extended network and to a further opening of the classroom walls. This will require schools to be willing to be held accountable, on a daily basis, for what is occurring within the school and to be willing to accept regular feedback and involvement from the home. It also requires those at home to understand that learning in the twenty-first century extends well beyond what they may have experienced.

A collaborative learning community requires highly committed and capable people at home who share and understand the vision of learning within the school. They must be willing to provide a home context that is equally focused on lifelong learning and development. This is where issues of equity are particularly relevant and where schools in low socio-economic communities may also have to commit to community education and to finding innovative ways for those at home to access and support their children. Examples of this could include utilising the church as a centre of learning, extending the operation of school homework centres to enable families to work with their children in these centres and providing access to computers for family members.

It should be noted that the capacity and willingness of the home to be involved could be problematic in high socio-economic schools. Not all students will have equal access to digital technologies at home and many homes may not value twenty-first century learning or understand the importance of digital technologies in schools. Those at home may need to be supported and pressured into shifting, into taking some direct responsibility for their child's education.

Whatever the solution to home access and involvement, the first step will be for schools to want to be held more transparently accountable to open their doors and to break down the current barriers, or protective walls. They will then need to take the lead and work with the home to ensure sufficient infrastructure, including ensuring that capable and willing human resources are available. This is no small ask, but the potential benefits are likely to be far-reaching.

Conclusion

The authors have highlighted in this chapter the extent to which many schools are now capable of taking the use of technology a step further and how they can use the digital technologies to meet the increasing demand for home–school partnerships and greater accountability for learning. What we have not considered is the extent to which they are ready to do so from an attitudinal viewpoint and it is this willingness, or lack of, that will remain the critical barrier to the development of networked, learning communities.

Currently the use of technology tends to be focused on the school or the home as two different entities or contexts, with instances where students are able to enrich what is occurring at school through their home resources. Schools are also providing students with access to the world beyond their immediate communities and attempting to break the digital divide that exists for many students. In this model, home and school are two separate contexts with only limited, and generally 'opportune', connections.

The next step is for schools to increase both the extent and nature of the information they provide to the home. Ideally, this will allow for greater two-way communication and direct involvement by the home in the learning experiences of their children. The bridge between school and home will become more permanent and stronger, with purposeful and meaningful communication based on evidence related to learning.

Finally, the home context should become an extension of the classroom so that the divisions between the two are blurred. This would occur through the digital network but also through a mutually agreed and shared vision for learning, with both home and school working in partnership to achieve their goals. This is not difficult to implement in a technological sense. The difficulty lies in changing attitudes and expectations. The issue lies in the extent to which both the home and the school are willing, aside from being able, to develop and maintain a collaborative learning community and to alter traditional relationships and role delineations.

Guiding questions

After reading this chapter, consider your context and propose your ideas in relation to the following guiding questions.

1   What are the major lessons/issues emerging from these case studies that are relevant to your school's context?

2   What schools do you know that have effectively enabled the homes to work closely with those schools in the teaching and learning?

3   Would you consider those schools to be networked school community pathfinders?

4   Could others learn from these? If so, how are or how could their innovative approaches be disseminated?

Key messages

- The successful digitising of schools should make home–school connection and collaboration, in the form of a learning partnership, easier to achieve.

- A networked learning community requires the home to be able to readily access the school network and for those at home to understand and value the role of contributing directly to the learning of their children at school. It also requires the school to commit to an extended network and to a further opening of the classroom walls.

- Aside from being able, both the home and the school need to be willing to develop and maintain a collaborative learning community and to alter traditional relationships and role delineations.

CHAPTER 11

Parent perspectives on the digital home–school nexus

BRENTON HOLMES

There is a need for principals and teachers to readily acknowledge and appreciate the role of the parents, not only as 'first educators' but as 'continuing educators', and to see a place for them in the educational life of the school. There is a need for parents to recognise and appreciate the power and importance of their educative role, and to see the value of the attributes they can bring to the education process.

For many people this means looking at the school–home relationship in an entirely new light. This will not happen overnight. It means changing many decades of attitudes and beliefs about who is responsible for what in the raising of children. This will take time, effort and considerable awareness-raising among parents and professionals alike.

It has also profound implications for the training of teachers and for the selection of principals.

Saulwick Muller Social Research (2006, p. 15)

The current state of the home–school nexus

As the opening quote indicates, we need to understand that the focus of education—the student—is the immediate, common interest shared between a school and a family. Parents are their children's first, and ongoing, educators. School is the dominant institution to which parents and children are connected for at least a decade, and often more, during childhood and adolescence. For parents and families, that connection can be weak or strong, but it is far from inconsequential.

Since the 1980s, the issue of how schools engage with families has been of burgeoning interest among both researchers and policy makers, especially in the US but also in the UK, some European countries and in Australia. The findings of the research are unequivocal and consistent, and support what commonsense and intuition would already tell us.

Young people's wellbeing, sense of purpose and capacity to achieve their potential are all increased when families, schools and communities engage effectively with one another. Indeed, students' learning and their levels of achievement have been shown to improve significantly when their parents are involved as partners in the education process (Villa-Boas 1993; Henderson 1987; Sanders 1997; Christian, Morrison & Bryant 1998; Epstein 2001; Henderson & Mapp 2002).

There are various ways in which parents might be 'involved' in their children's education, and that involvement may manifest itself more strongly in one domain than in another. For example, some parents' involvement may emphasise a physical presence in the classroom or school-based activities more generally. Others choose to enrich and extend their child's learning out of school via museums, libraries, exhibitions and travel. Some may supervise homework closely or ensure that the home has the computers, books, quiet space and time to enable the child to settle into autonomous learning activities. Some parents do all of these things. Some do none.

A major survey of meta-analyses of student achievement (Hattie 2009) sheds some valuable light on what kind of family involvement leads to improved student achievement. Hattie distinguishes parents who 'know how to speak the language of schooling' (p. 61) from those who don't, and stresses the significance of this distinction for young people's educational outcomes.

Various home factors—like conducive home surroundings, regularly discussing school progress, supervising and assisting with homework—all contribute positively to achievement, but the analyses show that, across all home variables, 'parental aspirations and expectations for children's educational achievement have the strongest relationship with achievement' (Hattie 2009, p. 70). It would appear that young people whose parents can articulate their expectations and aspirations in 'the language of schooling' are doubly advantaged.

On the policy front, Australian jurisdictions have in recent years been quite explicit in stating their commitment to schools working in partnership with parents and families. The joint ministerial *Adelaide Declaration on National Goals for Schooling in the Twenty-first Century* (Ministerial Council on Education, Employment, Training and Youth Affairs [MCEETYA] 1999) formally 'acknowledges the role of parents as the first educators of their children' and commits governments to 'strengthening schools as learning communities where teachers, students and their families work in partnership'. Most State and Territory education authorities issued policy statements encouraging strong engagement between schools and families, as have those in the non-government school sector.

An even more tightly focused commitment to family engagement was made by Australian governments with the cross-sector development and official dissemination of the *National Family–School Partnerships Framework* (Australian Government 2008). Copies of the Framework were sent to all schools, with a letter from the Federal minister which encouraged schools to use the Framework to explore new ways to form and sustain family–school partnerships for the benefit of students.

Broadly speaking, these formal undertakings have not issued in a dramatic change in partnership practices. The picture across Australian schools remains mixed. Whether genuine partnerships are established depends largely on the disposition of the school principal and is usually influenced by the degree of social capital that already exists within the community concerned. It is fair to say that the development of strong family–school relationships is an ad hoc rather than a systematic feature of Australian school education.

What remains certain is that parents are universally keen to have a positive relationship with their child's school. Principals and teachers are, on the whole, open to such engagement and many actively seek it. Despite this goodwill, both schools and parents often find it difficult to initiate, let alone sustain, regular and open communication. Given that communication is the fundamental requirement for the establishment of a relationship, in addition to a vibrant, ongoing and mutually supportive educational partnership, schools and families should actively pursue every available means to facilitate communication between them.

What parents expect from schools

Notwithstanding occasional national government surveys of parents and an increasing accountability requirement from schools to formally seek the views of parents, there is little coherent research and reporting about Australian parents' expectations of school education. For example, research commissioned in 1998 by the National Council of Independent Schools Association revealed that parents in those schools had high expectations (Saulwick & Muller 1998) and the report's authors declared those expectations to be shared by parents generally. Parents expect schools to:

- nurture their children with care
- allow their children to develop as well-rounded human beings
- imbue their children with, and reinforce, the values and culture of the home
- instil in their children self-discipline and respect for others
- teach their children how to learn, and
- give their children enough skills and knowledge to allow them to build a future, economically and socially.

Similar findings emerged from later research commissioned by the two peak parent organisations for government and non-government schools—the Australian Council of State School Organisations and the Australian Parents Council. Their research on family–school partnerships (Saulwick Muller Social Research 2006) and information from parent focus groups conducted in 2009 by their jointly sponsored Family–School and Community Partnerships Bureau have given quite a clear picture of what parents want and how well they think that the education system is delivering the goods. It is worth elaborating on that picture as a prelude to considering the potential development of a networked concept of family–school engagement.

The prime consideration for parents with respect to their child's school, at both the primary and secondary levels, is whether their child is happy. That happiness is seen overwhelmingly as a function of the child's relationship with their teachers, and of the leadership provided by the school principal in creating an ethos of care and an environment in which learning can proceed in an orderly, student-centred manner.

Parents are almost always well disposed towards their children's school, believe that teachers do a good job under trying conditions, and they lament the pressure and lack of resources that many schools confront as they try to fulfil their educational and social responsibilities. Parents are universally interested in their children's schooling, but the institutional qualities— the traditions, structures and hierarchies—that continue to surround most schools make it difficult for them to participate in, or even observe, their child's educational experience.

When it comes to relationships between school and home, parents rate the need for communication highly, but in practice the extent and effectiveness of communication varies greatly. Parents continue to value 'the regular newsletter', which for most schools remains a paper-based communication, conveyed by students to their families with variable success. In diverse communities, communication is often made more complicated by language barriers and a lack of familiarity with schools' traditional modes of communicating with parents.

This is not to deny that significant efforts are being made by many schools to greatly enhance their communication practices, which include greater openness to the presence of parents in the school, the appointment—albeit rarely—of family liaison officers, and in some cases the development of sophisticated websites, email lists and SMS alerts. But the majority of schools are a long way from establishing regular and effective networks of general communication between the school and the home, let alone more direct and frequent engagement between teachers and parents as partners in an educational enterprise.

Parents often entertain different imaginings about the state of their school's communication infrastructure and practices, and as a consequence have varying expectations of the school when it comes to liaising with and responding to parents. For instance, some parents assume that all teachers have their own workstation with computer and telephone access. This gives rise to expectations that parents should be able to readily exchange emails with teachers or arrange a phone conversation. In many schools, teacher access to computers and phones is extremely limited and calls to mobile phones are highly regulated, all of which militates against timely and easy communication with families.

Other parents, sympathetic to the pressures and lack of resources plaguing their school, know the difficulties involved in communicating beyond the school and consider it unfair, for example, to expect teachers to report to families regularly by email on each of their many students. Such parents are disappointed—but not surprised—when school websites do not contain up-to-date information about what is happening in their child's class.

Consistent with the prevailing ad hoc rather than systematic approach to family–school liaison and engagement, the application of digital technologies to communications with parents often relies on the enthusiasm and commitment of a particular teacher or principal within the school. When that person moves on, initiatives flounder. Relatively few schools have been able to establish robust technical maintenance schemes to support digital communications, and this undermines the efforts of even its most ardent proponents, whether teachers or parents.

The application of the digital technologies to better engage schools with families is potentially much greater than the convenient exchange of information and advice, by email and other means, important as that is. Given the increasing pervasiveness of these technologies in the home, the wealth of educationally valuable resources to which they give access and the extent to which digital technologies are thoroughly embedding themselves in the daily lives of students and the population at large, it is imperative that schools and families are enabled and encouraged to harness the power and enjoy the benefits of a digitally networked collaboration.

As discussed in Chapters 3, 7 and 12, active support from government—through policy, infrastructure and finance—will go a long way to making networked schools, families and communities a reality. But the nature of that reality must be determined by the needs, preferences and desires of citizens, as both parents and taxpayers. In the case of families with children in schools, that reality must be one in which parents and carers are able to fulfil their roles as 'primary and ongoing educators', and in which schools can carry out their vital educational function confident in the knowledge that their efforts are supported, understood and appreciated by parents. Such a condition will offer the best chance that students will find schools to be a place in which they are happy, where they can grow intellectually, socially and emotionally, and from which they can emerge as self-directing agents of their own lives, effective citizens and navigators of a networked world.

Towards a digitally networked home–school nexus

Before examining the needs, opportunities and necessities that a digitally animated world entails, we should be clear about the existing state of affairs regarding Australians' access to digital technology, the nature of their involvement in online activity, and the extent of the resources available to them. Only then can we develop a meaningful strategy for strengthening the home–school nexus by digital means.

Australian parents are as diverse in their backgrounds and circumstances as the Australian population as a whole. It is therefore reasonable to assume that in the case of data about people's engagement in the digital world, national statistics and the findings of research based on random sampling can be legitimately regarded as applicable to the cohort of parents who have school-age children. So, from official Australian Bureau of Statistics (ABS) data and other surveys, what do we know about Australian families' access to and use of digital technologies?

Online access and participation—how much and of what kind?

In its second report in the series *Australians and the digital economy*, the Australian Communications and Media Authority (ACMA) (2009a) addressed the issue of online participation. The report tells us that:

> Australians are increasingly using the Internet for applications such as email, instant messenger and chat, user-generated content services and voice-over Internet protocol and video applications. While adoption of these services is being driven by younger Australians, they are increasingly being used by all age groups. (p. 1)

Around 73 per cent of people aged 14 and over live in a household with an Internet connection, and 68 per cent of households enjoy broadband connection. The proportion of broadband connections is increasing and there is also a trend to adopt services with higher download speeds. It is estimated that only 13 per cent of Australians aged 14 years and over had never used the Internet, and these people tend to be older Australians, with nearly half being over the age of 50. If we assume that the bulk of parents of school-age children are younger than 50, there would be only a very small percentage of parents who have never used the Internet. Indeed, the ACMA (2009a) report indicates that people between the age of 14 and 49 are more likely to be heavy users of the Internet. As well, Australians who live in a household with a partner and children were more likely to have an Internet connection (83%), and this is more likely to be a broadband connection (68%).

A Swinburne University report mapping Internet use in Australia (Ewing, Thomas & Schiessl 2008) and the Pew Research Center's *Internet and American Life Project* (Rainie & Anderson 2008) both provide significant insights into why and how families use digital technologies. Australian respondents to the Swinburne survey were much more likely to say that Internet access had increased their contact with various groups. The majority thought that the Internet had increased their contact with family members. Similarly, the Pew survey found that families are among the keenest users of technology, with the Internet used often as social activity within families. Some 51 per cent of parents said they browsed the Web with their children. There is an emergence of new kinds of connectedness built around the Internet and mobile phones. Some 53 per cent said that new technologies had increased the quality of their contact with distant family members, while 47 per cent said it improved interaction with those they live with.

For Australian users, the Internet has become a very important source of information—more important than the traditional media of newspapers, radio and television. Fewer than seven in ten users described the Internet as 'important' or 'very important'. The proportion of users rating the Internet as 'very important' is more than double that for radio and newspapers and more than four times the figure for television. Interestingly, almost two-thirds of Australian Internet users believe that they spend the same amount of time reading books as they did before accessing the Internet. More than one in ten believe it has increased (Ewing, Thomas & Schiessl 2008).

The Pew findings (Rainie & Anderson 2008) reveal that the Internet is proving a valuable tool in helping American citizens make important decisions across multiple areas of their lives, including health, educational and financial decisions. The Internet ranks high among sources of information and advice that people are seeking. Eight in ten Internet users have looked online for health information, with many e-patients saying the Internet has had a significant impact on the way they care for themselves or for others. The Internet was the top source for material on personal coping strategies during the recession, with some 69 per cent of all American adults having gone online to get help with personal and economic issues.

A majority of Australian users in the Swinburne survey look for local community news on the Internet and well over a third do so at least weekly. Again respondents were quite positive about the use of the Internet for creative purposes. A majority of Internet users agreed that the Internet enabled them to share creative work they liked with others. The Pew study also found that many Americans have contributed their own content and commentary to various websites and through messaging networks such as Twitter.

Given the ABS and ACMA data, and to the extent that the Swinburne study is representative of, and the Pew study indicative of, the ways in which Australians use digital technologies, we can be confident that:

- Access to and active use of the Internet communications is a significant feature of the digital environment of the parents of Australia's school children;
- Home-based computers, often with broadband connections, are commonly available in most students' homes;
- Most families who use digital technologies regard them as an enhancement of inter-family connection, and parent–child engagement via these technologies is common;
- The Internet is increasingly regarded as a reliable and preferred source of information, including for community information; and
- Citizens of all ages are increasingly contributing content to digital networks via websites or messaging.

There are, however, some particular cohorts of families and individuals in Australia who are excluded from the digital landscape, paralleling overseas experience. In Australia, these include:

- Indigenous Australians: 69 per cent less likely than non-Indigenous people to have any Internet connection and half as likely to have broadband access;

- low-income Australians: income is the single largest determinant of Internet access and broadband, with the likelihood of having any Internet access for households earning $1000 to $1999 per week being about 2.7 times more than those earning less than $599 per week; lower-income families with children are much more likely to have access to the Internet than those without children;

- single-parent households with dependent children under 15 years: 77 per cent Internet and 52 per cent broadband access compared with 92 per cent and 68 per cent respectively for comparable dual-parent households.

Any strategies, policies or initiatives directed at establishing digitally enabled networks of schools, families and communities must take special care to ensure that those groups already under-represented in online participation are not further disenfranchised.

Is a digitally enabled network likely to enhance the home–school nexus?

Greater efforts to network families, schools and communities must continually be challenged by the question: What is the *real* significance and *potential practical benefit* of a serious investment in a digital home–school network? We have already referred to the extensive research that demonstrates unequivocally that parental involvement as partners with schools in the education of their children leads to significant improvements in academic achievement and overall wellbeing. We have also seen the extent to which digital technologies are becoming pervasive in most homes, with young 'digital natives' and older 'digital immigrants' both participating and collaborating in online and other digital communications.

It is worth reinforcing here that the 'digital natives' are, and will continue to be, the groundbreakers both in the way digital technologies are used and by being the ongoing teachers of the 'digital immigrants'. One of the most frustrating things for 'digital natives' to experience (and their parents to observe) is the failure of schools to recognise the range and depth of skills already possessed by young people. Too often schools try to restrict students' access to digital technologies, or teachers struggle to exploit the benefits of digital technologies, while in the meantime the bulk of young people are happily and effectively exploiting those technologies out of school hours as a learning resource.

But even if we accept that 'digital natives' are confident navigators of the digital world, is it necessarily the case that digital networks are an effective way to promote and facilitate home–school partnerships and stronger parental engagement in young people's learning? It is important that we have some justification for thinking so. The relationship between families and schools is too valuable a dog to be wagged by an uncritically adopted digital tail.

School–home communication

We have noted earlier parents' genuine desire for communication from their child's school about school activities in general and about how their child is progressing. Parents differ in the expectations they have about the sophistication, frequency and interactivity of schools' communications with them. In July 2008, the global educational publisher Pearson commissioned an online survey of US parents to determine the frequency and manner of communication that parents currently have with their child's school. The survey also gauged parents' attitudes on the impact of regular communication on overall student achievement (Pearson 2008).

The survey revealed that parents are seeking ways to become more involved in their child's progress at school through the use of technology. Additionally, parents widely viewed their involvement as a key factor in a child's overall achievement and indicated a strong desire to be more informed about overall progress, especially grades, in order to positively impact their child's school performance. Parents also acknowledged the benefits of better communication, specifically online communication, between school and home—namely the ability to afford earlier intervention opportunities to solve problems and as a motivating factor for their child to take on more responsibility with respect to the outcome of his or her academic performance.

The Pearson findings about what parents want are entirely in accordance with the views of Australia's peak parent organisations and the findings from their research into family–school partnerships. Given the relative abundance of digital technologies in homes, the increasingly routine use of email and other digital communications by Australian adults and children, and the increased investment by schools in digital technology, the signs are hopeful that routine communications and general information exchange between school and home should become a more universal practice.

Such a prospect somehow seems a very modest, if important, outcome. The question must still be asked: To what extent can a digital home–school network help bring about a more productive learning environment for students, improve students' educational outcomes, and enrich the opportunities for lifelong learning for all family members, not just school children?

Richer, deeper, more relevant, more equitable engagement

Beyond the basics of an efficient, digitally transmitted exchange of information between the school and the home lies the potential for a radically transformed reality for schooling. This reality is predicated upon the existence of networks of the kind that already prevail powerfully in many people's personal and professional lives, including the World Wide Web, social media platforms like Facebook and MySpace, and the plethora of message boards, wikis and other collaboration-driven technologies. Online and offline are increasingly just two modes of everyday being-in-the-world.

Many parents are vitally aware that their children's prowess as digital technology users is a key attribute of their future success as citizens, workers and agents of their own professional and personal destinies. Other parents sense that this is so, but are unsure about how best to support their children to that end. Parents expect, and teachers and principals acknowledge, that schools have a major role to play in preparing students for a digitally powered world. But almost everyone admits that, by and large, students are already navigating that world more effectively than their teachers, and (as discussed in more detail in Chapter 4) that in many respects homes are better equipped than schools to facilitate that navigation.

Schools are responding in a variety of ways to the expectations placed on them regarding digital technologies in classrooms. Some are using a tight regime of rules and filters to restrict students' access to the digital world, while others accept such access as a normal, inevitable and necessary aspect of young people's lives, and foster personal responsibility for that access.

Australian families seem broadly satisfied with the way their children use and access the digital technologies available at home. Levels of parental control vary, but generally speaking young people are trusted to use the technologies responsibly. There exists considerable evidence that young people are alert to the so-called 'dangers of cyberspace' and many families talk about such things as a matter of course. Broadly speaking, parents regard such discussion as much a part of their guardianship responsibilities as they would questions of sexual health, abuse of alcohol, vehicle use and a multitude of other social and moral issues.

While national curricula are being devised by education authorities, and will be adopted by schools, the resources available to support those curricula are increasingly to be found not only within the school and its community, but beyond them in the vastness and variability of the digital information universe. The richness of these multimedia resources is unprecedented, and they are potentially accessible to all. The tiny remote school, the impoverished inner-city school, the average suburban high school are potentially no longer confined to what is immediately and physically present in their classrooms and libraries.

Moreover, they are as accessible from the home (perhaps more so) than from the school, and parents are potentially able to enjoy those resources and learning experiences as much as their children—something that the traditional nexus between schools and homes has militated strongly against. Indeed, parents and children now potentially enjoy vastly greater opportunities for sharing an educational journey led by either. Relevance is something that both parents and children can consider jointly and be in a position to do something about on their own initiative. It is easy to over-egg the pudding in describing what is for most young people's schooling, and for their families, a potential—rather than an actual—reality. It remains the case, however, that the infrastructure for the new reality largely already exists or is being built, and in any event that new reality is already being inhabited by people in the non-school domains of their lives.

Moving the reality of schooling and its relationship to families from existing, traditional, rather nineteenth-century reality to its potential digital, twenty-first century, networked reality is less a question of desirability or feasibility and more a question of political will and the financial, organisational and professional changes to bring that will into effect. To be sure, these are no small considerations, but the scale and rapidity of what is occurring, and its implications for how we think about schools and the nexus between schools and homes, make such considerations imperative.

What is to be done?

In Australia, to some extent, and perhaps more so in some comparable countries, there are numerous striking examples of how schools, teachers, students, parents and communities are applying digital technologies in innovative and powerful ways to serve the interests of learning. They range from sophisticated websites where complete information about a school—its programs, resources, timetables—are all readily available, to highly interactive digital learning adventures linking schools and families and crossing the globe. Parent groups are using online simulators to conduct 'what if' analyses of various school budget scenarios. Social media and email lists are being used by parents to lobby decision makers, strengthen accountability and build a constituency for local, regional or national changes in education policy. The possible applications of digital tools are essentially limited only by people's imaginations.

These developments are very exciting, but also very threatening to many existing stakeholders. Traditional boundaries are being blurred, barriers dismantled, challenges mounted, opportunities created, inequities overcome, privileges undermined, questions asked, alternatives canvassed, sources diversified, surprising alliances forged and collaborations initiated. In short, an abundant and mind-boggling brave new digital world is at the disposal of those who wish to bend it to their purposes. The task is less a technical one than a strategic, moral and political one. This is hardly news to anyone who regards schooling as primarily a moral enterprise whose goal is to create the citizens and grow the entrepreneurs, scholars, inventors, artists and others who will lead flourishing personal and professional lives and will help shape our collective future.

Getting the technology strategy right

We noted earlier that we must not uncritically allow the digital tail to wag the education dog. We cannot afford to squander scarce public resources. Governments, let alone education authorities, must come to a very clear sense of the mission of schooling—preferably conceptualised in terms of lifelong learning—and of the outcomes that governments want schools to achieve. Properly contextualised decisions must then be made about which technologies and organisational arrangements will be most effective at delivering those outcomes at reasonable cost.

While flexible responses as to how services and outcomes are delivered are highly desirable, governments have a fundamental obligation to ensure fairness and an equitable distribution of benefits across communities, attempting to deliver as far as possible an equality of outcomes. We have identified earlier those individuals and groups in Australian society who are already disenfranchised or less well-served than others when it comes to accessing digital technologies. Digital exclusion will likely increasingly overlap with, and exacerbate, social exclusion.

Australian parents are notably concerned with questions of justice when it comes to education, and the concept of networked families, schools and communities necessarily invokes questions of equity in its realisation. Schools provide a convenient mechanism through which to identify and support those families who are less well-endowed with online access and digital resources. Governments must be prepared to support schools in responding to this need.

It goes without saying that schools themselves must be effectively digital before they can be networked with (often effectively digital) homes. Increased resources are being targeted at schools' digital requirements, but it is unlikely that schools will ever enjoy the kind of technological investment that will sustain them at levels comparable to what is happening in most homes, and the community more generally. It is not just a question of hardware and software, but a matter of maintenance, help-desk support and training for teachers and school administrators. This raises significant questions of how to provide such support cost-effectively. Can it be provided locally, or is a centralised system preferable, and so on.

Another important consideration to bear in mind, when thinking about networked home–school engagement, is that the devices through which that network will be activated are constantly changing. In particular, they are becoming smaller, more flexible and more mobile. These changes will themselves have an effect on how parents orient themselves to their participation in the home–school network.

Becoming comfortable with online interactions with the school—email, messaging and so on—from the computer on the desk at home is one thing. Manipulating handheld devices, using iPods and the like may well be another—and parents will invariably lag their children in becoming adept at using them. In short, even participating in a network will involve a constant learning by parents of new skills and information just to stay in the game. The same applies to schools and teachers. Only when the skills and access issues are bedded down can the serious content of engagement proceed, involving education, consultation, deliberation and participation.

Enabling the 'work' in networking

If networked schools and families are to prove viable, and in particular are to improve educational outcomes, parents must themselves be supported in developing their own skills as participants in a collaborative educational enterprise. Collaboration itself is something of an art and entails skills and dispositions that cannot be assumed to come naturally. Nor should it be forgotten that all such collaboration must involve the young people who are the focus and purpose of the exercise.

We have earlier noted Hattie's significant distinction between parents who can speak the language of schooling and those who cannot. For parents to be engaged in their children's schooling via a network, they must be inducted into the language of schooling. Principals and teachers are the obvious starting points, and outreach—by bringing parents into the school, visiting homes, or through well-designed online communications—will be crucial in identifying and helping those parents for whom the language of schooling may well be a foreign one.

Keeping the purpose of school and education in mind

Given that parents universally espouse the strong wish that their child's school experience be a happy one, the establishment of a networked home–school arrangement will be judged in no small way by parents according to its contribution towards that goal. Perhaps the importance of a child being happy at school has become a more significant consideration as families have increasingly seen both parents working outside the home and the school has become the prime, safe haven to whose care the child is daily consigned.

Moreover, as the socialisation of the child has become increasingly the remit of the school—as extended families and other socialising institutions like churches and clubs have waned—the physical presence of the child in the school and all the personal interactions that it entails have become a particular interest of parents. It is likely that parents would be significantly more distressed by having their child unhappy at school than by the school lacking the technology to sustain a networked link between home and school. Such a network will always be seen as valuable to the extent that it serves the child's happiness at school. The link between the two is unlikely to be immediately obvious to most parents, and indeed the link may prove neither a necessary nor sufficient one.

The point worth reiterating, however, is that a child's happiness at school will be significantly influenced by how relevant the school experience is to that child's interests, preferences and expectations. Today's digital natives are less likely to be happy if they are compelled to endure a school where their own digital norms are either not understood, are studiously ignored or actively rejected. To the extent that a digital home–school nexus is able to be forged, such a disjuncture between the child's and the school's norms can be largely avoided, and the chances of a happy school experience will rise accordingly.

We have seen that parents declare high expectations of schools around providing young people with the skills and knowledge to enable them to build a future socially and economically. This is also the constant refrain of governments and education ministers. Because digital technologies are increasingly embedded in both social and economic activity, schools are compelled to recognise and respond to digital challenges. Parents and their children reasonably expect that schools will be equipped physically and pedagogically to produce digitally proficient graduates.

Notwithstanding such reasonable expectations, we have discussed earlier the relatively disadvantaged digital condition of schools compared with many workplaces and with most homes, and the likelihood that such relative disadvantage will persist. It seems likely that, given parents' emphasis on the socialisation and personal growth aspects of school attendance, families might be willing to underwrite better digital access to learning resources from home if it somehow helped schools and teachers to put more time and effort into those vital, relational, face-to-face personal and communal activities in classrooms, playgrounds and on sporting fields. In the event that such arrangements emerged, supplementary digital help (as indicated in Chapter 12) would need to be provided to the homes of lower-income families and others currently excluded from mainstream online access.

For parents, talk of networked schools and families might also usefully be illuminated by concepts like 'scaffolding', which imply a sense of building upon what is already available, as well as providing a framework within which more extended educational opportunities are made available, not just for children, but also for adult family members. Such notions are consistent with the idea of lifelong learning to which parents are becoming increasingly accustomed in their own working lives. They also promote and sustain the idea of learning communities, which seems to have gained some traction in Australia, especially through environment preservation activity, neighbourhood renewal initiatives, the growth of study circles (notably among seniors), early childhood parenting programs and the like.

Once upon a future

An effective, digitally enabled home–school nexus is predicated upon a sufficiency of infrastructure and digital devices in both domains, and a commensurate level of skill and commitment by all participants.

Governments must decide the nature and the level of public investment in networks linking schools and homes, ensuring that the fundamental principles of equitable access are realised, and recognising that the private investment by families in establishing homes as digital nodes is not only a necessary feature of achieving networked engagement but an important contribution to the broader public good.

Students—largely already normalised into a digital world as 'digital natives'—are happy learners in schools where they can build capability and know that they are understood and supported. The more integrated their learning at school and at home, and the more their digital prowess can serve that integration, the more efficient their learning and the better their learning outcomes.

Parents—their 'digital immigrant' credentials on the up—anticipate an increasingly networked and digital future for themselves and especially for their children. They want engagement with schools on terms that reflect their status as co-educators of their children, and where communication between parents and teachers is conducted in a manner and through media familiar to them in their working lives and other relational areas.

Today's societies and economies, increasingly reliant on networks and digital technologies for its daily functioning, depend for their future success on citizens whose skills, values and creativity are given the maximum opportunity to flourish. This is achieved through a process of lifelong learning geared towards both civic and economically productive ends. Networked schools and communities are vital to realising that lifelong learning-infused society and economy.

A nation's contribution to global endeavours—political, environmental, economic, judicial, humanitarian and cultural—requires its effective participation in global networks. It is not far-fetched to suggest that the networked home–school nexus can be regarded as a prototype for—or version in miniature of—the larger negotiation of power and relationships between the public and private realms. It is a simple matter of fact that the digital technologies increasingly transact the bulk of the communications involved in such negotiations. In a democracy, a citizen's apprenticeship to such engagement via a digital home–school nexus seems eminently plausible and highly desirable.

Acknowledgement

The editors would like to acknowledge the support provided to Brenton Holmes, the author of this chapter, by the Family–School Community Partnership Bureau, that was in turn assisted by funding from the Commonwealth of Australia through the Department of Education, Employment and Workplace Relations—Quality Outcomes Programme.

Guiding questions

After reading this chapter, consider your context and propose your ideas in relation to the following guiding questions.

1   To what extent do parents regularly collaborate with the leadership in your school's development and decision-making processes? Where collaboration occurs, what proportion of parents do you think are engaged in this?

2   To what extent do students regularly collaborate with the leadership in your school's development and decision-making processes? Where collaboration occurs, what proportion of students do you think are engaged in this?

3   What are some examples that the school employs to collaborate online with parents and the students?

4   Propose strategies that you believe would strengthen the home–school nexus. In your proposal, indicate the areas that you think parents and students could be encouraged to have their say to create stronger home–school partnerships.

Key messages

- Young people's wellbeing, sense of purpose and capacity to achieve their potential are all increased when families, schools and communities engage effectively with each other. Students' learning and their levels of achievement have been shown to improve significantly when their parents are involved as partners in the education process.

- Greater efforts to network families, schools and communities must continually be challenged by the question: What is the *real* significance and *potential practical benefit* of a serious investment in a digital home–school network?

- An effective, digitally enabled home–school nexus is predicated upon a sufficiency of infrastructure and digital devices in both domains, and a commensurate level of skill and commitment by all participants.

CHAPTER 12

UK Home Access program:
A case study

RAY TOLLEY

The benefits for learners of having home access to technology will only be realised if there is agreed support for learners and their families from education practitioners and the wider community. In turn, education practitioners and the wider community will benefit from the improved and increased opportunities for engagement by learners.

By having access to technology in their home the learners and their families will be able to gain a greater understanding of:

- *what the learner is doing in their education and why*
- *what the education provider is doing to support them in their learning and why*
- *how digital technologies can support them to engage in activities that are meaningful to them and meet their needs and interests*
- *how and why the family can actively support learners*
- *how the education provider and the community can support them and how they can also benefit from the fact that learners have home access to technology.*

Becta (2008a, p. 20)

A pathfinder case study to show the way

Pathfinders help to show us the path to follow. This chapter provides the United Kingdom's Home Access initiative as a case study to provide an invaluable insight into the way forward to all those interested in furthering the nexus between the school and the students' home and the creation of a networked school community. The initiative builds on the vast effort the UK has made as a nation over the last two decades to better harness the undoubted power of technology to enhance the education of young people, and in so doing continues a national quest to dismantle the traditional school walls, to develop a mode of schooling in keeping with the contemporary world that educates all young people and to improve national productivity.

Most importantly, the initiative spells out in neon lights for all other nations—developed and developing—the vital contribution the students' homes play in the education of young people and the enhancement of national productivity, and that that education ought to be factored into any national educational developmental strategy. While the earlier chapters have made the point about the educative power of the students' homes very strongly, and when a major nation like the UK proclaims that importance, it is incumbent on all involved in school development—the educators, administrators, parents and the politicians—to heed the advice and to look closely at the move.

In providing this case study, one is very conscious that the program has just commenced and that time will be needed before one can critically reflect on the impact of the initiative. That said, it is possible to reflect on the considerable body of research the UK drew upon in formulating the program, to comment on the nature of the program being implemented, the advances made thus far and to draw upon the very considerable research now available globally to flag the kind of issues the UK and you are likely to encounter when mounting this kind of program.

What is important to appreciate is that no nation has as yet shown the educational courage or acumen to reach out and seek to collaborate with its students' homes on the scale of the UK, or indeed to venture into such uncharted waters. For once the public relations unit was correct when it prepared a media release that proclaimed 'England to lead the world in computer access for young people' (Department for Children, Schools and Families [DCSF] 2008). What also bears noting, as the senior program administrators regularly and openly attest, is that while the homework has been done, no one knows exactly what will be the full impact of the program, intended and unintended.

That is the reality of moves you make in your school, education authority or nation. What the UK is doing, as is advocated elsewhere in this book, is to build on the current developments and momentum, to take calculated risks, to move initially in a graduated manner, learning from those experiences, and to use the new technology to better perform the ways of old. Where it moves in time is as yet unknown.

Context

In examining the UK's Home Access program, like any you are considering for your school, it is important to view it in its context. Also important is appreciating that it is being introduced by a proactive government, after years of very considerable investment in digital technology in the nation's schools and in an educational culture where the use of the digital in schools has all but become normalised.

It also comes at a time when all the major arms of British government are accepting of the importance of education assisting to enhance national productivity and of ensuring that all its citizens, including the economically disadvantaged, can contribute to that improved productivity—an outlook you might find still missing from your own context. While the Leitch Review (Leitch 2006) in many respects set the ball rolling, the momentum was markedly increased in the first part of 2009 with the release in June of the Estelle Morris (2009) report, *Independent review of ICT user skills,* and Lord Carter's *Digital Britain—final report* (Department for Culture, Media and Sports [DCMS] & Department for Business, Innovation and Skills [DBIS] 2009). If one paragraph could be quoted from all of these works it might be from Estelle Morris (2009):

> *The challenge faced in helping 11.6m adults in England gain the skills they need to take full advantage of the social and economic benefits of technology in the 21st Century, is a significant one. (p. 37)*

The point to appreciate with the UK developments, as will become increasingly apparent in the consideration of the program objectives below, is that the nation's educational agenda is far, far broader than the narrow approach taken in other developed nations who are still preoccupied with the facility for the home computers to enhance young people's performance on often dated basic skills tests. The desire is to provide an appropriate, comprehensive education for the entire nation's young and their families in a digital and networked world.

Research

Anyone contemplating a home–school nexus or developing a networked school community can learn much from the research undertaken in the UK as a precursor to the launch of the Home Access program. What one sees in the UK from the mid 1990s onwards is a growing body of research both accompanying the moves to better harness the capacity of the technology and as a precursor to major policy initiatives. The national department of education (which has gone through several name changes) and Becta (http://www.becta.org.uk) have commissioned much of that research. Similarly, the higher education research community as represented by the Joint Information Systems Committee (JISC) has published a large body of excellent research that has been of help to the school communities (JISC 2009). In contrast to many other situations where the spin-doctors' take on the scene is the only information available, the UK has over the last decade compiled a sizeable body of objective research on the use of technology in education. Virtually all is readily available for download from the Internet.

Probably the easiest entry point to that research is the report prepared by the Ministerial Task Force assembled to advise on the shape of the Home Access program. Entitled *Extending opportunity* (Becta 2008a), this report not only provides a summary of the major research, but also a lead into further, more specific reading. The work of Comber et al. (2002), Desforges and Abouchaar (2003), Hart, Bober and Pine (2008), Kent and Facer (2004), Passey (2005), Reynolds (2006), Schmitt and Wadsworth (2004), and Somekh et al. (2005) collectively cover most aspects of the students' home use of digital technology and as such are well worth a read. Fuller details can be found at the Becta Home Access website at http://www.becta.org.uk/homeaccess.

Objectives

The program objectives are succinctly detailed in the Ministerial Task Force report and in the media releases that accompanied the formal commencement of the initiative in September 2008. As indicated, the program objectives are wide-ranging and of a type that would be applicable in most forward-thinking school communities. As well as the intention expressed in the opening quote to this chapter, the core vision of the Home Access Taskforce is:

> Home access to technology providing all learners with access to learning where and when they need it, achieved through providing:
>
> – increased opportunities for all learners to engage with the curriculum and interact with its resources beyond the confines of the school day;
>
> – increased opportunities for all learners to extend their learning into areas that match their personal interests, abilities and aspirations;
>
> – increased opportunities for all learners to develop the skills they need to pursue and drive their learning independently;
>
> – increased opportunities for all learners to become more involved in supporting their own and their families' learning; and
>
> – increased opportunities for families of learners to maintain the skills needed to participate in their communities and an increasingly 'connected' world.
>
> (Source: Becta 2008a, p. 19)

The objectives transcend the minutiae that have characterised the initial efforts of other education authorities. At the program launch, the following excerpts from the speech by the then Schools Minister Jim Knight highlighted the following:

> *A computer with Internet access is now as essential as a pen and paper in modern learning.*
>
> *Children from jobless and low-income families will receive a free computer and free broadband access under major plans to close the digital divide among young people.*
>
> *The £300m investment will help make England one of the first countries in the world to ensure every single young person can use a computer and the Internet at home for their education.*
>
> *Home access to ICT has educational, economic and social benefits. In fact, it is now clear that pupils without Internet access are at a disadvantage to their peers. Home access is increasingly becoming an essential part of a good education and having a computer with Internet access should be seen as equally essential as having a school bag, a uniform or a pen and paper. Many of us could not have even dreamed of having a computer in our*

own home when we were at school, but times have changed and young people are now at a significant disadvantage if they do not have a computer and access to the Internet. They are no longer luxury items, but are essential for a good education.

It is unacceptable that the digital divide is growing with 35 per cent of families having no access to the Internet and around a million children having no computer at home. That's why we are taking this unprecedented step.

But this isn't simply about handing out laptops and plugging them into broadband. Of course this is central to our plans but a laptop that's never used will not close the digital divide. What's important is what young people use computers for. I want young people using the Internet to study and research their school work and to find information that would normally be difficult to get hold of.

What I find particularly exciting is that young people can then show their parents and grandparents how to use the Internet so they can benefit from the vast amount of information available at their fingertips.

(Source: DCSF 2008)

The involvement and development of the total family, and not just the school-age children, was in fact crucial. Neil McLean, an Executive Director within Becta, underscored this thrust when speaking at the e-Learning Foundation conference in May 2009. The aim was to have the parents and students mutually develop their digital competencies. In expressing this desire, the UK recognises the considerable benefits that can come from a collaborative mode of education, from the parents and young people working together in a mutually supportive learning culture. It also appreciates that a significant proportion of the disadvantaged will be single parents and, like in most other developed nations, new arrivals often deficient in the language of their new land.

Nature of the program

The Schools Minister announced that the initial Home Access package would include:

- broadband for all young people between seven and 19 years of age whose families are eligible;
- a free laptop or other computer with relevant software and hardware bought with a 'Home Access' voucher; and
- support covering important areas such as Internet safety, effective use of technology for learning and a technical support help line.

(Source: DCSF 2008)

The program began in November 2008 with targeted funding available for all local authorities to provide home access for groups such as looked-after children and others for whom the authority has special responsibility. The wider program was then piloted in early 2009 in two local authority areas, with an expansion to the rest of England due to start in the autumn of

2009. Families in receipt of income support or unemployment benefits were able to apply for a 'Home Access' grant, which they can use to purchase a package from accredited suppliers.

The aim was to work towards universal home access by 2011. Oldham and Suffolk were selected as the initial pilot situations. Since the launch of the pilots in February 2009, over 7500 applicants have been successful in the pilot areas, prompting the government to extend the deadlines such that more families could benefit. Of note is that by mid July 2009, the Becta site was indicating that all funds had already been committed and that the only chance for those who had missed out was to apply in 2010. The ongoing funding of the initiative is clearly an issue and one that is addressed more fully later in the chapter.

The sample of the feedback received by Becta on the Oldham and Suffolk pilots is very positive:

> *The children now have their new laptops and are over the moon with them. I have never seen so much studying done in one evening... just brilliant!*

> Birtles (2009)

Further examples of feedback received from families in Oldham and Suffolk are:

> *My daughter was desperate to have the Internet for her schoolwork but we cannot afford it. She is doing well in school but it is always a battle to have to take her somewhere to do her homework. Thank you so much.*

> *The scheme has to be the most positive steps I feel there has been made towards children's education I have experienced in my lifetime.*

> Birtles (2009)

Alexandra Birtles from Becta noted on their Collaboration Forum that what has been most striking about the feedback is the recognition among parents that technology plays an important part in learning and that they feel having access at home will help their child's education. With the feedback of the Oldham and Suffolk trials collated, Doug Woods (2009) from Becta noted:

> *The final data from all the LAs [Local Authorities] involved in the Home Access project is now being collated. The first piece of good news is that I can now confirm that over 20,000 learners will benefit from the project. These are learners who will receive kit and access directly but obviously there are also siblings, families and carers who can also benefit, so the number of beneficiaries will eventually be higher.*

> *... However, behind the figures there must be a lot of 'good news' stories about how learners are starting to use the kit, how learners who might never have online access can now benefit from it, or how learners can now make use of the kit in interesting ways.*

If you'd like to see for yourselves what some parents think of the program, you can watch a film made for parents in the pilot at http://www.becta.org.uk/homeaccess.

Home access specifications

The package on 'offer' to the eligible families appears quite strictly defined, but there is in fact plenty of room for variation as they state:

- pre-setup to make it easier, and quicker, to get going
- all the ready-to-use applications you need—create documents, spreadsheets and much more
- pre-set with parental controls; this means unsuitable content is blocked from the first time you turn it on
- three-years anti-virus protection to keep your computer safe
- a national rate or cheaper phone number to call if you need help
- warranty and re-instatement so you are covered if it breaks or is stolen
- loaded with *Know IT all*, the safety guide for parents.

(Source: Next Generation Learning 2009)

If the family does not need a full package (maybe they already have a computer at home and just want the Internet), then they can just get the bits they want. Any of the suppliers approved to sell these packages will be able to help choose what's right. A quick look at the site of one of the chosen providers, that of the Hughes stores (http://www.centerprise.co.uk/ha/), reveals the streamlined nature of the acquisition process.

There are some limitations as to what can be provided. For instance, there should be a viewable screen and an appropriate keyboard. Software is not specifically named, which therefore allows the use of low-cost open-source products. Families who qualify for the grant are provided with a 'smart card' to pay for their selected package.

The issues for schools and homes

Government recognition

One of the main issues to emerge from this initiative for all associated with school development is the UK Government's recognition and active endorsement of the fundamental role the students' homes play today in the education of all the nation's young people, the contribution that education is expected to play in enhancing national productivity and that all UK schools ought to be working more collaboratively with their homes. It is a message that all associated with schooling should heed, but it is particularly important for those in school leadership roles, for it is one many do not appear to have accepted.

The UK is saying clearly that today's education of young people should entail an appropriate nexus and indeed collaboration between the school and the home. Allied is the desire to create a collaborative learning culture in all homes where all the family members and the students' carers should collectively acquire the competencies to make the most of the ever-evolving technology. It is also indicating that the state does have a vital role in educating all young people in the school and in ensuring that the economically disadvantaged are looked after in their homes. Interestingly, the UK Government is not pretending it has all the answers but approached astutely and gradually the best way forward will be found.

Onus on the school and its community

While a national government can provide the direction and the support, ultimately the onus will always be on the school principal and the particular school community to adopt a mode of schooling appropriate to its situation. What the government literature does not say is that across Britain, like all other nations, there is an immense diversity of school settings—small and large, rural and urban, historic and modern—where many have 'quite challenging' relationships between the school and the students' homes. As indicated earlier, the current home–school relationship will have a major impact on how quickly and far the school bonds with the homes. If the school has highwire fences to protect it from its neighbourhood, it is starting well behind the small rural school with close community ties.

Removing the technology barrier

The Home Access program, in the not too distant future—particularly when coupled with the digital market take-up trend discussed earlier—will go a long way to allowing the UK's state-funded schools to work on the assumption that all their students have in their homes the technology needed to undertake the online or digital study set by the school. While (as mentioned in Chapter 4) that situation already exists in the vast majority of homes, this initiative removes that digital divide. However, there will invariably be some families who do not believe in using the technology, sometimes for religious or cultural reasons, and others who will never get their act together.

The UK's state-funded schools should by 2011 be able to plan on the knowledge that all their students have in their homes the technology needed to operate networked school communities. What is important to recognise is that while the UK Government is going a long way to removing the technological divide, what it can never do is change the learning culture within the home, get all families to appreciate the importance of education and provide the informal 'teaching' of the more astute parents and carers.

Graduated implementation

An important part of the UK initiative is the graduated implementation strategy adopted. Not only is the UK taking advantage of the Oldham and Suffolk pilots, it is building on years of national investment in school technology and research, and a national culture which now accepts that the technology is integral to student learning. The graduated approach, particularly when coupled with an appropriate monitoring and evaluation strategy, allows both the schools and government to minimise the risks of venturing into the unknown and to consistently learn during the journey forward.

Using the new to better perform the ways of old

Allied to the graduated implementation is the focus—at least initially—on using the home technology, and indeed the bond with the homes, to better perform the ways of old, be it homework, achievement in the national curriculum or student reporting. There are at this stage no calls to fundamentally change the nature of British schooling or the national curriculum even though the way is opened to this possibility. One senses the recognition that it is wise for schools and their communities to become confident with the new and then in time to begin using it in new and more effective ways.

Teaching and learning opportunities

The teaching and learning opportunities provided in the school and the home, and by the school working in collaboration with the homes (and as indicated in the other chapters) are already immense and growing steadily. However, what the Home Access program does— even if unintentionally—is to focus on the nature of teaching and learning in the homes of the economically disadvantaged, and schools and education authorities are required to consider how best they can assist parents, grandparents and carers who look after young people after school to make the best use of their digital technology.

Administration and communication

Having the technology and Internet connectivity in all the students' homes also opens the way to markedly enhance the efficiency and effectiveness of the school's administration and communication with its homes. As indicated in Chapter 3, much school administration and communication fall well short of that used in other medium-sized enterprises. When all homes have Internet access, why would schools be generating and distributing reams of paper for such items as newsletters, teaching materials, permission notes, excursions or student reports? Schools and their communities should markedly rethink their operations, significantly reduce their photocopying, printing, administration and postage costs and re-deploy those savings.

Preparing the homes

One senses the UK and its individual school communities need to give far more thought to preparing the homes and, in particular, the homes of the disadvantaged to make best use of the new digital technology. While a central authority like Becta can provide important direction and support, such as the video mentioned earlier, the real impact will come at the individual school level, with the school working with its parents and carers, giving them the understanding and help required to develop the competencies needed. Mention was made in Chapter 7 of the desirability of providing parents with the skills and understanding to enhance the students' informal education, while Chapter 8 makes mention of using the technology skills of the older students to assist the homes in need. It is advisable to be looking to local initiatives like these to prepare the homes.

A very real risk schools and education authorities need to watch is the propensity to impose middle-class values, and in the instance of digital technology often dated and simplistic views, on how to best use the technology with the disadvantaged. The advice and the support offered ought to be developed collaboratively, involving the parents and most assuredly the students concerned and take on board the very considerable digital capacity already in the home. As indicated, it is wrong to assume that because a home does not have a computer it lacks digital capacity and competence. Becta's September Home Access presentation (2009b) provides parents, students and the community with encouraging information on the educational and social benefits of the new technology, along with how the Home Access program will provide low-income families with the necessary practical and financial support to embrace the new technology.

Activating the parents

Probably the greatest shortcoming of the Home Access program at this stage of its development is the planned involvement of parents. The message that comes from the program literature is that the parents are seen as largely passive receivers of the direction and support coming from the education professionals. It is appreciated that that might not be the intention, but when one analyses the background research and the planned roll-out of the program one sees little mention of the parents, either the disadvantaged or the wider parent community of the school playing an active role in the education.

As indicated in earlier chapters, two under-used resources are the students' parents and the digital capacity of the home. The UK initiative as it currently stands seeks to make limited use of the parents or to harness their under-used contribution. There is, for example, no mention of them having any voice in the Home Access program at the school, authority or national level, even though the homes of the disadvantaged will have the technical wherewithal to make a significant contribution.

If schools and nations are to make the most of the home's capacity, they do need to begin using the new universal parental access and the online tools and draw the parents, the carers and in many instances the students into the educative process. As Brenton Holmes notes in Chapter 11 and Clay Shirky (2008) forewarns in *Here comes everybody*, parents now have in the near universal Internet access, an immense, if as yet underused, political weapon that is better deployed in a positive, collaborative mode than as a coercive tool, and which could, if used astutely, lead to the dismissal of school principals and education authority CEOs.

Unintended developments and benefits

The open-ended nature of the UK initiative provides the chance for English school communities to explore almost boundless opportunities with all students, particularly when the school reaches the digital stage and its staff is comfortable and ready to begin dismantling the school walls and work more collaboratively with the students' homes. In essence, the government has given schools and their communities the green light and a largely unimpeded road to begin exploring how best to use the digital capacity of both the school and the home, whatever form it might take.

Funding

A major concern about the current UK Home Access program is its limited funding. At this stage the funding runs out in 2011. As mentioned, it is already apparent that there are funding constraints and more than a suggestion that some deserving homes will miss out. While by 2011 a significant proportion of the UK's disadvantaged homes ought to have the technology, the reality is that the computers in the existing homes will need to be upgraded in four to five years; in 2010 and 2011 respectively another batch of disadvantaged homes will require support; and all the homes will need the funds to pay for appropriate Internet usage.

While the market cycle and the reducing equipment prices should lessen the number of families in need of support, there will nonetheless be a sizeable number of UK families always requiring state support. The Ministerial Task Force flagged the importance of the Home Access program having the requisite ongoing monies (Becta 2008a). That becomes ever-more important once the program is operational and the schools and their communities come to rely on it. It is appreciated the government is exploring a private–public funding model to provide the requisite ongoing funding, and indeed the likes of Microsoft has already made a contribution to that fund (Fiveash 2009), but the distinct impression is that this arrangement is a long way off providing all the requisite funds. The UK might do well to consider some of the ideas suggested in Chapter 7 on how the technology could be funded.

Evaluation and research

While Becta's track record would suggest the initiative will be appropriately evaluated and the research published, it is also incumbent on each school community to monitor and reflect upon the impact of the program in its homes, and early in the piece identify, by working collaboratively with its parents and the students affected, how it might make even better use of the technology.

Conclusion

As indicated at the outset, this UK initiative is one that parents and school leaders globally should watch with interest and learn from. While the UK context may well be different to yours, there will undoubtedly be important insights that can be gleaned and contacts for further investigation made.

Guiding questions

After reading this chapter, consider your context and propose your ideas in relation to the following guiding questions.

1   What are the most important messages relating to your school that emerge from the UK initiative?

2   Can you identify areas in your school community needing improved access?

3   What might your school community do to improve Internet access of your socio-economically disadvantaged students—in the short, medium and longer terms?

Key messages

• The UK's Home Access initiative is discussed as a case study to provide all interested in furthering the home–school nexus.

• No nation has as yet shown the educational courage or acumen to reach out and seek to collaborate with its students' homes on the scale of the UK.

• This UK initiative is one that parents and school leaders globally should watch with interest and learn from.

CHAPTER 13

Teaching and learning opportunities: Possibilities and practical ideas

JASON ZAGAMI & GLENN FINGER

We know that young people's access to technology to support learning beyond the classroom is critical to their educational success. Home access will help involve those that know the pupil best in supporting progress, for example, parents and members of the wider community. This will also ensure that evidence of learning gathered beyond the classroom provides a broad view of the whole learner.

... [this] carries significant opportunities and implications for learning and teaching in schools, including how homework, coursework, communication and assessment are managed in the future. This includes opportunities for supporting parental engagement, extended and remote learning, and greater use of learning platforms and technology-supported learning more generally

Becta (2009a, p. 8)

The changing nature of digital technologies for teaching and learning

Throughout the various chapters of this book there are references made to the pathfinder schools, which are characterised as schools undertaking early exploration of the learning and teaching opportunities of new and emerging digital technologies. The pathfinders are focused on the constant drive to search for those teaching and learning opportunities, and they have made the shift to becoming a digital school by making the important movement from reflection to action (Lee & Gaffney 2008). However, in *Leading a digital school*, Lee and Gaffney noted that, even where schools had obtained digital take-off, most schools continued to operate as isolated entities, and they urged that a key principle of leading a digital school is developing a connection between students' homes and their schools. They encourage you to consider the following questions:

- What moves has your organisation made to create a networked school community through the use of technology?
- Do you have a policy or plan to create such a community; or have your efforts—at least to this point—been rather spasmodic without any overarching framework?

(Source: Lee & Gaffney 2008, p. 181)

To become networked school communities, and to reposition the importance of learning in the home, pathfinder schools have adopted digital technologies in ways that technologies became 'must-haves'. Lee and Gaffney (2008) observed that laptop computers, access to the Internet and interactive whiteboards are examples of digital technologies that often appeared initially in an isolated pathfinder classroom or school, and then the uptake occurred usually as the technology's capability and reliability increased, while costs decreased. Internationally, there is increasing evidence that digital technologies provide teaching and learning opportunities for strengthening the relationship between the learner, home and school.

This chapter explores the teaching and learning opportunities afforded by creating a networked school community through the following discussion that examines the changing nature of digital technologies for teaching and learning. Specifically, the technological convergence of the home–school nexus is presented. Subsequently, the chapter signals emerging opportunities of paradigm changing curriculum tools, the potential for social networks to become transformed to learning networks, and the implications for teaching and parenting in a 'new' world. Advice is provided for filtering the deluge of new opportunities and re-defining the scope of learning opportunities. The framing of exploring future teaching and learning opportunities is provided through the three adoption horizons used by the New Media Consortium and the EDUCAUSE Learning Initiative in *The Horizon Report: 2009* (Johnson et al. 2009).

What changes in digital technologies are occurring? What are some of the implications of those changes for moving towards a home–school nexus? Answers to those questions require a disposition for educators to constantly adopt a futures-oriented approach that is focused on identifying opportunities for teaching and learning. That disposition can be guided by using the three adoption horizon timeframes which *The Horizon Report: 2009* uses for the entrance of technologies into mainstream use for teaching, learning, research or creative applications; namely:

> *The first adoption horizon assumes the likelihood of entry into the mainstream of institutions within the next year; the second, within two to three years; and the third, within four to five years. (p. 3)*

The Horizon Report identified the following digital technologies for each of those adoption horizons:

- First adoption horizon: *mobiles* and *cloud computing*
- Second adoption horizon: *geo-everything* and the *personal web*
- Third adoption horizon: *semantic-aware applications* and *smart objects*.

That report notes that mobiles and cloud computing are evident now in what the authors refer throughout this book as the pathfinder schools. While others might not be aware of these technologies, some schools—particularly in those schools that are banning student use of mobiles—are aware but tend to resist any examination of their possibilities for teaching and learning.

A key challenge is to ensure that there are mechanisms and opportunities for exploring and identifying the possibilities. We suggest that the Horizon Reports are a means for doing this. Visit http://www.nmc.org/horizon regularly to keep abreast of the new and emerging technologies. These reports adopt a methodology that narrows down to identifying two technologies drawn from hundreds of technologies for each adoption horizon. The reports usefully explore the teaching and learning possibilities for each of the technologies. At the launch of the Australian and New Zealand edition in September 2009, Larry Johnson, CEO of The New Media Consortium, proposed that seven 'metatrends' were evident throughout the series of Horizon Report issues; namely:

Metatrend 1:   **The people**—the people are the network;

Metatrend 2:   **The network is everywhere**—too big for any person, nation or entity to control; e.g. cloud computing, private clouds, cell phone network with 1.1 billion new phones sold in 2007, 1.2 billion new phones sold in 2008, and 1.1 billion in 2009, which represents one new phone for every six people on the planet each year;

Metatrend 3:   **Collective intelligence**—re-purpose massive unorganised data sets (often produced by the public) to provide rich meaningful information; e.g. semantic applications;

Metatrend 4:   **Content is everywhere**—intellectual property and copyright are becoming increasingly irrelevant, with new information being co-created by many on the Web; e.g. geolocations;

Metatrend 5:   **Keyboards are for old people**—moving towards intuitive and natural interfaces with others, for various purposes and tasks; e.g. emergence of gesture-based computers, smart objects;

Metatrend 6:   **Serious games**—evident in the increasing focus of advanced training systems; and

Metatrend 7:   **Computing in three dimensions**—moving towards visualisations, and currently 3D visualisations.

The development of networked school communities aligns well with understanding that the people are the network, that networks are everywhere, collective intelligence is apparent, and content is everywhere. This differs markedly from confining learning to 'a place called school'.

Technological convergence—towards a home–school nexus

The availability of computer hardware in schools and homes has not tended to develop synchronously and in partnership with each other. Generally, while schools have made attempts to provide greater access for students to computers and the Internet in schools, there is now compelling evidence that for many students access to computers and the Internet in their home exceeds what was available in schools. While there have been fluctuations in access, there are still schools that provide relatively restricted access to computers for many students. As indicated in Chapter 4, this can be viewed as a difference to be capitalised on rather than being viewed as a digital divide.

Today, many homes have several computers and many more equivalent devices ranging from games consoles, media centres and mobile phones. Similar fluctuations have occurred with access to the Internet and software. Provision of computers and Internet access for students at home can be attributed to some extent by parents having the desire to maximise the productive learning of their children. Increasingly, students need access to a computer, the Internet and a printer in their homes to do their school assessment tasks. While there is a difference between home and school access that provides opportunities for schools to leverage, schools are also being pressed to provide students with greater access to digital technologies at school, to replicate and be relevant to industry and professional settings beyond the school.

This convergence between home, school and industry contexts has also required schools to introduce educational technologies of a more specialised nature. For example, interactive whiteboards have been widely adopted, learning management systems are being introduced, online course delivery is being explored, and a variety of specialised technologies such as scientific data probes, biometric feedback sensors and GPS systems are being introduced that exceed what is available in most homes. Likewise, home use of computer games, brain training software, mobile technologies, social networking and online tutoring greatly exceed their use in schools. The convergence and the differences present opportunities.

Ubiquitous access to digital technologies—u-learning

The uptake of technology in both the school and at home is increasing, with technology becoming incorporated into every aspect of modern life. Decreasing cost has led to a more widespread adoption of personal mobile phones, Netbooks, cable and wireless networks. Mobile devices and the Internet have changed the way we communicate and search engines have changed the way we access and think about information. These technologies have moved to become ubiquitous, and when used for learning it is referred to as 'u-learning' (Nalder 2009). As discussed in Chapter 5, u-learning is a combination of e-learning and m-learning, where the learner can be mobile yet immersed in a digital ecosystem. This contrasts markedly to the earlier structures of the one stand-alone computer sitting in a classroom, disconnected from the home, from the learner, and often from the world beyond the classroom.

This can be taken even further to envision the learner interfacing with projectors, cameras and hand gestures to interact with everyday objects and situations (Mistry, Maes & Chang 2009), while others might conjecture interaction directly from and back to the brain. Information becomes available when and how we require it, communication becomes rich and continuous, and access is readily available to the computational power we need to perform tasks, access information and communicate in ways beyond what is available today. Emerging trends include online data storage, software and operating systems—cloud computing—which are continuing to decouple users from desktop computing (Horrigan 2008), while mobile technologies, location aware or geolocation (Johnson, Levine & Smith 2009) and mixed-reality interactions with the environment will change the way information, businesses and people continuously interact with the embodied and digital representations of ourselves and our world.

Emerging technologies—the opportunities

Paradigm changing curriculum tools

The emergence and adoption of technological innovations are fundamentally challenging and transforming the existing curriculum in schools. The Web, digital texts, blogging, micro-blogging, texting, podcasting and video sharing are changing the nature of the English language curricula throughout the world to transform and complement existing modes of communication. This is only an example of a wider transformation of curriculum that is likely to continue. For example, while the Internet has transformed how students access, manage and use information, *The Horizon Report: 2009* (Johnson et al. 2009) indicates that currently online data is available for searching but its meaning is not, and suggests in its third adoption horizon—four to five years—that the vision for the semantic web is that it will do more in understanding the context in which key words are used:

> A typical search on the term 'turkey', for instance, might return traditional recipes, information about the bird, and information about the country; the search engine can only pick out key words, and cannot distinguish among different uses of the words.
>
> ... Semantic-aware applications are tools designed to use the meaning, or semantics, of information on the Internet to make connections and provide answers that would otherwise entail a great deal of time and effort. (p. 23)

Semantic websites are appearing, such as *WolframAlpha* (see www.wolframalpha.com/), which provides the ability to complete and document complex mathematical problems using natural language and, as such, offers challenges to the mathematics curriculum as did the introduction of calculators and spreadsheeting software applications. Similarly,

SemantiFind (see www.semantifind.com) is a plug-in for use with Google and provides a drop-down menu that prompts the user to select the semantic sense to improve the search results (Johnson, Levine & Smith 2009). The semantic web already needs to be factored into curriculum redesign.

To illustrate further examples of digital technologies that are curriculum-changing tools, the increasing sharing of live experimental data, data visualisation techniques, computer modelling and simulations to replace laboratory experiments present challenges to the science curriculum as much as it is challenging the field of science. Moreover, online mapping, access to live data collections, geocoding and ubiquitous GPS systems are revolutionising the nature of the geography curriculum. Teachers who are using interactive whiteboards and GoogleEarth have transformed the way geography is accessed by students and taught by teachers. An example of this is the National Geographic-led *My wonderful world* (National Geographic Society 2007a; see www.mywonderfulworld.org/index.html) which, in addition to having links for *Educators* and for *Kids and Teens*, also welcomes parents, and states, 'Parents, it's in your power to make sure your kids are getting the most out of our wonderful world' (National Geographic Society 2007b).

The way-back machine and the growing depth of digital footprints are changing the nature of the history curriculum from one of scarce primary source material to over-abundance. Biometrics, video analysis, Wii entertainment consoles and fitness trackers in cell phones are challenging the nature of physical education, and automatic language translators for websites and the spoken word challenges the nature of foreign language education. Computer education, long charged with directly meeting the educational challenges of technological innovation, is transforming from a study of how to use computers and software application, to developing the creativity and innovation required to flourish in a world of rapid technological change, with information literacy, visual literacy and technological literacy seen (Johnson, Levine & Smith 2009) as essential new elements of a modern curriculum.

Transformation of social networks to learning networks

In homes, the ways in which young people communicate with each other is also undergoing rapid change. These need to be better understood by educators (as discussed in Chapters 4 and 5). For example, the use of mobile phones by young people produced the unanticipated effect of a reduced use of these for voice calls, with young people embracing the use of SMS. Similarly, email is not the major communication device used, as young people use online chat tools such as MSN, micro-blogging such as Twitter, social networking websites such as MySpace and Facebook, and networked computer games. While schools have tended to focus on the negative influences of these tools at home, such as cyber-bullying discussed in Chapter 18, pathfinder schools are exploring their use to facilitate professional communication and networking. This shift in thinking translates to examining the opportunities for students to use and transform social networks to become powerful learning networks.

Social networking tools are increasingly being used as an alternative source of information and advice over traditional search engines. Young people are able to use their social networks as an extended resource when learning at home, but as yet few schools have embraced the potential that learning networks could provide to support learning at school, seeing the social nature of such communication solely as a distraction to the formal learning process. Some guidance is provided by Warlick (2009) in his identification of three main types of personal learning networks (PLNs):

- *Personally maintained synchronous connections*—the traditional network which can be enhanced using tools such as iChat, Skype, uStream, Twitter, Second Life;

- *Personally and socially maintained semisynchronous connections*—for networked learners, 'semisynchronous' refers to collaboration not having to happen in real time; online communities can engage when it suits them, and can use tools such as mailing lists, wikis, Google Docs, Twitter, and comment on blogs;

- *Dynamically maintained asynchronous connections*—Warlick suggests that while the first two connect us with one another, this PLN connects us with content sources that we identify as being valuable; the key tool is the RSS aggregator, and examples include Google Reader, Netvibes and Pageflakes.

Warlick's differentiation enables us to see a paradigmatic shift in the *dynamically maintained asynchronous connections* PLN whereby this has 'inspired a shift from a hunting-and-gathering information economy to the domestication of the information landscape' (Warlick 2009, p. 14).

Teaching and parenting in a 'new' world

While we know that teaching has been limited in the past to available educational resources such as books, pencil and paper, the Internet has fostered the widespread sharing of educational resources and become an essential component of learning design and implementation. Publishing models that once restricted access to high-quality resources are now challenged by open education policies that make resources more freely available legally to remix, improve and redistribute, including videos, images, audio recordings, books, lesson plans, games, simulations and full courses (Borgman et al. 2008).

Excellent examples have been learning object repositories developed locally, nationally and internationally, which complement the vast array of learning resources made freely available to teachers by organisations as diverse as the Learning Federation, NASA, the BBC and MIT. Coupled with the proliferation of open-source software, online software applications and system-wide purchasing negotiations, access to high-quality educational content, tools and environments is now more widely available to all schools with high bandwidth.

As countries make available more universal broadband there will come a wealth of new learning and teaching opportunities. For example, in Australia, the Fibre to the Home (FTTH) network through the roll-out of the National Broadband Network is planned to provide '90 per cent of homes, schools and businesses a connection of 100 megabits a second, 100 times faster than now' (*ABC News* 2009). The evolutionary changes that we have witnessed in communications can be enhanced by universal broadband enabling new opportunities for creating the home–school nexus. Again, pathfinder schools are already recognising the importance of authentically engaging their parents' and their students' learning in the home through online newsletters, emails, websites, SMS messages, and social networking tools such as Twitter and Facebook.

All Australian schools are required to provide annual reporting of school statistics online, but there seems to be limited use by schools in providing regular online versions of their paper-based newsletters to communicate with parents via email or school websites. While parents are increasingly using email to individually communicate to schools, other than responding to parent inquiries, few schools have initiated direct communication with parents on an individual basis as a means of supporting student learning (Becta 2009c). As referred to in Chapter 14, there are examples of online reporting emerging that improve parental engagement and are more effective for teachers than traditional practices. For example, see Becta (2008e), *Exploiting ICT to improve parental engagement: Moving towards online reporting*, at http://publications.becta.org.uk/display.cfm?resID=38170). Online digital portfolios, class websites and blogs, learning management systems, online attendance and standards reporting systems provide structured means to record and make available information on student progress and achievement.

Parental access to such data provides opportunities for improved learning to occur in the home, particularly when coupled with increased communication between parents and teachers. The latter is important and repositions parents as the originators and key participants, rather than waiting for an invitation from the school. Recorded by students and parents, educational activities and outcomes achieved in the home could also contribute back to such online recording systems, providing an improved overall understanding of a student's learning. In this way, increased parental involvement in school-based learning would enable interdependence, with parents and students being viewed as partners in learning.

With greater parental involvement in schools, the challenge for parents will be for them to inform change as well as gain greater awareness of the fundamental changes occurring in education. Those changes might be different from educational practices they were familiar with in their schooling. In a world where books were probably dominant, schools focused on selecting the most effective mix of texts to support student learning. School libraries contained collections of age-appropriate resources on topics deemed suitable and of interest to students, and most homes included a prized set of encyclopaedia.

In *Harnessing technology for next generation learning: Children, schools and families implementation plan 2009–2012*, Becta (2009a) has as one of its four core goals 'Strengthened relationships between families, schools and learners—with an emphasis on the adoption of information systems and use of online tools to improve parental involvement' (p. 4). It notes parental engagement as one of the strategy's key challenges:

> ... there is strong demand among parents and carers for online information and communication which is not yet being met. This can support better learning relationships between schools and parents. Many schools require further support and guidance to achieve what we know is possible with technology. (p. 9)

Disappearing walls of the classrooms and bedrooms

Since the inception of the Internet there has been concern over the intrusion of the online world into the privacy of young people's homes. This concern has extended to schools, with an initial response being to ban access, establish tightly managed environments and impose Internet filtering. While dubiously effective for a time, they were circumvented by proxy servers, personal email accounts and the ever-expanding range of online tools and websites. The greatest challenge, however, comes from the widespread adoption of mobile devices. As outlined throughout this book, a control and coercion approach is neither desirable nor possible due to the disappearing protection of classroom and bedroom walls.

Modern mobile phones, PDAs, iPods, laptops and handheld gaming consoles are increasingly being used by young people to achieve personal access to online tools and resources that schools and parents might seek to restrict. National online content-filtering solutions will limit access to only the smallest fraction of material of concern to schools and parents, and will undoubtedly be as easily circumvented as currently imposed restrictions. Schools will soon face an environment in which students using personal Internet-enabled devices will completely bypass school-based restrictions. As consistently argued in Chapter 18 by Kevin Larkin, Glenn Finger and Roberta Thompson, banning their use will continue to be ineffective as both parents and their children are increasingly reliant on mobile communication to manage their lives in an increasingly hectic world, and place greater trust in their ability to intervene or seek assistance in an emergency over that which was previously entrusted to schools.

Where the use of the Internet has matured and students, parents and schools are increasingly confident in their capacity to minimise potential dangers, these concerns are then responsibly balanced against the opportunities afforded by online access. Classroom learning can extend to involve schools, students and experts from across the globe seamlessly. Warlick's (2009) *Personally maintained synchronous connections, Personally and socially maintained semisynchronous connections* and *Dynamically maintained asynchronous connections* personal learning networks can be enabled. Students at home can engage in meaningful learning through virtual field trips, accessing, managing and analysing rich online content sourced to enhance classroom learning, and students can share and celebrate their learning with friends, family and global audiences.

At home, young people are already adapting to a world of online environments involving huge online communities (e.g. Facebook, MySpace), massive multi-player online role-playing games (e.g. World of Warcraft), and virtual worlds (e.g. Second Life) (Barab et al. 2007). The hype of Internet and online gaming addiction can be put in perspective with the many obsessive passions of youth, and balanced against the opportunity to develop the skills they will need to successfully operate in a world enmeshed in digital media and communication.

The removal of boundaries—the dismantling of the classroom and the bedroom walls—that protect and isolate the home and school from the intrusion of the outside world also allow young people to engage with this increasingly digital, networked world. Education, isolated and institutionalised, has the opportunity to re-engage with the world in which young people will live, and that world extends globally. At home young people can seamlessly communicate, play and learn with their friends in ways that are not limited by suburb, sunset or the perceived dangers of outside play.

As these boundaries and barriers are inevitably re-defined and removed, the distinction between school and home needs to be seen as a difference rather than a divide. Learning can occur and be valued when and where young people have opportunities to learn, both physically and virtually. Young people will have access to personal learning networks and networked learning spaces, as discussed by Kay Kimber and Claire Wyatt-Smith in Chapter 17. They will collaborate with teachers, peers, parents and their community, facilitated by technologies such as email, social networking, online games and audio- and video-conferencing. Such reframing of learning requires a rethink of the role of the professional educator and of their relationship with parents and students.

Roles for the professional educator

Through the years, many technological innovations have been accompanied by advocates foretelling the irrelevancy of teachers and schools as we saw the appearance of new technologies, such as books, recordings, film, television, computer-based training, the Internet, online education and most recently, social networking. Lee and Winzenried (2009) make the important observation in *The use of instructional technology in schools*:

> *... with the introduction of each of the emerging technologies is a surprising lack of implementation strategies with an underlying educational vision ...*
>
> *Rather, what one finds are implementation strategies that focus on the technical, with scant regard for the human change component. (p. 16)*

Educators, as with learners themselves, adapt and respond to the challenges advanced by technology, but education—with the exception of the pathfinders—has proven to be conservative in nature, assuming the role of inculcating each new generation and preparing them for a role within society. Until recently, education has lacked the intense market pressures that force the immediate changes needed to remain competitive in business. However, with increased transparency and accountability, resistance to change is no longer sufficient in a competitive, globalised knowledge economy. In Australia, even early childhood education is now linked to the Australian Government's productivity agenda.

Knowledge and skill acquisition in narrow and traditional discipline fields can no longer be the prime focus of formal education; what is learned is no longer as important as developing and strengthening the capabilities involved in learning, problem solving, communicating and creativity. Modern life and work are too complex, diverse and subject to change to be accommodated by a narrow discipline-focused curriculum of common skills and knowledge. For example, the *Framework for 21st Century Learning* 'presents a holistic view of 21st century teaching and learning that combines a discrete focus on 21st century student outcomes (a blending of specific skills, content knowledge, expertise and literacies) with innovative support systems to help students master the multi-dimensional abilities required of them in the 21st century' (Partnership for 21st Century Skills 2009).

The Framework indicates that the twenty-first century requires new roles of educators to develop learning and innovation skills of creativity and innovation, critical thinking and problem solving, and communication and collaboration. Developing these in pen-and-paper based classrooms is inadequate. Rather, they need to be coupled with information literacy, media literacy and ICT literacy, along with life and career skills as an overarching extension to traditional disciplines. The Partnership for 21st Century Skills (2009) suggests that teachers and students need to use these as contexts to develop the vital skills, knowledge and expertise that students need to master in order to work and live in the twenty-first century. Within such a framework, curriculum decisions can increasingly be focused on general learner capabilities instead of long lists of required knowledge and skills.

For this transformation to be sufficient, the authors suggest that all educators need to adopt at least the minimal position of researching the work of the pathfinders to draw upon the transferability of what is being designed, implemented and learned to continually renew and redesign their role and practice. The authors suggest that the best way to achieve this is to engage and model being a member of a networked community of learners and for educators to develop and engage in their PLN.

Students are increasingly becoming '24/7 learners', merging entertainment and social activities with learning opportunities, and increasingly they are supported by complex systems of mentors: teachers, parents, siblings, relatives, friends, work colleagues, tutors, psychologists, therapists, personal trainers, and life coaches—to name some existing possibilities. The development of PLNs that provide advice, guidance and support will challenge the mass transmission model dominant in most classrooms and lecture theatres. The importance of teachers will undoubtedly remain, but as experts on how to learn, not on what is being learned.

The very scope and range of educational possibilities available with new digital technologies, their ability to occur in pathfinder projects and move to more widespread, ubiquitous implementation, and the flexibility in how students can now learn, liberate the ability of educators to schedule and designate what is learned, when, where and how. Increasingly, the converse can occur if there isn't a fit for purpose between the school's offering and young people's identity, and engagement with the world in which they live and will work. The impact might be that young people will disengage from traditional schools and curriculum. This disengagement might occur not just from perceived or actual irrelevance, but from the ease at which they can accomplish what is mandated by formal curriculum. Focused increasingly on learning what they want to learn, the formal curriculum may increasingly be looked upon with the mix of sympathy, apathy and frustration, which might well be how many young people look on the use of digital technologies in schools today. Anecdotally, we have heard stories from parents of conscientious, high-performing students that their children have said they 'tolerate' school and can't wait to get home to get into some serious work on their assignments where they don't have to wait for a timetable to allow them to engage online.

Redefining the scope of ubiquitous learning opportunities

Globalisation is challenging traditional concepts of education, online courses are available from and to anywhere on the globe, highly qualified tutors from developing nations are available online, the quality of online educational resources are increasing to where they do not need teachers to facilitate their use, and computer games are increasingly drawing upon educational domains to provide contexts and challenges. Many computer games now offer educational experiences far beyond the reach of schools. Simulations have evolved from the likes of *Sim City* and are now available in dozens of curriculum domains, from learning how to manage a farm, theme park or movie studio, to complex geopolitical simulations spanning nations and galaxies. Such games rely on problem solving as the inherent driver to the entertainment experience, and as problem solving becomes central to the educational process, increasing recognition will be given to such simulations and game play.

The World Wide Web is defined by the ways in which individuals can express themselves creatively. Students can publish online—often just to their friends, but potentially to billions. The effort and creativity they put into their MySpace environments, websites and YouTube creations often greatly exceed their classroom projects, particularly in terms of their engagement and the amount of time devoted to these. As personal online spaces become more complex and interactive, and the tools more accessible and intuitive, students will increasingly engage creatively with 3D modelling, programming, digital music making and film production. Traditional arguments that students engage only superficially with such tools and that formal learning is required to progress them beyond basic usage, is not sustainable in light of self-instruction tutorials, guides, supportive online communities and the increasingly intuitive nature of the tools developed to support these activities. Photo editing, movie making and 3D modelling were the domain of expensive and specialised software tools only a few years ago, now each is possible using online websites, designed for intuitive and untutored use.

While these points relate closely to problem solving and creativity, the third key aspect of the *Framework for 21st Century Learning* is communication and collaboration. Web 2.0 encompasses tools and processes for ubiquitous communication and collaboration. Traditional educational concepts of individual and group tasks are passé when students are naturally drawing upon their personal networks to complete learning tasks at home, and wherever they can get away with it at school. Young people are increasingly experiencing the world as a shared mixed-reality experience, in constant electronic contact with friends that can be dispersed globally. Multi-player games and virtual 3D environments provide opportunities to share entertainment experiences and creative expression.

The constant online sharing of the minutiae of young people's lives through MySpace, Facebook and Twitter replicate coffee shop meet-ups, but continuously and with dozens to hundreds of friends; sleep is becoming described as a *network interruption*. They naturally view challenges and educational tasks within such collaborative frameworks and draw upon their networks to assist them in learning and problem solving. This collaborative world view sees the attempts of antiquated copyright and intellectual property frameworks to keep pace with new technologies and forms of communication with undisguised derision. Young people freely share their creative contributions and expect to be able to freely access what they need to further their own creativity and learning. They are not averse to spending freely on the tools and infrastructure to enable this to occur, and see the commercialisation of online content as outdated and obstructive to an environment that has been built on the free exchange of ideas and creative works.

Conclusion

During the past decade, the sciences of how people learn and the technologies available to support learning, teaching and education have begun to productively co-evolve (Borgman et al. 2008). This chapter has identified some of the teaching and learning opportunities afforded by the development of a networked school community and creating an effective home–school nexus of interaction. The authors suggested that it was useful to continually examine the 'horizon technologies' through the three adoption horizons used in *The Horizon Report: 2009* (Johnson, Levine & Smith 2009). In addition, it was suggested that educators research the work of the pathfinders to continually inform their practice, and to identify the opportunities.

In the discussion about the convergence of digital technologies, it was established that educators, parents and students are now faced with a wealth of learning and teaching opportunities, which are needed to be embraced to transform the deficiencies of traditional education structures that work from a school–home digital divide to adopt a home–school difference. This can be capitalised on through the tools and practices that have become ubiquitous for students beyond the classroom and bedroom walls.

The chapter provided practical ideas that can be explored further—such as PLNs—and that demonstrated the central importance of the continuing educative role needed to be played by parents, teachers and schools as learning partners in networked school communities. Increases in the professionalism and expectations of teachers in the twenty-first century, in a context of rapidly emerging technologies, can facilitate the optimal learning conditions for students, both within and outside of school. Teachers themselves will need to learn new approaches to teaching and learning in order to achieve such benefits and this will be a fundamental change, and the shift required of many will be substantial.

It can only be achieved when teachers embrace and model the use of digital technologies to support their own learning, engaging fully with emerging technologies—online communications, simulations, mobiles, games, online communities, virtual worlds and personal learning networks. Teachers have managed to adapt to email and the WWW, though this took longer than most aspects of society and, indeed, some are still questioning and struggling with the change. Just as technological literacy is essential for the students of the twenty-first century, it is vital for our educators if they are to continue to retain relevancy to the learning processes of their students.

Beyond pedagogical practice, teachers will continue to increasingly use technology to manage the learning process through measurement, diagnosis and evaluation. As formal educational practice becomes more complex, verifiable and robust, requiring detailed and continuous analysis of numerous measurable variables, the capacity for parental understanding of the processes involved will diminish. However, opportunities to extend these new capacities to optimise student learning to all facets of a student's life will involve the home and all non-school environments. An increasing component of a child's learning will involve non-school activities, and while schools and parents may guide aspects of this learning, increasingly young people will direct their own learning afforded by technology and individual interests.

Increased trust in the professionalism of teachers to manage and support student learning can be supported by increased transparency and the open involvement of the whole community. Schools, teachers, parents and most of all students require trust in an educational system to which alternatives exist. Parents and students must recognise the professional contribution of schools and teachers, and likewise professional educators must recognise and value the contribution to be made by the home and the decision-making capacity of students as the best guide for their interests and passions. Despite the challenges involved, a home–school nexus of digital technology supported interaction is well placed to support an effective educational environment for students in the twenty-first century.

Guiding questions

After reading this chapter, consider your context and propose your ideas in relation to the following guiding questions.

1   What are some of the digital technologies mentioned in the chapter that you believe your school should be adopting?

2   By adopting those digital technologies, what kind of learning and teaching opportunities would you like to see it explore in the short and longer term?

3   How could the new and emerging digital technologies assist personalise learning?

4   What ideas in relation to the 'disappearing walls of the classroom and the bedroom' do you think could improve student learning?

5   What new roles for educators do you think are needed?

Key messages

- Emerging opportunities for learning and teaching are available through paradigm changing curriculum tools, and the potential for social networks to become transformed to learning networks.

- Warlick's *Personally maintained synchronous connections*, *Personally and socially maintained semisynchronous connections* and *Dynamically maintained asynchronous connections* personal learning networks (PLNs) can be enabled.

- Students are increasingly becoming '24/7 learners' operating in PLNs, merging entertainment and social activities with learning opportunities, and increasingly they are supported by complex systems of mentors: teachers, parents, siblings, relatives, friends, work colleagues, tutors, psychologists, therapists, personal trainers and life coaches.

CHAPTER 14

Teacher readiness: TPACK capabilities and redesigning working conditions

GLENN FINGER & ROMINA JAMIESON-PROCTOR

The quality of an education system cannot exceed the quality of its teachers.

McKinsey Report (Barber & Mourshed 2007, p. 13)

We argue that intelligent pedagogical uses of technology require the development of a complex, situated form of knowledge we call Technological Pedagogical Content Knowledge (TPCK). At the heart of TPCK is the dynamic, transactional relationship between content, pedagogy and technology. Good teaching with technology requires understanding the mutually reinforcing relationships between all three elements taken together to develop appropriate, context-specific strategies and representations.

Matthew Koehler, Punya Mishra & Kurnia Yahya (2007, p. 741)

Teacher readiness—networked school communities and expectations of teachers

The quotation from the McKinsey Report focuses the reader's attention on the importance of quality teachers. Chapter 1 drew attention to the differentiation between *quality teachers* and the more sophisticated concept envisioned by the creation of networked school communities of *quality teaching* where teaching is seen as a shared responsibility. The networked school community vision recognises the importance of quality twenty-first century teachers being ready and having the capabilities to assume the new roles required. In this chapter, drawing on the contemporary work of Mishra and Koehler (2006) and Koehler and Mishra (2008), we present the conceptualisation of Technological Pedagogical Content Knowledge, now being referred to as TPACK (formerly TPCK)—'the total package'—to inform teacher readiness.

In addition, the chapter urges that we need to redesign teachers' working conditions—their roles, the buildings and their classrooms. A redesign is also needed of the largely nineteenth- and twentieth-century rigid timetable based as it is upon an industrial model of schooling.

This means a 'dismantling of the classroom walls' and a challenging of the 9–3 timetable punctuated by playground duty, and the assumption that learning occurs predominantly in the classroom, to embrace the digital technologies and learning in the home through understandings of the emergence of learners being immersed in healthy digital ecosystems. This chapter explores the question: What does this mean in terms of teacher readiness and redesigning working conditions?

What expectations are there for teacher capabilities in networked school communities? Given the central importance of quality teachers in improving student learning, what does this mean for teacher readiness?

For teaching in the twenty-first century, teacher capabilities need to include technological knowledge (Hughes cited in Roblyer & Doering 2009) for enabling learning to take place in an increasingly networked, digital world. This quest has been reflected in the development of a range of standards, expectations for teachers, and the proliferation of reports, the growth of 'computer education', 'ICT' and 'technology' professional associations, and journals focusing on sharing and improving professional knowledge and practice using digital technologies. In Australia, in 2002, the report *Raising the standards: A proposal for the development of an ICT competency framework for teachers* (DEST 2002) mapped Australian developments and international trends in considering strategies for developing a national framework for describing teacher ICT competency standards, which could be used by teacher education institutions, teacher employers and professional associations to develop ICT standards relevant to their purposes and contexts.

Internationally, ISTE has developed The ISTE national educational technology standards (NETS•T) and performance indicators for teachers (ISTE 2008) organised according to five standards, with each having four performance indicators:

1   Facilitate and inspire student learning and creativity.

2   Design and develop digital-age learning experiences and assessments.

3   Model digital-age work and learning.

4   Promote and model digital citizenship and responsibility.

5   Engage in professional growth and leadership.

Of direct relevance to networked school communities, in modelling digital-age work and learning, ISTE includes performance indicators which state that teachers are expected to 'collaborate with students, peers, parents and community members using digital tools and resources to support student success and innovation', and to 'communicate relevant information and ideas effectively to students, parents and peers using a variety of digital-age media and formats' (ISTE 2008, p. 1).

ISTE also developed a set of standards for administrators—*ISTE NETS for administrators* (ISTE 2002)—according to six standards: Leadership and vision; Learning and teaching; Productivity and professional practice; Support, management and operations; Assessment and evaluation; and Social, legal and ethical issues. Interestingly, through the NETS Refresh Project, these were updated in June 2009 to become Visionary leadership; Digital Age learning culture; Excellence in professional practice; Systemic improvement; and Digital citizenship (ISTE 2009). In the revised set of expectations relating to excellence in professional practice, a performance indicator is for educational administrators to 'facilitate and participate in learning communities that stimulate, nurture and support administrators, faculty, and staff in the study and use of technology' (ISTE 2009). This implies readiness for teachers to move beyond the traditional classroom and school boundaries.

In Australia, Arthur (2009), in his article 'Experience the Digital Education Revolution', argues that the Australian Government's Digital Education Revolution vision will require 'well-trained teachers' (p. 49). He notes that, 'Teacher pre-service education coverage is varied' (p. 52), and that teacher professional development programs are required to 'integrate ICT into pedagogical practice' (p. 52). This is to be assisted through the Australian Government's $11.25 million school-based professional development, with strategic advice from the Teaching for the Digital Age initiative. Clearly, it is no longer sufficient for teachers to be trained from an earlier era prior to digital technologies. The following section proposes the TPACK conceptualisation to develop teacher readiness for networked school communities.

Technological pedagogical content knowledge (TPACK) capabilities

The design of most teacher education programs—both pre-service and continuing professional development programs—is informed by Shulman's pedagogical content knowledge (PCK), described by Shulman (1987) as 'the special amalgam of content and pedagogy that is uniquely the province of teachers, their own special form of professional understanding' (p. 8). Teacher readiness in relation to PCK highlights the importance of teachers' deep knowledge of the curriculum, and the pedagogical knowledge needed to teach this disciplinary knowledge successfully. Few (including Shulman) would have been able to envision the technological changes that have occurred since the late 1980s.

For teachers to have the readiness to effectively design and engage in networked school communities, there is growing support for technological knowledge to complement content knowledge and pedagogical knowledge. Koehler and Mishra (2005) have introduced Technological Pedagogical Content Knowledge (TPCK)—now referred to as TPACK, with the connotation of TPACK being the *total package* as a way of representing what teachers need to know about technology, content and pedagogy. Elsewhere, Schrum et al. (2007) note that until the pedagogical approaches take advantage of a technology's pedagogical affordances to achieve content-specific learning objectives and these are identified, it will not be possible to prepare teachers to make effective use of current and emerging technologies.

According to Mishra and Koehler (2008) teachers with TPACK have knowledge of content, pedagogy and technology, as well as understanding of the complex interaction between these knowledge components. They argue that teachers who have this type of understanding are characterised by the creative, flexible and adaptive ways in which they navigate the constraints, affordances and interactions within the TPACK framework.

> *The TPACK framework suggests that the kinds of knowledge teachers need to develop can almost be seen as a new form of literacy … Viewing teachers' use of technology as a new literacy emphasizes the role of the teacher as a producer (as designer), away from the traditional conceptualization of teachers as consumers (users) of technology.*

Mishra & Koehler (2008, pp. 10–11)

Consequently, teacher readiness for networked school communities can be framed in terms of TPACK capabilities, with the teacher positioned as curriculum designer (envisioned in Figure 2.1 in Chapter 2). This readiness provides teachers with the capabilities required to take advantage of the digital, networked technology, and become participants in a more collaborative, networked and inclusive operational mode involving the wider community in the provision of a quality education appropriate for the digital future.

TPACK capabilities and networked school communities

TPACK, as displayed in Figure 14.1, appropriately represents the central proposition that 'at the heart of good teaching with technology are three core components—content, pedagogy and technology, and the relationships between them' (Mishra & Koehler 2008, pp. 11–12).

Importantly, TPACK enables you to understand how the selection of technologies, the development of your digital technologies infrastructure and your planning to move to become a digital school, and subsequent move to create a networked school community, require pedagogic and content considerations to inform the technological decisions. Whether or not you introduce interactive whiteboards, virtual learning environments, learning management systems, or understand the implications of digital ecosystems (discussed in Chapter 13), your decisions and design of learning should focus on the intersection of technology, pedagogy and content. Where initiatives have failed and been ineffective we suggest that this can usually be explained in terms of the 'total package'—TPACK—not informing that thinking, design and implementation.

In addition, TPACK understands that context matters, and that solutions require 'nuanced understanding that goes beyond the general principles of content, technology and pedagogy' (Koehler & Mishra 2008, p. 23) to gain a deeper understanding of how those knowledges are situated 'in particular contexts (including knowledge of particular students, school social networks, parental concerns, etc.)' and 'imparts the kind of flexibility teachers need in order to succeed' (p. 23). Figure 14.2 positions TPACK within the context of networked school communities where 'a place called school' displays TPACK required for teacher readiness, but also open, networked learning communities rather than a closed 'school' context.

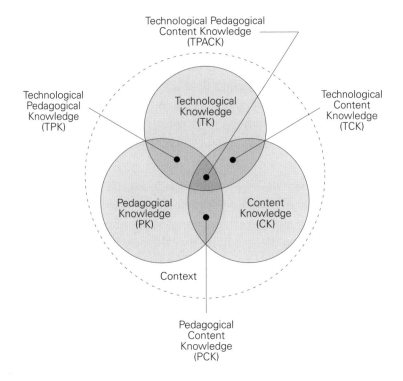

Figure 14.1 TPACK conceptualisation
(Adapted from Mishra & Koehler 2008)

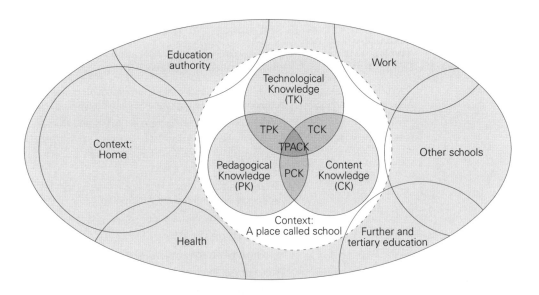

Figure 14.2 Context of a place called school—TPACK and the networked school
communities vision

Teacher readiness and redesigning working conditions

There are links between teacher readiness for moving from a largely Industrial Age model to the Information Age model of schooling; for example, in moving from a paper-based to a digitally based paradigm of schooling (Lee & Gaffney 2008). A move from a digital school to networked school communities is accompanied by a redesign of teachers' working conditions—how, when and why learning takes place. As displayed in Figure 14.2, 'a place called school' becomes part of a richer, more comprehensive understanding of networked, legitimate learning spaces.

Stages of teacher development have been proposed to explain teacher adoption of digital technologies for teaching and learning. For example, Newhouse, Clarkson and Trinidad (2005) suggest that teachers might move through stages of inaction, investigation, application, integration and transformation. They indicate that the defining move from application to integration requires movement through a 'critical use border'. We suggest that, for moving to a digital school or digital take-off, teacher readiness requires teachers to move through the 'critical use border' to be able to integrate digital technologies. To create a networked school community, we suggest, needs teacher readiness to move beyond integration to transformation. Table 14.1 builds upon Newhouse et al.'s (2005) stages of teacher development to portray teacher readiness and Lee and Gaffney's (2008) characteristics of traditional paper-based and digitally based paradigms of schooling (see also Chapter 1, Table 1.1), and gives insights into redesigned working conditions for teachers.

Table 14.1 Stages of teacher development, and relationship to digital schools and networked school communities

Stage of teacher development	Stages of school development (TPACK features)	Characteristics of and implications for redesigned working conditions for teachers
Inaction	Traditional Industrial Age model of school organisation (Focus on pedagogy and content)	General lack of leadership, interest and/or action in acquiring and/or using digital technologies Schools operating as discrete, largely stand-alone entities Segmented organisational structure, with a widespread division of labour Discrete and constant instructional technologies in paper, the pen and the teaching board Individual lesson preparation Reliance on mass media Staffing hierarchical, with fixed roles Well-defined and long-lasting jobs Slow segmented paper-based internal communication and information management Long-established operational parameters

Stage of teacher development	Stages of school development (TPACK features)	Characteristics of and implications for redesigned working conditions for teachers
Investigation	Early stages of understanding of Information Age (Focus on pedagogy and content—some exploration of digital technologies to enhance learning and teaching)	Some leadership and vision emerging Teachers beginning to develop some interest and starting to act on this interest with using digital technologies with their students Teachers still largely dependent—lack of resources and time seen as barriers Some professional development provided to some teachers
Application	Exploration of digital technologies (Focus on technology applications, pedagogy and content largely within existing curriculum frameworks)	Teachers advocating for purchase of digital technologies; e.g. interactive whiteboards Recognition of the importance of professional development provided
Critical use border		
Integration	Digital school—'digital take-off' (Focus on technology, pedagogy and content)	Teacher readiness for integrating digital technologies to enhance learning Evidence of school networks Transition occurring as schools move from becoming digital schools Some evidence of networked school communities
Transformation	Networked school communities, incorporating the total school community and its homes (TPACK is fully embraced— sophisticated understandings of the intersection of technology, pedagogy, and content and context)	Strong interdependence, particularly between home and school Integrated synergistic operations Suite of changing, increasingly sophisticated, converging and networked digital instructional technologies Increasing collaborative lesson development Interactive multimedia Changing flexible team-oriented staff roles Uncertainty, untapped potential, rising expectations and frequent job changes Instant communication and management of digital information across the organisation Few established operational parameters

(Adapted from Newhouse, Clarkson & Trinidad 2005, and Lee & Gaffney 2008)

Teacher readiness—key messages

The following key messages are provided to guide your thinking about teacher readiness for developing networked school communities.

1   **Understand TPACK—the 'total package'.** This can be used as the conceptualisation to understand the intersection of technology, pedagogy and content to:

   - inform professional development to enable teacher readiness;

   - inform the selection of digital technologies based upon pedagogic and content considerations; and

   - inform a problem-seeking, problem-solving and knowledge-generation approach to developing networked school communities.

2   **Understand your contextual considerations.** Refer to Table 14.1 to identify the stages of teacher development and school development where you think you are at. How far down the path are you and other teachers in realising the vision of a digital school? How far beyond being a digital school are you?

3   **Understand the learning in the home and 'beyond a place called school'.** What digital technologies are students using at home and at school? What learning is occurring in the home? How can you authentically engage parents, carers and the community?

4   **Capitalise upon existing networks and develop new networks.** What networks already exist that promote learning? What networks do you want to develop? How can you network with other schools, the home, further and tertiary education, education authorities, health organisations and the world of work (as shown in Figure 14.2)?

Redesigning working conditions: twenty-first century learning spaces and digital ecosystems

In their book *Why not the best schools?*, Caldwell and Harris (2008) suggest that for Australian schools to become the best schools in the world, large numbers of school buildings built in the last century need replacing or refurbishing, and argue that this applies in particular to public sector schools which generally compare poorly with those facilities of the private schools. They make the case that:

> ... their design is simply ill-suited to the curriculum and pedagogies of the 21st Century. They are not attractive places for students and staff to work in. ... there is nothing on the scale of England where most secondary schools will be rebuilt or replaced over the next decade. Schools in Finland are designed well and hold pride of place in their communities. (p. 170)

In the move to networked school communities, the vision sees learners being immersed in the architecture of digital ecosystems. Of direct relevance here in developing and sustaining a digital education ecosystem is the framework presented by Ingvarson and

Gaffney (2008), and their chapter in the book *Leading a digital school* (Lee & Gaffney 2008) is recommended reading. They refer those interested in pursuing the movement towards digital ecosystems to examine the history of virtual learning environments (VLEs) in Wikipedia at http://en.wikipedia.org/wiki/history_of_virtual_learning_environments. This provides a chronological account of the early developments in computer-assisted learning, which preceded learning management systems (LMS) and learning content management systems (LCMS). They noted that intranets and local area networks (LANs), which use passwords and usernames, are commonly used by learning organisations and will continue to be part of the architecture for VLEs.

The more recent movement has occurred through VLEs that is 'less didactic, more open application of digital technology, which is more directed at learning and less about management and control' (Ingvarson & Gaffney 2008, p. 149). This movement aligns with the movement towards creating a home–school nexus. Rather than a school-centred, hierarchical approach characterised by command and control, this reflects what Husband (2008) refers to as 'wirearchy'—'a dynamic two-way flow of power and authority based on information, knowledge, trust and credibility, enabled by interconnected people and technology' (p. 1). Husband appropriately indicates that:

> The last thirty years have been about the building of the technical infrastructure that provides an interconnected world. The integrated platform for a transformation to economies and a world driven by the communication and exchange of information is now solidly in place. The next fifty years will be about learning how we will behave in an interconnected world and workplace. (p. 1)

This is being played out in schools' VLEs through interoperability between student management systems and administration systems, and the architecture now enables us to go beyond this to connect the home and school through developing networked school communities. Ingvarson and Gaffney (2008) provide examples such as Blackboard (2009), Moodle (2009), Drupal (2009) and SharePoint (Microsoft 2009). Elsewhere in industry, which has adopted new technologies more quickly than education systems, the Cisco-led Information Age Partnership study (cited in Directorate General Information Society and Media of the European Commission, n.d.) conceptualised the progression towards digital ecosystems as follows:

1. Email—for effective internal and external communications

2. Websites—for visibility in the global marketplace, and for the diffusion and gathering of information

3. e-Commerce tools—for ordering and paying online, for reducing transaction costs and to maximise accessibility to new markets

4. e-Business tools—for supply chains integration, realising value in the supply-chain integration, and reducing costs

5   Environments for networked organisations—for outsourcing, for enabling new business models, and virtual enterprises

6   Digital ecosystems—for global dynamic connection and aggregation of businesses, sharing of knowledge, ideas and capacities, and spontaneous selection and evolution among services and solutions.

In an increasingly digital, networked world, schools might also follow these trends to becoming networked organisations and move to become part of digital ecosystems. These ecosystems need to enable both educators and the learners to ubiquitously engage in connected ways characterised by interoperability between the VLEs, which are usually managed systems, and systems outside of those environments so that the learning platform can integrate aspects important to learning, such as the learner's home, work and their formal education. According to Ingvarson and Gaffney (2008), 'healthy' digital ecosystems 'can provide a more responsive, personalised, effective, equitable and efficient learning experience for each student' (p. 152). This vision of healthy digital ecosystems remains elusive at this stage, and unless the way they are designed and informed by educationally sound rationales to justify what they are attempting to achieve,

> *we may end up wasting resources and developing 'sick digital ecosystems' that contain the pathological entities intent on undermining the vision and culture of the school or system. Examples of the latter would include ... applications that ... control processes or performance with no appreciable benefit in effectiveness, efficiency ... for staff and students.*
>
> Ingvarson & Gaffney (2008, p. 152)

Essential to the move to networked school communities is a redesign of teachers' working conditions. The following are provided as discussion starters to provoke thinking about the redesign possibilities.

1   **Redesign professional development**. Considerable research findings have demonstrated that teachers need to be the leading learner, with agency for lifelong and life-wide learning. The move to networked school communities enables and promotes online communities of learners where teachers are active members of professional associations and networks. These can be initiated by the teacher, as well as by the more usual school- or systems-initiated professional development. Professional development can be seen more as professional learning where the locus of control is with the teacher.

2   **Engage parents and the community**. It is important to note the distinction between *involvement* and *engagement*. Engagement needs to be more than the occasional newsletter to parents and/or invitation to the annual speech night or class play. Networked school communities should emphasise the home–school nexus enabled by digital technologies to have greater interactions between students, teachers, parents and the community.

3   **Exploit digital technologies for redesigning teachers' roles to improve productivity**. Continually investigate and identify opportunities for more effective and efficient uses

of teachers' time and professional expertise to maximise productivity in terms of student learning. A redesign of teacher use of time for other than professional roles is long overdue. Current organisation of schooling imposes a large opportunity cost for both students and professionals. What other organisational arrangements could be implemented which increase student learning productivity and enable better use of teachers' time?

4   **Redesign learning spaces**. Consider the design of buildings and explore innovative learning spaces such as the redesigning of libraries to learning centres. New classrooms are becoming designed to capitalise upon digital technologies. Beyond those redesigned buildings are contemporary conceptions of networked learning spaces—from anywhere and at any time, irrespective of building design. What do your learning spaces currently look like? What might they become?

Some pathfinder examples and possibilities

The following provide some interesting examples of the use of networked, digital technologies to develop a home–school nexus. Consider how you might create something similar, and the implications of these for teacher readiness and working conditions.

Improving parental engagement: Ranvilles Infant School, Fareham, Hampshire (Hampshire Local Authority), United Kingdom

This project was the Winner, ICT Excellence Award 2007 (Becta 2008f) in the 'Extending learning opportunities (primary)' category. For more details, see http://awards.becta.org.uk/display.cfm?resID=34519.

Through use of a VLE to extend learning beyond the classroom, this UK infant school used digital technologies to its advantage to keep parents involved with their child's education. As many of the children's parents are in the Navy, the VLE enables progress tracking and answering questions while they are at sea. There is strong encouragement of parents to contribute ideas online. Reports completed throughout the year are shared with the parents, culminating in end-of-year reports, which include photographs of achievement and attainment. The school has an 'open door' policy that is complemented by the online chat rooms for parents, pupils and staff. Online forums are used to talk to parents and, in particular, the children.

Online reporting

There are examples of online reporting that improve parental engagement and are more effective for teachers than traditional practices. For example, see Becta (2008e), *Exploiting ICT to improve parental engagement, moving towards online reporting,* at http://publications.becta.org.uk/display.cfm?resID=38170

Use of Zoomerang online surveys

For more details, see Zoomerang's *Education Survey Resource Centre*, at http://www.educationsurveyresources.com/.

Zoomerang is an online survey tool that opens up possibilities for schools that are genuinely interested in gathering feedback from parents, carers and the community to inform school decision making. The site claims that a 2006 survey of Zoomerang users from the education sector reported that Zoomerang feedback had impacted program changes, that they gained a better understanding of student concerns, replaced largely ineffective paper surveying and enhanced administration policies. In *Parents want more technology in schools* (Zoomerang 2008), results of a nationwide parent survey regarding online access, mobility, gaming and safety within the school environment showed that 92 per cent of the parents surveyed said that they would like to have online access to the same content distributed to their children, but only 49 per cent reported that their schools provide such access. The study also reported that the most important perceived benefits to parents of online access are access to missed work assignments and the ability for parents to be more involved. A scan of the first 20 entries for Australian web pages using the search terms 'zoomerang survey schools' indicated that Zoomerang is being used for a variety of online surveys. These include the following.

- The development of an online Zoomerang survey to ascertain current levels of ICT available to students at home, expertise of students and parents, perceptions of ICT use in the school and desired future directions. This was part of an action research study 'Future directions in ICT' at Rooty Hill High School, New South Wales by Beverley Powell (see https://www.det.nsw.edu.au/proflearn/areas/sld/research/powell.htm).

- *Edna for Schools Newsletter*, Issue 20, 16 October 2008 drew attention to an online survey using Zoomerang by indicating that the Australian Government through the AICTEC Secretariat is undertaking research into learners' and educators' views of learning with technologies. Teachers are asked to encourage parents and students to complete the surveys (see http://www.lists.edna.edu.au/lists/lists/viewmessages;jsessionid=76D8FD7 4E37E009CFE3F716C93EE7973?list=edna-for-schools&mid=800141).

- NSW Primary Principals' Association members are being urged to complete an APPA Zoomerang survey seeking feedback to the draft Primary School Charter in 2007 (see http://www.nswppa.org.au/nswppa/documents/wh2007t3w5.doc).

- Online lessons from the Victorian State Education Department are urging children to use Zoomerang to construct surveys (see 'bring a healthy lunch to school' http://www.education.vic.gov.au/teacher/healthylunch.htm).

- Social service agencies such as Young Carers Australia are using Zoomerang to survey young people (see http://www.youngcarers.net.au/Carers/content.aspx?id=32).

Use of social network—create a Ning

Educators have become aware of the power and potential of Web 2.0 technologies—social networking. In establishing networked school communities, it is worth considering creating a Ning. Some examples include teachers who:

- have created online spaces for parents and teachers to communicate using Web 2.0 tools (see http://www.ourschool.ca/category/featured-teacher);

- use technology to communicate with their students; e.g. an Australian teacher who sends homework (involving videos) to students via phone MMS messaging (see http://mrrobbo.wordpress.com/2009/02/18/sending-homework-to-a-phone-via-mms-messaging).

Examples of Ning sites worth visiting include:

- West Meadows Parents: A communication network for West Meadow School Parents (see http://wmsparents.ning.com/)

- People for Education's Community Online: Using a Ning network to connect parents to a school (see http://schools-at-the-centre.ning.com/group/parentsaspartners/forum/topics/using-a-ning-network-to)

- People for Education's Community Online: What is the role of community's in creating the Canada we want (see http://schools-at-the-centre.ning.com/forum/topics/cost-effective-communication)

- Independent School Educators Network (see http://isenet.ning.com/)

- Black Parents Association of Columbia Public Schools (see http://bpacps.ning.com/)

- Classroom 2.0 Teaching parents how to use Web 2.0 Tools (see http://www.classroom20.com/forum/topics/649749:Topic:127758)

- Classroom 2.0 – (see http://www.classroom20.com/). This is a professional development Ning for teachers.

- Developing Networked School Communities (see http://networkedschooling.ning.com). This Ning accompanies this book.

Conclusion

This chapter indicated the central importance of quality teachers who now require TPACK capabilities—technological knowledge, pedagogic knowledge and content knowledge—to enable the realisation of the networked school community's vision. TPACK allows the reader to examine the nuances of their own context and to become a problem seeker, problem solver and knowledge generator. By synthesising the stages of teacher development and stages of school development in becoming a digital school, and then moving beyond that to developing a networked school community enables the reader to undertake a self-analysis to consider where they and their school are at with regard to its current stage of development.

The move to networked school communities requires new expectations for teachers, a redesign of their working conditions, a redesign of learning spaces, and engaging parents, homes and communities to capitalise upon the capacity of digital technologies beyond those provided by the school.

Guiding questions

After reading this chapter, consider your context and propose your ideas in relation to the following guiding questions.

1 Do you think that teachers at your school have sufficient technological knowledge to be ready for being part of a networked school community?

2 Where would you position the staff of your school in Table 14.1?

3 Where would you position your school in Table 14.1?

4 What strategies would you suggest to develop teacher readiness?

5 What is your vision for learning spaces in the twenty-first century?

6 Outline your vision for redesigning the working conditions of teachers. Consider current activities that are time-consuming, out-dated practices that need to be discarded and replaced by more effective, professional practices more appropriate for twenty-first century learning and teaching.

Key messages

- The networked school community vision recognises the importance of quality twenty-first century teachers being ready and having the capabilities to assume the new roles and develop the home–school relationships required in realising this vision.

- Understand TPACK—the 'total package'—as the conceptualisation to understand the intersection of technology, pedagogy and content to inform professional development and enable teacher readiness; to inform the selection of digital technologies based on pedagogic and content considerations; and to inform a problem-seeking, problem-solving and knowledge-generation approach to developing networked school communities.

- The move to networked school communities requires new expectations for teachers, a redesign of their working conditions, a redesign of learning spaces, and engaging parents, homes and communities to capitalise upon the capacity of digital technologies beyond those provided by the school.

CHAPTER 15

Middle school students and digital technology use: Implications from research

LYN COURTNEY, NEIL ANDERSON & COLIN LANKSHEAR

The complexity of the 21st century middle school student can be challenging. Students who would rather text message than talk to each other makes for a different world ... They are talking on their cell phone, sending messages on their computer, talking to their friends and doing homework at the same time. It has made middle school an interesting place to try to keep students focused on learning. Middle school students have become accustomed to a fast-paced day. It's time to fill their lives with experiences that make middle school a place to run too [sic] not from. Let's take the middle school years as a tremendous opportunity to help students to encounter a whole new journey to their future.

Stephen Jones (12 March 2009)

Context and challenges

The effective use of digital technologies in schools has been a major focus of Australian and international educational initiatives for the last 25 years. Driving this has been the recognition that the world has evolved into a 'knowledge economy', and the 'digital age' has created an innovative workplace that schools need to prepare students to enter (Ministerial Council on Education, Employment, Training and Youth Affairs [MCEETYA] 2008; Queensland Government 2005). *The Melbourne Declaration on Educational Goals for Young Australians* (Australian Education Council [AEC] 2008) noted the 'rapid and continuing advances in ICT are changing the ways people share, use, develop and process information technology' (p. 5) and recommended that 'in this digital age, young people need to be highly skilled in the use of information and communications technologies (ICT). While schools already employ these technologies in learning, there is a need to increase their effectiveness significantly over the next decade' (p. 5).

What has been challenging is how digital technologies can be used by schools in ways that promote equity, inclusiveness and excellence in educational outcomes and career pathways

(Anderson et al. 2009; Anderson et al. 2008; Anderson et al. 2007; Baskin & Williams 2007; Courtney et al. 2009; Heemskerk et al. 2005; Jamieson-Proctor et al. 2006). Specifically, this chapter notes two key challenges—teacher confidence and competence issues, and the home–school differences that impact on the effective use of digital technologies in schools. These challenges complement the identification in Chapter 14 of the importance of teacher readiness for developing networked school communities:

This chapter provides evidence from preliminary analyses of a pilot study concerning attitudes towards digital technologies by upper middle school students (Years 8, 9 and 10). This study was conducted recently in Queensland, Australia by the research team at James Cook University. In relation to informing and creating the home–school nexus, findings from this study revealed some of the barriers to the effective uptake of digital technologies by students in the school environment, which adds weight to previous research into the home–school nexus reported elsewhere in this book. The focus of this chapter is on the experience of the middle school student, the learner. The learner's experience in the school environment is strongly influenced by the teacher's confidence and competence with digital technologies.

Tensions between young people's digital technology use and teacher confidence

The recent *Digital Life Survey* (Synovate 2008) and the previous *Global Media Survey* (New Paradigm 2007) have emphasised the fundamental changes in how school-age students and young adults participate in digital technology-rich home environments. For example, young people report enthusiastic uptake of multi-tasking involving an increasing number of web-connected devices and an overwhelming rejection of passive activities in favour of connectivity, interaction and personal contribution (Huws 2007; Victorian Education and Training Committee 2006). That trend is at odds with how digital technologies are often used in the classroom to support traditional pedagogical approaches. Recently, Jamieson-Proctor and Finger (2008) concluded that teacher confidence in using digital technologies has a significant impact on their students' uptake of new technology to enhance classroom learning. They reported that teachers who felt more confident to use digital technologies with their students 'reported that their students currently used ICT more than students of less confident teachers. Further, more confident teachers also preferred their students to use ICT more for teaching and learning than did less confident teachers' (n.p.). Elsewhere, Dale, Robertson and Shortis (2004) found that school principals pinpointed teacher confidence and competence as more important factors in the uptake of digital technologies in classrooms than resources. One principal commented that 'getting the staff to embrace the potentiality of ICT has proved to be more difficult than getting it in' (p. 465).

The previous chapter demonstrated the importance of teacher readiness and highlighted the need to redesign traditional learning spaces. In particular, TPACK—the intersection of technology, pedagogy and content—was now required for teacher pre-service education and for professional development of practising teachers. According to *The ICT Impact Report* (Balanskat, Blamire & Keefala 2006), the lack of ICT competence (referred to in the TPACK conceptualisation as TK—technological knowledge) impacts negatively on teacher confidence and creates boundaries against seamless in-school and out-of-school technology use. As summarised in Table 15.1, that report identified the following teacher, school and system level barriers:

Table 15.1 Teacher, school and system level barriers

Teacher level barriers	School level barriers	System level barriers
Lack of ICT skill Lack of motivation and confidence using ICT Inappropriate training	Absence and poor quality of ICT infrastructure Lack of high-quality hardware and suitable educational software Limited access to ICT equipment Limited project-based experience and experience in project-based learning	Rigid structure of the traditional schooling system

Progress in encouraging optimal use of digital technologies has been disappointing. Jamieson-Proctor and Finger (2008) referred to the 2006 Organisation for Economic Cooperation and Development (OECD) statistics to illustrate that only one in five 15-year-old Australian students indicated that they used computers almost every day. In a recent Greek study (Vekiri & Chronaki 2008), it was determined that over 90 per cent of students use computers at home on a daily basis, but only 58 per cent of students used computers regularly in their school environment despite adequate school technological resources. In the US, Cuban (2000; 2006) criticised the under-utilisation of ICT in education and the lack of value for the large investment undertaken by education systems.

The literature does provide some guidance that might be helpful in building a confident and competent mindset. These areas include:

- effective professional development;
- teacher laptop ownership programs;
- ongoing support in the form of competent experienced peers and ICT coordinators; and
- access to reliable and wide broadband and overcoming gender issues.

(Source: Cuban 2000; 2006)

Programs that increase teacher confidence and competence should be sensitive to gender preferences, particularly when female teachers typically display less confidence in using ICT than their male counterparts (Jamieson-Proctor et al. 2006), and where teachers in rural and remote areas are often required to teach out of their area of specialisation and have less access to professional development than their city-based peers (Anderson et al. 2007).

Home–school nexus—understanding the 'middle school turn-off'

Despite the considerable uptake of digital technologies in young people's personal lives and enormous investments being made into education to equip students as 'new millennium learners' (Department of Education, Science and Training [DEST] 2005; MCEETYA 2008), data continues to suggest that girls are still under-represented in fields such as science, physics and ICT (see Brotman & Moore 2008). To illustrate, the former Department of Communications, Information Technology and the Arts (DCITA) (2005), now called the Department of Broadband, Communications and the Digital Economy (DBCDE), reported that, while 80 per cent of new ICT undergraduates were male, 53 per cent of higher education students were female (Australia Bureau of Statistics [ABS] 2006). This is also reflected in declining female participation rates in high school, and Anderson and co-researchers (2007; 2008; 2009) revealed that it was in the middle school years that girls reported they were 'turned off' school-based ICT.

This book is premised on the assumption that both girls and boys use digital technologies ubiquitously as part of their personal and home lives. Furthermore, there is the accompanying encouragement for a better understanding of this difference and to capitalise on the home–school difference, rather than the perpetuation and deepening of a digital divide between home and school. It is in the middle school years, or early adolescence, that engagement with learning reportedly declines (Hill & Russell 1999). However, it is also during the early adolescent years that young people become more engaged with digital technologies. Research comparing in-school and out-of-school technology use suggests that differences change over time as new applications and program capacities emerge. For example, the scope of Internet usage at home expanded hugely as broadband was introduced.

Also, differences within and across school and out-of-school contexts have varied to some extend by gender, age and socio-economic status (Kent & Facer 2004). For example, until recently the gender gap between boys and girls was apparent, with boys using computers and the Internet more than girls as well as having more computer experience (OECD 2007). However, that gap has almost become insignificant due to the increasing female use of social computing tools, though decent broadband access is not available everywhere. For example, in Australia, equity issues remain between the 'information rich' and 'information poor' families (Neal 2008, p. 80), but we need to recognise that 86 per cent of students aged 15 reported using a computer at home (OECD 2007).

Furthermore, while uptake is strong, the decline in female participation in advanced level ICT subjects and career pathways has been the subject of extensive international research

(Anderson et al. 2007; 2008; 2009; American Association of University Women [AAUW] 2001; Millar & Jagger 2001). The overall trend that Kent and Facer (2004) identified still holds true—that is, young people use digital technologies more at home than at school and enjoy home use more. Kent and Facer have documented that with home use of digital technologies young people acquire:

- a wider range of skills and strategies;

- more problem solving;

- more development of thinking skills; and

- more exercises of perseverance, imagination and memory exploration.

Many researchers (such as Hull & Schultz 2001; Kent & Facer 2004; Lankshear & Knobel 2003, 2006; Leander 2005) have cautioned against setting up a false dichotomy between 'in-school' and 'out-of-school' activities. However, Hull and Schultz (2001) observed that 'one should expect to find, and should attempt to account for, movement from one context to the other' (p. 577), while at the same time recognise that the school environment has evolved into a 'particular, specialized institution' (p. 5), and that it is important to identify features that seem to be distinctively characteristic of it, particularly in relation to learning. They recommended that 'doing so will allow us to reconsider what we have grown accustomed to taking as natural and normal and to recognize [school's particular brand of learning] as an artefact of a particular kind of learning that is associated primarily with schooling' (p. 577).

Researchers have observed different kinds of cross-over from in-school to out-of-school contexts and vice versa. For example, Kent and Facer (2004) suggested that young people's uses of computers at home through Instant Messaging (IM) and social networking provides 'a "virtual" social context in the home, shaped by their expectations of social contact formed in the classroom at school, that draws on many of the characteristics of the interactions they describe with physically co-present peers in school' (p. 452). Alternatively, software and digital technology processes introduced at school may be 'played with' at home and fed back into use at school. Therefore, a clear delineation between home and school computer use is becoming more difficult to ascertain, as are the distinctions between formal and informal learning. Black (2009) contrasted the print-centric basic skills orientation of schooling with the non-formal access to twenty-first century skills (Jenkins 2006) that young people routinely leverage within affinity spaces (Gee 2004) where they spend considerable time and energy redesigning and reverse-engineering. In this arena, young people experience diverse forms of peer reviewing and expert-like feedback that is not typically encountered in school-based learning experiences (Black 2009). Students enjoy rich 'tech savvy' opportunities as they select technologies appropriate for different purposes.

Transforming schooling with the assistance of a digital technology infused curriculum was the aim of the Department of Education and Training in Western Australia (WA). This resulted in an initiative whereby student-owned Notebooks were introduced into a number of schools. In an evaluation of John Willcock College, one of the middle schools participating in the computer program, with approximately 660 students and 23 per cent of students from Aboriginal heritage, Newhouse (2008) reported that this program led to dramatic changes in computer use in schools. For example, in the first year, computer use rose from 16 to 45 per cent, with student use of computers in school almost doubling from one hour to almost two hours per day, and most teachers and students (80%) reported accessing online information routinely. While the student-owned Notebook program in WA demonstrated a very successful integration of computers into schools, this research also noted that it was not merely the Notebooks alone that contributed to its success. Rather, a professional learning approach with school leadership and technical support was involved, which contributed to a significant increase in teacher confidence and competence in the three years of the program, which contributed to its success (Newhouse 2008).

Research has also found support for the hypothesis that digital skills are acquired primarily through experimental learning at home rather than from formal instruction at school as high school students' 'home access to Internet and domestic use of e-mail and education software were found to be positively related to students' achievements' (Kuhlemeier & Hemker 2005, p. 476). Elsewhere, in a review of the literature relating to ICT use and attainment, Cox et al. (2004) reported that in today's school, students are encouraged to use digital technologies for homework. Not surprisingly, several studies have revealed that ICT use at home differs from ICT use at school (Kent & Facer 2004; Sutherland, Facer & Furlong 2000), especially the way in which students' digital technology use in school is controlled by the school, and often is at odds with how young people use technology in their daily lives (Neal 2008).

Limitations in the use of school computers were highlighted by Kent and Facer's (2004) findings from a large survey study of over 1800 students and group interviews with over 190 students, conducted in the UK in 2001 and 2003, which revealed that in relation to use of the Internet 'young people's critiques of school activities were most vocal. Class activities involving Internet searches were criticized as overly prescriptive … and the use of filters in school was singled out for particular criticisms' (Kent & Facer 2004, p. 452). Those criticisms highlight the 'growing frustration of young people used to fast and functioning equipment in the home and the fundamental difficulties of introducing potentially disruptive technologies [like] the Internet into the schoolroom' (Kent & Facer 2004).

The following section presents a summary of a pilot study that investigated the attitudes of students towards digital technologies in middle schools to inform deeper understandings of the negative attitudes reported elsewhere.

Research study: The middle school experience

The research summarised here functions as a pilot study to the Australian Research Council (ARC) Linkage Grant investigating middle school students' attitudes towards ICT and some of the barriers to using computers effectively at school. This study endeavoured to elucidate some of the factors that contributed to senior high school girls' negative attitudes towards ICT, as reported in previous research by this team (e.g. Anderson et al. 2009; Courtney et al. 2009; Courtney, Timms & Anderson 2006), whereby the middle school years were identified as the years that girls reported being 'turned off to computers' (Anderson et al. 2007).

The research design

The pilot study employed a mixed-method approach, involving survey (quantitative data) and focus group interviews (qualitative data), which was similar to the research design used in the 2006–2008 ARC Linkage study into the declining participation rate of senior high school girls' participation in ICT career pathways (Anderson et al. 2009; Courtney, Timms & Anderson 2006). Findings from this pilot study will be used to inform the research design for the 2008–2010 ARC Linkage research into middle school girls' negative perceptions of ICT subjects and career pathways.

The participants

The participants in this study were purposively selected and consisted of 162 upper middle school students enrolled in two government (public) schools located in Queensland, Australia: one rural school ($n = 99$) and one remote school ($n = 63$). There were 86 males (53%) and 76 females (47%) enrolled in Year 8 ($n = 51$), Year 9 ($n = 54$) and Year 10 ($n = 57$). Forty-two students were not taking ICT subjects and 120 students were enrolled in ICT subjects.

The materials

The short paper-based questionnaire comprised of three demographic questions (gender, middle school grade, and taking or not taking computer subjects); and seven forced-response questions using a five-point Likert scale (1 = Strongly Disagree; 2 = Disagree; 3 = Neither Disagree or Agree; 4 = Agree; 5 = Strongly Agree); namely:

A   I enjoy using computers at school.

B   Computer subjects are boring.

C   Computer subjects are interesting.

D   I have a lot of experience using computers.

E   I like what I learn in computer subjects or the computer parts of other subjects.

F   I would want to learn about computers even if computing was not taught in school.

G   I would like to change the computer subjects if I could.

In addition, two open-ended questions were included in the questionnaire: 'Please write what you enjoy most about using/learning about computers at school' and 'Please write what you enjoy least about using/learning about computers at school.'

The procedure

Information letters and school agreement forms were sent to the principals of two government schools in Queensland (one rural and one remote). The principals of the schools agreed to participate in this research. Subsequently, information letters, information forms and consent forms were mailed to the two schools to be sent home with all students enrolled in Years 8, 9 and 10. The surveys were administered to the students by a researcher during regular class time and the demographic and forced-response data were subjected to quantitative analyses using Statistical Package for the Social Sciences (SPSS), Version 17. The students' responses to the two open-ended questions on the survey, 'What do you enjoy most about using/learning about computers at school?' and 'What do you enjoy least about using/learning about computers at school?', were open coded (Strauss & Corbin 1998; Yin 1994), and themes were identified by using comparisons within and between interviews (Boeije 2002; Tesch 1990).

In addition to completing the short surveys, six students from each school were asked to participate in a 45-minute focus group interview. Also, the principal, ICT heads of department (HODs) and four teachers participated in face-to-face interviews. However, the focus group and individual interview data are currently being analysed and will not be presented in this chapter.

Some key results and discussion

Quantitative analysis of the results was extensive and various significant findings were identified. This discussion will summarise the findings and highlight areas that converge or diverge from the literature. There was a statistically significant difference between attitudes towards enjoyment of using computers at school, with both boys and girls enrolled in the middle school grades of Years 8, 9 and 10 agreeing that they enjoyed using computers at school, but over the three years this enthusiasm declined. This supports previous findings from Anderson and colleagues (2007; 2008; 2009) that high school girls (Year 11 and 12) enjoyed using computers in primary school and became 'turned off' school-based ICT in their junior secondary school years. High school girls (Years 11 and 12) reported that they did not enjoy using computers and would rather engage with people than machines (Courtney, Timms & Anderson 2006). The item 'Computer subjects are boring' was derived from the previous ARC research (Anderson et al. 2009; Anderson et al. 2008; Courtney, Timms & Anderson 2006; Courtney et al. 2009) findings that high school girls (Years 11 and 12) found computer subjects boring. Both boys and girls slightly disagreed that computer subjects were boring in Year 8; however, by Year 10 these students slightly agreed that computer subjects are boring, which confirms a trend that has been emerging from the literature (Anderson et al. 2008; Courtney, Timms & Anderson 2006; Neal 2008). That is, the change seems to develop throughout the middle school years.

Interestingly, the results in relation to experience using computers verified previous research that there is no substantial gender difference in expertise with computers, which diverges from the literature (e.g. OECD 2007). However, the results indicated that there was an overall decline in the interest in computing subjects as students moved through their middle school years, again supporting previous findings reported by Anderson and colleagues (2007; 2008). This lack of interest in computer subjects seems to be confirmed, with additional results reflecting some apathy towards the content of computer subjects despite reporting that these subjects held declining interest to students. This may reflect the general lack of educational motivation reported by Hill & Russell (1999), or perhaps better reflects an attitude of 'it's too hard to use computers at school', 'school computers don't work' and 'I can't access anything on them' as was reflected by participants of this study. It seems that, while students use digital technologies increasingly throughout the middle years of schooling at home and in their personal lives, the design and demands of computer subjects do not appear to engender similar positive attitudes.

It was, however, in the content of the open-ended questions that clues began to emerge regarding the factors that contribute to the interest and disinterest in ICT and computer subjects. Twenty-seven per cent of the students who answered the question, 'Write what you enjoy **most** about using/learning about computers in school' answered that computers helped with assignments and school work. Unsurprisingly, students preferred using computers for online communication and enjoyment/games (70%), whereas 40 per cent of students disliked using computers for assignments, which was exacerbated by the content being considered boring (16%) or confusing (8%), both of which may be attributed to teacher confidence or competence, as highlighted by Jamieson-Proctor and Finger (2008) and Reynold et al. (2003). Teachers demonstrating competence and confidence in e-learning should be able to extend students' learning experiences beyond the confines of the traditional classroom by bringing the world to the student and personalising learning in a way that fosters excitement in learning and diminishes negative attitudes towards digital technologies. The following examples of answers provided reflect the positive ways in which students approach the use of digital technologies.

- 'When I am on the computer I can get my work done quicker and it's easy.' (Year 8 girl)
- 'I like using emails, Google Earth and look up stuff on Google.' (Year 8 boy)
- 'When we do learn about computers, I love everything.' (Year 9 girl)
- 'I like computers because they are fun and lots of great things are on it (e.g. Microsoft PowerPoint, music, games, etc.).' (Year 9 boy)
- 'Typing is neater than writing.' (Year 10 boy)

Barriers to using computers at school were highlighted by students who answered the question, 'What do you enjoy **least** about using/learning about computers in school?', with 34 per cent of students noting slow, inadequate bandwidth, school restrictions or computer malfunctions (e.g. computers freezing or losing work). The benefit of bringing digital technologies into schools is offset by the frustrations of trying to use this technology effectively in the school environment, which supports findings reported by Kent and Facer (2004) and Neal (2008) that the school restriction and control mechanisms (e.g. firewalls and site bans) inhibit the effective use of digital technologies by students in school. The initial findings from the pilot study support conclusions suggested by Hayes (2007) that successful integration of digital technologies in schools would benefit from whole-school approaches that may require 'fundamental shifts in core activities of schools' (p. 385). The following are examples of responses that indicate some frustrations with restrictions, filtering, limitations with the school computer's capabilities, and the repetitive nature of school tasks.

- 'Computer restrictions.' (Year 8 boy)
- 'When our work gets deleted and the computers freeze.' (Year 9 girl)
- 'The Internet blocks that are on them. You can't access anything on them.' (Year 9 boy)
- 'The computers are too slow and you can't use them for anything.' (Year 10 boy)
- 'Doing the same thing over and over again.' (Year 10 girl)

The findings discussed here from the pilot study are intended to provide some basis upon which the reader can consider the transferability of the findings to her/his context rather than the generalisability of the results. What is happening with students in the middle years? Is there a disconnect between school and home use of digital technologies? Why is this occurring?

Conclusion

This chapter initially built upon the importance of teacher readiness discussed in the previous chapter, by emphasising teacher confidence and competencies in digital technology use that contribute to the students' engagement with digital technologies in the classroom. In order to keep up with the speed of technological innovations, it becomes essential that the educational sector is at the cutting edge of digital technologies in order to best equip young learners to meet the demands of a technological workplace. Preliminary analysis of the pilot study revealed that middle school boys and girls indicated a decline in interest in using computers at school. It also revealed an increase in the perception of school-based computing as boring. A synergy between technology, teaching and learning continues to be elusive. This study cautions us that, in relation to formal computing subjects at school, it is the middle school years that provide a crucial 'turning point' from being engaged with digital technologies to disengaging with them for formal school requirements. This represents a major disconnect from their positive and increasingly ubiquitous use at home and in the students' personal lives.

Therefore, this chapter strengthens the argument for creating a home–school nexus, and the importance of developing networked learning spaces in which the home–school differences are capitalised upon to turn around the middle school turn-off. It is expected that findings from the larger ARC Linkage research to be completed in 2010 should elucidate factors that contribute to the middle school 'turn-off' to ICT subjects at school. With the desired outcome of preparing young learners for effective participation in the networked world, the home–school nexus may provide the gateway to unravelling these challenges.

Guiding questions

After reading this chapter, consider your context and propose your ideas in relation to the following guiding questions.

1   By referring to Table 15.1, are these barriers present in your school context? How might these be overcome?

2   Do you agree that there is a 'middle school turn-off'?

3   Do you agree that young people engage more in digital technologies during early adolescence?

4   Do you think that, generally during middle years of schooling, there is a disconnect between young people's decreased engagement with formal schooling and their increased engagement with digital technologies beyond formal schooling? If yes, what role might the creation of a home–school nexus play in addressing this disconnect?

Key messages

*   It is in the middle school years, or early adolescence, that engagement with learning reportedly declines, while students become more engaged with digital technologies.

*   Research comparing in-school and out-of-school technology use suggest that differences change over time as new applications and program capacities emerge.

*   Barriers identified by students include slow, inadequate bandwidth, school restrictions or computer malfunctions (e.g. computers freezing or losing work).

*   The benefit of using digital technologies in school is offset by the frustrations of trying to use this technology effectively in the school environment, such as the school restriction and control mechanisms (e.g. firewalls and site bans) that inhibit the effective use of digital technologies by students in school.

*   Creating a home–school nexus and developing networked learning spaces are needed to turn around the middle school turn-off.

CHAPTER 16

Student Internet usage in a networked school community: The challenge

DAMIAN MAHER & MAL LEE

You have a generation who's faced with a society with fundamentally different properties, thanks to the Internet. We can turn our backs and say this is bad or we don't want a world like this. But it's not going away. So instead of saying that this is terrible, instead of saying, 'Stop MySpace, stop Facebook', you know, 'Stop the Internet', it's a question for us of how we teach ourselves and our children to live in a society where these properties are fundamentally a way of life. This is public life today.

danah boyd (2008)

Most notable, however, were the marked inconsistencies between the policies adopted by various reactive schools and education authorities. Facilities as diverse as email, social networking, YouTube, Flickr, Skype and computer games were prohibited by some authorities and endorsed by others. We found it difficult to work out the logic behind some of the decisions to prohibit or endorse and were little surprised that teachers living in a networked nation expressed so much frustration.

… We also found inconsistencies in the way reactive education authorities controlled school Internet sites, with some controlling all school Internet sites centrally and determining what is prohibited or endorsed, while other similarly inclined authorities gave each school control of its own site.

Mal Lee & Pru Mitchell (2009, p. 27)

Networked school communities and student Internet usage

Fundamental to an education in a networked school community is the facility for students to use the Internet when required, whether it is at home, on the move or in the classroom. While this facility is being readily provided in the home and increasingly on the move, in many schools in parts of the developed world students' use of the Internet in class is markedly constrained. In developing a networked school community that draws increasingly on the digital capability of the home and makes extensive use of collaboration and social networking, it is vital that your school addresses very early the home–school difference and adopts a solution appropriate to your situation.

The current contrast between the home and the school, particularly with the more reactive situations, is indeed dramatic. The trend in many instances is seemingly escalating the difference, even at a time when the research on Internet safety and on the schools' desire to make greater use of the online in their teaching is pointing strongly to the educational desirability of all schools and education authorities making astute use of the plethora of educational opportunities available. It would not be unreasonable to suggest that in certain situations around the world concerns about Internet safety in schools have become paranoiac and have lost all semblance of rationality. While it is apparently acceptable for young people to have largely free access to the Web up to the classroom door, somehow the actual use within the classroom in countries like the US, the UK and Australia has to be tightly controlled (Moyle 2009), with students' human rights thus being ignored. The sad reality is that while vested interests in the aforementioned nations can pressure public authorities about what happens in the schoolroom, they have no such sway in democratic societies over private citizens.

In considering how best to provide the desired Internet access for your students, bear in mind that there is now a very considerable and potentially lucrative market in school network control, and that it is in the interest of those companies to fan the current concerns, even if most are not valid. As Lee and Winzenried (2009) indicate, technology industries are constantly seeking to shape the school's use of technologies, usually to the advantage of the companies concerned and not the schools.

The challenge in creating your networked school community is to identify how the new entity is going to provide the desired high-level access while at the same time addressing the genuine concerns that come from operating digitally and online. It will of necessity be a balance and this is likely to change over time. In striking that balance, it will be important once again to undertake a far more reasoned, holistic examination of the situation than the myopic view that much of the media, and currently many schools, education authorities and governments, are holding today. History reveals a remarkably consistent anxiety about all new technologies, and those anxieties disappear as the use of the particular technology is normalised and becomes ubiquitous. It is nonetheless disappointing to see so many in positions of authority perpetuate the mistakes of the past.

What is also disappointing has been the failure of many in positions of responsibility, and in particular the public policy developers, to identify—let alone address—the major issues, resulting in the adoption of remarkably inconsistent, illogical stances on Internet access by both students and teachers within the classroom. One of the first issues you will need to address is who is it within the school who decides on the nature of the Internet access, and in turn ensure that the Internet usage policy accords with the desired educational purpose of the school. The identification, or simply the reiteration of the school's underlying educational philosophy, is fundamental to determining the school's approach to Internet access. The importance of this shaping philosophy is evidenced in the very different approach taken to Internet access by Sweden, Denmark and the Netherlands, where the focus is on education and learning rather than on simplistic technical solutions (Moyle 2009).

What appears to be happening in many situations, and possibly in your school, is that this approach is in many instances not being driven by educational considerations. It is important then that the participants in different layers, including teachers, executive or support staff outside the school, have a clear, shared understanding of what is desired and what is the best way to achieve that end. This can only come through ongoing dialogue. As you will see below, decisions are being made in many instances by middle managers for technical and administrative rather than for any educational reasons. In a networked school community, to create an effective home–school nexus, various interests will need to be met. There are legislative requirements, such as the rights of its citizens to be observed, and very real technical issues relating to network security as well as the desired educational outcomes. All the competing interests have to be considered. As indicated throughout the book, one of the major differences between the traditional and networked school community is the nature of the decision making, where the former is strongly hierarchical and the other far more collaborative. While ultimately it will be the principal in most instances who makes the final decision on the nature of Internet access, it will be important to ensure that the decision is arrived at collaboratively and is well informed.

As flagged, the approach adopted at a point in the life cycle of the technology will likely need revisiting as the technology becomes normalised and the research and experience allays the constraining initial fears. Currently, young people's homes are generally working from a position of trust, while many schools and education authorities appear to be more stringent in the use of controls than is warranted. While there will be some young people who misuse the system, the majority will be honest and it is for these young people that the systems need to be developed and operated. If your school is one of the growing number of proactive ones mentioned in Chapter 3 that have opted to use their caring culture and trust their students, you are a long way ahead. If it is not, major shifts in thinking will be needed in an increasingly networked world where control, coercion and compliance are largely ineffective.

It would appear that most reactive schools, education authorities and governments operate on the assumption that the best approach is to shield the young people from any association with the 'nasty' parts of the Internet, while the proactive schools and education authorities are generally operating on the belief that schools should use their 'protected' learning environment to educate their students for life and work in a digital future where the use of the Internet will be pervasive. Outside of the place called school, young people have learned how to operate within a networked world and have incorporated the use of the Internet into their everyday lives. What many in authority don't appear to have grasped is that young people have of their own volition accommodated the everyday use of the Internet into their schema and lives, 24 hours a day, seven days a week, and 365 days a year (Australian Communications and Media Authority [ACMA] 2007). The use is part of their everyday existence, yet while they have normalised its use, schooling is struggling to do so.

The challenge within a networked mode of schooling is how to reconcile the differences. It may well be that there will be need to have separate arrangements within the classroom and outside those rooms, but that is something young people have shown themselves very adept at handling. The key is to identify and employ practical operational parameters that all can work within and are consistent with the school's educational philosophy. An important issue that relates to all the previous points is the extent to which networked school communities should be incorporating digital citizenship, as discussed more fully in Chapters 9 and 18. As long as 20 years ago, John Gilmore made the telling observation, known as Gilmore's Law, that 'the net interprets censorship as damage and routes around it' (*Wikipedia* 2009g). That observation still holds today. Young people universally have become very apt in circumventing the controls imposed. The sooner many in authority recognise that reality and collaborate with young people and their parents to provide the best possible path forward, the sooner real progress will be made.

Home Internet usage

As indicated in earlier chapters, young people's use of the Internet outside the classroom is pervasive and normalised in their everyday existence. That access is often through the desktop computers in the home, but increasingly also through their games consoles, laptops, Smart phones and digital television set-top boxes. The vast majority of teenagers and a rapidly growing number of upper primary school students now have web-enabled Smart phones that they use most days of the year, invariably leaving the phone on all day.

The trend is very much for young people outside the classroom to have use of increasingly sophisticated technology and a wider access to broadband networks via ever-faster wireless. The Smart phones, particularly since the advent of the second-generation iPhone in 2008, have increasingly become wireless handheld computers. They have long since ceased being mere cell phones. The vast majority of young people appear to be trusted by their parents and carers to access the Internet when they wish, and to do so sensibly. While there is obviously a continuum of parent controls employed—from the tightly filtered through to complete freedom—the reality is that most young people have relatively free use of the Internet via the home technology. Once one moves to access the Internet via the Smart phones, usage is generally only controlled by the charges imposed by the ISP.

One has only to reflect on the situation with the young people whom we know personally to appreciate the level and nature of home Internet use by young people across the developed and the developing world. The situation in your home is not likely to be all that different to those in Taiwan, Japan, India, Israel, Norway, England or the US.

School Internet usage

Internet use in the vast majority of the world's schools is far from being ubiquitous. Let us remember that the school might never be able to provide the same kind of Internet access as the home. The school only operates for a portion of the day, usually for five days a week, for approximately 200 days a year. Within that limited time, the school has many other important things to do other than provide Internet access. Given this context, you can see why the authors commented earlier on the minuscule access provided for Internet use in the school, when compared with the hours available outside. It does make one wonder at times why all the concerns about the few school hours of access, while little is said about all the other hours of use outside the classroom.

While the more proactive schools are moving to provide ubiquitous student access, the majority in many nations are still a long way off and remain ill-equipped to maximise the more significant opportunities of the networked school community. The reasons are varied, with some relating to the funding, the network infrastructure and the instructional technology needed to provide ready access by all students and teachers to the Internet. Others relate to the stage of the technology in the developmental cycle and the associated paranoia of Internet dangers, while some are cultural and others have to do with the current bureaucratic control of schooling, the power exercised by some 'ICT coordinators' and network managers, and the lack of leaders equipped to lead digital and networked schools (Moyle 2006; Lee & Gaffney 2008). Disturbingly, many schools continue operating as discrete entities increasingly divorced from the real, ever-changing networked world.

The main reasons are often human and not technological. That is, leadership has universally failed to adopt a positive outlook towards the networked world, seek to capitalise upon the educational opportunities being opened, adopt a guiding vision for the desired educational future and be willing to mount a holistic long-term implementation strategy to realise the vision. This is reflected at the school, education authority and national levels. Alternatively, as indicated in Chapter 3, schools that have adopted a proactive, visionary approach have been able to overcome most of the very real hurdles confronting them and provide their students with ready access to the Internet at school and more specifically in the classroom. The constraints inherent in running a school, such as those identified in Table 6.1 (p. 106), do mean classrooms will rarely be able to provide the same kind of access as the home, but they can provide far readier access than is now apparent in many schools.

What is the situation regarding Internet access at your school? How does it compare with the other schools nearby? Does it fall at the proactive or reactive ends of the continuum detailed in Table 3.1 (pp. 38–9)? If your school is at the proactive end, you might use the following section as a checklist to judge how proactive your school is. However, if your school is within the reactive zone, you will need to overcome the following hurdles.

The human hurdles

Negative outlook of leadership

The first major hurdle you will need to address in seeking to achieve the desired Internet access in the school is the attitude of the leadership in the school. If the school's leadership—and in particular the principal—does not see the educational potential of the digital and networked worlds, you have some serious work to undertake. As flagged on numerous occasions, the role of the principal in taking the school forward is fundamental. Fortunately, most school leaders are amenable to change if they are offered the kind of reasoning used throughout this book, and in particular the rationale for various options provided in Chapter 8.

Lack of direction

The negative outlook is invariably expressed in a general lack of direction in the organisation, the absence of any shaping vision, the propensity for different people within the organisation to make decisions, the adoption of often illogical and irrational decisions, and a generally reactive approach where the school responds in isolation to each new development. While significant research has yet to be undertaken on the scene globally, the picture obtained by Lee and Mitchell (2009) on the Australian scene (and cited in the opening quote to this chapter) is similar from all accounts to the situation found in the US, the UK and New Zealand, and possibly in your school. This lack of direction and uncertainty are clearly unhelpful when one is mounting a concerted implementation strategy that requires all within the school community to know the operational parameters.

Historic technological paranoia

History provides numerous examples of deep concern associated with the introduction of most new technologies. It is thus worth reminding ourselves of the history of innovation and the surrounding hysteria about the safety of young people, and thus putting the current societal anxiety in its wider context. Film, radio and television all brought with them great promises of social and educational benefits but, at the same time, were accompanied by great concern for young people's exposure to harmful and inappropriate content. In the case of film, concerns gave rise to calls for censorship and for restricting the distribution of films that might 'corrupt the morals of children or adults or incite to crime' (*The Outlook*, 20 June 1914, p. 185). This led to approximately 40 educational and religious groups in the US calling for federal regulation of motion pictures by 1931 (Wartella & Jennings 2000). Exactly the same concerns were raised for film, radio and television, and similar concerns are now being raised about the Internet. Cassell and Cramer (2008) provide an invaluable insight into the perceived impact of the aforementioned technologies on young women and the need for society to protect their morality. In commenting on the outcry of letting women in the late nineteenth century perform the role of telegraph operators, they noted:

> *Not only were they incapable of technical competence, young women, most vulnerable to losing their virtue, were also thought to be the most vulnerable to the vice of the telegraph. Interestingly, these very same young women were the most likely to be hired as telegraph operators, and the quickest to pick up the technical skills, despite the rhetoric about women's incompetence in the face of the technology ... These themes of parental technical deficiency and ensuing parental loss of control in the face of a daughter's appropriation of the technology for her own ends are common in the literature and publicity surrounding all the communications technologies. The telephone produced anxiety to an even greater extent than the telegraph. (p. 60)*

It this kind of thinking that one has to overcome if the school is to provide the desired ready access. It is simply a case of viewing the developments in their holistic context and appreciating that, in time, the fears regarding this technology move on.

'Cyber safety' movement

The issues of 'cyber safety' and, in particular, 'cyber bullying' need to be viewed in context and with some rationality in a world hungry for sensationalism. As indicated below, one needs to be aware of the 'carpet baggers' who have moved into the market and have joined with the Internet filter industry and the sensationalism of the media to present their views about educating young people for a digital world. There are indeed significant issues relating to the education of young people in the digital world that should be addressed by a networked school community through its instructional program, but to suggest the issues will best be addressed by banning Internet access in the few hours of schooling while it is being used as a normal part of the everyday lives of young people is to abrogate the educational responsibilities of schools by not seeing their students as digital citizens.

Schools are appropriately concerned about the safety of students online; however, information is being relied on to justify the use of filters and passwords which in many cases, is not credible. For example, a much publicised case of a 12-year-old British school girl who ran away with a US marine she met over the Internet (McDougall 2003) was reported through television, radio, newspapers and online media and was cited as an example of the dangers of the Internet. This report and others like them focus on the shocking, and present singular events as typical online interactions and are therefore misleading.

Research shows that while there are some risks associated with online interactions, this can be managed through online participation of parents and teachers, not by limiting access to appropriate sites and networks that young people actively participate in at home and at school, as commented on by Maher (2008) and as pointed out by danah boyd from the Harvard Berkman Center for Internet & Society in the opening quote to the chapter. A telling conclusion reached by the recent study undertaken by the Berkman Center at Harvard for the US State Attorneys-General bears noting that 'A poor home environment that includes conflict and poor parent–child relationships is correlated with a host of online risks (Wolak et al. 2003; Ybarra and Mitchell 2004b)' (Berkman Center 2008, p. 21).

Research also suggests that the majority of young people who use the Internet do it in a responsible and honest way, and that 'Most online communication is with local friends: Being in constant contact with friends is highly valued, and there is little interest contacting strangers' (Livingstone & Bober 2005, p. 2). Parents, teachers and administrators have to give our young people some credit in being able to handle networked technologies. Currently, it seems that many believe that young people do not have any skills at all in navigating online, and adults have to monitor every action they take for their safety. This raises the issue of how young people are being consulted about their views and experiences and this can inform the debate of providing access. It is almost as if students aren't part of the equation. It is vital that young people's views be taken into account when considering safety.

If you want to explore in greater depth the many issues associated with 'cyber safety', it is suggested you download the aforementioned Berkman Center study which provides a comprehensive analysis of the scene (Berkman Center 2008). It reinforces the approach taken here by the authors, that, if approached sensibly, the online poses no greater risk for young people than the offline. However, it is a world young people and their parents have to better understand. The authors would also suggest reading the overview of the global scene prepared by Moyle (2009) and contrast the reported stances adopted by European nations like the Netherlands, Denmark and Sweden, and nations like the US, the UK and Australia. While, as Moyle indicates, her observations come from a dinner conversation in mid 2009, the potentially contrasting stance on the use of technical controls is in itself highly revealing.

Bureaucratic control

The lack of positive direction and leadership by the school, coupled with the cyber safety paranoia, is combining in some situations to heighten the control and power of the educational bureaucrats. What bears remembering is that a bureaucrat's prime concern is to serve the senior member of the government of the day, be it the minister of education or the chair of the local authority. It is most assuredly not the education of young people. While that might sound cynical, any who have occupied a senior position in a bureaucracy and worked with bureaucracies around the world will know that is so. For example, if the relevant Minister of Education believes the line being promoted in the media, his/her bureaucrats will provide a simple—even if unworkable and inappropriate—solution.

The bureaucratic controls are most vividly expressed in the outright banning of certain technologies from being used within the classroom. Across the developed world, you will find a significant number of schools and education authorities banning the use in the school of Smart phones, laptops, computer games consoles, and online computer games, iPods, social networking sites, a range of Web 2.0 technologies, YouTube, and even Skype. However, many of the controls are more subtle, but equally as effective. Limits are placed on the amount of bandwidth that can be used by a faculty, restrictions are placed on the particular brand of equipment that can be connected to the network, and administrative controls are imposed that limit those entitled to use a facility. Collectively, these result in teachers not trying to get their students to access the Internet.

Diminution of democratic and legal rights

Allied to the increased bureaucratic control of student Internet access, and the failure to relate the level and nature of control to any underlying educational rationale, is the facility for the more extreme education authorities and schools to use their control of school Internet access to reinforce their particular religious or political beliefs, even if they breach their nation's human rights. At the time of writing, for example, litigation was being launched in the US by civil rights groups against those local education authorities that were blocking student access to sites that discussed the likes of gay and lesbian marriage and abortion (De Vise 2009). In brief, the local authorities were using their control of the Internet as a censorship tool. There is somehow the perception that if the control is imposed on young people it was not a breach of their rights. The same scant regard for the nation's laws is also evidenced in many schools' belief that it can confiscate a student's technology, even when it is the personal property of the student, or as indicated earlier intrude on the student's privacy if it is believed to be educationally desirable.

Distrust of students and teachers

Another hurdle is the assumption by some that they need to operate from a position of mistrust of both the students and the teachers. It is quite common in countries like Australia and the US for teachers to have to seek formal, often written permission to gain access to a particular site or online facility, with the underlying assumption that if they breach the trust their rights will be withdrawn. The contrast with the out-of-class situation is pronounced.

Cultural blockages

The early signs point to the national and related school teaching culture also impacting on the nature of Internet access. The cultural setting is clearly vital. In many schools, probably unintentionally, teachers tend to default to the ways of the culture they have only ever known in schools. One of the challenges, even for the clearest thinking of educational leaders, is to stop resorting to the ways of old. While it is only natural, it is a smaller hurdle that can soon trip you over.

Probably the vast majority of teachers and school administrators would not realise that they never let the students use any of the school's technology unless a teacher is overseeing its use. Even if the students know far more about that technology than the teacher they are invariably not trusted to use it alone. Think about the situation in your school. What is the school going to do when the students bring their own technology into the classroom?

Another significant cultural block is the belief that schools are discrete entities where the only real education happens within the walls of the school, and that if the school opts to block student Internet usage no access will be possible. In conducting a recent leadership seminar in the Northern Territory of Australia, Mal Lee encountered the situation where the local education authority in its quest to improve the lives of the Indigenous students in the Aboriginal lands had banned access to any type of pornography on the landline network serving the school. What they neglected to consider was the young people's excellent Smart phone access via a high-speed 3G mobile network.

The 'carpet baggers'

Many in schools and even education authorities are not conscious of the profound influence exerted by the technology companies and their marketing dollar on the technology used within schools. As Lee and Winzenried (2009) revealed, this has been so for the past century and continues today. From the early 1990s there have been technology companies worldwide that have viewed the introduction of networks in schools as a source of profits, often with no consideration of the educational validity of the move. Those companies use their extensive marketing and lobbying dollar very astutely to reinforce the line being projected in the media. Check, for example, the appendix of the aforementioned Berkman Center study to appreciate the kind of companies with a vested interest in promoting school filters. The sale of filtering software is big business around the world. On one site, it was reported that the global market for the storage and Internet safety industry is estimated at $US23 billion dollars (*People's Daily Online* 2008). The intent of these companies is to sell their products.

Finance and infrastructure

Many schools in the developed world are struggling financially to provide the digital, network infrastructure and support (see Chapters 3 and 7). Some fundamental changes need to be made if schools are going to have the technology in each classroom to allow the classes to readily access the Internet, even if much of its usage is blocked or constrained. This situation has been well documented in a US report published in 2005 by the National Center for Educational Statistics. The authors of the report found that only 35 per cent of primary schools they surveyed had a full-time, paid school technology director/coordinator (Parsad, Jones & Greene 2005).

The lack of ongoing support in schools means students and teachers often are required to wait lengthy periods of time before getting problems resolved. This has the effect of disrupting programs that have been put in place that rely on the technologies, and ultimately affects the learning opportunities for students. Interestingly, this type of limited support is usually not found in the educational bureaucracies that administer schools and demonstrates a lack of commitment to providing appropriate Internet access to schools.

The technical hurdles

In addition to the human hurdles, there is a set of technical hurdles apparent in most schools. Some are significant and will be impediments for some time, and are largely the result of the educational architects who are leading the schools not addressing whether these hurdles need to be in place.

Network operations and security

It is a given that the networks used in and by schools need to be secure, reliable and easily used. They need also to be future-proofed and able to withstand immense use, invariably in concentrated timeslots, and the inevitable external and internal attacks, particularly by way of viruses. There will thus always need to be reasonable controls placed on their use and on those who use them. That concern about control could be markedly minimised if schools were able to move, at least in time, to a type of network that allowed only a few highly skilled operators into the internal workings of the network and kept the vast majority of users in a position where they had no access to them. To use a car analogy, there would be much to be gained by allowing only a couple of highly skilled and accredited mechanics to access and fine-tune the engine, and restricting all others to inside the car and the controls. That is what happens with web facilities, and is evidenced in tools like Google Docs and the emerging cloud technology. Unfortunately many, if not most, school networks are of the vintage where both the mechanics and the drivers had access to the motor and hence are able to easily and unwittingly ruin the engine. While that vintage remains in use, some significant controls and precautions will be required. A further set of hurdles is placed in the way of student Internet access whose place warrants serious questioning.

Control by the centre

It would appear that the majority of education authority networks are configured such that the central authority controls all access rights, so reinforcing the power of the central network manager. The same networks could readily be configured—as, for example, it is with the Lismore Catholic Education authority in Australia—to allow the individual schools to decide on all the access rights for their community.

Passwords

School and education authority leaderships have seldom questioned the educational validity of using in schools network administration practices designed for the business office. Most schools in the English-speaking world use Microsoft-centric networks without seriously questioning the consonance of those networks' business settings with a school's educational agenda. The most pervasive of those settings is the unabashed embracement of passwords in K–12 settings. Why are they used in the way they are? Are there more educationally appropriate approaches that could be employed?

When early childhood students are required to change their password every two weeks, one needs to question the educational relevance of the hurdle. There are numerous problems with the use of passwords for both young people and parents, hurdles that could be readily removed with some lateral thinking. In classes in which Damian Maher taught as a primary school teacher, students were often required to remember a password to log into their accounts. While the students were all provided with the same password initially, the students would change them. They thus went to Damian indicating they had forgotten their password. However, as soon as he went to assist them, he found they had changed it and, not having administrator rights, he was unable to make the change. When this happened, students had to wait until the school's computer coordinator could reset the password, thus unnecessarily disrupting many lessons. Often passwords would not work, and if a new student came to the school it could take months before the student was looked after. To get around this problem, use was often made of another student's log-in that obviously completely defeated the purpose of the password log-in.

In many schools, even kindergarten students are required to log into computers. If you have ever been in a kindergarten class, you will know that the literacy level of an average five-year-old does not allow for a quick log-in. Damian remembers computer lessons with kindergarten students where they have 45 minutes to use the computers, yet in some instances it took 20 to 30 minutes before all the students could log themselves in to use a Paint program! Does this happen in your school?

The prime concern should be on facilitating ready student access to the Internet in the school, not adapting the educational process to fit in with an inappropriate computer system. It is about ensuring that the desired educational philosophy shapes the use of the technology, and not letting the technology dictate the usage as now happens in many schools.

Filters

Another of the hurdles facing ready Internet access is the level of control applied to the network filters. Every school network needs filters, even if only to ensure that the school abides with legally appropriate uses of digital technologies. What you need to check is the level of control, and by whom. In the more proactive schools, the filter controls are set in accordance with the school's educational vision. In the reactive settings, there is often no such guidance and it is left to the whim of the network manager. In a networked school community that kind of haphazard practice is inappropriate.

In many respects, the use of filters in the reactive schools and education authorities is allied to the earlier comments about bureaucrats and politicians aided by vested industries promoting usually expensive filtering 'solutions'. They can't. Aside from the fact that Gilmore's Law will circumvent the efforts, the actual filters can only go part-way from shielding young people from designated websites. In a study conducted by Kaiser Family Foundation (2002), the question asked was 'Does filtering block access to non-pornographic web sites?' The results of this study showed that the most restrictive level of filter setting blocked 25 per cent of legitimate health-related sites. Clearly then filters in themselves are not the answer in limiting unwanted access. This failure to block access to inappropriate sites while also preventing access to appropriate sites has been found in numerous other studies (Greeenfield, Rickwood & Tran 2001; Sutton 2005).

Filtering carries with it other problems. Once they are installed, they provide a perception of safety that is not accurate, as 'Filters can be circumvented or defeated in various ways: children may disable or uninstall them, go around them (e.g. through a proxy server)' (Flood & Hamilton 2003, p. 19). As capable Web users know, it is possible to use the likes of proxies to circumvent the blockages imposed by network filters. Moyle (2009), in reporting on the conversation about Internet safety filtering approaches with a cross-section of international technology educators, observed:

> They acknowledged the overall futility of using technical solutions to stop young people accessing blocked sites … To limit and control students' access to sites in schools seemed, however, a counter-productive measure doomed to failure. (p. 4)

At first glance, all these impediments appear immensely daunting. But then you quickly realise that the vast majority are human hurdles, and many link with the school leadership failure to set the direction and ensure all the school's operations support the vision.

The hurdles and developing the way forward

Table 16.1 summarises the human and the technical hurdles discussed in the preceding sections of this chapter, and provides the space for you to formulate appropriate responses to take a proactive approach. We encourage you to regularly return to complete this table, and some advice is provided here.

Table 16.1 Developing proactive approaches to the human and the technical hurdles

The human hurdles	Formulating your proactive approach
Negative outlook of leadership	Who are the decision makers?
Lack of direction	*Your response*:
Historic technological paranoia	
'Cyber safety' movement	
Bureaucratic control	
Diminution of democratic and legal rights	
Distrust of students and teachers	
Cultural blockages	How are you going to develop policy?
The 'carpet baggers'	*Your response*:
Finance and infrastructure	
	How are you going to engage the home and the school—and the students—in policy development?
	Your response:
The technical hurdles	
Network operations and security	How is the infrastructure and ubiquitous Internet access best managed and achieved?
Control by the centre	*Your response*:
Passwords	
Filters	

In planning the way forward, consider whether or not you are in the fortunate situation of already being in a proactive school, or in a reactive contextual setting that has still to remove a significant set of hurdles. Whatever your context, the key is to adopt the total teacher/parent/student community as part of a holistic implementation strategy that provides ready and reasoned access to the Internet. Remember that many young people already have ready access to the Internet in their homes. Many young people increasingly have ready access via their web-enabled, wireless mobile technology. These young people are very likely already part of networks, as networks are everywhere, and the people are the networks—as outlined in Chapter 13 which refers to Larry Johnson's seven 'metatrends' gleaned from examining the last eight years of the Horizon Reports.

If you are in a school that already provides students with excellent use of the Internet, you can move on to consider how best to address the enhancement of teaching and learning in a networked world. Those who are faced with what might appear to be many (and unnecessary) hurdles can readily address the issue of increasing access at the same time as removing and overcoming the hurdles. In a networked school community, the desire should be to adopt an approach that embraces both the in-school and out-of-classroom use of the Internet, while appreciating that ultimately there will be elements of the overall approach that apply more in parts of the networked community than the other.

In considering the way forward, bear in mind the observation made in Chapter 3 about the Japanese secondary school. Increasingly, young people will have the technology to completely by-pass the school network. Bear also in mind the potentially dramatically different approach to Internet use adopted by the Netherlands, Denmark and Sweden and their reliance on education and focus on learning as central to the way forward. The challenge as mentioned is to strike the appropriate balance.

The decision maker

One of the first tasks is to clarify who is ultimately responsible within the networked school community. Is it the network manager, the teacher librarian, the principal or a committee of the school council? We have a strong suspicion that in most situations it will be the principal, but your particular situation and governance arrangements might lead to another choice. What is vital is having that position of responsibility identified.

Policy development

Determine who develops the overall policy for the networked school community. It is suggested that ideally it should be a collaboratively developed policy made by involving the staff, the parents and the students—yes, the students! The policy development process can simultaneously lift your school community's understanding of and deflate the cyber safety concerns, and enhance the student learning in a digital, networked world. For an authentic home–school nexus, the home needs to be involved in the policy development early and at all phases.

'Selling' the policy

It will be important in developing the policy to also factor in the selling, the marketing of the proposition among the school's wider community, those overseeing its work and the key politicians. This will need to be ongoing and foregrounded throughout. An important facet of the sell will be the promotion of the total-community approach and the implementation, in conjunction with the homes, of an educational program that promotes educationally appropriate lifelong use of the Web.

Management

A central part of the reasoned approach is the wise management and use of the various digital technologies, and in particular those technologies that provide Internet access and those owned by young people that will be used on the move and in the classroom. The ideas on the management of that technology will require close scrutiny.

'Online' education

The most important aspect of the reasoned approach is the development of an educational program that equips the student to use the online world that can be woven into the networked school community's curriculum, and to understand and value both the formal and informal education provided by the networked school community.

Conclusion

It is important to understand that those wanting to provide the appropriate education of young people need to design and shape the desired future. In many respects, this is a consistent underlying theme throughout this book. If there is a lack of leadership and action, it is likely that schooling will drift and remain locked in an organisation designed for the last century. In addition, where this continues to occur, many schools find themselves encountering the many hurdles described earlier.

Take control and shape the path you would like and you will markedly minimise those hurdles. You will provide ready and educationally meaningful student Internet access, and assist in preparing young people for digital futures.

Guiding questions

After reading this chapter, consider your context and propose your ideas in relation to the following guiding questions.

1   What rules or restrictions are placed on student and staff use of the Internet at your school? Who is responsible for determining the controls placed on student and staff access? Does the school have the independence and authority to decide the kind of Internet access it believes is desirable?

2   Do the school's Internet access and use arrangements align with the school's educational purpose? If not, why do you think there is a mismatch, and what changes do you think need to be made?

3   To what extent are students accessing and using the Internet beyond school? More or less?

4   Are students already opting to forego the use of the school network because of the controls? If they are, what major hurdles need to be lowered or removed?

5   What kind of collaboration has taken place, or needs to take place, to ensure the school community, its students and parents have a say in determining the operational parameters?

Key messages

- One of the first issues you will need to address is who it is within the school who decides on the nature of the Internet access and, in turn, ensures that the Internet usage policy accords with the desired educational purpose of the school.

- The proactive schools and education authorities are generally operating on the belief that schools should use their 'protected' learning environment to educate their students for life and work in a digital future where the use of the Internet will be pervasive.

- There are both human and technical hurdles that proactive schools can overcome.

- If there is a lack of leadership and action, it is likely that schooling will drift and remain locked in an organisation designed for the last century.

CHAPTER 17

Student assessment and digital futures: How shall we know them?

KAY KIMBER & CLAIRE WYATT-SMITH

Shrinking resources and market pressures mean that education can no longer be the sole responsibility of governments … Reforming assessment is essential to enabling any systemic change in education. And change on a global scale is required to equip students of today with the skills they need to succeed in the workforce of tomorrow. The international education assessments in the Program for International Student Assessment (PISA) … focus on key competencies in reading, mathematics and science but we always wanted to extend the scope to cover important new skills. In PISA 2003, we took a step by adding an assessment of problem solving, but one limited to analogical reasoning. We hoped to add information and communications technology (ICT) competence in PISA 2006 but did not succeed … We all need now to work together to advance assessment practice.

Professor Barry McGaw (13 January 2009, p. 1)

Introduction

The invention of the printing press revolutionised access to information with widespread implications for learning. Developments in communication technologies in the last five years represent an even more radical shift, bringing unlimited access to knowledge at a rate unprecedented in former eras. Fisch, McLeod and Bronman (2006; 2008) have estimated that the 1.5 exabytes (1.5×10^8) of unique new information items generated across the world in 2006, eclipsing that of the previous 5000 years, had escalated to 4 exabytes (4×10^{19}) in just two short years. This is the everyday landscape in which today's young people are challenged to learn.

While education and the schooling sector in particular have struggled to keep pace, there are new signs of the incursions of telecommunication carriers into curriculum and assessment. For example, the proposed Assessment and Teaching of 21st Century Skills (ATC21S) project recently announced by the Federal Minister for Education will involve

Australia, Finland, Portugal, Singapore and Britain as global partners. This project, the first of its kind, aims to measure skills for the modern world, including 'cross-disciplinary analytical, creative, adaptive and problem-solving skills as well as their ability to work co-operatively' (Australian Labor Party 2009). Importantly, while the project is a pilot, it marks the entrée of a global computer partnership involving Cisco, Intel and Microsoft into the business of online testing, with an intention to link the project to the Organisation for Economic Co-operation and Development (OECD) program for international student assessment.

Given the rapidity of change in digital technologies, Leu et al. (2004) reminded us that our theoretical insights into reading and being literate with print do not readily transfer into a multimedia-saturated world: 'What we know about new literacies from the traditional research literature must recognize that we actually know very little' (p. 1571). Given our dual interests in this chapter in learning and assessment, it is also timely to reflect on Rowntree's (1977) provocation, some three decades ago, about the purposes and values of an educational system, as played out in its assessment procedures:

> If we wish to discover the truth about an educational system, we must look into its assessment procedures. What student qualities and achievements are actively valued and rewarded by the system? How are its purposes and intentions realised? To what extent are the hopes and ideals, aims and objectives professed by the system ever truly perceived, valued and striven for by those who make their way within it? The answers to such questions are to be found in what the system requires to **do** in order to survive and prosper. The spirit and style of student assessment defines the de facto curriculum. (p. 1) [emphasis in original]

Rowntree's questions above remain salient; however, the dominance of new technologies calls for a rethinking of assessment in schooling to match the new learning landscape for young people. The introduction of high-stakes, large-scale, technology-mediated assessment is inevitable and integral to credentialling structures. Further, it promises to be transformative within education in terms of what is taught and how it is taught. Our vision for assessment, however, is school-based, with a transformative possibility tied to its recognition of the complementary roles that both in-school and out-of-school learning spaces can play in young people's education. At its core is the belief that assessment practices should support and strengthen young people's capacities for acting with greater mindfulness when using or creating knowledge online. This belief is consistent with the current widespread movement of *assessment for learning* (Black & William 1998; Macintyre, Buck & Beckenhauer 2007) that promotes assessment as central to efforts to improve student learning.

The following section, 'Assessment opportunities—networked learning spaces (NLS)', begins with instances of young people's learning already occurring outside school, and outside current assessment practices. The issues of *connectivity, creativity and agency* are identified as critical for connecting school assessment domains and practices with out-of-school online learning. This section argues that as knowledge today has no fixed boundaries, school-based assessment needs to become more inclusive of other learning locales, creative in design and more supportive of young people's acquisition of *learner agency*.

The section on 'Assessment opportunities—essential digital learnings (EDL)', prioritises young people's critical, more mindful approaches to learning in NLS over technological proficiency or frequency of new media usage. The notion of 'essential digital learnings' (EDL) is explored with its goal of metalearning and its core elements of *e-credibility*, *e-designing* and *e-proficiency* (Kimber & Wyatt-Smith 2009). It is argued in this chapter that these requisite metacognitive and operational capacities work to strengthen young people's learner agency in their networked learning spaces. As such, these learnings have implications for what comes to be assessed and valued as demonstrations of learning. To this end, we present an assessment framework that seeks to relate digital learning and learning spaces in the understanding that the latter extend well beyond the classroom. We conclude by considering the potential of this framework for informing the design of tasks and related assessment criteria and standards in revisioning school-based assessment practices.

Assessment opportunities—networked learning spaces (NLS)

The term 'learning space' is taken to mean any physical or virtual location where an individual or group can engage in meaning making. In the traditional sense, a classroom is a designated place for learning and, hence, a type of 'learning space'. Our interest, however, is in those spaces that may (or may not) take a physical form and are connected via digitally mediated communications, hence 'networked learning spaces' or NLS. This concept resonates with directions currently being taken by some telecommunications carriers associated with Partnerships for 21st Century Skills (2009a). Their clear stance on learning environments is that in 'today's interconnected and technology-driven world, a learning environment can be virtual, online, remote; in other words, it doesn't have to be a place at all' (p. 3).

Understood broadly, NLS are digitally connected, potentially drawing home, school and community places in local and global locations into a boundless and dynamically connected learning landscape. Undoubtedly, NLS work to facilitate the interconnection of individuals anywhere in the world, at any time, in the gathering, creating or sharing of digital texts, whatever their form, usually in out-of-school contexts. However, while curriculum frameworks and materials that guide teaching and learning using digital technologies are just beginning to emerge (see http://www.thelearningfederation.edu.au/tlf2/), a pressing challenge is to help teachers bridge the gap between traditional print-dependent learning and digitally enabled learning. This is vital if the current major investment of funds in school technology is to benefit young people. Additionally, ways of assessing digital learning are given scant attention in national and state curriculum policy documents. Further, ways of enabling digital learning assessment to improve learning have not been the subject of sustained research over time.

Recent thinking in learning has, however, embraced the notion of schooling and curriculum redesign, extending beyond the classroom:

> *We must redesign schools that reach far beyond the traditional classrooms many adults experienced when they were young. The learning environments of the 21st century must encompass a rich mix of media and devices, varied cultures, and virtual and real-life relationships. Policy must serve as the steering mechanism to guide the creation of learning environments that are both more expansive and more inclusive—spaces for learning that offer more people more access to more places and information while also allowing for close-knit social relationships among community members to flourish. Making all this happen is the task before us. It will not be easy, inexpensive, or quick. But it is essential.*
>
> Partnerships for 21st Century Skills (2009a, pp. 27–28)

The above quote makes clear the need to move away from 'traditional classrooms' and their related authority structures. It also indicates how new learning environments make available more possibilities for young people to establish and maintain 'close-knit social relationships'. It points to the role of digital technologies in building social capital over time.

Before considering NLS in closer detail, the nature of online communication should be addressed. For many young people, online spaces mean instant communication, particularly through social networking sites as a popular vehicle for exchanging informal banter with friends or displaying their personal preferences or changing loyalties. The negative media publicity on the misuse and public display of inappropriate messages or mobile phone images as cyber-bullying does warrant adult-led discussions on ethical usage, empathy and responsible publication. However, for increasing numbers of young people, social networking sites have become the vehicle for sharing knowledge, developing expertise and expressing creativity. Characteristically, in these instances usage is self- and peer-monitored, for positive and useful purposes (see Ito et al. 2008; Jenkins 2006).

In fields ranging from cultural and new media studies to education, the social networking phenomenon has been the site for research and investigation. According to Lenhart et al. (2007), over 64 per cent of all American youth are active participants in social networking sites, and 59 per cent are active creators of online content. More recently, the Speak Up 2008 surveys (Project Tomorrow 2009b) found that over half of 280 000 American middle and high school students collaborated online for homework and school projects. Stern (2008) investigated young people's social network website creations and established their role in identity formation and technology skill development. Another study revealed how teenagers loved 'geeking out' every day with new media, a term that the authors described as 'self-directed, peer-based learning' (Ito et al. 2008, pp. 1–2). Jenkins (2006) noted the extent of young people's participation in these communities and their power in launching future careers. In such instances, self-motivated learning was fuelled and developed by peers or adults who shared those same interests.

Two vignettes follow as evidence of these participatory types of NLS. Martin and Hannah (fictional names), both Australian secondary students, recounted their online, out-of-school activities to the authors of this chapter.

Martin: local student, virtual journalist, international peace-keeper

Fifteen-year-old Martin, a computer enthusiast, was intent on an army career and passionate about real accounts of military deployments. At school, he studied modern and ancient history, learned about racial prejudice through Harper Lee's *To Kill a Mockingbird*, and statistics through mathematics classes. Interestingly, it was in his own bedroom that these diverse and seemingly discrete fields were fused into a more powerful learning experience.

Martin met Angus in an online community. A Scottish soldier who had recently returned from his second tour of duty in Afghanistan, Angus chatted 'live' with Martin about modern-day warfare, racial prejudice, and global politics—all tantalisingly enthralling topics for Martin.

With Angus's agreement, Martin invited his mother to join their conversation, sharing headphones and ideas. Martin was keen to initiate his mother into his online gaming chat room activities. Discussion ranged across everyday lifestyles in an occupied country, the lived beliefs and attitudes of occupying soldiers, peace-keeping forces, everyday lives for Afghani people, the role of women as change agents, soldier training, weaponry, cross-national interactions, and political intrigue.

Martin did not lack confidence in talking 'live' with an adult from another country and with a world of invaluable experiences to share. Moreover, Martin found the immediacy of the discussion about a global, peace-resolving issue stimulating.

Hannah: local student, virtual gallery director, international artist

Sixteen-year-old Hannah spent hours on her computer, creating and manipulating digital art. She was a member of five online communities and moderated her own online art group with school friends. They displayed work from over 20 contributing artists and invited comment and critique from members in Australia, Asia and America. Hannah believed that her online art community had hundreds of members and she claimed most of these as virtual friends.

Hannah basked in the pleasure of seeing what other members thought of her work, checking the viewing graphs that showed how many members had seen her work that day—the highest, 130, and the lowest, 20. These view graphs showed her, at a glance, the extent to which her work had been 'noticed', so helping establish her status as a digital artist.

In class, Hannah was reluctant to display her own written and creative work. At most, she might count a few of her classmates and her teacher as viewers of her creations. These viewings were within the four walls of her classroom.

Through Hannah's participation in and creation of digital art for her online community friends, her confidence in her artistic and technological ability grew proportionally to her skills and public recognition.

The characteristics of networked learning spaces (NLS)

Several aspects in both vignettes illustrate the wider phenomenon of young people's twenty-first century online practices. Each provides an opportunity to consider their potential for a broader notion of twenty-first century assessment practices. Both Martin and Hannah exercised agency in their choice of online community. Their entry, participation and manner of involvement were self-initiated. Both communities included international members with whom they could collaborate and share expertise. Their contacts were personally sought out or contacted, and helped to provide meaningful information with high immediacy of purpose.

Creativity was central to Hannah's community interactions, as was political and cultural consciousness to Martin's. Both Martin's and Hannah's activities were highly engaging, being sustained over several hours at a time. Their local and global *connectivity* was enabled via their own high-powered technology, at home, unblocked by web-filtering software or firewalls as in many schools. Selwyn's (2006) research into the 'digital disconnect' between home and school noted that most students found the school filters and blocks so annoying and restrictive that they chose to confine Internet-based activities to home usage.

In a similar vein, the Speak Up 2008 surveys (Project Tomorrow 2009b) identified communications, collaboration, creation and contribution as important themes in American teenagers' daily lives. Henry Jenkins (2006) argued that in this highly participatory culture, young people were developing the kinds of skills that were increasingly valued in the modern workplace. So it would appear that across the world the benefits of these types of NLS for future citizenship are considerable. However, certain aspects of these online learning practices offer ways for rethinking school assessment practices. Three factors that could guide the shaping of new assessment opportunities are identified and outlined below—that is, connectivity, creativity and agency.

Factor 1: Connectivity

The current disconnection between home and school learning needs to be bridged for assessment to match the twenty-first century learning landscape more closely. Schools need to find ways to value and include worthwhile learning, wherever it occurs. Consider, for example, how both Martin and Hannah had been active contributors to their online communities. Martin had learned valuable lessons about military operations, intercultural relationships, human rights, humanitarianism and political consciousness. Similarly, Hannah learned about collaboration and creative and proficient use of technology software, and developed her own creative status and confidence. Yet, in neither instance was there any evidence of their out-of-school, self-initiated learning being recognised or valued in school.

What of Martin's and Hannah's school learning? Here, their learning continued in discrete subject silos, each with its own core content and specific assessment mode—largely through print-based testing. What if Martin and Hannah had been able to negotiate their own project to build on their initial interests across two or three subject areas? Could a cross-disciplinary approach have sanctioned an interdisciplinary project, involving further digital research and the creation of multimodal records to be stored in an e-portfolio and evaluated by a panel of teachers, peers and knowledgeable others from the online communities? Furthermore, could not the global reach of their online activities have included perspectives from and about other cultures to enrich their learning?

As the Internet enables intricate patterns of connectivity, opportunities are presented for blending formal and informal learning, and cross-disciplinary learning. Suggett (2007) has noted the potential of interdisciplinary learning with digital technologies for enabling active learners with high levels of problem-solving skills. Also of note is increasing support for the potential of global connectivity for enriching intercultural communication, mutual respect and global citizenship. In the US, a white paper prepared by the Partnerships for 21st Century Skills (2009b) urges educators to interconnect rich core disciplinary content with twenty-first century skills and the important theme of 'global awareness' that includes:

- using twenty-first century skills to understand and address global issues;

- learning from and working collaboratively with individuals representing diverse cultures, religions and lifestyles in a spirit of mutual respect and open dialogue in personal, work and community contexts; and,

- understanding other nations and cultures, including the use of non-English languages.

(Source: Partnerships for 21st Century Skills, 2009b, p. 2)

In Australia, the first National Curriculum also advocates the development of greater depth and expertise in mandatory discipline knowledges, cross-disciplinary investigations, significant increases in technology skill development, innovation and the promotion of global citizenship (MCEETYA 2007). All these impact on how schooling prepares young people and prompt consideration of how connectivity might be a useful concept for rethinking assessment practices.

Factor 2: Creativity

The second identified factor of NLS is creativity, an aspect associated with originality and the creation of a new product from other materials.

To some extent, creativity is synonymous with innovation. Interestingly, 'create' has superseded 'analyse' as the most complex knowledge and cognitive process in the revised Bloom's Taxonomy (Anderson & Krathwohl 2001). It was defined as 'putting elements together to form a novel, coherent whole or make an original product', with three associated skills of 'generating, planning and producing' (Krathwohl 2002, p. 215).

In *Imagine Australia: The role of creativity in the innovation economy* (Prime Minister's Science, Engineering and Innovation Council 2005), creativity was linked to advancing both scientific knowledge and artistic creations for the nation, newly defined as 'the innovation economy'. The creative imagination was said to know 'no divide between science and art. It seeks the unknown and invents the future' (p. 1). This notion of creativity is mirrored in the shaping of the Australian national curriculum:

> *Creativity* refers to skills and orientations which enable the development of new ideas and their application in specific contexts. It includes generating an idea which is new to the individual; seeing existing situations in a new way; identifying alternative explanations; seeing links; and finding new ways to apply ideas to generate a positive outcome. Creativity is closely linked to innovation, and requires characteristics such as intellectual flexibility, open-mindedness, adaptability and a readiness to try new ways of doing things.
>
> National Curriculum Board (2009, p. 8) [emphasis in original]

If creativity begins with imagination and a willingness to experiment for innovations, Hannah exemplified that with her digital creations. Her skill development was fostered by her local and virtual art community primarily outside school. Increasingly, schools are expected to foster that creativity in school. According to McWilliam and Haukka (2008), 'If we cannot "transmit" creativity, we can certainly teach *for* creativity' (p. 654).

This means that whatever the subject area, teachers will be designing innovative approaches to curriculum delivery and finding ways to foster those skills alluded to in the above quotation, for individuals and collaborative teams. With creative problem solving encouraged among students, and the opportunity to find team solutions, young people are not just engaged in the activity but also challenged to find innovative solutions. Examples are presented in two scenarios below.

1 Online gaming scenario

McGonigal (2008) designed a problem-solving game, 'I Love Bees'. The game involved over 600 000 mainly teenage players who formed their own online community to share, track and analyse new puzzle pieces as they gradually solved the problem over a four-month period. The scenario drew them into several real-world locations across the globe and they used a range of media platforms to solve the puzzle:

> These massively distributed puzzle pieces were tracked down and documented by individuals, but compiled and analysed by the group. Once a new piece of content was turned over to the collective, it then would be analysed by thousands of players on dozens of different community forums. A single new clue detected on Dana's blog, for example, resulted in 2,401 new comments from players within days of being found.
>
> McGonigal (2008, p. 206)

This example of creative scenario-building illustrates how young people can collaborate in real and virtual space, find innovative ways to connect and solve clues, and sustain their engagement across time. Teachers across disciplines could:

- collaborate in devising the scenario, conditions and timeframe;
- be flexible in identifying learning moments and observing collaborative interactions;
- build in opportunities for teaching particular skills, whether discipline- or technologically based;
- share student-created artifacts produced in the process of unravelling the puzzle as evidence of learning; and,
- devise criteria and standards that account for the desired attainment levels.

2 New era of online assessments

Silva (2008) has recounted details of a range of innovative approaches to assessment that are involving young people collaboratively in problem-solving scenarios. One was the College Work and Readiness Assessment (CWRA). This test was completed in a 90-minute session by Year 9 students in Delaware, US. While the rationale of the single task was assessing students' creative approaches to solving real-world problems, it involved students accessing editorials, 20-page research reports, budgets and other documents. They were expected to demonstrate proficiency in several subject disciplines as well as 'broader and more sophisticated skills like evaluating and analysing information and thinking creatively about how to apply information to real-world problems' (p. 1). School officials believed that the task had value in prompting students to think critically, intelligently and in innovative ways, more so than in traditional pen-and-paper tests.

A second creative assessment task, River City, presented students with a problem for which they developed and tested hypotheses, analysed their findings and presented a report with recommendations—all in virtual space. Developers noted how the program allowed teachers to track individual students' movements and decisions at each step along the way, so providing a new type of evidence for assessing learning and individual progress. Perhaps something of these two online assessment possibilities will find a place within the new Assessment and Teaching of 21st Century Skills (ATC21S) project.

From all these perspectives, creativity becomes not just a capacity for developing young people for their twenty-first century lives, but also a challenge for teachers in their designing of creative activities and assessment tasks. Any consideration of how young people connect, communicate, collaborate and create in actual and virtual locations must address the quality and manner of their activity. This is reflected in the individual's capabilities in that environment and the paradox of the third critical factor of agency.

Factor 3: From 'agency' to 'learner agency'

While we define 'agency' as an individual's freedom and capacity for acting on personal decisions, this in itself is a paradox for educators who wish only to provide their students with opportunities to improve the quality of their decision making and their ability to make informed decisions. To illustrate, we re-examine the Martin and Hannah vignettes. Martin and Hannah exercised *personal agency* in locating or forming their like-minded community. Their learning was motivated by personal interests and the desire for developing expertise in their chosen areas. Above all, Martin and Hannah operated autonomously and sought out advice or other members' expertise to solve problems of their own finding at times when they needed it.

One might question, however, whether Martin and Hannah were exercising *learner agency* where issues of trust, critical reading and ethically responsible behaviours were elevated in the mindfulness of their online interactions. For example, did Martin verify that Angus actually *was* Angus and was Angus's account cross-checked for reliability? Was Hannah able to trust the claimed expertise of her critical friends? Lankes (2008) has argued that there is a distinct need for any user, but particularly youthful users, to apply reliability checks on a constant basis. Further, he placed both reliability and authority as anchors to a 'continuum of approaches to credibility' (p. 110).

According to Jenkins (2006), the main problems of online activities are of 'transparency' and an 'ethics challenge' (p. 3). The first highlights how young people need to become aware of how media and certain aspects of technology shape their perception of the world. The second concerns their participation as both 'media makers and community participants' (p. 3). Whether involved in curricular areas or out-of-school activities, young people should be able to apply, with confidence, more digital technologies-focused, metacognitive strategies as they engage with or interrogate particular aspects of their online environments. In these ways, young people's sense of personal agency can be elevated towards those more discriminating online practices associated with learner agency.

While *connectivity, creativity* and *agency* are considered as integral triggers for rethinking curriculum and assessment, they are not sufficient of themselves to guarantee that young people will become more discerning learners in their networked learning spaces. This is where educators need to foster desirable habits and capabilities for young people to acquire and enact, wherever they are learning. It is no longer enough for students to know *what*, but to know *how* to do certain things with that knowledge, and even *whom* to contact. Suggett (2007) has argued:

> *The rapidity of knowledge development, the immense capacity for storing and retrieving knowledge and increasing value of intangible assets has shifted the core focus in knowledge from know–what to know–how. The importance of relationships and collaboration also places a premium on know–who. (p. 5)*

This means that mindful, informed learner agency needs to be called for at any time, in any place. As such, personal skills with decoding, manipulating, synthesising and creating new knowledge are required across subject disciplines. Of high relevance here are research findings that question the level of young people's critical use of new technologies. Buckingham (2007) reported on research in the US and UK, noting the absence of critical depth in many young people's everyday activities out of school. He spoke of the banality and superficiality that characterised much of their interaction.

In Australia, one national study investigated students' proficiency with technology in schooling (MCEETYA 2007). Using a six-level literacy scale and proficiency standards to describe student performance, researchers established ICT proficiency levels and differentiated across the cohort in terms of gender, state and socio-economic context. As interesting as these comparative patterns of ICT proficiency are, of pertinence to this chapter is the conclusion:

> One should not assume that students are uniformly becoming adept because they use ICT so widely in their daily lives. The results of the assessment survey suggest that students use ICT in a relatively limited way and this is reflected in the overall level of ICT literacy. Communication with peers and using the Internet to look up information are frequent applications but there is much less frequent use of applications that involve creating, analysing or transforming information. There are substantial differences between Year 6 and Year 10 suggesting that considerable growth in ICT proficiency takes place over these four years. (p. x)

The 'relatively limited' manner of technology use in schooling also became evident in a longitudinal Griffith University Study (2003–2008) funded by the Australian Research Council, *Using and creating knowledge in the high school years: Performance, production, process and value-adding in electronic curricular literacy* (see http://www.griffith.edu.au/education/creating-knowledge). Part of this study involved evaluating over 800 student-created digital texts for their demonstrated online use and creation of knowledge.

Findings from this study showed that very few of the secondary school student participants were able to operate effectively across verbal, visual, kinaesthetic and technological modes. That is, when the students focused on the online content to construct their own multimodal text, many students were unable to present the information in a creative design sense at the same time. Conversely, if they chose to focus on designing an 'artistic' multimodal text, their depth in content was compromised. Of particular note was how only a very small number of students were able to demonstrate 'transmodal facility'; that is, a fine-tuned ability to work with and across source texts, technology platforms and modes of representation to create new digital texts where critical thinking about content and concepts is balanced with the aesthetics of design.

Whether taken individually or collectively, these studies indicate a pressing need for schools to set young people on the right path towards more mindful use of technologies in their daily lives, wherever or whenever they are engaged in learning. From the perspective of learner agency, we would expect young people to be self-regulated learners who are ready and able to make informed decisions about website authorship, the credibility and reliability of web sources, ethical use of source materials, and remain culturally sensitive in all their online activities. Further, they would be able to create their own texts where substance (well-synthesised, corroborated and ethically used content) was effectively combined with an aesthetic sense. That is, they would be exercising learner agency in a discerning and creative manner.

Assessment opportunities—essential digital learning (EDL)

Three key areas in online environments for identifying and developing leaner agency, particularly in terms of enhancing their metalearning and metacognitive capacities, are *e-credibility*, *e-designing* and *e-proficiency* (Kimber & Wyatt-Smith 2009).

e-Credibility

Young people range easily across actual and virtual spaces, on demand, from home, school or using mobile technologies. In so doing, they readily accept infinite opportunities for making their own choices of sites and contacts that could be friendly, benign, legitimate or covertly malign. This complex information universe creates complex issues and requires sophisticated reading skills. As a consequence, effective operation in a universe of information options requires more than technological proficiency, basic literacy or even collaborative teamwork. Critical reading and the ability to identify markers of reliability or values operating in the site are essential.

Understood broadly, 'e-credibility' in digital environments is closely linked to the ability to gauge the trustworthiness, believability or reliability of a person or source. Metzger and Flanagin (2008) have argued that credibility issues have become the greatest challenge facing a networked society, particularly with young people. Rather than applying their own credibility checks to the creators of source material, young people tend to seek corroboration of information from their online social networking 'friends' (Flanagin & Metzger 2008). There is a need to interrogate sources, seek corroboration and different perspectives, and attempt to discriminate in a systematic and informed manner. With practice, the student user could develop these analytical skills to the point of being able to operate autonomously, particularly when out of the classroom, and make informed decisions about site choices and actions.

e-Credibility takes on an ethical perspective, given the extent to which young people engage in re-mixing digital content. Interestingly, the importance of values education and ethical behaviours has gained more prominence in Australia's national curriculum documents, although consideration has not been given as yet to its place in assessment:

Ethical behaviour refers to a set of skills and orientations enabling students to understand and act in accordance with moral and ethical principles. It includes identifying right and wrong; understanding the place of ethics and values in human life; acting with moral and ethical integrity; acting with regard for others; and having a desire and capacity to work for the common good.

National Curriculum Board (2009, p. 9)

So whether selecting their own online sources or assembling their own digital texts, young people need to develop their meta-strategies for interrogating texts, seeking corroboration and arriving at informed decisions.

e-Designing

'e-Designing' refers to the creation of a digital product, but it also means active learning in digital worlds. It involves a dynamic crossing between mental and virtual spaces as the learner sources, connects and engages with ideas, information, images and other users to re/assemble or create a new digital creation. The very act of designing can help project the learner towards a deeper appreciation of the topic to become a value-adding component to learning. e-Designing involves a balance between creativity, a sense of the aesthetic and an ethical respect for others' creations. The earlier discussion on creativity takes on greater potency here, as the more advanced the e-designers become, the more digitally agile they are in moving across those different modes and platforms. Hence, transmodal facility will be a key marker of effective designing. Finally, with the ease of digital re-mixing, it is essential that young people develop and sustain a strong measure of ethical responsibility and personal pride to ensure that they do not misrepresent themselves or others.

e-Proficiency

With 'e-proficiency', young people are expected to operate at a more critical level than that of basic keyboard competency, software familiarity or Internet searching via one favoured search engine. e-Proficient users will be able to select the best search engine or database for a particular purpose, generate discriminating search terms, and be knowledgeable about tracking seemingly hidden aspects of the Web when locating sites and information (see Lankes 2008 and Metzger & Flanagin 2008).

In terms of the production or creation of knowledge products, the e-proficient user will be able to select from a wide range of options on display, but also have a fine sense of ethical responsibility. Rather than freely harvesting others' images, music or text, with little regard for copyright concerns, the e-proficient user will be constantly mindful of the extent and manner of use of others' creations. Furthermore, in moving purposely and fluently across different platforms, modes and genres, the e-proficient user will be exercising 'transmodal facility'. In all these ways, the e-proficient user will be intent on improving the quality of their digital knowledge use and production.

As explained above, each of the EDL is differentiated by particular attributes and details but understood to be interconnected. Together they constitute the nature of operating at a meta-level and the specific attributes of learner agency. Table 17.1 presents an assessment framework that relates the factors of NLS and the EDL, as discussed above. Three features of the design of the table are worth mentioning.

First, its design suggests the contextualising of learning in ways that go well beyond physicality and centre attention on connectivity, creativity and agency. This works to de-centre the traditional distinction between learning in and out of school and provides a new way to talk about contexts and performance.

Second, the table includes digital learning involving how young people (1) *use* existing knowledge texts or materials and (2) *create* and share new knowledge texts or materials. The inclusion of both ways of working—using and creating—challenges traditional notions in assessment that priority should be given to demonstrations of what knowledge students 'know'. The emphasis on creating and sharing new knowledge means, for example, that assessment of reading online involves far more than comprehension. It can properly extend to how young people read the Internet, locate and retrieve information, and ideally mine the sites to address issues of credibility and reliability, even ideology. Moreover, online reading and writing can be understood as interrelated, with Internet investigations as the basis for writing in a range of forms, including visual material.

Third, centrally placed in the table is the concept of 'transmodal facility' to represent its significance in terms of the fluidity, balance and dexterity with which the learner could operate across multiple modes and platforms, and for different purposes.

Conclusion—towards a new vision for assessment

In this final section, we explore the implications of the assessment framework for future efforts at rethinking assessment quality.

Exciting recent developments in e-assessment like those discussed under *creativity* herald the arrival of engaging and enriching classroom experiences. There is no doubt that systemic uses of large-scale, high-stakes assessment practices will continue to be valued for credentialling purposes, whether print-based or computer-oriented, but they are no longer sufficient for twenty-first century learning priorities. Any thinking about assessment practices in the twenty-first century must concern ways of incorporating digital technologies, capitalising on the connectivity of networked learning spaces, finding ways to encourage creativity, and being able to identify the effectiveness of young people's digital capabilities.

In saying this, we return to the title of this chapter. *How shall we know them?* If 'them' refers to young people in a wider learning landscape, as well as the knowledge products that they create, then the focus for ascertaining quality can be on demonstrations of learning. It will mean not just the quality of a completed product, but the quality of the learning

Table 17.1 An assessment framework relating digital learning and learning spaces

		e-proficiency	e-credibility	e-designing	
CONNECTIVITY	*Using existing knowledge texts or materials*	Ability to locate and retrieve information in written, visual, auditory, digital modes, using a variety of search engines, databases, and strategies. Ability to use a range of software efficiently and fluidly.	Ability to discern how values are operating in a source text, and how people and places are represented. Ability to make a discriminating selection of sources, balance viewpoints and find corroborating evidence.	Ability to identify/discern the potential of source material and to select for (1) new applications and (2) appropriate mode/s of display. Ability to keep efficient records of source texts and to utilise these ethically.	CREATIVITY
	Operating with transmodal facility Ability to work with and across source texts, technology platforms and modes of representation to create a new digital text where critical thinking about content and concepts is balanced with the aesthetics of design.				
	Creating and sharing new knowledge texts or materials	Ability to select software and mode of display appropriate for selected audience, the medium and type of content. Ability to exploit the potential of the software to engage audience and achieve particular effects in accordance with the intended audience/purposes.	Discriminating use of selected sources. Discriminating choice of material/resources for display or communication. Ethical/scholarly acknowledgment and use of all sources.	Ability to assemble, compose or design an aesthetic, creative combination/ transformation or treatment of existing sources/materials into a new representation or text.	

along the way. If 'we' extends beyond teachers, to parents, carers, knowledgeable others in the community—and the students themselves—then the necessity of widening assessment practices to be more inclusive is clear. Such a shift would call into question how teachers and students engage in feedback and the larger issue of quality.

At the heart of any rethinking of assessment should be the understanding that assessment is inherently social and cultural, as well as political. In these ways, it may be possible to see the social applications of the 'essential digital learnings' and how learners can co-contribute to the development of effective learner agency in others. By blending all sites of learning into a widened learning landscape, the contributions of learners, peers and community members can be accepted and valued. We suggest that such moves are vital if schooling and, more specifically, assessment in schooling are to remain relevant in the twenty-first century.

Postscript

Martin is fulfilling his dream. He has been accepted to the Royal Military College, Duntroon, Australia. One of Hannah's digital creations won a Minister's Award for Excellence in Art in her final year of secondary school. She is undertaking tertiary studies in creative technology.

Acknowledgments

The authors wish to acknowledge The Australian Research Council for funding to enable the research study 2003–2008 reported in this article, and the Principal of Brisbane Girls Grammar School for supporting the secondment of Dr Kimber to undertake this research.

Guiding questions

After reading this chapter, consider your context and propose your ideas in relation to the following guiding questions.

1 How can digital technologies in your school enable assessment *for* learning approaches?

2 What suggestions for assessment opportunities in your school would you like to see occur, in terms of networked learning spaces and essential digital learnings?

3 Discuss your understandings of e-credibility, e-designing and e-proficiency.

Key messages

- The dominance of new technologies calls for a rethinking of assessment in schooling to match the new learning landscape for young people.

- Our vision for assessment is school-based, with a transformative possibility tied to its recognition of the complementary roles that both in-school and out-of-school learning spaces can play in young people's education.

- Three key areas in online environments for identifying and developing learner agency, particularly in terms of enhancing their metalearning and metacognitive capacities, are e-credibility, e-designing and e-proficiency.

Student health and welfare in networked school communities

KEVIN LARKIN, GLENN FINGER & ROBERTA THOMPSON

> *As a culture, we've already made our decision: we've built our civilisation upon the unbounded access to information—good and bad. We can't go back and attack the root assumptions of the 21st century without bringing the whole thing down around us. Either information is free, or it is not. Either we rely on self-control, or we do not. This is the price we pay for living in a time of a nearly infinite capacity to learn and share.*

Mark Pesce (20 March 2009)

Aligning student health and welfare issues with the home–school nexus

The position taken by this book of the need for the development of networked school communities through creating a home–school nexus is based largely on an optimistic, positive positioning to capitalise on the educational opportunities of student use of new technologies, especially the rapid uptake and use of social networking. Regularly, the media has highlighted these new 'dangers' through headlines. For example, in the same issue of *The Sunday Mail* (24 May 2009), within the space of several pages, it carried the story with the headline 'Childhood innocence caught in a sinister web: Parents get the call to educate naive teens about the dark side of technology' (Sinnerton 2009), as well as the life-changing positive story about the 'iPod: The little machine that changed music forever' (*The Sunday Mail* 2009).

Given our position regarding the reality of the increasingly networked world in which young people are currently immersed, and that schools need to embrace and take advantage of this reality for educating their students, we have a responsibility as educators to teach them how to safely navigate such a world. To attempt to prevent student access to such technologies is neither an appropriate nor practical response. The aim of this chapter establishes the important considerations of student welfare in a networked world, premised on a central approach of educating students to become digital citizens.

Promoting and fostering the health and welfare of school children is rapidly becoming a worldwide concern. For example, in Europe, the ongoing World Health Organization's 'Health Behaviour in School-age Children' (HBSC) studies are undertaken on the premise that our future rests heavily on looking after the health of young people—and this encompasses physical, emotional and social wellbeing, which in turn results in long-term benefits for individuals and society (Currie et al. 2004). Moreover, national and state governments in Australia acknowledge the link between student health and wellbeing, academic success and safe and supportive learning environments through the *National Safe Schools Framework* (Australian Government 2007). An ongoing concern for the welfare of young people has led to extensive research into supportive school-based programs. Significantly, contemporary programs that aim to improve student health and welfare at school also emphasise the role of parents and the community. Positioning the health and welfare of young people into the networked school community therefore aligns well with our encouragement for creating a home–school nexus.

Importantly, the home–school nexus and the health and welfare of young people are both exacerbated by the ever-increasing challenges contemporary adolescents face during the transition to adulthood. Adolescence is typically a period of experimentation and working out a sense of identity. Above all, young people are taking on new peer relationships and simultaneously weakening the link to family (Sullivan, Cleary & Sullivan 2004). In the twenty-first century the exponential growth of digital technologies (Becker 2000b) and the rapid uptake of social networking parallel this transitional phase. Effectively, the technological interplay between young people, home and school amplifies the impact of a networked world. This seamless cyberspace interface influences home and school life in new and seriously challenging ways.

Student health and welfare and digital technologies

While we have generally assumed the school and the home to be the two safest places for young people, the rapid uptake of digital technologies among young people is presenting challenges to this perspective. Popular culture, media and digital technologies are becoming increasingly pervasive influences in the development of identities, and the establishment of new contexts for belonging, participation and maturation (Bornholt, Piccolo & O'Loughlin 2004). As discussed earlier in the book, young people's use of all manner of digital technology is all-pervasive.

The normalised use of digital technologies into early adolescent lives and cultures means that the 'local' and each individual's place within it are increasingly understood in ways that transcend grounded physical location (Carrington 2006). The picture that emerges is of young people spending long hours using digital technologies and thus limiting their time for human, real face-to-face interactions and, to some extent, discounting these (Donchi & Moore 2004).

Moreover, Gillespie (2006) suggests that cyber communication concerns are likely to persist because the use of technology among young people continues to grow. In particular, parents express concerns over the psychological effects of going online too often and believe children who spend too much time on the Internet develop antisocial behaviour (Turow 1999). More recently, a national survey of 500 Australian parents indicates that one in six parents nominate bullying as their biggest school-related concern over their child being a victim of crime (46%) or performing poorly at school (44%). Manocha says that online aggression is a significant component of bullying, which makes that study's findings important for agencies dealing with this form of youth aggression (Parenting Australia 2009).

As discussed, the common reaction by authorities is often the knee-jerk reaction of banning access. Nevertheless, research indicates that student use of digital technologies and social networking has a positive effect on social relationships and learning outcomes (Australian Government 2007). For example, Boneva et al. (2006) argue that student instant messaging (IM) patterns satisfy two major needs of adolescents—maintaining individual friendships and boosting group identity. They suggest Instant Messaging is popular with adolescents because it simulates spending time with friends offline without the rigidity of peer-group rules of acceptance. In addition, Greenfield et al. (2006) indicate adolescents use the anonymity of the Internet to find information and ask questions about personal problems and health concerns. In this way, the Internet provides a space for adolescents to explore their relationships without adult interference.

Importantly, there is overwhelming research-based evidence to demonstrate that digital technologies have become a medium through which adolescents construct meaning and develop social identities. This dates back as far as Turkle (1995) who noted that the Internet provided a place that facilitated self-expression, especially those feelings that often go unexpressed in everyday life. Similarly, Willard (2007) elaborates, suggesting the 'virtual' nature of the Internet and social network sites provide opportunity and space for young people to try different identities. However, Burbules (2004) argues the term 'virtual' implies that digital communication is something of less value—something not 'real' in relation to traditional face-to-face interaction. This can be problematic because the ambiguous space created by digital technologies allows young people to experiment and 'try on' identities and engage in social behaviour unpoliced.

Concerns of detection, social disapproval and punishment are diluted by an interactive world away from adult supervision. The subliminal suggestion that cyber communication is not 'real' associated with the anonymous nature of the Internet means that 'normal' behavioural restraints become lost or disregarded. Social cues are reduced and Internet behaviour becomes less inhibited, and is referred to as the 'disinhibition effect' (Suler 2004; Mason 2008). The 'disinhibition effect' strips away socially accepted roles and allows adolescents to loosen up and express themselves more openly (Willard 2005). While this phenomenon allows young people to explore, develop and resolve identity concerns, it also frees adolescents to be harsher, ruder and even threatening. Specifically, 'virtual' environments create a new medium for negative social interaction. Mason (2008) suggests that this disinhibition might contribute to cyber-bullying behaviours among adolescents.

Alternatively, Bhat (2008) suggests impulsivity during adolescence might be a contributing factor to inappropriate behaviour in networked spaces. She suggests young people may act without fully considering the consequences of their actions for themselves or others. There is an illusion of invisibility and a facelessness that does not encumber their actions (Suler 2004). Moreover, the reduction in social and affective cues and a lack of tangible feedback in digital spaces impede adolescent ability to empathise or be remorseful. Not having to deal with someone's immediate reaction can be freeing to a young person (Trolley, Hanel & Shields 2006; Willard 2005). In these instances, adolescents disassociate themselves from their real identity and take on a virtual identity, which Joinson (1998) refers to as an 'online-disassociated' real self. Ultimately, the distinction between reality and the virtual world becomes blurred. Dangerously, adolescent impulsivity and the online-dissociated real self can lead to health and welfare concerns for young people. In particular, Bhat (2008) suggests that there are links between cyber-bullying and intense levels of online retaliation to adolescent impulsivity in digital landscapes.

Research evidence remains inconsistent concerning the effects of digital technologies on student health and wellbeing. Kraut et al. (1998) appropriately suggest that the Internet can either undermine or foster student wellbeing depending on whether it supplants or expands the opportunity for meaningful, daily contact with friends. Gross, Juvonen & Gable (2002) suggest the advances in digital technologies and the continuing growth in youth access to the Internet explain discrepancies across studies. They urge researchers to take into account the social and developmental context of adolescent lives when addressing youth welfare and the Internet.

In terms of psychosocial development, Kraut and Patterson (cited in Donchi & Moore 2004) found increases in Internet use were associated with declines in the size of a person's social circle and family communication, and increases in depression and loneliness. The ability to process social information, regulate emotions in public situations and display acceptable and competent social behaviours are important aspects in gaining peer acceptance. The amount of time spent with media, digital technologies and mobile technologies may limit face-to-face social interactions, thereby reducing the proximity of the peer group and the opportunities for personal growth.

However, conflicting evidence shows that the Internet is often responsible for highly developed online relationships, some of which lead to offline social contacts, implying that social isolation may diminish with greater Internet use (Mazalin & Moore 2004). Digital communications are also opening up new avenues for creating and sustaining intimate social relationships that include, but also extend beyond, the family. According to Snyder et al. (2008), the most popular activity on home computers for the adolescents in their study was communicating with people (44%), with 57 per cent of the females surveyed indicating that communicating with friends was the most frequent use of home computers. The use of such communication technologies is acting to blur the boundaries between social and physical space as young people use them to create 'always on' networks of communication (Carrington 2006).

Whether or not increased use of digital technologies by adolescents is positive or negative, the reality is that adolescent use of the technology is characterised by increasing levels of mobility and global reach (Holmes & Russell 1999). In this interaction with the global world via the Internet adolescents are engaging with a variety of cultural artifacts and establishing a sense of self-identity that is beyond the control of traditional institutions such as families and schools. Adolescent use of technology is a substantial influence in the contemporary formation of adolescent identity, and one that has profound implications for current educational practice in the middle school (Holmes & Russell 1999; Snyder et al. 2008), especially in relation to behaviour management and pedagogic practice (Carrington 2006).

What is clear is that an appropriate educational response is needed to maximise the potential of young people using digital technologies for meaningful learning, while developing an appropriate response to managing the risks.

Understanding users in a networked world

The UK's *Social networking: A quantitative and qualitative research report into attitudes, behaviours and use* (Office of Communications 2008) reported that social networkers differ in their attitudes to social networking sites and in their behaviour while using them. Importantly, the report indicated that non-users of social networking sites also fall into distinct groups based on their reasons for not using social networking sites, namely:

- *Concern about safety*—people concerned about safety online, in particular making personal details available online
- *Technical inexperience*—people who lack confidence in using the Internet and computers
- *Intellectual rejecters*—people who have no interest in social networking sites and see them as a waste of time. (p. 6)

It might be reasonable for educators to adopt similar reasons for not using social networking. Some educators might feel inexperienced in engaging with Twitter, MySpace, Facebook or Bebo, and unsure about setting up wikis and blogs. We suspect that educators also appropriately need to be presented with convincing educational rationales for incorporating the use of new digital technologies. Whatever the reason for non-users, this is out of step with young people's use of social networking.

In contrast to non-users of social networking, site users tended to fall into five distinct groups based on their behaviours and attitudes:

- *Alpha socialisers*—(a minority) used sites in intense short bursts to flirt, meet new people and be entertained

- *Attention seekers*—(some) craved attention and comments from others, often by posting photos and customising their profiles

- *Followers*—(many) joined sites to keep up with what their peers were doing

- *Faithfuls*—(many) typically used social networking sites to rekindle old friendships, often from school or university

- *Functionals*—(a minority) tended to be single-minded in using sites for a particular purpose.

(Source: Office of Communications 2008, p. 6)

In a review of the literature *Harm and offence in media content: Updating the 2005 review*, the UK's Office of Communications (2006) found:

> *Research suggests young people may be aware of the risks, especially regarding social networking sites, but this awareness of these issues and problems is not always translated into action ... the widespread accessibility of the Internet, along with its affordability, anonymity and convenience appears to increase the likelihood of media harm ... This leads to concerns about the possibility of underestimating the unanticipated or future consequences of making private information public. (p. 15)*

The same literature review also noted that there is evidence that young people generally are not able to respond appropriately when they receive hostile, bullying or hateful messages. Similarly, 'parents are unclear how they can know about, or intervene in, risky behaviours undertaken—deliberately or inadvertently—by their children' (UK Office of Communications, p. 15). Therefore, the transformational change to a new paradigm required to enable the educational possibilities of networked school communities brings with it new risks and the need for new responses. This has historical precedents, just as the change to the industrial world brought with it new risks and responses, such as dangerous working conditions in the mines and factories and health-related risks due to increased population in the cities. The change from an industrial world to a networked world involves new risks and impacts already evident in changes in employment patterns and new legislation related to cyber crime such as identity theft and online fraud.

To do nothing is not an option, and a decision to undertake no action is a decision to leverage the increasing knowledge gap known as the 'digital divide'. This knowledge gap caused by limited digital technology literacy results in the absence of a range of skills that optimise digital technology use in a global knowledge economy, where those technologies are increasingly central and pivotal to effective functioning. Conversely, creating networked school communities enhances digital inclusion, which militates against situations where digital technology use for educational purposes is accessed primarily by the privileged who can afford schooling designed for the twenty-first century.

Just as schools in previous ages have prepared students for the requirements of their world, such as industrial models of schooling that prepared a ready workforce based on Industrial Age needs, in this digital age, schools must design and provide an appropriate model of schooling that meets the needs of our young people. This need has been recognised at an economic level and through a productivity agenda by numerous proactive national governments who have responded with comprehensive national strategies to harness the educational potential of the digital technologies directly into the hands of adolescents as part of that response.

While aware of the risks involved in operating in a networked world, these risks can be appropriately managed in much the same way that schools manage other risks through risk management approaches. Subsequently, the authors argue that it is no longer sufficient for educators to provide policies and implement actions through control and coercion to address the social, legal and ethical issues that the networked world poses.

In response to Pesce's quote in the opening to this chapter, we have no options other than to embrace the reality of our networked world and understand that parents/carers and young people in their homes can shape and respond to these challenges in educationally appropriate and transformative ways.

Social, legal and ethical issues

Given the limitations of space, this chapter highlights some of the issues rather than offer an exhaustive description of all social, legal and ethical issues. Issues relating to young people working in networked school communities include intellectual property, censorship, cyber plagiarism, privacy and surveillance technologies, inappropriate use of texting and email, cyber-bullying, and virtual actions with real-world consequences.

According to Baase (2007), new privacy issues that we have not had to deal with before have emerged, including 'access to our search queries and all sorts of data we ourselves put on the web, location tracking, high-tech surveillance systems, increasing risks of sensitive data stolen from businesses, and some anti-terrorism programs' (p. xiii). There are websites such as Wikileaks (see wikileaks.org) where anyone can anonymously post material that other people would rather have kept secret.

In addition, Internet safety has been the focus for some time and, in what proved to be a largely futile attempt to provide a filter for enhancing Internet safety, the Australian Government undertook the $189 million NetAlert scheme which included $84.4 million for the National Filter Scheme, plus funding for online policing, a help line and education programs. Interestingly, Tom Wood, a 16-year-old Melbourne schoolboy at the time, proved the futility of this narrow thinking and approach by taking just over 30 minutes to be able to de-activate the controls. According to a report in the *Herald Sun* (Higginbottom & Packham 2007), his technique also ensured that the software's toolbar icon was not deleted, leaving parents under the impression that the filter was still working. In the newspaper report, Wood was quoted as saying that 'filters aren't addressing the bigger issues anyway. Cyber-bullying, educating children on how to protect themselves and their privacy are the first problems I'd fix'.

Cyber-bullying is defined by Willard (2005) as the disseminating of harmful or cruel speech or engaging in other forms of social cruelty using the Internet or other digital technologies. Willard further suggests that cyber-bullying can be classified into seven different categories: Flaming, Online harassment, Cyberstalking, Denigration, Masquerade, Outing, and Exclusion.

Furthermore, the repetitive and unrelenting nature of traditional bullying is not always obvious in cyber-bullying cases and therefore the resulting harm is undermined. Often, mainstream explanations for this phenomenon adopt the notion that cyber-bullying is a glorified form of 'note passing'. For example, as indicated in a personal communiqué to one of the authors (Thompson 2009), cyber-bullying might be perceived as 'bitchy adolescent behaviour, something that has always been around. We outgrew it, so will they'.

Moreover, the anonymous nature and the facelessness of cyber-bullying tend to set it apart from other forms of youth aggression. In fact, Shariff and Hoff (2007) compare cyberspace to Golding's (1954) *Lord of the flies*. They suggest the chaos and deterioration of the unsupervised boys in Golding's novel parallels the deterioration of adolescent relationships in virtual space. As Golding's story unfolds, the boys realise it is easy to attack others when assuming a different identity, for example, when they painted their faces to hide who they were. Similarly, in cyberspace, adolescents use anonymity to govern friendship circles and enforce social boundaries.

Rigby, a key writer about bullying, suggests cyber-bullying now deserves special consideration as it is a recent phenomenon, and 'there has been much uncertainty in how to respond to the problem' (Rigby, 2007, p. 274). Rigby provides advice that focuses on school policies, staff knowledge, and lessons which deal with Internet use risks, and advises schools to help solve cyber-bullying. Even though cyber-bullying might occur independently outside of schools, these suggested approaches reflect a traditional response of school interventions, monitoring and control. We suggest that cyber-bullying challenges these rational approaches due to the connectivity, anonymity, and amplification which the Internet enables.

In addition, cyber-bullying can be intense and have high impact, even when it is a one-off incident. Adolescents know that their humiliation from a single taunt, a descriptive email or a text message can be amplified by being sent to countless others instantly. Furthermore, 3G handheld devices make it easy for unsuspecting students to be 'tricked' or 'outed' when their actions are uploaded to the Internet for many others to see (Patchin 2009a). The infinite audience (Shariff 2008) and the repetitive, rebounding nature of cyberspace multiply the severity of the cyber-bullying, and the consequences for young people can be devastating.

When I sat in front of my computer alone, gnawing away at my fingers watching the cruel lies in bold type being sent across the world, I felt such desperation. The machine transmitted information much faster than I could deny it. It seemed endless. It was stronger than me and would outlast me.

McCaffrey (2006)

As Conger (2009) suggests in relation to virtual worlds:

Social networking sites, enabled by Web 2.0 technologies and embodied in role-playing worlds are gaining in popularity ... Behavioral controls can be regulated through program code restrictions, rules of conduct, and local norms. Most vendor hosts of virtual worlds use code restrictions sparingly, restricting only overtly illegal activities. Otherwise, all worlds ... rely on the development of in-world local norms to regulate behaviour. As a result, many unethical forms of behaviour have arisen, including griefing, fragging, and industrial espionage. (p. 105)

'Griefing', for example, refers to unacceptable and usually unethical behaviours in virtual worlds that reflect real-life unacceptable behaviours, such as murder, stealing, rape and violent assaults. For 'griefing' to occur, three actions are involved:

1   The use or abuse of a game mechanic that was not intended by the game's developers.

2   The inability of the victim to exact some means of retribution beyond utilising similar unintended game mechanics.

3   The intended purpose of an act of griefing must be to negatively impact the gameplay of another person.

(Source: *Wikipedia* 2009h)

In some situations, virtual actions have resulted in serious real-world consequences. Warner and Raiter (2005) highlight an example where the violence of the World of Warcraft game, where stealing isn't forbidden but can be punishable through beatings, carried over into real life. A man was murdered in China as he was believed to have stolen a virtual sword. According to Conger (2009), this is clearly unethical and morally indefensible, and reflects the seriousness of the impact of immersive virtual world experiences carrying into real life. Conger (2009) also identifies instances of suicide:

... 13 year old Megan Meier committed real world suicide after first being befriended then receiving abusive remarks from a MySpace acquaintance thought to be a boy who turned out to be the parent [Lori Drew] of an ex-girlfriend.

Leonard, cited in Conger (2009, p. 109)

In relation to the above case, the outcome was that a jury in California convicted Lori Drew on misdemeanour charges, despite strong public sentiment that the conviction should have referred more specifically to Drew cyber-bullying Meier into committing suicide. She was found guilty of violating MySpace's terms of service (PBS Teachers 2008).

Consequently, Conger (2009) appropriately warns that this portrays a serious example of an extreme tragic consequence resulting from an online experience. In that incident, the adult deliberately engaged Megan Meier into a communicative relationship, then subsequently abused her without 'moral or ethical justification for the original deception, the false content, or the mean spirited abuse' (Conger 2009, pp. 109–110).

Implications for home

It is important to avoid thinking that the traditional control and coercive approach to surveillance and supervision of students are appropriate responses. In most chapters there is the recurring theme and internal consistency of argument that success in networked school communities will come primarily from astute and ongoing education that engages both the parents and the students.

The authors recommend that there needs to be more enlightened understandings about student use of digital technologies beyond the school, building on that knowledge of home use, and providing direction, values education and astute information literacy. Appropriate actions include working collaboratively in the networked world with the students and their parents. Throughout the book, it is made clear that a collaborative and networked mode that involves the home is appropriate, rather than control measures determined and regulated by the educators, with no role for the parents or the students other than to obey.

The reasons are compelling for enabling home and student agency, namely:

- Student use of the digital technologies in schools is substantially less than student use in the home where young people can choose to use digital technologies 24/7, every day of the year.
- The use of digital technologies in the home has long since normalised the use of the digital.
- As the ACMA study (2007) concludes, the vast majority of young people use the technology in a balanced way—and that it is the place called school that has the problem and not the home.
- The networked school's formal responsibilities are limited.
- There will inevitably need to be different digital technology procedures within the classroom and outside.

The caution (as discussed earlier in Chapter 9) is that when the coercive mode is used in schools the students opt to bypass it or do their work at home. Anecdotally, students are given their assessment tasks at school, tolerate the restricted access to digital technologies at schools, and undertake the intense, productive online engagement when they arrive home. A win-win situation for learning and teaching is created when the homes and the school work collaboratively to develop an approach appropriate to the particular school community and context.

Adopting a shared focus on digital citizenship that is developed, reinforced and supported by educators, the students and those in the home is a potentially more powerful paradigm than a concentration on the role of schools and teachers. This provides new roles, relationships and expectations for students and teachers. In terms of expectations for teachers, the US developed *National Educational Technology Standards (NETS•T) and Performance Indicators for Teachers* (International Society for Technology in Education [ISTE] 2008) identifies the fundamental concepts, knowledge, skills and attitudes teachers need in order to apply technology in educational settings. The expectations include the promotion and modelling of digital citizenship and responsibility; namely:

- **Promote and model digital citizenship and responsibility**: Teachers understand local and global societal issues and responsibilities in an evolving digital culture and exhibit legal and ethical behaviour in their professional practices. Teachers:

  a   advocate, model, and teach safe, legal and ethical use of digital information and technology, including respect for copyright, intellectual property and the appropriate documentation of sources;

  b   address the diverse needs of all learners by using learner-centred strategies and providing equitable access to appropriate digital tools and resources;

  c   promote and model digital etiquette and responsible social interactions related to the use of technology and information;

  d   develop and model cultural understanding and global awareness by engaging with colleagues and students of other cultures using digital-age communication and collaboration tools.

(Source: ISTE, 2008)

Similarly, ISTE provides the National Educational Technology Standards (NETS•S) and Performance Indicators for Students (ISTE, 2007), which includes digital citizenship:

- **Digital citizenship**: Students understand human, cultural, and societal issues related to technology and practise legal and ethical behaviour. Students:

  a   advocate and practise safe, legal and responsible use of information and technology;

  b   exhibit a positive attitude towards using technology that supports collaboration, learning and productivity;

  c   demonstrate personal responsibility for life-long learning;

  d   exhibit leadership for digital citizenship.

(Source: ISTE, 2007)

What is silent here are the new expectations of home use and expectations of and guidance for parents in this new world of networked school communities to focus more on the home. Central to the development of networked school communities and creating a home–school nexus is the shared approach between all who are connected to understand and enact the norms of digital citizenship.

The development of an educative approach underpinned by principles of digital citizenship can be implemented to make the significant shift to students and the home being the locus of decision making and responsibility. The typical response has been that schools have established policies such as Acceptable Use policies, student charters and IT codes of conduct, as well as explicit procedures for the positioning of computers, reporting of incidents of inappropriate use, password policies, and regular auditing of computer files and folders including reviews of temporary Internet files and Internet favourites. Those policies and procedures detail rules, responsible use of digital technologies, authorised access, respect for other users of digital technologies, privacy, copyright compliance and clear consequences for inappropriate use.

At home, as Mason (2008) suggests, there are likely to be low-level boundaries. Parents, carers and students adopt responsibilities for ensuring student safety, health and wellbeing in networked communities as this becomes a shared responsibility between home and school, with students and their parents having to play key roles in monitoring home use of digital technologies and their behaviour in those spaces.

To shift the focus on the home and understand its importance, a preventative, developmental, educative and consequential approach to assessing and minimising risk to students will be best achieved through parents/carers in homes:

- developing a vision of moving beyond the home–school divide to networked school communities;
- recognising the valuable investment in digital technologies being used in homes; and
- promoting and modelling digital citizenship with their children.

Conclusion

This chapter established that in relation to student health and wellbeing, networked school communities present new challenges and risks, as well as opportunities for improving learning and teaching. This requires new thinking and new approaches as it is neither practical nor desirable to adopt a traditional supervisory approach to student access and use of digital technologies. The approaches characterised by control and coercion are no longer appropriate. As we find ourselves in an increasingly networked world and students undertake learning in networked school communities, the knee-jerk reaction to ban access is unsophisticated at best, always ineffective, and at worst is a decision to abrogate an understanding of the networked world young people have to operate in now and their needs for effective participation in digital futures.

The development of digital citizenship at home has to become a shared, interdependent responsibility by schools, educators, students, their parents, carers and their communities. The move beyond a digital school to a home–school nexus can provide opportunities for new ways of interaction, collaboration, reflection and learning and teaching, accompanied by appropriate social, legal and ethical digital technology use by young people.

Guiding questions

After reading this chapter, consider your context and propose your ideas in relation to the following guiding questions.

1 What student health and welfare issues relate to Internet use at your school?

2 Explain your understanding of digital citizenship. How can this be promoted?

3 Describe your approach to supervision of young people's use of the Internet.

4 How would you describe the use of networking sites by a young person whom you know? *Alpha socialiser* who uses sites in intense short bursts to flirt, meet new people, and be entertained; *Attention seeker* who craves attention and comments from others, often by posting photos and customising their profiles; *Follower* who joins sites to keep up with what their peers are doing; *Faithful* who typically used social networking sites to rekindle old friendships, often from school or university; or *Functional* who tends to be single-minded in using sites for a particular purpose.

Key messages

- It is important to avoid thinking that the traditional control and coercive approach to surveillance and supervision of young people is an appropriate response in a networked world.

- Adopt a shared focus on digital citizenship that is developed, reinforced and supported by educators, the students and those in the home—the parents/carers and communities.

- Networked school communities present new challenges and risks as well as opportunities for improving learning and teaching. This requires new thinking and new approaches as it is neither practical nor desirable to adopt a traditional supervisory approach to student access and use of digital technologies.

PART D

Implementation

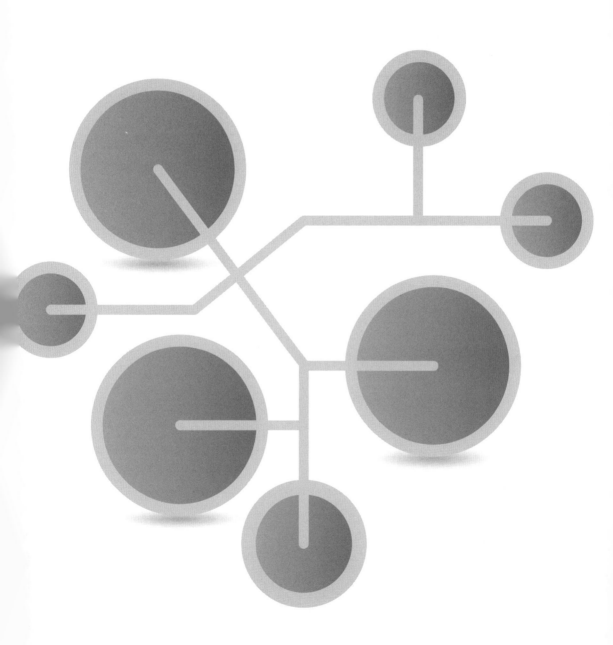

Implementing the shift

MAL LEE, GLENN FINGER & MARTIN LEWIS

Successful implementation of difficult technological changes requires visionary leadership that has carefully considered the benefits, consulted with influence leaders at all organisational levels to spot unintended consequences and sources of resistance, and developed a detailed plan and continuous quality assurance process to foster implementation over time.

John Luo, Donald Hilty, Linda Worley & Joel Yager (2006, p. 465)

The shift to networked school communities

The creation of the home–school nexus and the development of the networked school community need to be implemented wisely and in a manner befitting your school's situation, the desired collaborative nature of the organisation, and the shift from a mass to more individualised mode of schooling. The model you choose to use will have to work within an environment of ongoing, uncertain and consciously engineered change, where those leading the development will be obliged to navigate uncharted waters, while at the same time convince teachers and parents used to a known form of schooling to embrace the new ways. The challenge of providing surety while gradually attuning their thinking to a style of schooling that will be ever-evolving and changing will be considerable.

The irony is that the world of constant change and excitement is one in which the young people already thrive beyond schools and classrooms. How you address this conundrum and draw the parents, teachers, educational administrators and, ultimately, the politicians into the real world where ongoing change is required to provide the requisite contemporary education will be one you have to grapple with as you seek to move to the networked phase of schooling.

Implementing the shift—twelve key guiding principles

It is with this in mind that we reiterate that the shift to the networked mode should be undertaken primarily by those proactive, pathfinding schools that have succeeded in achieving digital take-off (Lee & Gaffney 2008) and getting a critical mass of teachers to use digital technologies in their everyday teaching. One is talking about schools that are working within the digital phase and have the readiness (as outlined in Chapter 14) to flourish within the new environment. When you are ready to begin the task of moving to a networked mode and creating a home–school nexus, we suggest that there is a suite of twelve key guiding principles to be addressed, displayed in Table 19.1 below. While it is understood that these are still embryonic days, these principles should provide guidance for you in your endeavours to implement the shift. Overlaying these considerations are the now well-understood factors that influence bringing about major organisational change, articulated by researchers such as Michael Fullan (2007; 2008) and evident in works such as *Our iceberg is melting* (Kotter & Rathgeber 2006).

Table 19.1 Guiding principles for implementing the shift

1	Opt for graduated, balanced and engineered change.
2	Plan and implement holistically.
3	Identify and pursue the unifying vision and underlying principles.
4	Implement the principles in the management of the technology.
5	Openly use the new to improve the old.
6	Act independently—within parameters.
7	Meet government responsibilities.
8	Develop readiness.
9	Politic the change.
10	Sell the concept.
11	Attend to the administration.
12	Measure your attainments.

It is vital that you factor the latter thinking into the design of your school's implementation strategy and remember that the most important variable will always be the quality and preparedness of the school principal to lead the implementation strategy. The principal will be the one who will ultimately have to gauge the current relationship between the school and its homes, and where the school should make its initial moves to further that relationship. Furthermore, the principal should be the one to ensure the development of the desired collaboration is factored into all the school's moves and an appropriate supportive learning culture is created and sustained.

Understanding that you will be commencing your work within the context of the current staff and organisational structures, it is going to be imperative that the existing principal is committed to the idea of shifting to the networked mode. Without that leadership the journey might be constrained to a small shift. Integral to the shift to the networked mode is the importance of enabling the individual units—the school, the principal, the teacher and the student—greater independence and freedom to respond appropriately to an ever-changing learning environment. This development, in turn, needs to be embodied in the school's management of the digital technologies, particularly as it begins to make greater use of the student's technology. It needs to align with the paradigm shift away from the mass educational model where the centre decides what is appropriate to one where the independent units have a major say in the decision making and are able to use—particularly for their personal use—the mobile technologies they find appropriate.

All the signs are that a shift—even a part shift—from the traditional model could have significant implications, all of which need to be considered even if operationally they prove not to be a concern. As indicated earlier, there are very considerable educational, social, organisational and economic benefits that will flow from the school taking advantage of the students' mobile technology. However, the benefits will only flow if the use of that technology is managed astutely within the desired operational principles. At this point in time there is insufficient research available to provide guidance on this, as most research—such as that by Dieterle, Dede & Schrier (2007), Brown and Metcalf (2008), JISC (2008) and Newhouse (2008)—relates to the use of mobile technology owned by the organisation. The ethical, legal, educational or logistical issues relating to the students' use of their own technology in the classroom need to be considered.

Implementation guidance

We provide the following guidance for implementing the shift.

Opt for graduated, balanced and engineered change

We recommend that the plan should be for a graduated and balanced implementation strategy that consciously promotes the earlier advocated ongoing and successful change within the organisation. Use a series of thoughtfully evaluated trials to enhance your understanding and to clarify the school's relationships with its homes and facility to use the networks and collaboration such that you can continue to retain the support of the wider school community, while instituting the changes and movement towards a networked schooling vision. The organisational literature provides cautions about over-reaching.

In essence, start off by making incremental change, and then proceed in manageable ways. This will be particularly important in managing the move to include students' use of their technology in the school. Remember that the changing of the traditional mode of schooling has until recently been very difficult and the challenges immense. However, when schools achieve digital take-off and move into the digital phase of schooling, many of the old constraints disappear as the appreciation by teachers, students and the parents of the opportunities opened by the digital networked mode become increasingly evident.

While the movement forward is possible, there will still be many hurdles to overcome, not least of which will be the propensity for the organisation to embrace the new approach as the norm—to reposition the organisation. Therefore, it is important in the initial graduated moves that you acquire the understanding required, consistently attune the school's operations to ongoing change, and secure support of the leadership at senior levels of your education system and from the community. This support is needed to overcome the human and the technical hurdles referred to in Chapter 16.

Make change a strategy

Give yourself time to get the enhancements right and, most importantly, have them accepted by your wider school community and the key politicians needed to support the change. Deliberately use the early graduated moves to navigate the political dimensions in leading the way forward for more substantial initiatives. History reveals there will be outside challenges to your initiatives. Ready yourself for those inevitable criticisms. Occasionally, this might mean some degree of patience in being an early adopter, and checking how successful the early adopters have been in winning community-wide support.

In the early stages when no structural change is required, many of the incremental moves to create a greater home–school nexus should be easy to make, but in time as you run into the various structural impediments, making the shift is likely to be more difficult. Adopt not only a graduated approach, but also a balanced, carefully nuanced approach, appreciating that on occasions you may have to make compromises to remain on track. For example, you are likely to have to strike a balance between the following tensions:

- those facets of the informal education that are included in the formal curriculum and are best left to be developed in the informal zone;
- the aspirations of the school community and those of the current government;
- the amount of technology to be provided by the home and the school;
- the home and school access to the Internet;
- the school's and the centre's hosting of services;
- those aspects of the learning best addressed in the social context of the school, and those more effectively undertaken privately in the home;
- when to push forward with an initiative and when to hold back; and

- the independence required by a teacher and his or her obligations to fulfilling the unified purpose of the community.

The principal's role and the role of the school leadership team in maintaining that balance will be vital.

Plan and implement holistically

In a networked world where all facets of the school's operations form an increasingly integrated, interconnected eco-system, it is imperative to use a holistic planning and implementation approach that simultaneously addresses all the relevant variables. Lee and Gaffney (2008) discuss the importance and nature of this style of planning and implementation at length in *Leading a digital school*. As schooling moves from the digital to networked phase, employs an even more collaborative and team-based approach and takes advantage of increasingly convergent technology, the integrated holistic approach becomes ever-more important.

Avoid the adoption of a discrete networked schooling plan, bolted onto the existing school plan and imposed on the school by a bureaucracy playing the latest political game. Weave all facets of the development of the networked mode into the existing school plan and ensure each of the developments relates to the realisation of the desired school outcomes. While collaboration with all stakeholders is important, ultimately it is the school's leadership who will need to ensure that they are not distracted from achieving their vision. This seeming paradoxical use of the hierarchical within the networked mode was touched upon earlier. In the real world, there has to be a person with the higher-level people management skills responsible for coordinating and overseeing all the implementation strategy.

In moving away from the traditional operational parameters associated with the school, it will be important to factor into the planning time to explain and gain acceptance of the new arrangements. Allied will be the necessity to clarify, particularly for the parents, which facets of young people's education are formal and which are informal, and that they are the parents' responsibility and not that of the school. That could become challenging at times. For example, while the school might provide advice and support of the students' use of a learning program outside the traditional school year, it would need to be stressed that it is entirely up to the students and their parents to heed that advice.

Identify and pursue the unifying vision and underlying principles

The importance of early identification of the vision and purpose of the school and the key principles guiding the school's operation is greater than ever. The purpose and the associated operational principles are the glue that holds the school and its community together.

'Organisations that are built to change have a clear sense of who they are and what they stand for.' (Lawler & Worley 2009, p. 193)

All within the new school community have to understand and actively work towards fulfilling the unifying purpose and observing the key principles, and that includes the principal, the school staff, the parents and the students. In the examples of pathfinding schools across the world, there are often seemingly disjointed efforts by schools and education authorities seeking to take advantage of the opportunities opened by both the networks and the facilities within the home to enhance the students' education. It is highly likely that many school leaders and parents will be asking which of these initiatives advance the purpose of the school and accord with the core principles and how it is applied.

One of the more important roles that the networked school community can play is to help place these many developments in a macro context. It can assist in identifying which ones are worth continuing with and enabling each school to identify its educational vision within the wider networking schooling mode. Therefore, it is important in your planning that you:

- schedule the early identification of the school's vision, and its underlying principles;
- adopt an identification process consistent with the desired networked and collaborative mode;
- ensure all the staff, and especially each new appointment, understand the organisation's underlying purpose and its operational principles; and
- ensure you build in the flexibility and the ongoing review processes that allow the vision to be refined over time.

As indicated in earlier chapters, many of the tools and facilities of the online world provide the ready opportunity for busy people to contribute to the identification of both the unifying vision and the underlying principles. Allow yourselves time to both identify the vision and have the networked school community understand what is required. The identification of the operational principles is equally important. What are the principles you want to operate on in a democratic school, working within a networked and collaborative environment? Aside from according respect and recognition for all students, what are the other principles you wish to be observed?

Appreciate that you will want to weave the attainment of the vision and respect for the principles throughout all facets of the developmental planning, implementation, the curriculum, the management of the technology and the selling of the concept. One of the newer challenges of a networked school community will be the ever-evolving nature of the school, the impact of more sophisticated technologies, and the increased expectations of all members of the school community, including the changing expectations of the students.

One of the realities of emerging technologies is that uses made of the technology when first introduced are very soon superseded. Solutions that you thought at the time were mind-blowing become taken for granted within six months. This makes the identification of the desired educational outcomes challenging, particularly if you have not identified the underlying principles and processes. It needs to be stressed that the technology is there for a serious purpose, though paradoxically it is often the sheer playfulness and attractiveness of the technology that will engage students.

Implement the principles in the management of the technology

This is fundamental in the management of both the school's and the students' technology. The technology management has to accord with the school's purpose and its operational principles. That should be evident from the first trial onwards. While you will have idiosyncratic technology issues, the astute management of technology requires a consistent alignment between the underlying principles and the deployment of the technology. Without that alignment the problems occur as the home–school nexus is compromised.

The vision and the principles of the organisation should shape the choice, deployment and use of the technology. While most schools know how to manage their own technology, few have had any experience in managing the simultaneous use of both the student and school technology. A vital first step in any move to the networked mode is to identify your operational principles and desired outcomes. Leave aside for the moment the actual technology. To illustrate, consider the flow-on of your school embracing the following principles.

- Use of the digital technologies should be normalised and ubiquitous in all school operations.
- Use of the digital technologies by all the school community should work from a position of trust rather than mistrust, assuming innocence but astutely monitoring transgressions.
- Decisions on the management of the technology should be made collaboratively involving stakeholders, including the students, though ultimately the final decision will be made by the school principal.
- All students have home access to the Internet.
- The school strives to provide ready student access to the Internet across the school campus, while recognising its legal obligations, every day, all year round.
- The school endeavours to provide 24/7 operability of its network.
- The individual, be it a staff member or a student, will decide which mobile computing technology they wish to use, including the backup of critical data.
- Students will be responsible for the care, operation and maintenance of their own technology.
- The school community, including the students, parents and the staff, will collaboratively identify the parameters for the students using their technology on the school campus.
- The school educates the community on availability of open-source applications and online data storage.

- The school maintains onsite storage for mission critical or sensitive data.

- The school clearly states appropriate digital contact times during the day, and agreed response times between members of its community.

- The school implements an identity management system so that the inevitable myriad of contact numbers, addresses, handles and nicknames can be readily accessible. Ideally, this will be a system that allows clients to change their own details.

- The school shifts its communications to being fully digital, including communications with parent bodies, alumni and governance.

We appreciate there will be others you will want to add, and we emphasise that before you make your first steps through trials or pilot programs, make sure that you identify the key principles and understanding that you will review, and refine them over time. It might also be opportune to reflect on some of your current technology management practices and ascertain whether they are consistent with those principles. We recommend that you access two excellent sources for information on the emerging technology for use in education: the regularly released Horizon Reports (see, for example, Johnson et al. 2009) and Becta's series on emerging technologies (Becta 2009a, 2009d).

Openly use the new to improve the old

In your planning, appreciate that all new technology will be used initially to try and better perform the old ways. It happens in aspects of life and work, and not simply education (Naisbitt 1984). Also understand that in the initial stages most of the initiatives to implement the home–school nexus and to shift increasingly to a networked mode of schooling will emanate from the more proactive, visionary educational professionals in both the schools and the education authorities. Consequently, it will be important to factor this appreciation into your planning and your expectations. Understand that quality educational professionals should have the best interests of their students as their focus at all times. They have the responsibility, the expertise and the time to ensure that the best possible education is provided, and as such can be expected to play that leading role. If there are not any benefits for student learning, then ask why the investment should not be redirected.

They too will be the ones that should want to shift to a model that harnesses the resources of the home and the school, and wider networked world, to provide an education appropriate for a rapidly evolving world. The initial efforts by those professionals to make best use of the new technologies will invariably be to use the technology to better perform the ways of old. Understand that this can be expected and is useful, as it allows the staff time to get to know the technology and its possible uses. Consequently, it allows staff to identify how the technologies might be better deployed. History and experience have consistently demonstrated this in a host of industries, and in the future the technology will be used in significantly different ways.

It means you will need to allow time for the desired changes to be made and embedded into the normal operations of all the staff, and indeed to be accepted as the norm by your community and political overseers. While it is tempting to be impatient and want the instant adoption of completely new ways, it is important to be realistic and appreciate that sometimes it might take some time to get all the teachers on staff using the new technology, to become comfortable with it, particularly in the classroom, and then to appreciate the value of using it in new and untried ways.

Think through the time it takes to set up trials, to conduct and learn from them, and then in turn to have the whole staff adopt and embed the new approach. The trials alone could take nine to 12 months and the wider school uptake of the initiative another couple of years for the new technology to be used in significantly new ways. Initially this will happen only with the early adopters. A strategic horizon of three to five years to bring about a fundamental change in school operations is a reasonable expectation. Plan realistic timelines and ensure that adequate, sustained support is normalised in the school's operations.

Act independently, within parameters

Schools operating within a networked, collaborative mode, where a significant proportion of the technology the school uses will be owned by its families, require a large degree of independence to conduct their own operations. Similarly, the school's principal, teachers and students also will need considerable independence in their work and decision making. In many situations this kind of independence will run counter to the kind of central control being exercised by the hierarchy, network managers, educational administrators and often the elected officials. It is now common globally to see examples of the elected officials, the ministers of education and the chairs of local authorities micro-managing the daily operations of the schools. While the use of that power might make the officials concerned feel powerful, the organisational literature will attest that it will serve only ever to lower the effectiveness of the schools.

Examine your situation and decide early what you will need to do. If you already have the desired school independence and agency, you can implement the shift. However, if you haven't, you and the wider school community—and possibly a broader set of 'like school' communities—will need to begin negotiating and, if necessary, politicking the desired change with the higher-level elected officials. As you will appreciate, the teaching staff usually will not be able to be involved in that politicking, but the wider community can.

The reasons for the independence are to be found not only in each school community having control over the deployment of its resources, but in the recognition that:

- the onus for change ultimately always rests with the individual school, with it being able to adopt a way forward that addresses its unique context;
- within the networked mode, each school's networks will be distinct, as will be the collaboration, and as such need to be controlled by the school; and

- in a rapidly, uncertain world the school, the teachers and the students need to work within a culture that encourages responsiveness to the ever-changing circumstances, calculated risk taking and the facility to trial the way forward through uncharted waters.

It is the individual school with its unique situation that ultimately has the task to make the shift to a networked mode of schooling, and make the shift in a way that best suits its staff and students and the current circumstances. All the schools have a set of obligations they should fulfil and they should be given direction and support by the education authority. The difference in a networked world is that each school requires the independence to develop a solution that satisfies its community, which actively encourages it to maintain a long-term collaboration and where the parent community is encouraged to continue its significant investment. In a model of schooling where the parents of the school are providing a significant proportion of the school's digital resources, they are entitled to have a significant say in the school's operations.

Whether your context is the two-teacher school in the bush, the urban charter school catering for a highly multicultural new arrivals community, the primary school in a coastal community with its beach culture, or the historic K–12 independent school in a regional centre, it will have its own distinct settings and opportunities for collaboration and networking. Only the people in that context, with its particular mix of staff and students, know what is best for their community and are in a position to generate the social and intellectual capital crucial to the success of a networked school community.

As indicated, some educational bureaucrats and governments might have trouble with the concept of organisational independence (so powerfully enunciated by Lipnack & Stamps 1994), but it is as important for the school principal and the individual staff within the school to have their independence and freedom to best contribute to the development of their school. The importance of the role of the principal within the networked school will be as great, possibly more so, than ever. To fulfil that role she or he has to have the freedom as the principal educational architect of the new organisation to respond rapidly and flexibly to ongoing change. The principal has to be able to:

- deploy the school's limited funds wisely;
- work closely with the parents and students in the best use of their digital contribution;
- collaborate with surety in a networked mode with the school's community;
- regularly attune the school's operations to the ever-changing circumstances; and
- decide on the approach to be taken.

The same independence should be accorded the staff and the students. The move to the networked mode signals in many respects the departure from a mass mode of teaching and learning to one that is appreciably more individualised and reflects personalised learning. It recognises that young people outside the classroom are already experiencing that independent, personalised learning and that the school's operations need to shift accordingly. Schools have been very slow to acknowledge young people as digital natives (Prensky 2006) who have a distinct and considerable awareness of digital technologies not always shared by the digital immigrants, and who could contribute much to the school's development.

This shift needs to be particularly noted by the variously termed 'ICT' or network managers who have long worked in the hierarchical 'control over' mode, providing a mass solution for all. The support of independent members, each with their particular needs and requirements, will oblige them to adopt a very different approach, not least of which will be to work collaboratively and accommodate an ever-more diverse range of hardware and software. This diversity will pose problems in terms of support, but the shift in financial outgoings will save monies that can be directed into this support role.

Schooling has a long tradition of constancy and resistance to change. The networked school community, in contrast, will be an organisation that undergoes regular change and its members must have the facility, the independence, to respond rapidly and appropriately to the changing circumstances. A hierarchical bureaucracy remote from the school's homes and community micro-managing the school's operations is inappropriate. In many situations, moving even some control away from the bureaucracy will be difficult, but it needs to be foregrounded in your planning. This is why the use of the political route below is suggested.

Meet government responsibilities

Foreground the school's responsibilities to government in your planning. It is appreciated that those responsibilities will vary across the developed world and across education systems. The reality is that increasingly all schools will be expected to play a role in enhancing the nation's productivity and to ensure young people can make a meaningful contribution in an increasingly knowledge-based world. One of the eternal challenges is the balancing of the educational—one might say the political—outcomes dictated to schools, with those outcomes held to be more important by the school community. The challenge can become very marked with those governments that set short-term, highly political targets that run counter to what the school believes is more appropriate. The challenge can also be significant in those schools that have both provincial and national government obligations, particularly when the respective governments are of a different political persuasion.

It is an eternal game all schools need to play in determining what counts, but in recent years school accountability and transparency of student outcomes have grown. In addition, there is a plethora of legislative and accountability obligations the school will need to meet. As school funding and the tenure of the school principal and the teachers have become increasingly tied to governments making judgements based on often narrow student outcomes data, the importance of this has grown. How appropriate many of the current specified educational outcomes are for your networked school community, you will need to decide. If you believe they are markedly out of step with the school's thinking, you can either look to addressing them or enter into the debate with the policy makers and the politicians. There is a very high chance that some of these more bureaucratic obligations could be counterproductive and you will need to decide how they are best addressed.

Develop readiness

Chapter 14 highlighted the vital importance of teacher readiness in having the TPACK capabilities in being able to make the move to the networked mode. However, it is not simply the teachers that need to be readied for the shift to the networked mode. It also includes the students, the parents, the carers and the education bureaucrats. A reasonable expectation would be that the majority of the staff, the full-time and casual teachers, the school leadership and the professional support staff all should have normalised the everyday use of digital technologies in their work before the school can begin to embark on the quest to develop a networked school community and create the desired home–school nexus. In brief, as indicated throughout this book, the school should have achieved digital take-off (Lee & Gaffney 2008) and moved into the digital phase as a platform for implementing the shift into being networked.

When one begins making the shift, it will be imperative for all of the staff to be provided with the time and resources required to maintain their ongoing personal and professional learning. Give the early adopters opportunities for action research to demonstrate the success or otherwise of trials. There is a high probability that much of that development will have to do with human relationships as well as the ongoing development of technological competencies. Working collaboratively, in a networked mode and possibly within teams, requires a collaborative, open disposition to share and test ideas and co-construct new knowledge. It is highly likely their enhancement and the ongoing development of TPACK will be required. When this occurs, there is a powerful understanding of collective intelligence and that content is being co-created and shared.

As indicated in Chapter 14, the ongoing enhancement of the staff's digital competencies— referred to as technological knowledge (TK)—is important. The speed of the technological development makes it essential that the provision of the requisite training and support is normalised in the school's everyday operations. Historically, schools, education authorities and national programs have generally allocated insufficient resources for training and support. It is very easy, particularly for community members, to forget it costs schools significant monies to provide teachers with the time required to undertake effective training and professional development. In a networked world, though, the provision of professional development should not be seen as being hierarchical. Be prepared for and encourage teachers to self-direct their own professional learning, particularly by being members of online communities of interest and online communities of practice.

A facet of the staff readiness that is fundamental to the continual evolution of the school is the selection of staff, teaching and support. Ensure that all the duty statements and selection criteria enable the attraction, selection and recruitment of staff who have the desire and capabilities to foster ongoing change in the organisation. The observations about the school staff hold equally with the central office staff. Few will have the experience of or the understanding required to work within a networked mode. Part of the 'sell' and the 'politicking' mentioned below should be channelled towards readying the bureaucrats for the shift.

If the parents and carers are to play an enhanced role in the formal and informal education of their children, and to be involved in the ongoing development of their school, they too will need to be prepared to play that role. While the adoption of an open, collaborative, networked mode of operation will undoubtedly assist that preparation, the school should consciously and authentically engage with the parents. Much of that preparation will be cultural, will entail changing attitudes, and will reinforce the importance of the home in the teaching and learning process, the contribution that the balanced use of digital technologies plays, and the recognition that the education of the children goes on every day, all year round.

Bear in mind that this might need some repositioning as the parents and carers may have been shut out of the school's operations and might hold anti-school feelings. Understand that there will be a range of parent views and perspectives that will require consideration as the school prepares them to play a more engaged, inclusive and meaningful role. The aim should be to further the bond between the homes and the school, and build a relationship and learning culture within the networked school community that will assist in providing the desired learning.

Remember that in a world where most parents work and life is complex and demanding, schools need to be smart and use the tools of the online world if they are to gain the support of both the parents and the children's carers. As established in Chapter 4, given young people's digital technology access and use in their homes, it would suggest that the group that will require the least preparation for the shift to the networked mode will be the students—the digital natives already thriving in the digital and networked environment. Interestingly, the facet of their readiness that could require particular attention is their willingness to express their needs and to contribute their understanding of the digital, networked world to the discussions on the development of the networked mode of schooling. For example, the report Project Tomorrow (2008) suggests that it is only in recent years that young people have been called upon to contribute their expertise and that, in 2009, it was still unusual for schools to invite the students at all levels to contribute their digital awareness.

Politic the change

In all that you do as a school community, politic each of the significant enhancements you make. It is appreciated that this call is not normally made in a publication on educational change. However, it is important in a democracy that the parent and student community uses democratic processes and communicate with the elected representatives as an everyday facet of the school development process through:

- drawing the families into playing a significant role in the daily operation of the school,

- markedly shifting the control of the school's operations from solely the education hierarchy to a more collaborative model where each school requires considerable independence and the parents require a voice in how their digital resources are deployed; and

- involving the students.

It is appreciated that most government employees are not permitted to participate in the politicking of their school and that the role has to be played by the school's families. As the professionals charged with providing the best possible education, one could argue that the professional staff—the public servants—are responsible for providing the parents with the requisite educational advice. In the early stages, as the senior bureaucrats and elected political representatives adjust to the idea of the parents having an active voice in the working of their networked school community, it would be advisable to be extra cautious in protecting the school leadership from the potential negative consequences of challenging the constraining bureaucracy. The preference is that they should be able to perform a more open professional advisory role for the school community.

In your politicking, use all the traditional, acceptable avenues open in a democracy, and communicate with the major local and regional elected representatives as well the supportive educational bureaucrats. However, as Clay Shirky (2008) makes clear, be aware that in a networked world some of democracy's most powerful new tools are the Web 2.0 facilities. Every networked school community should be using those facilities to grow the school, to communicate, to inform, to collaborate, to politic the desired changes and to maintain the development of the school. Conscious of the bureaucracy's potential control of the official school website, your community might need to consider using one of the free social networking facilities like a Ning (http://www.ning.com) to perform the above-mentioned roles.

Sell the concept

Closely aligned with the politicking of the change is the importance of promoting the overall concept of the networked school community—to sell the concept. We encourage you to market each of the major enhancements made and relate how those enhancements can provide the best possible education for a digital future. The ongoing promotion of the initiatives is integral to the overall organisational change process. It is a fundamental part of securing wider community acceptance and the embedding of the changes being made. While there are many valid reasons for making the changes, those reasons have to be sold, and sold well and professionally over a concerted period of time.

Education has, and in particular many politicians have, a strong propensity to recycle ideas, and we notice there is a regular advocacy by some to return to the working of the past. To illustrate, this has been evidenced by calls that texting is damaging literacy, that Wikipedia is not a reliable source of information, and that pencil-and-paper examinations are the most appropriate form of all assessment of student achievement. If the developmental collaboration is well handled, you should have your own community developing more sophisticated understandings of the reasons for change. You will appreciate, though, that there are other stakeholders who will need to be convinced. Look for opportunities to use the 'smarts' of the networked, digital world to help in that selling, but don't neglect to make use also of the better traditional face-to-face promotional opportunities and ensure you very publicly celebrate each of the major advances you make.

Attend to the administration

While it might not be appealing, attention to detail needs to be given to ensure the astute, efficient administration of the evolving networked school community. An ever-developing networked school community that relies on working closely with the home and networked world needs highly user-friendly, smart, efficient systems and processes appropriate to the changing world. Most importantly, the staff need the employer to assist in providing them with the technology and the resources to operate within a networked and mobile world where they are able, when desired, to operate independently.

Many school administration and communication systems lag well behind comparable mid-sized business and public sector enterprises. Most seem to be designed to reinforce the power and control exerted by the educational bureaucracy. It is essential that the school use systems and processes that can be readily upgraded to the changing circumstances. Often hierarchical organisations reward those staff who don't rock the boat and who favour maintaining the status quo. You will want a structure that rewards those able to work in project teams, who collaborate closely, who take some risks, who understand the ever-evolving needs of the home, and who actively promote ongoing change and learning within the organisation.

The authors' strong suspicion is that it will be the school's questioning of the appropriateness of the current administration system that will most rankle the bureaucracy. It will be necessary from the outset to understand the political context of dealing with these tensions, and to politic the planned changes.

Measure your attainments

Build into all your implementation strategies an accompanying evaluation approach that includes the measurement of the achievements. Appropriate hard data, particularly longitudinal data and trends, will be required to support the ongoing development, the politicking, the selling and most importantly the fulfilment of the school's government responsibilities. The school will thus need to have—and to regularly use—its information systems. One of the key and underused functionalities of the shift to digital technologies is the amount of data available and the ease of analysing that data.

There is thus much to be said for providing the wider school community with regular feedback on the school's attainment of the key performance indicators it has compiled in its identification of the desired outcomes. The feedback should be succinct, readily understood by all parents, regular, and able to be accessed online at any time by everyone interested. Schooling has had a poor reputation (Lee & Winzenried 2009) for being willing to provide the hard, readily quantifiable data, particularly as it relates to the use of technology. That situation has changed markedly in most countries in the past decade, but there are still those reluctant to gather and publish the data. To implement the shift to create the home–school nexus and to develop a networked school community, it is necessary to measure and openly publish the data on the school's attainments to inform future planning and actions aimed at engaging the parents, students and the wider community.

Conclusion

The task of changing the model of schooling has never been easy. While the last decade has shown it is possible for the leadership and vision to make significant changes, those changes have largely tended to occur within the existing school walls. Moving from a traditional paper-based model of schooling to a digital school, while difficult, is necessary for teaching and learning in the twenty-first century. Becoming a digital school provides the platform for implementing the shift to becoming a networked school community. When the walls are extended or dismantled in ways that learning is understood to occur beyond the classroom walls as well as within them, the parents, students and the community are all involved in an organisation of schooling that needs to be implemented wisely and strategically. The need for this shift is compelling and the benefits for students can be immense and exciting.

Guiding questions

After reading this chapter, consider your context and propose your ideas in relation to the following guiding questions.

1   Which of the 12 guiding principles are already evident in your school?

2   Which of the 12 guiding principles are not evident at all?

3   To implement the shift to a networked school community, outline:

   a   your vision

   b   networked school community collaboration strategies to be undertaken

   c   implementation principles that you believe are most important for you to realise your vision in your context.

Key messages

- The creation of the home–school nexus and the development of the networked school community need to be implemented wisely, astutely and in a manner befitting your school's situation, the desired collaborative nature of the organisation, and the shift from a mass to more individualised mode of schooling.

- There is a suite of 12 key guiding principles, as displayed in Table 19.1, that need to be considered and can guide the implementation of the shift.

- The need for this shift is compelling and the benefits for students can be immense and exciting.

chapter 20

Conclusion: The journey continues

MAL LEE & GLENN FINGER

Every day you may make progress. Every step may be fruitful. Yet there will stretch out before you an ever-lengthening, ever-ascending, ever-improving path. You know you will never get to the end of the journey. But this, so far from discouraging, only adds to the joy and glory of the climb.

Winston Churchill (n.d.)

The next phase of the journey—becoming a networked school community

Our intention has been to provide the signposts showing you that the networked school community will characterise the next phase of schooling. It is already apparent in the visionary pathfinding schools, education authorities and nations. The emergence of the new networked school community mode created through a strengthening of the home–school nexus is well underway. As Larry Johnson has identified, the two most significant megatrends evident are that the people are the network and that the network is everywhere. Schooling needs to understand this and capitalise upon these trends.

Schooling in the proactive situations has moved from its traditional paper-based form to a digital mode. This move was well articulated in the book *Leading a digital school* (Lee & Gaffney 2008). The pathfinders are leading the way into the networked mode. The potential of the mode is immense, and there is little doubt that as schools, parents, students, educational and government leaders come to more fully understand and embrace the benefits, the development of networked school communities will occur at an increasing pace.

The great advantage of the networked school community, and the associated collaboration with the students' homes in particular, is the facility for existing schools to use the new playing field to complement the existing school offerings, enrich and give greater relevance to those offerings and assist in redressing the many structural shortcomings of the traditional mode of schooling. Schools have to cater well for every young person. Most struggle with the challenges in these new times and new challenges. It is taking some time for those associated with schools and their long-established ways to appreciate the significant structural and cultural shortcomings of the traditional, stand-alone model of schooling. As the work and successes of the pathfinders come to be better known and the ripple effect is amplified by the networked world, so more and more will appreciate the many diverse benefits of schools shifting to the new mode.

What will become increasingly apparent with the networked mode is its overall unified purpose, the interconnectedness of the key elements and the synergies possible by consistently giving due attention to those elements and the resulting collective intelligence, content being co-created and ideas being tested and shared. We are encouraged through the evidence that increasingly schools across the world are achieving digital take-off (Lee & Gaffney 2008). In the process of moving into a digital operational mode they have begun to significantly change the nature of the schooling, the style of the teaching and the operation of the organisation, and to move from a state of resistance to change to one of innovation. The change thus far in the operation of those schools has been one of ongoing renewal.

Central to the change has been the emergence of a critical mass of staff who have normalised the use of digital technologies in their teaching and in the learning by their students. Having teachers who appreciate the possibilities of digital technologies to enhance the quality and effectiveness that the schooling provide, and who have the skills and desire to harness the digital to enhance this human endeavour, is fundamental to any successful move into the networked mode.

With that understanding and the willingness to carefully push the envelope, virtually any type of networked school community is possible. However, to achieve this vision they will need to collaborate with, engage and value their community—in particular their students and parents—and acknowledge the home–school difference as an opportunity. Most importantly, the quest to realise the vision can be undertaken gradually with the total school community learning together as it pursues its goals.

In the early, pre-structural change, most schools will be able to incrementally and relatively easily initiate these moves. Those schools tightly managed and constrained will find it more difficult. For example, some schools might need to navigate the constraints posed by a powerful educational bureaucracy and industrial agreements, or where the school's relationship with the students' homes is not cooperative and mutually respectful.

We suggest that, over time, as structures and legislative and embedded cultural impediments are modified, this will make possible the new opportunities for significant development. In all your planning it will be important to always balance the moves towards the vision with the everyday realities of your community, and at time compromises need to be made. One of the realities facing all schools, including virtual schools, is that they play a vital social role in all developed societies. It is important to recognise that schools make a significant contribution to learning, but that greater learning can be achieved through the creation of a home–school nexus.

This book makes the salient point that the investment in digital technologies presents a largely overlooked opportunity for schools to capitalise on. Viewed as a home–school difference rather than a digital divide, the investment in the home in partnership with the investment by schools provides a more powerful conceptualisation. As the pathfinders move to work collaboratively with homes to develop networked school communities, we caution that there is the growing divide between the proactive schools, education authorities and nations, and the reactive. That divide is likely to increase, with the students in the reactive schools being ever-more disadvantaged.

While there are schools moving forward into the networked mode, there are many still in the traditional paper-based mode providing a dated and increasingly irrelevant education. Look around and you will see schools still using the same kind of teaching that was employed when you went to school, and proclaiming the virtue of their work. While those schools, and sometimes their education authorities and governments, are quick to provide the 'spin' that they are providing a great traditional education, they are becoming irrelevant in the twenty-first century networked world. Where are you positioned now?

Within a democratic society and a networked world when the professionals charged with providing a quality education for the contemporary world fail to deliver, the community is justified in using the democratic processes and the collaborative tools available online to seriously question the work of the school, the leadership and, where appropriate, the educational bureaucrats and the elected officials. Shirky (2008) observed when commenting on the political power of the Internet:

> Our electronic networks are enabling novel forms of collective action, enabling the creation of collaborative groups that are larger and more distributed than any other time in history. The scope of work that can be done by non-institutional groups is a profound challenge to the status quo. (p. 48)

In writing this book, the team of authors is very aware of the immense challenge taken on by attempting to enunciate a vision for a mode of schooling still in its early stages of being conceptualised. Some years ago, the focus might have been on integrating ICT within a formal curriculum and physical school setting. More recently, it might have been focused on digital take-off by staff within the school. We trust that this provokes your thinking about the next phase—about what is available now that can create the networked school community. The various chapters individually and collectively aim to provide insights and guidance for you, your school and/or education authority to implement the shift to realise that vision.

The team was very aware of the significant challenge of bringing about changes in the nature, purpose and organisation of formal schooling. We believed it was vital to encourage you throughout your reading of this book to adopt a bird's-eye perspective, to get you to look at the macro scene, to appreciate the major influences at play, and thus relate this to your context—to enable your school community to take advantage of the immense and ever-emerging opportunities to enhance the quality of schooling.

Schools make a great contribution to society, but schooling is an 'industry' like all others that has to move with the times if it is to continue to play its desired role. The authors' intention has been to float a concept, to provide a rationale for the adoption of the concept, to suggest the form it might take, and to provide some practical ideas on how schools might go about building on their current early moves and create a mode of schooling that will best prepare their young people for life and work in a digital future.

To assist the refinement of your thinking and that of the writing team we have ourselves taken advantage of the tools of the networked world and created a Ning where collaboratively we can discuss the way forward. Please feel free to join us in the ongoing evolution of this new and ever-evolving mode of schooling.

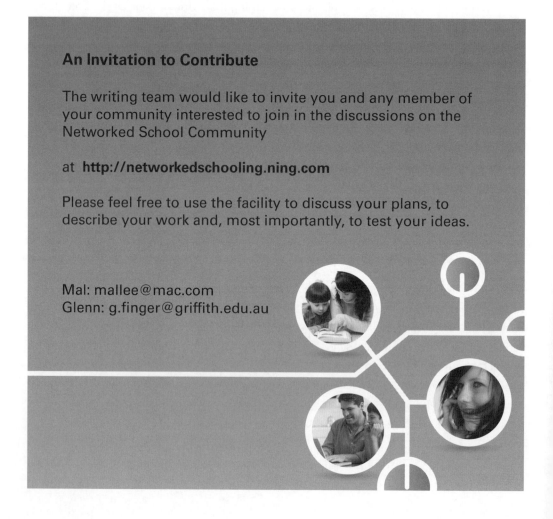

An Invitation to Contribute

The writing team would like to invite you and any member of your community interested to join in the discussions on the Networked School Community

at **http://networkedschooling.ning.com**

Please feel free to use the facility to discuss your plans, to describe your work and, most importantly, to test your ideas.

Mal: mallee@mac.com
Glenn: g.finger@griffith.edu.au

Conclusion

Our hope is that in examining the potential form of the networked school community and forming a closer nexus between the teaching and learning in the home, you will come to appreciate the very immense potential of this mode of schooling and the very considerable gains that can be achieved by all associated with the school's community—the students, the parents, government, the politicians and, in particular, the educational professionals charged with providing the best possible education.

It is a potential outcome rarely achieved in the history of schooling. The shift to the networked mode most importantly signals a move from the mass form of schooling associated with the Industrial Age to one that is far more personalised, all-encompassing and relevant for a networked world and digital future.

Guiding questions

After reading this chapter, consider your context and propose your ideas in relation to the following guiding questions.

1   Where is your school in terms of becoming a digital school?

2   Where is your school in terms of moving beyond a digital school to becoming a networked school community?

3   What steps do you think should be taken to move to the next phase of your school's journey?

Key messages

- Balance the moves towards the vision with the everyday realities of your community and recognise that, at times, compromises will need to be made.

- The investment in digital technologies in the home presents schools with a largely overlooked opportunity to capitalise upon. Viewed as a home–school difference, rather than a digital divide, the investment in the home in partnership with the investment by schools provides a more powerful conceptualisation.

- The authors' intention has been to float a concept, provide a rationale for the adoption of the concept, suggest the form it might take, and offer some practical ideas on how schools might go about building on their current early moves and create a mode of schooling that will best prepare their young people for life and work in a digital future.

- Engage online at http://networkedschooling.ning.com.

Bibliography

Note: All links were active as at November 2009, unless otherwise indicated.

AAPT 2007, *Research finds new technology is challenging the Australian family*, viewed 20 October 2009, AAPT, <http://www.aapt.com.au/our-company/news/2007/Research_finds_new_technology_is_challenging_the_Australian_family>.

ABC News, 2009, *Factbox: Key points about national broadband network*, viewed 23 October 2009, ABC, <www.abc.net.au/news/stories/2009/04/07/2536815.htm>.

Abrahams, N & Dunn, V 2009, 'Is cyber-bullying a crime?', BizTech, Technology, *The Age*, 21 May 2009, viewed 19 September 2009, <http://www.theage.com.au/news/technology/biztech/is-cyberbullying-a-crime/2009/05/21/1242498854929.html>.

Acquisti, A & Gross, R 2006, 'Imagined communities: Awareness, information sharing, and privacy on Facebook', *Privacy enhancing technologies*, Springer-Verlag, Berlin, pp. 36–58.

Aisbett, K 2001, *The Internet at home: A report on internet use in the home*, viewed 23 October 2009, Australian Communications and Media Authority, <http://www.acma.gov.au/webwr/aba/newspubs/documents/internetathome.pdf>.

American Association of University Women (AAUW) 2001, *Educating girls in the new computer age*, AAUW, Washington, DC.

Amis, D 2002, *Kids will be kids*, viewed 22 October 2003, <http://www.netfreedom.org/news.asp?item=186>

Anderson, L & Krathwohl, D 2001, *A taxonomy for learning, teaching and assessing: A revision of Bloom's taxonomy of educational objectives*, Allyn-Bacon Longman, New York.

Anderson, N, Courtney, L, Timms, C & Buschkens, J 2009, *Equity and information communication technology (ICT) in education*, Peter Lang, New York.

Anderson, N, Lankshear, C, Courtney, L & Timms, C 2007, 'Because it's boring: Why high school girls avoid professionally-oriented ICT subjects', *Journal of Computers & Education*, vol. 50, pp. 1304–318.

Anderson, N, Timms, C, Courtney, L & Lankshear, C 2008, 'Girls and information communication technology (ICT)', in N Yelland, G Neal & E Dakich (eds), *Rethinking education with ICT*, Sense Publishers, Rotterdam, The Netherlands, pp. 181–221.

Anderson, R 2006, 'Away from the "icebergs"', *OCLC Newsletter*, no. 2, viewed 19 September 2009, <http://www.oclc.org/nextspace/002/2.htm>.

Anderson, RE & Becker, HJ 1999, *Teaching, learning and computing: 1998 national survey*, Center for Research on Information, Technology and Organizations, University of California and University of Minnesota.

Apple, MW & Beane, JA 1999, Democratic schools: *Lessons from the chalkface*, Oxford University Press, Buckingham.

Arafah, S, Levin, D, Rainie, L & Lenhart, A 2002, *The digital disconnect: The widening gap between Internet-savvy students and their schools*, viewed 19 September 2009, <http://www.pewinternet.org/Reports/2002/The-Digital-Disconnect-The-widening-gap-between-Internetsavvy-students-and-their-schools.aspx>.

Arthur, E 2009, 'Experience the Digital Education Revolution', *Education Technology Solutions*, April/May issue 29, pp. 49–52.

Atkinson, M, Lamont, E, Gulliver, C, White, R & Kinder, K 2005, *School funding: A review of existing models in Europe and OECD countries*, LGA Research Report, NFER, Slough, UK.

Australian Bureau of Statistics (ABS) 2001, 2001 *Census: Computer and Internet use*, Australian Bureau of Statistics, viewed 23 October 2009, <http://www.ausstats.abs.gov.au/ausstats/subscriber.nsf/0/54127FB5498012DCA257125001824C6/$File/29350_2001.pdf>.

Australian Bureau of Statistics (ABS) 2006, *Education and work, Australia*, Australian Bureau of Statistics, viewed 3 March 2009, <http://www.absgov.au/AUSSTATS/abs@nsf/mf/6227.0?>.

Australian Communications and Media Authority (ACMA) 2007, *Media and communications in Australian families*, ACMA, Canberra, viewed 16 July 2008, <http://www.acma.gov.au/webwr/_assets/main/lib101058/media_and_society_report_2007.pdf>.

Australian Communications and Media Authority (ACMA) 2009a, *Online Participation*, Australians and the digital economy, report no. 2, ACMA, Canberra, viewed 23 October 2009, <http://www.acma.gov.au/WEB/STANDARD/pc=PC_311655>.

Australian Communications and Media Authority (ACMA) 2009b, *Click and connect: Young Australians' use of online social media 01*, Qualitative research report, ACMA, Canberra, viewed 16 July 2009, <http://www.acma.gov.au/WEB/STANDARD/pc=PC_311797>.

Australian Communications and Media Authority (ACMA) 2009c, *Click and connect: Young Australians' use of online social media 02*, quantitative research report, ACMA, Canberra, viewed 16 July 2009, <http://www.acma.gov.au/WEB/STANDARD/pc=PC_311797>.

Australian Education Council (AEC) 2008, *The Melbourne Declaration on Educational Goals for Young Australians*, Australian Education Council, viewed 30 May 2009, <http://www.curriculum.edu.au/mceetya/melbourne_declaration,25979.html>.

Australian Government 2007, *National Safe Schools Framework*, Department of Education, Science and Training, viewed 23 October 2009, <http://www.dest.gov.au/sectors/school_education/publications_resources/profiles/national_safe_schools_>.

Australian Government 2008, *Family-School Partnership Framework: A guide for schools and families*, Australian Government Department of Education, Employment and Workplace Relations 2008, available at <http://www.dest.gov.au/sectors/school_education/publications_resources/profiles/Family_School_Partnerships_Framework.htm>.

Australian Government 2009a, *Digital Education Revolution*, Department of Education, Employment and Workplace Relations, viewed 18 September 2009, <www.deewr.gov.au/SCHOOLING/DIGITALEDUCATIONREVOLUTION/Pages/default.aspx>.

Australian Government 2009b, *Education tax refund*, viewed 16 July 2009, <http://www.australia.gov.au/educationtaxrefund>.

Australian Labor Party 2009, *Assessment and teaching of 21st century skills*, media statement, Australian Labor Party, viewed 10 June 2009, <http://www.alp.org.au/media/0609/msed090.php>.

Baase, S 2007, *A gift of fire: Social, legal and ethical issues for computing and the Internet*, 3rd edn, Prentice Hall, New Jersey.

Balanskat, A, Blamire, R & Kefala, S 2006, *The ICT impact report: A review of ICT impact on schools in Europe*, Insight, viewed 1 May 2000, <http://insight.eun.org>.

Barab, S, Sadler, T, Heiselt, C, Hickey, D & Zuicker, S 2007, 'Relating narrative, inquiry, and inscriptions: Supporting consequential play', *Journal of Science Education and Technology*, vol. 16, no. 1, pp. 59–82.

Barber, M & Mourshed, M 2007, *How the world's best performing school systems come out on top*, McKinsey & Company, viewed 30 August 2009, <http://www.mckinsey.com/clientservice/socialsector/resources/pdf/Worlds_School_Systems_Final.pdf>.

Baskin, C & Williams, M 2007, 'ICT integration in schools: Where are we now and what comes next?', *Australasian Journal of Educational Technology*, vol. 22, no. 4, pp. 455–73.

Bazley, N 2009, 'Cyberbullying', *Behind the news*, episode 11, 12 May 2009, viewed 19 September 2009, ABC, <http://www.abc.net.au/news/btn/story/s2564784.htm>.

Becker, HJ 2000a, 'Pedagogical motivations for student computer use that lead to student engagement', *Educational Technology*, September/October, pp. 1–16.

Becker, HJ 2000b, 'Who's wired and who's not: Children's access to and use of computer technology', *Future of Children*, vol. 10, no. 2, pp. 44–75.

Becta 2006, *The Becta Review 2006*, Becta, viewed 16 July 2008, <http://publications.becta.org.uk/display.cfm?resID=25948>.

Becta 2007a, *Harnessing Technology review 2007: Progress and impact of technology in education*, summary report, Becta, viewed 16 July 2008, <http://publications.becta.org.uk/display.cfm?resID=33980>.

Becta 2007b, *Harnessing Technology delivery plan*, Becta, viewed 16 July 2008, <http://publications.becta.org.uk/display.cfm?resID=28223>.

Becta 2008a, *Extending opportunity*, final report of the Minister's Taskforce on home access to technology, Becta, viewed 19 September 2009, <http://partners.becta.org.uk/upload-dir/downloads/page_documents/partners/home_access_report.pdf>.

Becta 2008b, *Universal access: A guide for school leaders*, Becta, Coventry.

Becta 2008c, *Benefits of ICT use outside formal education*, interim report, The learner and their context, Becta, viewed 30 August 2009, <http://partners.becta.org.uk/upload-dir/downloads/page_documents/research/reports/learner_context_interim.pdf>.

Becta 2008d, *Harnessing Technology review 2008: The role of technology and its impact on education*, Becta, viewed 19 September 2009, <http://publications.becta.org.uk/display.cfm?resID=38751>.

Becta 2008e, *Exploiting ICT to improve parental engagement: Moving towards online reporting*, Becta, viewed 30 August 2009, <http://publications.becta.org.uk/display.cfm?resID=38170>.

Becta 2008f, *ICT excellence awards 2007: Extending learning opportunities (primary)—Winner*, Becta, viewed 30 August 2009, <http://awards.becta.org.uk/display.cfm?resID=34519>.

Becta 2009a, *Harnessing Technology for next generation learning: Children, schools and families implementation plan* 2009–2012, Becta, viewed 19 September 2009, <http://publications.becta.org.uk/display.cfm?resID=39547>.

Becta 2009b, *Home Access presentation*, Becta, viewed 23 October 2009, <http://collaboration.becta.org.uk/docs/DOC-1842>.

Becta 2009c, *Engaging parents*, Becta, viewed 19 September 2009, <http://www.becta.org.uk/engagingparents>.

Becta 2009d, *Home Access*, Becta, viewed 19 September 2009, <http://www.becta.org.uk/homeaccess>.

Bell, A, Crothers, C, Goodwin, I, Kripalani, K, Sherman, K, Smith, P 2007, *World Internet Project New Zealand*, AUT, Auckland.

Belsey, B n.d., *Cyberbullying.ca: Always on? Always aware!*, viewed 23 October 2009, <http://www.cyberbullying.ca/>.

Berkman Center for Internet & Society 2008, *Enhancing child safety and online technologies*, final report of the Internet Safety Technical Task Force, Berkman Center for Internet & Society, Harvard University, viewed 6 October 2009, <http://cyber.law.harvard.edu/pubrelease/isttf/>.

Betcher, C & Lee, M 2009, *The interactive whiteboard revolution: Teaching with IWBs*, ACER Press, Melbourne.

Bhat, CS 2008, 'Cyber bullying: Overview and strategies for school counsellors, guidance officers, and all school personnel', *Australian Journal of Guidance and Counselling*, vol. 18, no. 1, pp. 55–66.

Bielefeldt, T 2005, 'Computers and student learning: Interpreting the multivariance analysis of PISA 2000', *Journal of Research on Technology in Education*, vol. 37, no. 4, pp. 339–47, viewed 19 September 2009, via Eric database, <http://www.eric.ed.gov/ERICDocs/data/ericdocs2sql/content_storage_01/0000019b/80/2a/0d/4c.pdf>.

Birtles, A 2009, 'What do parents think?', Becta Collaboration—blogposts in Home Access, viewed 1 July 2009, <http://collaboration.becta.org.uk/community/homeaccess/blog/2009/07/13/what-do-parents-think>.

Bishop, G 2006, 'Advocacy: A ripple effect', *OCLC Newsletter*, no. 2, viewed 19 September 2009, <http://www.oclc.org/nextspace/002/advocacy.htm>.

Black, P & Wiliam, D 1998, *Inside the black box: Raising standards through classroom assessment*, King's College, London.

Black, R 2009, 'English-language learners, fan communities and 21st century skills', *Journal of Adolescent and Adult Literacy*, vol. 52, no. 8, pp. 688–97.

Blackboard 2009, *Increase the impact: Transform the experience*, viewed 30 August 2009, <http://www.blackboard.com/>.

Blanchard, M, Burns, J & Metcalf A 2007, *Bridging the digital divide: Creating opportunities for marginalised young people to get connected*, Research Report No. 1, Inspire Foundation and ORYGEN Youth Health Research Centre, University of Melbourne, Melbourne.

Boeije, H 2002, 'A purposeful approach to the constant comparative method in the analysis of qualitative interviews', *Quality and Quantity*, vol. 36, pp. 391–409.

Boneva, BS, Quinn, A, Kraut, RE, Keisler, S & Shklovski, I 2006, 'Teenage communication in the instant messaging era', in R Kraut, M Brynin & S Keisler (eds), *Computers, phones, and the Internet*, Oxford University Press, New York, pp. 201–18.

Borgman, C, Abelson, H, Dirks, L, Johnson, R, Koedinger, KR, Linn, MC, Lynch, CA, Oblinger, DG, Pea, RD, Salen, K, Smith, MS & Szalay, A 2008, *Fostering learning in the networked world: The cyberlearning opportunity and challenge*, a 21st century agenda for the National Science Foundation, viewed 23 October 2009, <http://www.nsf.gov/pubs/2008/nsf08204/nsf08204.pdf>.

Bornholt, LJ, Piccolo, A & O'Loughlin, M 2004, 'Understanding "identity of place" for young Australians: Thoughts and feelings on local, regional and national identity for adolescents and young adults in urban contexts', in HW Marsh, J Baumert, GE Richards & U Trautwein (eds), *Self-concept, motivation and identity: Where to from here?*, proceedings of the 3rd International Biennial SELF Research Conference, Berlin, 4–7 July 2004, SELF Research Centre, University of Western Sydney, Sydney, viewed 20 October 2009, <http://www.self.ox.ac.uk/Conferences/2004_Proceedings_All_Papers.htm> and <http://www.self.ox.ac.uk/Conferences/2004_Bornholt_Piccolo_OLoughlin.pdf>.

boyd, danah 2007, 'Why youth (heart) social network sites: The role of networked publics in teenage social life', in D Buckingham (ed.), MacArthur Foundation series on digital learning: *Youth, identity, and digital media volume*, MIT Press, Cambridge, MA.

boyd, danah 2008, cited in transcript from *Growing up online* by R Dretzin, Frontline, WGBH Educational Foundation, viewed 20 October 2009, <http://www.pbs.org/wgbh/pages/frontline/kidsonline/etc/script.html>.

Bradbrook, G 2008, Meeting their potential: *The role of education and technology in overcoming disadvantage and disaffection in young people*, Becta presentation, viewed 23 October 2009, <http://events.becta.org.uk/content_files/corporate/resources/events/2008/november/b6_potential_bradbrook.pdf>.

Bradwell, P 2009, *Edgeless university: Why higher education must embrace technology*, Demos, viewed 19 September 2009, <http://www.demos.co.uk/files/Edgeless_University_-_web.pdf?1245715615>.

Broch, E 2000, 'Children's search from an information search process perspective', *School Library Media Research*, no. 3, viewed 19 September 2009, <http://www.ala.org/Content/NavigationMenu/AASL/Publications_and_Journals/School_Library_Media_Research/Contents1/Volume_3_(2000)/childrens.htm>.

Brotman, JS & Moore, FM 2008, 'Girls and science: A review of four themes in science education literature', *Journal of Research in Science Teaching*, vol. 45, no. 9, pp. 971–1002.

Brown, D 2009, 'Mobiles OK in class', *The Mercury*, 3 February, viewed 23 October 2009, <http://www.themercury.com.au/article/2009/02/03/53181_tasmania-news.html>.

Brown, J & Metcalf, D 2008, *Mobile learning update*, The Learning Consortium, viewed 23 October 2009, <http://www.masieweb.com/p7/MobileLearningUpdate.pdf>.

Brydolf, C 2007, 'Minding MySpace: Balancing the benefits and risks of students' online social networks', *The Education Digest*, October, pp. 4–8.

Buckingham, D 2007, *Beyond technology: Children's learning in the age of digital culture*, Polity Press, Cambridge, UK.

'Bullying', 2009, *The Guardian*, viewed 22 October 2009, <http://www.guardian.co.uk/education/bullying>.

Burbules, NC 2004, 'Rethinking the virtual', *Informatica na Educacao: Teoria & pratica*, vol. 7, no. 1, pp. 89–107.

Caldwell, B & Harris, J 2008, *Why not the best schools?*, ACER Press, Melbourne.

Carrington, V 2006, *Rethinking middle years: Early adolescents, schooling and digital culture*, Allen & Unwin, Crows Nest.

Carter, H 2009, 'Teenage girl is first to be jailed for bullying on Facebook', *The Guardian*, 21 August 2009, viewed 19 September 2009, <http://www.guardian.co.uk/uk/2009/aug/21/facebook-bullying-sentence-teenage-girl>.

Carvin, A 2008, *Lori Drew convicted in Megan Meier case*, PBS Teachers, viewed 23 October 2009, <http://www.pbs.org/teachers/learning.now/2008/12/lori_drew_convicted_in_megan_m.html>.

Cassell, J & Cramer, M 2008, 'High tech or high risk: Moral panics about girls online', in T McPherson (ed.), *Digital youth, innovation, and the unexpected*, The John D. and Catherine T. MacArthur Foundation Series on Digital Media and Learning, The MIT Press, pp. 53–76, viewed 19 September 2009, <http://www.mitpressjournals.org/doi/abs/10.1162/dmal.9780262633598.053>.

Chien, C, Sen-chi, Y, Chao-hsiu, C & Huan-Chueh, W 2009, 'Tool, toy, telephone, territory, or treasure of information: Elementary school students' attitudes toward the Internet', *Computers & Education*, vol. 53, pp. 308–16.

Childnet International 2008, *Young people and social networking services: A Childnet International research report*, Childnet International, viewed 19 September 2009, <http://www.digizen.org/downloads/fullReport.pdf>.

Christian, K, Morrison, FJ & Bryant, FB 1998, 'Predicting kindergarten academic skills: Interactions among child care, maternal education, and family literacy environments', *Early Childhood Research Quarterly*, vol. 13, no. 3, pp. 501–21.

Church, AP 2005, 'Virtual school libraries: The time is now!' *MultiMedia & Internet@Schools*, vol. 12, pp. 8–12.

Churches, A 2009, *Bloom's digital taxonomy* (Version 3.01), viewed 20 October 2009, <http://edorigami.wikispaces.com/file/view/bloom%27s+Digital+taxonomy+v3.01.pdf>.

Cohen, P, Kulik, J & Kulik, C 1982, 'Educational outcomes of tutoring: A meta-analysis of findings', *American Educational Research Journal*, vol. 19, pp. 237–48.

Comber, C, Watling, R, Lawson, T, Cavendish, S, McEune, R & Paterson, F 2002, *Learning at home and school: Case studies*, DfES, London.

Committee of Inquiry into the Changing Learner Experience 2009, *Higher education in a Web 2.0 world*, report of an independent committee of inquiry into the impact on higher education of students' widespread use of Web 2.0 technologies, viewed 20 October 2009, <http://www.jisc.ac.uk/media/documents/publications/heweb20rptv1.pdf>.

Commonwealth Department of Education, Science and Training (DEST) 2002, *Raising the standards: A proposal for the development of an ICT competency framework for teachers*, DEST, viewed 23 October 2009, <http://www.dest.gov.au/NR/rdonlyres/B35D8670-5447-4DFC-8388-1C81F3329113/1574/RaisingtheStandards.pdf>.

Commonwealth Department of Education, Science and Training (DEST) 2003, *Implementation manual for National Safe Schools Framework: Implementation manual*, DEST, Canberra.

Conger, S 2009, 'Web 2.0, virtual worlds, and real ethical issues', in P Candace Deans (ed.), *Social software and Web 2.0 technology trends*, Information Science Reference, Hershey, New York, pp. 105–117.

Connell, J 2007, 'Bedrooms as classrooms', John Connell blog entry, 13 October 2007, viewed 20 October 2009, <http://www.johnconnell.co.uk/blog/?p=542>.

Conole, G, de Laat, M, Dillon, T & Darby, J 2006, 'An in-depth case study of students' experiences of e-Learning: How is learning changing?', paper presented at the 23rd annual conference of the Australasian Society for Computers in Learning in Tertiary Education (ASCILITE): Who's learning? Whose technology?, viewed 20 October 2009, <http://www.ascilite.org.au/conferences/sydney06/proceeding/pdf_papers/p127.pdf>.

Cook, B 1995, 'Managing for effective delivery of information services in the 1990s: The integration of computing, educational and library services', paper presented at the ALIA Information Online & On Disc 95 conference, Sydney.

Courtney, L, Lankshear, C, Timms, C & Anderson, N 2009, 'Insider perspectives vs. public perceptions of ICT: Toward policy for enhancing female student participation in academic pathways to professional careers in ICT', Policy Futures in Education, vol. 7, no. 1 (online publication), viewed 23 October 2009, <http://www.wwwords.co.uk/pfie/content/pdfs/7/issue7_1.asp>.

Courtney, L, Timms, C & Anderson, N 2006, '"I would rather spend time with a person than a machine": Qualitative findings from the girls and ICT survey', in A Ruth (ed.), *Quality and impact of qualitative research*, 3rd annual QualIT conference, Institute for Integrated and Intelligent Systems, Griffith University, Brisbane, pp. 51–57.

Cox, M, Abbott, C, Webb, M, Blakeley, B, Beauchamp, T & Rhodes, V 2003a, *ICT and attainment: A review of the research literature*, Becta, viewed 19 September 2009, <http://partners.becta.org.uk/upload-dir/downloads/page_documents/research/ict_attainment_summary.pdf>.

Cox, M, Abbott, C, Webb, M, Blakeley, B, Beauchamp, T & Rhodes, V 2003b, *ICT and pedagogy: A review of the research literature*, Becta, viewed 19 September 2009, <http://partners.becta.org.uk/upload-dir/downloads/page_documents/research/ict_pedagogy_summary.pdf>.

Cox, M, Webb, M, Abbott, C, Blakeley, B, Beauchamp, T & Rhodes, V 2004, *A review of the research literature relating to ICT and attainment*, Becta, London.

Cox, S 2008, 'A conceptual analysis of technological pedagogical content knowledge', PhD thesis, Brigham Young University, viewed 30 August 2009, <http://contentdm.lib.byu.edu/ETD/image/etd2552.pdf>.

CTV News 2009, B.C. *principal unplugs illegal cellphone jammer*, CTV, viewed 22 May 2009 <http://www.ctv.ca/servlet/ArticleNews/story/CTVNews/20090401/cellphone_jammer_090401/20090401?hub=SciTech>.

Cuban, L 1986, *Teachers and machines: The classroom use of technology since 1920*, Teachers College Press, New York.

Cuban, L 2000, *So much high-tech money invested, so little use and change in practice: How come?*, edtechnot.com blog, viewed 22 April 2009, <http://www.edtechnot.com/notarticle1201.html>.

Cuban, L 2001, *Oversold and underused: Computers in the classroom*, Harvard University Press, Cambridge, MA.

Cuban, L 2006, 'Laptops transforming classrooms? Yeah sure ....', *Teachers College Record*, 31 October, viewed 16 June 2009, <http://www.tcrecord.org>.

Currie, C, Roberts, C, Morgan, A, Smith, R, Settertobulte, W, Samdal, O & Rasmussen, V (eds) 2004, *Young people's health in context: Health behaviour in school-aged children (HBSC) study*, international report from the 2001/2002 survey, World Health Organization, viewed 23 October 2009, <http://www.euro.who.int/eprise/main/who/informationsources/publications/catalogue/20040518_1>.

Dale, R, Robertson, S & Shortis, T 2004, 'You can't not go with the technological flow, can you? Constructing "ICT" and "teaching and learning"', *Journal of Computer Assisted Learning*, vol. 20, pp. 456–70.

Danesh, A, Inkpen, K, Lau, F, Shu, K & Booth, K 2001, 'Geney™: Designing a collaborative activity for the Palm™ handheld computer', paper presented at the Conference on Human Factors in Computing Systems, Seattle, WA.

Davidson, CN & Goldberg, DT 2009, *The future of learning institutions in a digital age*, The John D. and Catherine T. MacArthur Foundation, viewed 20 October 2009, <http://www.scribd.com/doc/13476078/The-Future-of-Learning-Institutions-in-a-Digital-Age>.

Dede, C (ed.) 1998, 'Six challenges for educational technology', *Learning with technology*, viewed 20 October 2009, <http://www.docstoc.com/docs/4991034/educational-technology>.

Department for Children, Schools and Families (DCSF) 2008, *Broadening horizons: England to 'lead the world' in computer access for young people*, DCSF, viewed 23 October 2009, <http://www.dcsf.gov.uk/pns/DisplayPN.cgi?pn_id=2008_0208>.

Department for Culture, Media and Sports (DCMS) & Department for Business, Innovation and Skills (DBIS) 2009, *Digital Britain—final report*, viewed 23 October 2009, <http://www.culture.gov.uk/images/publications/digitalbritain-finalreport-jun09.pdf>.

Department of Communications, Information Technology and the Arts (DICTA) 2005, Participation summit: overview paper, viewed 3 March 2009, <http://www.archive.dcita.gov.au/2005/09/participation_summit/breakout-groups/overview_paper>. The document can now be viewed at http://www.archive.dcita.gov.au/__data/assets/pdf_file/0009/31599/Overview_Paper_for_Breakout_Groups.pdf.

Department of Education and Training 2005, *Smart classrooms*, Queensland Government, viewed 1 June 2009, <http://education.qld.gov.au/smartclassrooms/strategy/ sp_census_learning.html>.

Department of Education and Training 2009, *OneSchool guiding principles*, Queensland Government, viewed 30 August 2009, <http://education.qld.gov.au/oneschool/gprincipals.html>.

Department of Education, Science and Technology (DEST) 2001, *Making better connections: Models of teacher professional development for the integration of information and communication technology into classroom practice*, viewed 21 May 2008, <http://www.dest.gov.au/schools/publications/2002/MBC.pdf>.

Department of Education, Science and Technology (DEST) 2002, *Raising the standards: A proposal for the development of an ICT competency framework for teachers*, viewed 30 August 2009, <http://www.dest.gov.au/NR/rdonlyres/B35D8670-5447-4DFC-8388-1C81F3329113/1574/RaisingtheStandards.pdf>.

Desforges, C & Abouchaar, A 2003, *The impact of parental involvement, parental support and family education on pupil achievement and adjustment, literature review*, DfES Research Report 433, viewed 19 September 2009, <http://www.nationalliteracytrust.org.uk/familyreading/ParentalInvolvement.doc>.

Devaney, L 2008, 'CoSN to school leaders: "Think before you ban"', *eSchool News*, 21 January 2008, viewed 22 October 2009, <http://www.eschoolnews.com/news/top-news/index.cfm?i=51725>.

De Vise, D 2009, 'Students crave a break on cellphone ban', *Washington Post*, 1 June 2009, viewed 23 October 2009, <http://www.washingtonpost.com/wp-dyn/content/article/2009/05/31/AR2009053102533.html?wpisrc=newsletter&wpisrc=newsletter>.

Dewey, J 1916, *Democracy and education*, Macmillan, New York.

Dieterle E, Dede C, Schrier KL (2007) '"Neomillennial" learning styles propagated by wireless handheld devices', in M Lytras & A Naeve (eds), *Ubiquitous and pervasive knowledge and learning management: Semantics, social networking and new media to their full potential*, Idea Group, Inc, Hershey, PA, pp. 35–66.

Dikeos, T 2009, 'Teen's death highlights cyber bullying trend', *7.30 Report*, video, 23 July 2009, ABC, viewed 22 October 2009, <http://www.abc.net.au/news/stories/2009/07/23/2633775.htm>.

DiMaggio, P & Hargittai, E 2001, *From the 'digital divide' to 'digital inequality': Studying Internet use as penetration increases*, Princeton University Center for Arts and Cultural Policy Studies, Princeton, New Jersey.

Directorate General Information Society and Media of the European Commission n.d., *Digital ecosystems: The enabling technologies and paradigms for fostering endogenous local development , local capacity building and knowledge sharing processes providing tailored and personalized ICT services to citizens and business networks*, viewed 23 October 2009, <http://www.digital-ecosystems.org>.

Donchi, L, & Moore, S 2004, 'It's a boy thing: The role of the internet in young people's psychological wellbeing', *Behaviour Change*, vol. 21, no. 2, pp. 76–89.

Dretzin, R & Maggio, J (producers) 2008, *Growing up online*, video, PBS, viewed 6 March 2009, <http://www.pbs.org/wgbh/pages/frontline/kidsonline/>.

Drupal 2009, *Drupal.org*, viewed 30 August 2009, <http://drupal.org/>.

Dyer, J 2001, 'Library volunteer and service providers: A prototype for creating a grace space', *An information odyssey ... a long and eventful journey*, 11th National Library Technicians' Conference, Hobart, August 2001, available from <http://conferences.alia.org.au/libtec2001/papers/dyer.html>.

Ebersole, S 1999, 'Adolescents' use of the World-Wide Web in ten public schools: A uses and gratifications approach', unpublished PhD in Communication Dissertation, Regent University, Virginia Beach, VA, viewed at <http://faculty.colostate-pueblo.edu/samuel.ebersole/diss/dissertation_final.pdf>.

Eckert, P 1989, *Jocks and burnouts: Social categories and identity in the high school*, Teachers College Press, New York.

Epstein, J 2001, *School, family, and community partnerships*, Westview Press, Boulder, Colorado.

Epstein, JL & Sanders, MG 2006, 'Prospects for change: Preparing educators for school, family and community partnerships', *Peabody Journal of Education*, vol. 81, no. 2, pp. 81–120.

eSchool News 2009, *ACLU sues over blocked web sites*, eSchool News, viewed 19 September 2009, <http://www.eschoolnews.com/news/top-news/index.cfm?i=58845>.

Estyn 2009, *Good practice in parental involvement in primary schools*, Estyn, viewed 19 September 2009 <http://www.estyn.gov.uk/thematicreports/good_practice_in_parental_involvement_in_primary_schools_april_2009.pdf>.

Ewing, S, Thomas, J & Schiessl, J 2008, CCI Digital *Futures report: The Internet in Australia*, Swinburne University of Technology, Melbourne

Fairlie, RW 2005, *Are we really a nation online? Ethnic and racial disparities in access to technology and their consequences*, report for the Leadership conference on Civil Rights Education Fund, viewed 19 September 2009 <http://www.civilrights.org/publications/nation-online/digitaldivide.pdf>.

Feinstein, L & Symons, J 1999, 'Attainment in secondary school', *Oxford Economic Papers*, vol. 51, pp. 300–21.

Fieser, J & Dowden, B 2009, 'Yin Yang', *The Internet Encyclopedia of Philosophy (IEP)*, viewed 22 October 2009, <http://www.iep.utm.edu/y/yinyang.htm>.

Findahl, O 2008, *The Internet in Sweden*, World Internet Institute (English Edition), viewed 14 October 2009 <http://www.iis.se/docs/the_internet_in_sweden_2007.pdf>.

Fisch, K, McLeod, S & Bronman, J 2006, *Shift happens. Did you know?*, The Digital Blur, video viewed 13 June 2009, <http://thedigitalblur.com/2008/11/08/did-you-know-shift-happens-by-karl-fisch/>.

Fisch, K, McLeod, S & Bronman, J 2008, *Did you know?*, YouTube, video, viewed 13 June 2009, <http://www.youtube.com/watch?v=jpEnFwiqdx8&feature=related>.

Fiveash, K 2009, *UK schools chief begs for Home Access scheme cash*, The Register, 14 January 2009, viewed 22 July 2009, <http://www.theregister.co.uk/2009/01/14/home_access_computers_internet_pork_barrel/>.

Flanagin, A & Metzger, M 2008, 'Digital media and youth: Unparalleled opportunity and unprecedented responsibility', in M Metzger & A Flanagin (eds), *Digital media, youth and credibility*, The John D. and Catherine T. MacArthur Foundation Series on Digital Media and Learning, The MIT Press, Cambridge, MA, pp. 5–28.

Flood, M & Hamilton, C 2003, *Regulating youth access to pornography*, discussion paper no. 53, The Australian Institute, viewed 23 October 2009, <http://www.tai.org.au/documents/dp_fulltext/DP53.pdf>.

Foo, F 2009 'BYO laptops trend extends office', *The Australian*, 22 September, viewed 23 October 2009, <http://www.australianit.news.com.au/story/0,24897,26105149-15317,00.html>.

Ford, D 2008, 'Cyberbullying in schools', *Professional Educator*, vol. 7, no. 4, pp. 38–41.

Forrester, B 2008, 'Web 2.0 and ADL', *ADL Newsletter for Educators and Educational Researchers*, June, viewed 19 September 2009, <http://adlcommunity.net/mod/resource/view.php?inpopup=true&id=669>.

FreshMinds 2007, *Digital Inclusion: A discussion of the evidence base*, viewed 20 October 2009, <http://docs.google.com/gview?a=v&q=cache:tQydN9XTyroJ:research.freshminds.co.uk/files/u1/shminds_report_understandingdigitalinclusion.pdf+FreshMinds+(2007).+Digital+Inclusion:+a+Discussion+of+the+Evidence+Base.+London:+UK+Online+Centres+-&hl=en&gl=au&pid=bl&srcid=ADGEESiUNhu47rJrS8JgZZoghyhdqWHgPzhDWTQJtxdLhI7irO3FAOXeVCP5LKh2z2zGqMsYmw-S6oz5eh65XHxdx6s-U490s2kRZHZQpgfVXLYLAOJkIS66S6PrrMC0egTF4EagyQ3R&sig=AFQjCNEcSROAHzEYLv01Kl0X22f2-yIoWA>.

Friedman, T 2006, *The world is flat*, 2nd edn, Farrar, Straus Giroux, New York.

Frontline 2008, *Growing up online*, Frontline, viewed 23 October 2009, <http://www.pbs.org/wgbh/pages/frontline/kidsonline/>.

Fuchs, T & Woessmann, L 2004, *Computers and student learning: Bivariate and multivariate evidence on the availability and use of computers at home and at school*, CESifo working paper no. 1321, CESifo Group Munich, viewed 23 October 2009, <http://ideas.repec.org/p/ces/ceswps/_1321.html>.

Fullan, M 2007, *The new meaning of educational change*, Teachers College Press, New York.

Fullan, M 2008, *The six secrets of change*, Jossey Bass, San Francisco.

Futuresource Consulting 2009, 'Quarterly insight', state of the market report, quarter 1, unpublished presentation.

Gee, J 2004, *Situated language and learning: A critique of traditional schooling*, Routledge, London.

Gee, J 2005, *An introduction to discourse analysis*, Routledge, London.

Gee, JP 2007, *What video games have to teach us about learning and literacy*, 2nd edn, Palgrave Macmillan, New York.

Gee, L 2006, 'Human-centered design guidelines', in D Oblinger (ed.), Learning spaces: *An EDUCAUSE e-book*, viewed 30 August 2009, <http://www.educause.edu/LearningSpaces>.

Gerstner, LV, Semerand, RD, Doyle, DP, & Johnston, WB 1995, *Reinventing education: Entrepreneurship in America's public schools*, Penguin, New York.

Gibbs, G 1995, *Assessing student centred courses*, Oxford Centre for Staff Learning and Development, Oxford.

Gillespie, A 2006, 'Cyber-bullying and harassment of teenagers: The legal response', *Journal of Social Welfare & Family Law*, vol. 28, no. 2, pp. 123–36.

Gilster, P 1997, *A primer on digital literacy*, John Wiley & Sons, Mississauga, Ontario.

Golding, W 1954, *Lord of the flies*, Penguin Putnam Inc., New York.

Gore, A 1994, 'Super highway' speech, viewed 16 July 2008, <http://artcontext.com/calendar/1997/superhig.html>.

Greenfield, PM, Gross, EF, Subrahmanyam, K, Suzuki, LK & Tynes, B 2006, 'Teens on the Internet: Interpersonal connection, identity, and information', in R Kraut, M Brynin & S Kiesler (eds), *Computers, phones, and the Internet: Domesticating information technology*, Oxford University Press, New York, pp. 185–200.

Greenfield, P, Rickwood, P & Tran, H 2001, *Effectiveness of internet filtering software products*, viewed 20 October 2009, <http://www.acma.gov.au/webwr/aba/newspubs/documents/filtereffectiveness.pdf>

Gross, EF, Juvonen, J, & Gable, SL 2002, 'Internet use and well-being in adolescence', *Journal of Social Issues*, vol. 58, no. 1, pp. 75–90.

Gross, M & Latham, D 2007, 'Attaining information literacy: An investigation of the relationship between skill level, self-estimates of skill, and library anxiety', *Library and Information Science Research*, vol. 29, no. 3, pp. 332–53.

Guardian 2009, 'Bullying', viewed 22 October, 2009, <http://www.guardian.co.uk/education/bullying>.

Haddon, L 2004, 'Explaining ICT consumption: The case of the home computer', in R Silverstone & E Hirsch (eds), *Consuming technologies: Media and information in domestic spaces*, Routledge, London, pp. 82–96.

Hargittai, E 2003, *The digital divide and what to do about it*, viewed 28 February 2009, <http://www.eszter.com/research/pubs/hargittai-digitaldivide.pdf>.

Harris, C 2006, 'School library 2.0', *School Library Journal*, vol. 52, no. 5, pp. 50–53.

Hart, R, Bober, M & Pine, K 2008, *Learning in the family: Parental engagement in children's learning with technology*, Bakewell Intuitive Media Research Services, Bakewell, UK.

Hattie, J 2009, *Visible learning: A synthesis of over 800 meta-analyses relating to achievement*, Routledge, Abingdon.

Hauser, J 2007, 'Media specialists can learn Web 2.0 tools to make schools more cool', *Computers in Libraries*, vol. 27, no. 2, pp. 6–8, 47–48.

Hawkins, L 2009, 'e-Learning Foundation spring conference', email distributed on Becta's ICT Research Network, 10 March 2009.

Hay, L 2001, 'Information leadership: Managing the ICT integration equation', *Computers in New Zealand Schools*, vol. 13, no. 3, pp. 5–12.

Hay, L 2004, 'Information issues and digital learning: Rewriting the rules of engagement?' in S La Marca & M Manning (eds), *Reality bytes: Information literacy for independent learning*, School Library Association of Victoria, Carlton, pp. 49–66.

Hay, L 2005, 'Student learning through Australian school libraries. Part 1: A statistical analysis of student perceptions', *Synergy*, vol. 3, no. 2, pp. 17–30.

Hay, L 2006a, 'Student learning through Australian school libraries. Part 2: What students define and value as school library support', *Synergy*, vol. 4, no. 2, pp. 27–38.

Hay, L 2006b 'Are Internet–savvy kids@home the new information poor? Rethinking the digital divide', refereed paper presented at Visions of Learning: ASLA Online II Conference Proceedings, May 2006, Australian School Library Association Inc, Zillmere.

Hay, L 2006c, 'School libraries as flexible and dynamic learning laboratories … that's what Aussie kids want', *Scan*, vol. 25, no. 2, pp. 18–27.

Hay, L 2008, 'Moving beyond the rhetoric: What the research tells us about Web 2.0 & student learning', presentation, 23 February 2008, ASLANSW State Library Day.

Hay, L (in press), 'Using Web 2.0 technologies to support student learning through the guided inquiry process', PhD Thesis, Charles Sturt University.

Hay, L & Foley, C 2009, 'School libraries building capacity for student learning in 21C', *Scan*, vol. 28, no. 2, pp. 17–26, viewed at <http://www.curriculumsupport.education.nsw.gov. au/schoollibraries/assets/pdf/Schoollibraries21C.pdf>.

Hay, L & Kallenberger, N 1996, 'The future role of the school information services unit in the teaching/learning process', paper presented at ITEC Electronic Networking and Australasia's Schools Conference, Sydney, 12–13 April 1996, viewed 20 October 2009, <http://athene.csu.edu.au/~lhay/ISU/InfoServiceUnit.html>.

Hayes, D 2007, 'ICT and learning: Lessons from Australian classrooms', *Computers and Education*, vol. 49, pp. 385–95.

Hayward, B, Alty, C, Pearson, S & Martin, C 2003, *Young people and ICT 2002: Findings from a survey conducted in Autumn 2002*, Department for Education and Skills and British Educational Communications and Technology Agency (BECTA), London, UK.

Hedestig, U & Söderström, M 2009, *A user centred approach to inform learning space design*, viewed 30 August 2009, <http://www.ou.nl/Docs/Campagnes/ICDE2009/Papers/Final_ paper_090hedestig.pdf>.

Heemskerk, I, Brink, A, Volman, M & ten Dam, G 2005, 'Inclusiveness and ICT in education: A focus on gender, ethnicity and social class', *Journal of Computer Assisted Learning*, vol. 21, pp. 1–16.

Heinström, J 2006, Fast surfing for availability or deep diving into quality: Motivation and information seeking among middle and high school students, Information Research, vol. 11, no. 4, paper 265, viewed 22 October 2009, <http://informationr.net/ir/11-4/paper265.html>.

Heinström, J & Todd, RJ 2006, 'Uncertainty and guidance: School students' feelings, study approaches, and need for help in inquiry projects', *Scan*, vol. 25, no. 3, pp. 28–35.

Henderson, A 1987, *The evidence continues to grow: Parent involvement improves student achievement*, annotated bibliography, National Committee for Citizens in Education, Columbia, MD.

Henderson, AT & Mapp, KL 2002, *A new wave of evidence: The impact of school, family, and community connections on student achievement*, Southwest Educational Development Laboratory, Austin, Texas.

Hesselbein, F & Goldsmith, M (eds) 2009, *The organizations of the future visions, strategies, and insights into managing in a new era*, Jossey-Bass, San Francisco.

Higginbottom, N & Packham, B 2007, *Student cracks government's $84m porn filter*, viewed 23 October 2009, <http://www.news.com.au/story/0,23599,22304224-2,00.html?from=public_rss>.

Hill, PW & Russell, VJ 1999, 'Systemic, whole-school reform of the middle school years of schooling', paper presented at the National Middle Years of Schooling Conference, Melbourne.

Hinduja, S & Patchin, J 2008, 'Cyberbullying: An exploratory analysis of factors related to offending and victimization', *Deviant Behaviour*, vol. 29, pp. 129–56.

Hinduja, S & Patchin, JW 2009, *Bullying beyond the schoolyard: Preventing and responding to cyberbullying*, Corwin Press, Thousand Oaks, California.

Holloway, S & Valentine, V 2003, *Cyberkids: Children in the Information Age*, Routledge, London.

Holmes, D & Russell, G 1999, 'Adolescent CIT use: Paradigm shifts for educational and cultural practices?', *British Journal of Sociology of Education*, vol. 20, no. 1, p. 10.

Horan, T 2001, 'Digital places: Design considerations for integrating electronic space with physical place', DISP, no. 144, pp. 12–19.

Horrigan, J 2008, *Seeding the cloud: What mobile access means for usage patterns and online content*, viewed 30 August 2009, <http://www.pewinternet.org/pdfs/PIP_Users.and.Cloud.pdf>.

Hull, G & Schultz, K 2001, 'Literacy and learning out of school: A review of theory and research', *Review of Educational Research*, vol. 71, pp. 575–611.

Husband, J 2008, Wirearchy: *Social architecture for the wired world*, viewed 23 October 2009, <http://www.wirearchy.com/>.

Huws, U 2007, *EU research in social sciences: Information society*, viewed 1 May 2009, <ftp://ftp.cordis.europa.eu/pub/citizens/docs/eur23167_final_en.pdf>.

Illinois Institute of Design (ID) 2007, *Schools in the digital age*, Illinois Institute of Technology, viewed 16 July 2008, http://www.id.iit.edu/635/documents/MacArthurFinalReport1.pdf.

Ingvarson, D & Gaffney, M 2008,'Developing and sustaining the digital education ecosystem: The value and possibilities of online environments for student learning', in M Lee and M Gaffney (eds), *Leading a digital school: Principles and practice*, ACER Press, Melbourne, pp. 146–67.

International Society for Technology in Education (ISTE) 2002, *NETS for Administrators 2002*, viewed 30 August 2009, <http://www.iste.org/Content/NavigationMenu/NETS/ForAdministrators/2002Standards/NETS_for_Administrators_2002_Standards.htm>.

International Society for Technology in Education (ISTE) 2007, *The ISTE National Educational Technology Standards (NETS•T) and Performance Indicators for Students*, viewed 23 October 2009, <http://www.iste.org/Content/NavigationMenu/NETS/ForStudents/2007Standards/NETS_for_Students_2007_Standards.pdf>.

International Society for Technology in Education (ISTE) 2008, *The ISTE National Educational Technology Standards (NETS•T) and Performance Indicators for Teachers*, viewed 30 August 2009, <http://www.iste.org/Content/NavigationMenu/NETS/ForTeachers/2008Standards/NETS_T_Standards_Final.pdf>.

International Society for Technology in Education (ISTE) 2009, *NETS for Administrators 2009*, viewed 30 August 2009, <http://www.iste.org/Content/NavigationMenu/NETS/ForAdministrators/2009Standards/NETS_for_Administrators_2009.htm>.

Internet Industry Association (IIA) 2009, *Stronger defence against cyber bullying*, IIA security portal, viewed 20 October 2009, <http://www.security.iia.net.au/index.php/media-centre/news-room/56-stronger-defence-against-cyber-bullying-28-may-2009.html>.

Internet World Statistics 2009, *Internet usage statistics: The Internet big picture*, viewed 19 September 2009, <http://www.internetworldstats.com/stats.htm>.

Ito, M, Horst, H, Bittani, M, Boyd, D, Herr-Stephenson, B, Lange, P, Pascoe, C, Robinson, L with Baumer, S, Cody, Martínez K, Perkel, D, Sims, C & Tripp, L 2008, *Living and learning with new media*, summary of findings from the Digital Youth Project, The John D. and Catherine T. Macarthur Foundation Reports on Digital Media and Learning, viewed 13 June September 2009, <http://digitalyouth.ischool.berkeley.edu/files/report/digitalyouth-WhitePaper.pdf>.

Jackson, L, von Eye, A, Biocca, F, Barbatsis, G, Zhao, Y & Fitzgerald, H 2006, 'Does home Internet use influence the academic performance of low-income children?', *Developmental Psychology*, vol. 42, no. 3, pp. 1–7.

Jamieson-Proctor, RM, Burnett, PC, Finger, G, & Watson, G 2006, 'ICT integration and teachers confidence in using ICT for teaching and learning in Queensland state schools', *Australasian Journal of Educational Technology*, vol. 22, no. 4, pp. 511–30.

Jamieson-Proctor, R & Finger, G 2008, 'ACT to improve ICT use for learning: A synthesis of studies of teacher confidence in using ICT in two Queensland schooling systems', proceedings of Computers in Education Conference 2008 (ACEC'08), Canberra.

Jenkins, H, with Clinton, K, Purushotma, R, Robinson, A & Weigel, M 2006, *Confronting the challenges of participatory culture: Media education for the 21st century*, viewed 20 May 2009, <http://digitallearning.macfound.org/atf/cf/%7B7E45C7E0-A3E0-4B89-AC9C-E807E1B0AE4E%7D/JENKINS_WHITE_PAPER.PDF>.

Jenkins, T 1997, 'Children squabble: It's a fact of life, not always a case for the helpline', paper presented at the Childhood and Friendship in a Fearful World Conference.

JISC 2008, *Innovative practice with e-Learning*, viewed 23 October 2009, <http://www.jisc.ac.uk/uploaded_documents/publication_txt.pdf>.

JISC 2009, *Innovation in the use of ICT for education and research*, viewed 23 October 2009, <http://www.jisc.ac.uk/>.

Johnson, GM & Bratt, SE 2009, 'Technology education students: e-Tutors for school children', *British Journal of Educational Technology*, vol. 40, no. 1, pp. 32–41.

Johnson, L, Levine, A & Smith, R 2009, *The Horizon Report: 2009*, The New Media Consortium, Texas.

Johnson, L, Levine, A, Smith, R, Smythe, T & Stone, S 2009, *The Horizon Report: 2009*, Australia New Zealand edition, viewed 23 October 2009, <http://www.nmc.org/pdf/2008-Horizon-Report-ANZ.pdf>.

Johnstone, B 2002, *Discourse analysis*, Blackwell Publishing, Oxford, UK.

Joinson, A 1998, 'Causes and effects of disinhibition on the Internet', in J Gackenbach (ed.), *The psychology of the Internet: Intrapersonal, interpersonal, and transpersonal implications*, Academic Press, New York, pp. 43–60.

Jonassen, D 2000, *Computers as mindtools for schools engaging critical thinking*, 2nd edn, Merrill Prentice Hall, Columbus, Ohio.

Jones, S 2009, *Middle school students caught in the middle*, Ning in Education, viewed 23 October 2009, <http://education.ning.com/profiles/blogs/middle-school-students-caught>.

Kaiser Family Foundation 2002, *See no evil: How internet filters affect the search for online health information*, Kaiser Family Foundation, viewed 3 March 2009, <http://www.kff.org/entmedia/20021210a-index.cfm>.

Kennedy, T, Smith, A, Wells, A & Wellman, B 2008, *Networked families*, viewed 25 February 2009, <http://www.pewinternet.org/pdfs/PIP_Networked_Family.pdf>.

Kent, N & Facer, K 2004, 'Different worlds? A comparison of young people's home and school ICT use', *Journal of Computer Assisted Learning*, vol. 20, pp. 440–55, viewed 1 May 2009, via Informit database.

Kent, N & Facer, K 2008, *How do boys and girls differ in their use of ICT?*, Becta, viewed 19 September 2009, <http://partners.becta.org.uk/upload-dir/downloads/page_documents/research/gender_ict_briefing.pdf>.

Kimber, K & Wyatt-Smith, C 2009, 'Valued knowledges and core capacities for digital learners: Claiming spaces for quality assessment', in A Burke & R Hammett (eds), *Assessing new literacies: Perspectives from the classroom*, Peter Lang Publishing, Canada, pp. 133–55.

Kitchen, S, Finch, S & Sinclair, R 2007, *Harnessing technology schools survey 2007*, Becta, viewed 16 July 2008, <http://partners.becta.org.uk/index.php?section=rh&catcode=_re_rp_02&rid=14110>.

Klopfer, E, Squire, K & Jenkins, H 2003, 'Augmented reality simulations on handheld computers', paper presented at the 2003 American Educational Research Association Conference, Chicago, IL.

Koehler, M & Mishra, P 2005, 'What happens when teachers design educational technology? The development of technological pedagogical content knowledge', *Journal of Educational Computing Research*, vol. 32, no. 2, pp. 131–52.

Koehler, M & Mishra, P 2008, 'Introducing TPCK', in AACTE Committee on Innovation and Technology (ed.), *Handbook of technological pedagogical content knowledge (TPCK) for educators*, Routledge/Taylor & Francis Group, New York, pp. 3–29.

Koehler, M, Mishra, P & Yahya, K 2007, 'Tracing the development of teacher knowledge in a design seminar: Integrating content, pedagogy and technology', *Computers & Education*, vol. 49, pp. 740–62.

Kotter, J & Rathberger, H 2006, *Our iceberg is melting*, St Martin's Press, New York.

Krathwohl, D 2002, 'A revision of Bloom's Taxonomy: An overview', *Theory into Practice*, Autumn, pp. 212–18.

Kraut, R, Patterson, M, Lundmark, V, Kiesler, S, Mukopadhyay, T & Scherlis, W 1998, 'Internet paradox: A social technology that reduces social involvement and psychological well-being?', *American Psychologist*, vol. 53, pp. 1017–31.

Kraut, R, Scherlis, W, Mukhopadhyay, T, Manning, J & Kiesler, S 1996, 'The HomeNet field trial of residential Internet services', *Communications of the ACM*, vol. 39, no. 12, pp. 55–63.

Kuhlemeier, H & Hemker, B 2005, 'The impact of computer use at home on students' internet skills', *Computers & Education*, vol. 49, no. 2, pp. 460–80.

Kuhlthau, C 2004, *Seeking meaning: A process approach to library and information services*, 2nd edn, Libraries Unlimited, Westport, Connecticut.

Kurti, A, Spikol, D & Milrad, M 2008, 'Bridging outdoors and indoors educational activities in schools with the support of mobile and positioning technologies', *International Journal of Mobile Learning and Organisation*, vol. 2, no. 2, pp. 166–86.

Kvavik, R 2005, 'Convenience, communications, and control: How students use technology', in D Oblinger & J Oblinger (eds), *Educating the Net Generation*, EDUCAUSE Center for Applied Research and University of Minnesota.

Lankes, RD 2008, 'Trusting the internet: new approaches to credibility tools', in M Metzger & A Flanagin (eds), *Digital media, youth and credibility*, The John D. and Catherine T. MacArthur Foundation Series on Digital Media and Learning, The MIT Press, Cambridge, MA, pp. 101–21.

Lankshear, C & Knobel, M 1997, 'Literacies, texts and difference in the electronic age', in C Lankshear (ed.), *Changing literacies*, Open University Press, Buckingham & Philadelphia, pp. 133–63.

Lankshear, C & Knobel, M 2003, *New literacies: Changing knowledge and classroom learning*, Open University Press, Buckingham, UK.

Lankshear, C & Knobel, M 2006, *New literacies: Everyday practices and classroom learning*, Open University Press, New York.

Large, A 2006, 'Children, teenagers and the web', *Annual Review of Information Science and Technology*, vol. 39, no. 1, pp. 347–92.

Lawler, ER & Worley, CG 2009, 'Designing organizations that are built to change', in F Hesselbein & M Goldsmith (eds), *The organizations of the future visions, strategies, and insights into managing in a new era*, Jossey-Bass, San Francisco, pp. 188–202.

Leander, K 2005, *Fieldnotes from the SYNchrony project*, Vanderbilt University, Nashville.

Lee, M 1995, 'Harnessing the power of the home', *The Practising Administrator*, vol. 17, no. 2.

Lee, M 1996a, 'The educated home', *The Practising Administrator*, vol. 18, no. 3.

Lee, M 1996b, 'Close the library: Open the information services unit', *The Practising Administrator*, vol. 2, p. 7.

Lee, M 2000, 'Chaotic learning: The learning style of the 'Net Generation', in G Hart (ed.), *Readings and resources in global online education*, Whirligig Press, Melbourne.

Lee, M 2004, The school 'Chief Information Officer': *Their centrality and importance*, ASLA Online I conference proceedings, May 2004, Australian School Library Association Inc., Zillmere, Qld.

Lee, M & Boyle, M 2003, *The educational effects and implications of the interactive whiteboard strategy of Richardson Primary School: A brief review*, viewed 16 July 2008, <http://www.richardsonps.act.edu.au/interactive_whiteboard_initiative>.

Lee, M & Gaffney, M (eds) 2008, *Leading a digital school: Principles and practice*, ACER Press, Melbourne.

Lee, M & Mitchell, P 2009, 'Rollercoaster: Education and online access', *Professional Educator*, vol. 8, no. 2, pp. 25–27.

Lee, M & Winzenried, A 2009, *The use of instructional technology in schools: Lessons to be learned*, ACER Press, Melbourne.

Leitch 2006, *Prosperity for all in the global economy: World class skills 2006*, viewed 1 July 2009, <http://webarchive.nationalarchives.gov.uk/+/http:/www.hm-treasury.gov.uk/d/leitch_finalreport051206.pdf>.

Lenhart, A, Kahne, J, Middaugh, E, Macgill, A, Evans, C & Vitak, J 2008, *Teens, video games and civics*, Pew Research Center, viewed 19 September 2009, <http://www.pewinternet.org/Reports/2008/Teens-Video-Games-and-Civics.aspx>.

Lenhart, A & Madden, M 2007, *Social networking websites and teens*, Pew Research Center, viewed 19 September 2009, <http://www.pewinternet.org/Reports/2007/Social-Networking-Websites-and-Teens.aspx>.

Lenhart, A, Madden, M, Smith, A & Macgill, A 2007, *Teens and social media*, Pew Research Center, viewed 16 January 2008, <http://www.pewinternet.org/Reports/2007/Teens-and-Social-Media.aspx>.

Leu, D Jr, Kinzer, C, Coiro, J & Cammack, D 2004, 'Towards a theory of new literacies emerging from the Internet and other information and communication technologies', in R Ruddell & N Unrau (eds), *Theoretical models and processes of reading*, International Reading Association, Newark, DE, pp. 1570–613.

Levin, D & Arafeh, S 2002, *The digital disconnect: The widening gap between Internet-savvy students and their schools*, Pew Research Center, viewed 23 October 2009, <http://www.pewinternet.org/Reports/2002/The-Digital-Disconnect-The-widening-gap-between-Internetsavvy-students-and-their-schools.aspx?r=1>.

Levin, T & Wadmany, R 2006, 'Listening to students' voices on learning with information technologies in a rich technology-based classroom', *Journal of Educational Computing Research*, vol. 34, no. 3, pp. 281–317.

Levine, H, Glass, G & Meister, G 1987, 'A cost-effectiveness analysis of computer assisted instruction', *Evaluation Review*, vol. 11, pp. 50–72.

Lewin, T 2009, 'In a digital future, textbooks are history', *The New York Times*, August 9, viewed 22 October 2009, <http://www.nytimes.com/2009/08/09/education/09textbook.html?_r=2&em>.

Lipnack, J & Stamps, J 1982, *Networking: The first report and directory*, Doubleday, New York.

Lipnack, J & Stamps, J 1988, *The networking book: People connecting with people*, Routledge, Kegan & Paul, New York.

Lipnack, J & Stamps, J 1994, *The age of the network: Organizing principles for the 21st century*, John Wiley & Sons, Inc., New York.

Lippincott, J 2006, 'Net Generation students and libraries', *EDUCAUSE Review*, March/April, p. 57.

Lipsett, A. 2009, 'Cyberbullying "affects 1 in 10 teachers"', *The Guardian*, 4 April 2009, viewed 20 October 2009, <http://www.guardian.co.uk/education/2009/apr/04/cyber-bullying-schools-teachers-survey>.

Livingstone, S 2002, *Challenges and dilemmas as children go on-line: Linking observational research in families to the emerging policy agenda*, 3rd annual dean's lecture, The Annenberg School for Communication, University of Pennsylvania, viewed 19 September 2009, <www.lse.ac.uk/collections/media@lse/pdf/AnnenbergLecture.pdf>.

Livingstone, S 2007, *UK Children go online: Balancing the opportunities against the risks*, MEDIA@ LSE Electronic Working Papers No. 10, viewed at <http://www.lse.ac.uk/collections/media@lse/study/pdf/EWP10_final.pdf>.

Livingstone, S & Bober, M 2005, *UK children go online*, final report of key project findings, viewed 20 October 2009, <www.lse.ac.uk/collections/children-go-online>.

Loertscher, D & Todd, R 2003, *We boost achievement: Evidence-based practice for school library media specialists*, Hi Willow Research & Publishing, Salt Lake City, Utah.

Lomas, C & Oblinger, D 2006, 'Student practices and their impact on learning spaces', in D Oblinger (ed.), *Learning spaces: An EDUCAUSE e-Book*, viewed 30 August 2009, <http://www.educause.edu/LearningSpaces>.

Lonsdale, M 2003, *Impact of school libraries on student achievement: A review of the research*, report for the Australian School Library Association, Australian Council for Educational Research, viewed 20 October 2009, <http://www.asla.org.au/research/research.pdf>.

Luo, J, Hilty, D, Worley, L & Yager, J 2006, 'Considerations in change management related to technology', *Academic Psychiatry*, vol. 30, no. 6, pp. 465–69.

McCaffrey, K 2006, *Destroying Avalon*, Fremantle Arts Centre Press, Fremantle.

McDougall, D 2003, 'From internet chats to international schoolgirl hunt', *The Scotsman*, 17 July, viewed 30 June 2004, <http://news.scotsman.com/shevaunpennington/From-internet-chats-to-international.2444412.jp>.

McGaw, B 2009, cited in *News Release: Cisco, Intel and Microsoft collaborate to improve education assessments*, 13 January 2009, viewed 20 October 2009, <http://www.atc21s.org/Assets/Files/de10c023-ead5-4ccf-8a08-cbb273bb14fb.pdf>.

MacGill, AR 2007, *Parent and teen Internet use*, Pew Research Center, viewed 19 September 2009, <http://www.pewinternet.org/Reports/2007/Parent-and-Teen-Internet-Use.aspx>.

McGonigal, J 2008, 'Why I love bees: A case study in collective intelligence gaming', in K Salen (ed.), *The ecology of games: Connecting youth, games, and learning*, The John D. and Catherine T. MacArthur Foundation Series on Digital Media and Learning, The MIT Press, Cambridge, MA, pp. 199–228.

Macintyre Latta, M, Buck, G & Beckenhauer, A 2007, 'Formative assessment requires artistic vision', *International Journal of Education & the Arts*, vol. 8, no. 4, pp. 1–22.

McWilliam, E & Haukka, S 2008, 'Educating the creative workforce: New directions for twenty-first century schooling', *British Educational Research Journal*, vol. 34, no. 5, pp. 651–66.

Madrid, J n.d., *Why technology is failing in public schools*, video presentation, viewed 27 September 2009, <http://www.slideshare.net/jamadrid/why-technology-is-failling-in-public-schools?>.

Maher, D 2008, 'Cyberbullying: An ethnographic case study of one Australian upper primary school class', *Youth Studies Australia*, vol. 27, no. 4, pp. 32–39.

Mandry, RL, Inkpen, KM, Bilezikjian, M, Klemmer, SR & Landay, JA 2001, *Supporting children's collaboration across handheld computers*, paper presented at the Conference on Human Factors in Computing Systems, Seattle, WA.

Marsh, J 2004, 'The techno-literacy practices of young children', *Journal of Early Childhood Research*, vol. 2, pp. 51–66.

Mason, KL 2008, 'Cyberbullying: A preliminary assessment for school personnel', *Psychology in the Schools*, vol. 45, no. 4, pp. 323–48.

Mazalin, D & Moore, S 2004, 'Internet use, identity development and social anxiety among young adults', *Behaviour Change*, vol. 21, no. 2, pp. 90–102.

Megalogenis, G 2009, 'Cost of mobiles hits home', *The Australian*, 21 September 2009, p. 1.

Meredyth, D, Russell, N, Blackwood, L, Thomas, J & Wise, P 1998, *Real time: Computers, change and schooling*, Department of Education, Training and Youth Affairs, Canberra, viewed 30 August 2009, <http://www.dest.gov.au/archive/schools/Publications/1999/realtime.pdf>.

Metzger, M & Flanagin, A (eds) 2008, *Digital media, youth, and credibility*, The John D. and Catherine T. MacArthur Foundation Series on Digital Media and Learning, MIT Press, Cambridge, MA.

Microsoft 2009, *Microsoft Office SharePoint Server 2007*, viewed 30 August 2009, <http://www.microsoft.com/Sharepoint/default.mspx>.

Millar, J & Jagger, N 2001, *Women in ITEC courses and careers*, Department of Education and Skills, London.

Ministerial Council on Education, Employment, Training and Youth Affairs (MCEETYA) 1999, *The Adelaide Declaration on National Goals for Schooling in the Twenty-first Century*, viewed 9 October 2009, <http://www.dest.gov.au/sectors/school_education/policy_initiatives_reviews/national_goals_for_schooling_in_the_twenty_first_century.htm>.

Ministerial Council on Education, Employment, Training and Youth Affairs (MCEETYA) 2007, *National Assessment Program: ICT literacy Years 6 and 10 Report*, 2005, viewed 4 July 2008, <http://www.curriculum.edu.au/verve/_resources/NAP_ICTL_2005_Years_6_and_10_Report.pdf>.

Ministerial Council on Education, Employment, Training and Youth Affairs (MCEETYA) 2008, *Melbourne Declaration on Educational Goals for Young Australians*, viewed 11 April 2009, <http://www.curriculum.edu.au/mceetya/melbourne_declaration,25979.html>.

Mishra, P & Koehler, M 2006, 'Technological pedagogical content knowledge: A framework for teacher knowledge', *Teachers College Record*, vol. 108, no. 6, pp. 1017–54.

Mistry, P, Maes, P & Chang, L 2009, 'WUW—Wear Ur World: A wearable gestural interface', in proceedings of the 27th international conference Extended Abstracts on Human Factors in Computing Systems, Boston, USA, pp. 4111–116, viewed 23 October 2009, <http://portal.acm.org/citation.cfm?doid=1520340.1520626>.

Moodle 2009, *Welcome to the Moodle community!*, Moodle, viewed 30 August 2009, <http://moodle.org/>.

Morris, E 2009, *Independent review of ICT user skills*, viewed 1 July 2009, <http://www.dius.gov.uk/~/media/publications/I/ict_user_skills>.

Moyle, K 2006, 'Leadership and learning with ICT. Voices from the profession: What Australian school leaders say', in E Pearson & P Bohman (eds), *Proceedings of World Conference on Educational Multimedia, Hypermedia and Telecommunications 2006*, EdITlib/AAVE, Chesapeake, VA, pp. 89–96, viewed 16 July 2008, <http://www.editlib.org/p/22999>.

Moyle, K 2009, *Varying approaches to Internet safety: The role of filters*, viewed 19 September 2009, <www.cosn.org/.../Varying%20Approaches%20to%20Internet%20Safety.pdf>.

Murray, J 1999, 'An inclusive school library for the 21st century: Fostering independence', paper presented at the 65th IFLA Council and General Conference, Bangkok, Thailand, 20–28 August 1999.

Nair, P & Gehling, A 2007, 'Foreword', in S La Marca (ed.), *Rethink!: Ideas for inspiring school library design*, School Library Association of Victoria, Carlton, pp. 5–6.

Naisbitt, J 1984, *Megatrends*, Futura, London.

Naismith, L, Lonsdale, P, Vavoula, G & Sharples, M 2004, *Mobile technologies and learning*, report 11, Futurelab, viewed 19 September 2009, <http://www.futurelab.org.uk/resources/publications-reports-articles/literature-reviews/Literature-Review203/>.

Nalder, J 2009, *The dawn of uLearning: Near-future directions for 21st century educators*, abstract, Scribd, viewed 20 October 2009, <http://www.scribd.com/doc/12398804/The-dawn-of-uLearning-Jonathan-Nalder-Masters-thesis>.

National Curriculum Board 2009, *The shape of the Australian curriculum*, National Curriculum Board, viewed 19 June 2009, <http://www.ncb.org.au/verve/_resources/Shape_of_the_Australian_Curriculum.pdf>.

National Geographic Society 2007a, *My wonderful world*, National Geographic Society, viewed 30 August 2009, <http://www.mywonderfulworld.org/index.html>.

National Geographic Society 2007b, *My wonderful world—Parents: Welcome*, National Geographic Society, viewed 30 August 2009, <http://www.mywonderfulworld.org/parents_welcome.html>.

Neal, G 2008, 'Meaningful learning with ICT in the middle-years', in N Yelland, G Neal & E Dakich (eds), *Rethinking education with ICT*, Sense Publishers, Rotterdam, The Netherlands, pp. 79–109.

Newhouse, PC 2008, 'Transforming schooling with support from portable computing', *Australian Educational Computing*, vol. 23, no. 3, pp. 19–23.

Newhouse, P, Clarkson, B & Trinidad, S 2005, 'A framework for leading school change in using ICT', in S Trinidad and J Pearson (eds), *Using ICT in education: Leadership, change and models of best practice*, Pearson Education Asia, Singapore, pp. 148–64.

New Paradigm Global Media Survey 2007, *77% of the world's online youth would rather live without TV than live without the Internet*, CNW Group, viewed 4 May 2009, <http://www.newswire.ca/en/releases/archive/July2007/11/c5356.html>.

New Zealand Ministry of Education 2005, *Making a bigger difference for all students: Hangaia he huarahi hei whakarewa ake i nga tauira katao: Schooling Strategy 2005–2010*, Ministry of Education, Wellington.

Next Generation Learning 2009, *Computer and Internet packages: The choice is yours!*, Home Access, Becta viewed 1 July 2009, <http://www.nextgenerationlearning.org.uk/Home-Access/Computer-and-internet-packages/>.

Norris, P 2001, *Digital divide: Civic engagement, information poverty, and the Internet worldwide*, Cambridge University Press, New York.

NSBA 2008, *2008 T+L Conference annual survey: Technology use in your district*, viewed 19 September 2009, <http://vocuspr.vocus.com/VocusPr30/Newsroom/ViewAttachment.aspx?SiteName=NSBANew&Entity=PRAsset&AttachmentType=F&EntityID=111140&AttachmentID=1fc6c388-7ab5-4f8e-a04d-92d6a544c894>.

Obama, B 2009, *Organizing for America*, viewed 23 October 2009, <http://www.barackobama.com/index.php>.

Oblinger, DG (ed.) 2006, *Learning spaces*, Educause, Washington, DC, available from <http://www.educause.edu/LearningSpaces>.

Oblinger, DG & Oblinger, JL 2006, *Educating the Net Generation*, Educause, viewed 16 July 2008, <http://www.educause.edu/educatingthenetgen>.

Oden, RA Jr, Temple, DB, Cottrell, JR, Griggs, RK, Turney, GW & Wojcik, FM 2001, 'Merging library and computing services at Kenyon College: A progress report', *EDUCAUSE Quarterly Articles*, no. 4, viewed 20 October 2009, <http://www.educause.edu/ir/library/pdf/EQM0141.pdf>.

Office of Communications 2006, *Harm and offence in media content: Updating the 2005 review*, viewed 23 October 2009, <http://www.ofcom.org.uk/research/telecoms/reports/byron/annex6.pdf>.

Office of Communications 2008, *Social networking: A quantitative and qualitative research report into attitudes, behaviours and use,* Ofcom, viewed 23 October 2009 <http://www.ofcom. org.uk/advice/media_literacy/medlitpub/medlitpubrss/socialnetworking/report.pdf>.

O'Neill, G, Moore, S, McMullin, B (eds) 2005, *Emerging issues in the practice of university learning and teaching,* AISHE, Dublin.

Online Computer Library Center Inc. (OCLC) 2005, *Perceptions of libraries and information resources. A report to the OCLC membership,* OCLC, viewed 20 October 2009, <http:// www.oclc.org/reports/2005perceptions.htm>.

Organisation for Economic Co-operation and Development (OECD) 2007, *PISA 2006: Science competencies for tomorrow's world,* viewed 22 March 2009, <http://www.oecd.org/ dataoecd/30/17/39703267.pdf>.

Organisation for Economic Co-operation and Development (OECD) 2009, *Households with access to the Internet in selected OECD Countries,* viewed 22 July 2009, <http://www.oecd. org/sti/ICTindicators>.

Outlook 1914, 20 June 1914, p. 185.

Owen, S & Moyle, K 2008, *Students' voices: Learning with technologies; Students' expectations about learning with technologies: A literature review,* viewed 30 August 2009, <http://www. aictec.edu.au/aictec/webdav/site/standardssite/shared/Learner_Research_Literature_ Review.pdf>.

Parenting Australia 2009, *Bullying bigger fear than binge drinking for Australian parents,* Parenting Australia, viewed 23 October 2009, <http://www.parentingaustralia.com. au/.../227-bullying-bigger-fear-than-binge-drinking-for-australian-parents>.

Parr, JM & Ward, L 2004, *Evaluation of the digital opportunities project Far Net: Learning communities in the Far North,* Ministry of Education, Wellington, New Zealand.

Parsad, B, Jones, J & Greene B 2005, *Internet access in U.S. public schools and classrooms: 1994– 2003,* viewed 27 February 2009, <http://docs.ksu.edu.sa/PDF/Articles11/Article110232. pdf>.

Partnerships for 21st Century Skills 2009a, *21st Century learning environments: White paper,* Partnerships for 21st Century Skills viewed 19 June 2009, <http://www.21stcenturyskills. org/documents/le_white_paper-1.pdf>.

Partnerships for 21st Century Skills, 2009b, *P21 Framework definitions explained: White paper,* Partnerships for 21st Century Skills viewed 19 June 2009, <http://www.21stcenturyskills. org/documents/p21_framework_definitions_052909.pdf>.

Partnerships for 21st Century Skills 2009c, *Framework for 21st century learning,* Partnerships for 21st Century Skills viewed 19 September 2009, <http://www.21stcenturyskills.org/ index.php?option=com_content&task=view&id=254&Itemid=120>.

Passey, D 2005, *Aston pride ICT project phase 1: Evaluation report on the 'ICT in the home pilot' in Prince J/I School,* Lancaster University, viewed 19 September 2009, <http://www.bgfl.org/ bgfl/custom/files_uploaded/uploaded_resources/12590/Evaluation.doc>.

Passey, D & Rogers, C, with Machell, J & McHugh, G 2004, *The motivational effect of ICT on pupils*, DfES, viewed 19 September 2009, <http://www.dfes.gov.uk/research/data/uploadfiles/RR523new.pdf>.

Patchin, J 2009a, *Re: Cyberbullying legislation: Clarification of my position and invitation to participate*, blogpost 19 May, viewed 23 October 2009, <http://cyberbullying.us/blog/>.

Patchin, J 2009b, Re: *Public radio discussion on proposed cyberbullying legislation*, blogpost 13 May, viewed 23 October 2009, <http://cyberbullying.us/blog/>.

Patten, KB & Craig, DV 2007, 'Ipods and English-language learners: A great combination', *Teacher Librarian*, vol. 34, no. 5, pp. 40–44.

PBS Teachers 2008, *Lori Drew convicted in Megan Meier case*, viewed 1 October 2009, PBS Teachers, <http://www.pbs.org/teachers/learning.now/2008/12/lori_drew_convicted_in_megan_m.html>.

Pearson Education 2008, *Survey*, Pearson, viewed 23 October 2009, <www.pearsonschoolsystem.com/survey>.

People's Daily Online 2008, 'Huawei, Symantec launch storage, Internet safety joint venture', People's Daily Online, 18 February, viewed 4 March 2009, <http://english.peopledaily.com.cn/90001/90776/6356167.html>.

Perelman, L 1992, *School's out*, Avon Books, New York.

Pesce, M 2009, *Web of secrecy*, ABC, viewed 20 October 2009, <http://www.abc.net.au/unleashed/stories/s2521717.htm>.

Peters, T 1987, *Thriving on chaos: Handbook for the Management Revolution*, Alfred Knopf, New York.

Pines, S 2007, 'Foreword', in EE Gordon, RR Morgan, CJ O'Malley & J Ponticell (eds), *The tutoring revolution: Applying research for best practices, policy implications, and student achievement*, Rowman and Littlefield, Lanham, MD.

Porter, B 2002, 'Grappling's technology and learning spectrum', in B Porter (ed.), *MAPPing tools for organizing and assessing technology for student results*, viewed 22 October 2009, <http://www.bjpconsulting.com/products/grappling2002/spectrum.html>.

Prensky, M 2001, 'Digital natives, digital immigrants', *On the Horizon*, vol. 9, no. 5, p. 6.

Prensky, M 2006, *Don't bother me Mum, I'm learning*, Paragon House, St Paul, Minnesota.

Prime Minister's Science, Engineering and Innovation Council 2005, *Imagine Australia: The role of creativity in the innovation economy*, viewed 23 October 2009, <http://www.dest.gov.au/NR/rdonlyres/B1EF82EF-08D5-427E-B7E4-69D41C61D495/8625/finalPMSEICReport_WEBversion.pdf>.

Project Tomorrow 2008, *Leadership in the 21st Century: The new visionary administrator*, Blackboard, viewed 19 September 2009, <http://www.blackboard.com/K12/education21c>.

Project Tomorrow 2009a, Learning in the 21st Century: *Parents' Perspectives, Parents' Priorities*, Blackboard/Project Tomorrow, viewed 19 September 2009, <http://www.blackboard.com/Solutions-by-Market/K-12/Learn-for-K12/Leadership-Views/Education-in-the-21st-Century.aspx>.

Project Tomorrow 2009b, *Selected National Findings: Speak Up 2008 for Students*, Teachers, Parents and Administrators, Speak Up/Project Tomorrow, viewed 19 June 2009, <http://www.tomorrow.org/speakup/pdfs/SU08_findings_final_mar24.pdf>.

Pushor, D 2007, *Parent engagement: Creating a shared world*, viewed 30 August 2009, <http://www.edu.gov.on.ca/eng/research/pushor.pdf>.

Q Magazine 2009, July, p. 80.

Queensland Government 2005, Smart *Queensland: Smart state strategy 2005–2015*, viewed 1 May 2009, <http://www.smartstate.qld.gov.au/strategy/ strategy05_15/world.shtm>.

Rainie, L & Anderson, J 2008, *The future of the Internet III*, Pew Research Center, viewed 3 March 2009, <http://www.pewinternet.org/Reports/2008/The-Future-of-the-Internet-III.aspx>.

Ramaley, J & Zia, L 2005, 'The real versus the possible: Closing the gaps in engagement and learning', in D Oblinger & J Oblinger (eds), *Educating the Net Generation*, EDUCAUSE Center for Applied Research and University of Minnesota.

Reynolds, D, Treharne, D & Tripp, H 2003, 'ICT—the hopes and the reality', *British Journal of Educational Technology*, vol. 34, no. 2, pp. 151–67.

Reynolds, J 2006, *Parents' involvement in their children's learning and schools. How should their responsibilities relate to the role of the state?*, Family and Planning Institute, UK.

Rigby, K 2007, *Bullying in schools and what to do about it*, ACER Press, Melbourne.

Roberts, D, Foehr, U & Rideout, V 2005, *Generation M: Media in the lives of 8–18 year olds*, a Kaiser Family Foundation Study, viewed 30 August 2009, <http://www.kff.org/entmedia/upload/Generation-M-Media-in-the-Lives-of-8-18-Year-olds-Report.pdf>.

Roblyer, MD & Doering, AH 2009, *Integrating educational technology into teaching*, 5th edn, Pearson, Boston.

Rogers, Y, Price, S, Fitzpatrick, G, Fleck, R, Harris, E, Smith H, Randell, C, Muller, H, O'Malley, C, Stanton, D, Thompson, M & Weal, M 2004, *Ambient wood: Designing new forms of digital argumentation for learning outdoors*, proceedings of the 2004 Conference on Interaction Design and Children: Building the Community, ACM, Maryland, 1–3 June.

Rohrbeck, C, Ginsburg-Block, M, Fantuzzo, J & Miller, T 2003, 'Peer-assisted learning interventions with elementary school students: A meta-analytic review', *Journal of Educational Psychology*, vol. 95, pp. 240–57.

Rowlands, I & Nicholas, D 2008, *Information behaviour of the researcher of the future*, CIBER Briefing Paper, UCL, viewed 20 October 2009, <http://www.bl.uk/news/pdf/googlegen.pdf>.

Rowntree, D 1977, *Assessing students: How shall we know them?* Harper & Row, London.

Saettler, P 1990, *The evolution of American educational technology*, Information Age Publishing, Connecticut.

Sanders, MG 1997, *Building effective school–family–community partnerships in a large urban school district*, Report No. 13, Center for Research on the Education of Students Placed at Risk, Baltimore, MD.

Sanders, M & Epstein, J 1998, 'School-family-community partnerships and educational change: International perspectives', in A Hargreaves (ed.), *Extending Educational Change*, vol. 2, Springer, New York, pp. 202–24.

Saulwick, I & Muller, D 1998, *What parents want from their children's education in independent schools*, AISV, viewed 23 October 2009, <http://www.isca.edu.au/html/PDF/what_parents_want.pdf>.

Saulwick Muller Social Research 2006, *Family–School Partnerships Project: A qualitative and quantitative study*, Department of Education, Science & Training, Australian Council of State School Organisations and Australian Parents Council, Canberra.

Schibsted, E 2005, 'Way beyond fuddy-duddy: Good things happen when the library is the place kids want to be', *Edutopia Magazine*, 26 September 2005, viewed 20 October 2009, <http://www.edutopia.org/design>.

Schmitt, J & Wadsworth, J 2004, *Is there an impact of household computer ownership on children's educational attainment in Britain?*, CEP discussion paper no. 625, viewed 19 September 2009, <http://cep.lse.ac.uk/pubs/download/dp0625.pdf>.

Schön, D 1987, *Educating the reflective practitioner*, Jossey-Bass, San Francisco.

Schrum, L, Thompson, A, Maddux, C, Sprague, D, Bull, G & Bell, L 2007, 'Editorial: Research on the effectiveness of technology in schools: The roles of pedagogy and content', *Contemporary Issues in Technology and Teacher Education*, vol. 7, no. 1, pp. 456–60, viewed 30 August 2009, <http://www.citejournal.org/articles/v7i1editorial1.pdf>.

Scrimshaw, P 2004, *Enabling teachers to make successful use of ICT*, Becta, viewed 19 September 2009, <http://partners.becta.org.uk/page_documents/research/enablers.pdf>.

Selwyn, N 2006, 'Exploring the "digital disconnect" between net-savvy students and their schools', *Learning, Media and Technology*, vol. 31, no. 1, pp. 5–17.

Shanahan, D & Rowbotham, J 2007, 'Howard on internet porn crusade', *The Australian*, 10 August 2007, viewed 19 September 2009, <http://www.australianit.news.com.au/story/0,24897,22218715-15306,00.html>.

Shariff, S 2008, *Cyber-bullying: Issues and solutions for the school, the classroom and the home*, Routledge Taylor & Francis Group, New York.

Shariff, S & Hoff, DL 2007, 'Cyber bullying: Clarifying legal boundaries for school supervision in cyberspace', *International Journal of Cyber Criminology*, vol. 1, no. 1, pp. 76–118, viewed 23 October 2009, <http://www.cybercrimejournal.co.nr/>.

Sheldon, S 2003, 'Linking school-family community partnerships in urban elementary schools to student achievement on state tests', *The Urban Review*, vol. 25, no. 2, pp. 149–165.

Shirky, C 2008, *Here comes everybody: Organizing without organizations*, Penguin, New York.

Shirky, C 2009, *Clay Shirky's writings about the Internet*, viewed 23 October 2009, <http://www.shirky.com/>.

Shulman, L 1987, 'Knowledge and teaching: Foundations of the new reform', *Harvard Educational Review*, vol. 57, no. 1, pp. 1–22.

Siemens, G 2008, *New structures and spaces of learning: The systemic impact of connective knowledge, connectivism, and networked learning*, viewed 30 August 2009, <http://elearnspace.org/Articles/systemic_impact.htm>.

Silva, E 2008, *Measuring skills for the 21st century*, Education Sector Reports, viewed 19 September 2009, <http://www.educationsector.org/usr_doc/MeasuringSkills.pdf>.

Silverstone, R & Hirsch, E (eds) 2004, *Consuming technologies: Media and information in domestic spaces*, Routledge, London.

Sinnerton, J 2009, 'Childhood innocence caught in a sinister web: Parents get the call to educate naive teens about the dark side of technology', *The Sunday Mail*, 24 May 2009, pp. 50–51.

Snyder, I n.d., *New literacies for the twenty-first century: From page to screen*, Connected Learning: The Learning Technologies in Schools Conference, Melbourne.

Snyder, I, Wise, L, North, S & Bulfin, S 2008, *Being digital—in school, home and community*, Monash University, Melbourne.

Solomon, G & Schrum, L 2007, Web 2.0: *New tools, new schools*, International Society for Education in Technology (ISTE), Eugene, OR.

Somekh, B, Underwood, J, Convery, A, Dillon, G, Lewin, C, Mavers, D, Saxon, D & Woodrow, D 2005, *Evaluation of the DfES ICT Test Bed Project: Annual Report 2004*, viewed 19 September 2009, <http://www.evaluation.icttestbed.org.uk/files/ict_test_bed_evaluation_2004.pdf>.

Stanton, R 2003, 'Toward supported "communities of interest" in digital environments', in *Emerging visions for access in the twenty-first century library: Proceedings of a conference*, Council on Library and Information Resources, Washington, DC, August, pp. 33–43, viewed 20 October 2009, <http://www.clir.org/pubs/reports/pub119/pub119.pdf#page=39>.

Statistics New Zealand 2007, *Household use of Information and Communications Technology: 2006*, viewed 16 July 2008, <http://www.stats.govt.nz/browse_for_stats/industry_sectors/information_technology_and_communications/HouseholdUseofInformationandCommunicationTechnology_HOTP06.aspx>.

Steinkuehler, C & King, E 2009, 'Digital literacies for the disengaged: Creating after school contexts to support boys' game-based literacy skills', *On the Horizon*, vol. 17, no. 1, pp. 47–59.

Stephen, C, McPake, J, Plowman, L & Berch-Heyman, S 2008, 'Learning from the children: Exploring preschool children's encounters with ICT at home', *Journal of Early Childhood Research*, vol. 6, no. 2, pp. 99–117.

Stern, S 2008, 'Producing sites, exploring identities: Youth online authorship', in D Buckingham (ed.), *Youth, identity, and digital media*, The John D. and Catherine T. MacArthur Foundation Series on Digital Media and Learning, The MIT Press, Cambridge, MA, pp. 95-118, viewed 10 January 2008, <http://www.mitpressjournals.org/doi/pdfplus/10.1162/dmal.9780262524834.095>.

Strauss, A & Corbin, J 1998, *Basics of qualitative research*, 2nd edn, Sage, Thousand Oaks, CA.

Subrahmanyam, K, Greenfield, P, Kraut, R & Gross, E 2001, 'The impact of computer use on children's and adolescents' development', *Applied Developmental Psychology*, vol. 22, no. 1, pp. 7–30.

Suggett, D 2007, *21st century learning: Curriculum and assessment policy in Victoria, Australia*, Shanghai Education Commission Forum, viewed 19 June 2009, <http://www.eduweb.vic.gov.au/edulibrary/public/publ/research/publ/21C_Learning-Curriculum_and_Assessment_Policy_in_Victoria-Paper.pdf>.

Suler, J 2004, 'The online disinhibition effect', *Cyber Psychology and Behaviour*, vol. 7, no. 3, pp. 321–26.

Sullivan, K, Cleary, M & Sullivan, G 2004, *Bullying in secondary schools: What it looks like and how to manage it*, Paul Chapman Publishing, London.

Sunday Mail 2009, 'iPod: The little machine that changed music forever', 24 May 2009, p. 53.

Sutherland, R, Facer, K & Furlong, J 2000, 'A new environment for education? The computer in the home', *Computers & Education*, Special Edition, vol. 34, pp. 195–212.

Sutton, L 2005, 'Experiences of high school students conducting term paper research using filtered internet access', PhD Thesis, Graduate School of Wayne State University, viewed 22 October 2006, via http://digitalcommons.wayne.edu/dissertations/AAI3166752/

Synovate 2008, *Synovate EMS Digital Life survey shows highly varied multi-tasking media consumption amongst the elite Europeans*, viewed 23 October 2009, <http://www.synovate.com/news/article/2008/09/synovate-ems-digital-life-survey-shows-highly-varied-multi-tasking-media-consumption-amongst-the-elite-europeans.html>.

Syvänen, A, Beale, R, Sharples, M, Ahonen, M & Lonsdale, P 2005, 'Supporting pervasive learning environments: Adaptability and context awareness in mobile learning', proceedings from the Third IEEE International Workshop on Wireless and Mobile Technologies in Education, Tokushima, Japan.

Szoka, B & Thierer, A 2009, 'Cyberbullying legislation: Why education is preferable to regulation', *Progress on Point*, vol. 16, no. 12, pp. 1–26, viewed 20 October 2009, <http://www.pff.org/issues-pubs/pops/2009/pop16.12-cyberbullying-education-better-than-regulation.pdf>.

Tabs, ED 2003, *Internet access in US public schools and classrooms*, NCES, Washington.

Tapscott, D 1996, *The digital economy: Promise and peril in the age of Networked Intelligence*, McGraw Hill, New York.

Tapscott, D 1998, *Growing up digital: The rise of the Net Generation*, McGraw Hill, New York.

Tesch, R 1990, *Qualitative research: Analysis types and software tools*, Falmer Press, New York.

Thomas, J, Ewing, S & Schiessl, J 2008, *CCi Digital Futures Report: The Internet in Australia*, ARC Centre of Excellence for Creative Industries and Innovation, Swinburne University of Technology.

Thompson, RA 2009, personal communication, 5 March.

Timperley, H & Robinson VMJ 2002, *Partnership: Focusing the relationship on the task of school improvement*, NZCER, Wellington.

Todd, RJ 2007, 'Evidence-based practice and school libraries' (ch. 4), in S Hughes-Hassell & VH Harada (eds), *School reform and the school library media specialist*, Libraries Unlimited, Westport Connecticut, pp. 57–78.

Tondeur, J, van Keer, H, van Braak, J & Valcke, M 2008, 'ICT integration in the classroom: Challenging the potential of school policy', *Computers & Education*, vol. 51, pp. 212–23.

Trilling, B 2009, *Report: Reinvent schools for digital age*, eSchool News, viewed 14 October 2009, <http://www.eschoolnews.com/resources/building-a-cost-effective-digital-classroom/building-a-cost-effective-digital-classroom-articles/index.cfm?rc=1&i=56922>.

Trolley, BC, Hanel, C & Shields, L 2006, *Demystifying and deescalating cyber bullying in the schools: A resource guide for counselors, educators, and parents*, Booklocker.com, Inc, Bangor, ME.

Turkle, S 1995, *Life on the screen: Identity in the age of the Internet*, Simon & Schuster, New York.

Turow, J 1999, *The Internet and the family: The view from the parents, the view from the press*, Report No. 27, Annenberg Public Policy Center of the University of Pennsylvania, Philadelphia.

Unmuth, KL 2009, 'Keller's Trinity Meadows Intermediate School fifth-graders use cellphones as classroom computer', *The Dallas Morning News*, 20 February, viewed 4 March 2009, <http://www.dallasnews.com/sharedcontent/dws/dn/education/stories/DN-schoolphones_20met.ART.State.Edition1.4c6afb9.html>.

USC Annenberg School for Communication 2004, *Surveying the digital future*, Center for the Digital Future, University of Southern California, viewed 16 July 2008, <http://www.digitalcenter.org/pdf/DigitalFutureReport-Year4-2004.PDF>.

USC Annenberg School for Communication 2008, *Digital Future report*, Center for the Digital Future, University of Southern California, viewed 16 July 2008, <http://www.digitalcenter.org/pages/current_report.asp?intGlobalId=19>.

Usher, I 2009, 'Five ways to use your VLE/LP to support homework', *Changing the game?*, available from <http://moodlea.blogspot.com/2009/06/five-ways-to-use-your-vle-lp-to-support.html>.

Valentine, G, Marsh, J & Pattie, C 2005, *Children and young people's home use of ICT for educational purposes: The impact on attainment at key stages 1–4*, viewed 28 February 2009, <www.dcsf.gov.uk/research/data/uploadfiles/RR672.pdf>.

Valenza, J 2003, 'A letter to parents about the Internet', *Library Media Connection*, vol. 22, no. 3, pp. 30–31.

Valenza, JK 2005/2006, 'The virtual library', *Educational Leadership*, Dec/Jan, pp. 54–59.

Van Alstyne, M 1997, 'The state of network organization: A survey in three frameworks', *Journal of Organizational Computing*, vol. 7, no. 3, pp. 88–151, viewed 19 September 2009, <http://ccs.mit.edu/papers/CCSWP192/CCSWP192.html>.

Vancouver Sun 2008, 'District wakes up from laptop dream', 26 May, p. 1.

Vekiri, I & Chronaki, A 2008, 'Gender issues in technology use: Perceived social support, computer self-efficacy and value beliefs, and computer use beyond school', *Computers & Education*, vol. 51, pp. 1392–404.

Victorian Education and Training Committee 2006, *Final report: Education in the net age—new needs and new tools*, report on the inquiry into the effects of television and multimedia on education in Victoria, viewed 1 May 2009, <http://www.parliament.vic.gov.au/etc/reports/multimedia/Prelims.pdf>.

Villa-Boas, A 1993, *The effect of parent involvement in homework on student achievement*, Unidad, Winter, Issue 2, Baltimore Center on Families, Communities, and Children's Learning, John Hopkins University.

Wang, J, Iannotti, RJ & Nansel, T R 2009, 'School bullying among adolescents in the United States: Physical, verbal, relational, and cyber', *Journal of Adolescent Health*, vol. 45, no. 4, pp. 368–75.

Wang RR 2006 'Yinyang (Yin-yang)', in J Fieser & B Dowden (eds), *The Internet Encyclopedia of Philosophy (IEP)*, viewed 10 September 2009 <http://www.iep.utm.edu/yinyang/>.

Warlick, D 2009, 'Grow your personal learning network: New technologies can keep you connected and help you manage information overload', *Learning & Leading with Technology*, vol. 36, no. 6, pp. 12–16.

Warner, D & Raiter, M 2005, 'Social context in massively-multiplayer online games (MMOGs): Ethical questions in a shared space', *International Journal of Information Ethics*, vol. 4, pp. 46–52.

Wartella, E & Jennings, N 2000, 'Children and computers: New technology—old concerns', *The Future of Children—Children and Computer Technology*, vol. 10, no. 2, pp. 31–43.

Washington Post 2009, video, viewed 28 May 2009, <http://www.washingtonpost.com/wp-dyn/content/video/2009/05/26/VI2009052602555.html?wpisrc=newsletter>.

Wellington, J 2001, 'Exploring the secret garden: The growing importance of ICT in the home', *British Journal of Educational Technology*, vol. 32, no. 2, pp. 233–44.

Wesch, M 2007, *A vision of students today*, video, YouTube, viewed 19 September 2009, <http://www.youtube.com/watch?v=dGCJ46vyR9o>.

Wikipedia 2009a, *Collaborative Networked Learning*, viewed 21 May 2009, <http://en.wikipedia.org/wiki/Collaborative_Networked_Learning>.

Wikipedia 2009b, *Virtual Learning Environment*, Wikipedia, viewed 18 September 2009, <http://en.wikipedia.org/wiki/Virtual_learning_environment>.

Wikipedia 2009c, *Videocassette recorder*, Wikipedia, viewed 14 October 2009, <http://en.wikipedia.org/wiki/Videocassette_recorder>.

Wikipedia 2009d, *iPod*, Wikipedia, viewed 6 March 2009, <http://en.wikipedia.org/wiki/IPod>.

Wikipedia 2009e, *History of video games* 2009, Wikipedia, viewed 4 March 2009, <http://en.wikipedia.org/wiki/History_of_video_games>.

Wikipedia 2009f, *Facebook*, Wikipedia, viewed 13 March 2009, <http://en.wikipedia.org/wiki/Facebook>.

Wikipedia 2009g, *John Gilmore (Activist)*, Wikipedia, viewed 20 October 2009, <http:en.wikipedia.org/wiki/John_Gilmore_(activist)>.

Wikipedia 2009h, *Griefer*, Wikipedia, viewed 23 October 2009, <http://en.wikipedia.org/wiki/Griefer>.

Wikipedia 2009i, *Global Internet usage*, Wikipedia, viewed 2 July 2009, <http://en.wikipedia.org/wiki/Global_internet_usage>.

Wikipedia 2009j, *Network-centric organization*, Wikipedia, viewed 25 February 2009, <http://en.wikipedia.org/wiki/Network-centric_organization>.

Wikipedia 2009k, *Social network service*, Wikipedia, viewed 4 March 2009, <http://en.wikipedia.org/wiki/Social_networking>.

Willard, N 2005, 'Cyberbullying and cyberthreats', paper presented at the Office of Safe and Drug Free Schools National Conference, Washington.

Willard, N 2007, *Cyberbullying and cyberthreats: Responding to the challenge of online social aggression, threats, and distress*, Research Press, Champaign, Illinois.

Williamson, A 2006, *Computers in homes: Literature review*, The 2020 Communications Trust, viewed 23 October 2009, <http://www.computersinhomes.org.nz/pdf/CIH-2020-Lit-Review.pdf>.

Woods, D 2009, *Good news: Becta's collaboration forum*, 17 September 17 2009, Becta, viewed 27 September 2009, <http://collaboration.becta.org.uk/message/3301#3301>.

Woolfolk, A 2001, *Educational Psychology*, 8th edn, Allyn & Bacon, Boston.

Yin, R 1994, *Case study research: Design and methods*, 2nd edn, Sage, Beverly Hills, CA.

Zamaria, C & Fletcher, F 2008, *The Internet, media and emerging technologies: Uses, attitudes, trends and international comparisons 2007*, University of Waterloo, viewed 19 September 2009, <http://www.ciponline.ca/en/docs/2008/CIP07_CANADA_ONLINE-REPORT-FINAL%20.pdf>.

Zevenbergen, R & Logan, H 2008, 'Computer use by preschool children: Rethinking practice as digital natives come to preschool', *Australian Journal of Early Childhood*, vol. 33, no. 1, pp. 37–44.

Zoomerang, n.d., *Education Survey Resource Centre*, viewed 30 August 2009, <http://www.educationsurveyresources.com/>.

Zoomerang 2008, *Parents want more technology in schools*, viewed 30 August 2009, <http://zoomerang.wordpress.com/2008/12/08/parents-want-more-technology-in-schools/>.

Index

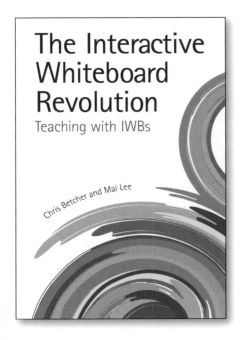

The Interactive Whiteboard Revolution
Teaching with IWBs
Chris Betcher and Mal Lee
ACER Press, 2009

Interactive whiteboards are not just another classroom technology. As the first digital technology designed specifically for teaching and learning, they have the potential to radically alter the way we learn. IWBs also facilitate the integration and ready use of all other digital technologies — hardware and software. Just as the blackboard was the symbol and transformative technology of the 19th century classroom, the interactive whiteboard will be the centrepiece of the 21st century digital classroom.

The Interactive Whiteboard Revolution: Teaching with IWBs provides a wealth of information on:

• Getting your school started with IWBs

• Selecting the right IWB technology

• Principles and strategies for effective IWB teaching

• Lesson design and software tools

• Professional development, training and support.

This book contains eight case studies about leading educators describing how they use IWBs.

Above all, **The Interactive Whiteboard Revolution** makes the point that IWBs are great tools to help great teachers do what they do best.

About the authors

Chris Betcher, aka betchaboy, has taught in a variety of classroom settings both in Australia and overseas and now works with teachers and students to help them use technology in engaging, effective and pedagogically sound ways. He is a frequent speaker on interactive whiteboards and other digital learning technologies and is currently the ICT Integrator at Presbyterian Ladies College in Sydney, Australia.

Mal Lee is an educational consultant specialising in the development of digital technology in schools. He is a former director of schools and secondary school principal, who has written extensively on the effective use of ICT in teaching practice.

TO ORDER
w: http://shop.acer.edu.au
e: sales@acer.edu.au

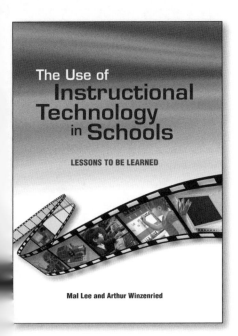

The Use of Instructional Technology in Schools

Lessons to be Learned

Mal Lee and Arthur Winzenried
ACER Press, 2009

The Use of Instructional Technology in Schools examines teachers' use of the major instructional technologies over the last century — from the days of silent film, radio and slide shows through to the modern interactive whiteboard and the Web. It explores the reasons why so few teachers have used these technologies and why, even in today's digital world, the most commonly used classroom tools are the pen, paper and teaching board.

The book provides decision makers with an invaluable insight into the million dollar question: What is required to get all teachers across the nation using the appropriate instructional technology as a normal part of everyday teaching? Without question, student learning is enhanced by adopting these new technologies.

About the authors

Mal Lee is an educational consultant specialising in the development of digital technology in schools. He is a former director of schools and secondary school principal, who has written extensively on the effective use of ICT in teaching practice.

Arthur Winzenried has taught in a wide variety of library and classroom settings, from primary to tertiary, and has been responsible for innovative developments in school ICT over a number of years. He is a frequent national and international speaker on knowledge management and is currently Lecturer in Information Systems at Charles Sturt University, NSW, Australia.

TO ORDER
w: http://shop.acer.edu.au
e: sales@acer.edu.au

Leading a Digital School
Principles and Practice
Mal Lee and Michael Gaffney
ACER Press, 2008

This book informs educational leaders about current developments in the use of digital technologies and presents a number of case studies demonstrating the value and complexity of these technologies. It encourages leaders to engage in the process of successful change in their own school community by providing guidelines and advice drawn from emerging research.

Leading a Digital School is a rich source of information about joining the new 'education revolution'. It shows clearly and concisely how schools can integrate digital technologies creatively and wisely in order to enliven teaching and support student learning.

About the authors

Mal Lee is an educational consultant specialising in the development of digital technology in schools. He is a former director of schools and secondary school principal, who has written extensively on the effective use of ICT in teaching practice.

Professor **Michael Gaffney** is Chair of Educational Leadership at the Australian Catholic University. Mike has wide experience as a teacher, an education system senior executive, and as a researcher, consultant and policy adviser to Australian governments in areas of education policy, curriculum and teaching practices appropriate to 21st century schooling.

TO ORDER
w: http://shop.acer.edu.au
e: sales@acer.edu.au